THE GREAT WAR

SALISBURY SOLDIERS

THE GREAT WAR

SALISBURY SOLDIERS

RICHARD BROADHEAD

To Mick
Best Wishes

Richard Broadhead.

TEMPUS

A French postcard, commemorating the general mobilisation on 2 August 1914. It depicts the allies Nicholas II, Tsar of Russia, Monsieur Raymond Poincare, President of France, and King George V of Great Britain.

Frontispiece:

Top: *British troops going into action at the Battle of the Somme.*

Bottom: *British troops in trenches at Gallipoli.*

First published 2007

Tempus Publishing
Cirencester Road, Chalford,
Stroud, Gloucestershire, GL6 8PE
www.tempus-publishing.com

Tempus Publishing is an imprint of NPI Media Group

British Library Cataloguing in Publication Data.
A catalogue record for this book is available from the British Library.

ISBN 978 0 7524 4428 4

Typesetting and origination by NPI Media Group
Printed in Great Britain

Contents

	Introduction	6
Chapter 1	The War of Hate, 1914	7
Chapter 2	1915 – The War that should have been over by Christmas	21
Chapter 3	Gallipoli	35
Chapter 4	Loos	50
Chapter 5	Jutland	67
Chapter 6	The Somme	72
Chapter 7	1917	108
Chapter 8	Arras	118
Chapter 9	Paschendaele	136
Chapter 10	Cambrai	155
Chapter 11	1918	162
Chapter 12	Kaiserschlact	169
Chapter 13	A Black Day for the German Army	196
Chapter 14	Armistice Day – Monday 11 November 1918	222
Chapter 15	Remembrance	241
	Maps	246
	A–Z of Memorials	250
	Bibliography	256

INTRODUCTION

A few years ago I attended a Remembrance Service during which a spokesman read out a list of names that were engraved on the war memorial. Whilst the initials and surnames of the fallen were being read out, I thought to myself 'how can we remember these men, when we know so little of them?'

Who was John Smith? The only man to have a Christian name detailed on the Salisbury 1914–19 War Memorial? Where did he live? How old was he? What happened to him? These were some of the questions I would have liked to have known the answers to and, as the years progress, all we are left with is a list of the names of men who fell in the First World War.

Lists are not always accurate, and are only as good as the people who compiled them. As for John Smith, on one listing he is recorded as Joseph and another just as the initial J. How can such important information be lost or inaccurately displayed?

How can we, as the descendants of the fallen of the First World War, remember them when our national lists contains such mistakes? This is where my book really started.

I have tried to give the reader an indication of who these men were; where they lived; who their wives and parents were and where they lie today. Even for those with no known grave, I have tried to give an indication of where they fell and where it is likely their remains lie today. For each man I have identified in this book I have tried to cross reference with other sources to ensure that the information is correct, but I apologise now for any mistakes made through information I have researched. For each man on the Salisbury War Memorial I have tried to not only identify them, but also to find a connection with Salisbury. Where no connection has been identified or verified I have not included them in this book. To do so would be based on a hunch or a guess, and not supportable research. These men deserve far more than a hunch. An example of this would be F. Sayers who was most likely Frank Sayers who died while serving on HMS *Nubian* in 1916 and had connections with Fordingbridge. I found no connection with Salisbury, and therefore you will not find him listed in the main body of this book.

This is not simply a book about those men listed on the Salisbury War Memorial, mainly because Salisbury Memorial is an incomplete list of those who died during the conflict. Included, however, are those who died while serving in the Salisbury area and are buried in local cemeteries and who will always remain a part of Salisbury, whether they are listed on the memorial or not.

I would like to thank those who gave me assistance while writing this book, inlcuding The Royal Gloucestershire, Berkshire & Wiltshire Regiment Museum, Salisbury. With special thanks to Martin McIntyre, Richard Long-Fox and Lt-Col. (rtd) David Chilton.

Most of all I would like to thank my long-suffering wife, Anita, who has supported me beyond the call of duty during the writing of this book and of course to my two lovely boys, Jack-Harry and Tom-Tom who were kind enough to give me leave from playing games with them, and whom I sincerely hope never have to serve their country in such a way as those listed herein.

This book is not about the battles of the First World War or the men who directed the battles, it is a book about the great men who left their towns, whether as a volunteer or a conscript, to fight for our future. If we forget their sacrifice we open the door for future conflicts, which will mean that their deaths were to have been in vain.

Lest we forget.

1

THE WAR OF HATE, 1914

In August 1914 the fuse was lit that would ignite a conflict that would change the world; it was to be given many names: the Great European War; The Great War for Civilisation and simply the Great War being but a few. There were many reasons for the commencement of hostilities, but once mobilisation of men had started it triggered a domino effect throughout Europe and then on across the world.

Patriotism spread through countries like a plague and, like a plague, it almost immediately claimed its victims. Men volunteered to fight for good and God against evil, in a war where keen, willing participants would be home for Christmas. The British Army was small, but well trained, and had been developed to protect and control the British Empire, while relying on the powerful British Navy to protect the world-trade routes.

In the August of 1914, soldiers of the British Expeditionary Force marched across Belgium, a country that Great Britain had treaty to protect, across fields where 100 years earlier, the Duke of Wellington had defeated Napoleon Bonaparte. They marched to the town of Mons and the First World War had begun.

23 AUGUST 1918 – THE BATTLE OF MONS, BELGIUM

Salisbury's First Casualty

Capt. Walter Richard Aston Dawes	*1st Battalion Wiltshire Regiment*
Place of birth: Salisbury, Wiltshire	Home country: England Age: 36
Date of death: 23/08/14	Cause of death: Killed in action
Memorial: Salisbury, Wiltshire	
War cemetery: Nouvelles Communal Cemetery, Belgium	
Theatre of war: Belgium	
Next of kin: Muriel Gertrude (wife); Frederick Aston & Mary Isabella Dawes (parents)	
Address: Hilary House, 20 Mill Road, Salisbury, Wiltshire	

On the afternoon of Thursday 3 September 1914, the first news of casualties started to reach Salisbury. Mr A. Whitehead of Salisbury, Capt. Dawes's solicitor, received a telegram stating that Lord Kitchener regretted to intimate that it had been officially reported to him that Capt. W.R.A. Dawes had been killed in action and expressed his deepest sympathy. Mr Whitehead proceeded to Hampshire Cross, Tidworth, where Capt. Dawes' widow and child lived, and conveyed the sad news to Mrs Dawes. Capt. Dawes was well known to many people in Salisbury, his native city.

Capt. Dawes was the son of the late Mr Frederick Aston Dawes, Official Receiver at Salisbury. He was educated in Salisbury and subsequently spent some years in his father's office. He joined the First Wilts Volunteer Rifle Corps as a private, and obtained a commission in the same corps; when the war broke out in South Africa, and service companies from each volunteer battalion were asked for, he volunteered. He served through the war, during which he became a sergeant and at its termination he obtained a commission in the Wiltshire Regiment with which he

Capt. Walter Richard Aston Dawes poses for a photograph seated on the right of the front row.

served in India and South Africa. In January 1911 he was promoted to captain. Before leaving Salisbury, Capt. Dawes took a deep interest in various local organisations and was for some years a member of the Salisbury Volunteer Fire Brigade. On the morning of 4 September 1914 the following sympathetic message from the King and Queen was received by telegram:

> Buckingham Palace
> To Mrs Dawes, c/o A. Whitehead Esq. 35 Canal, Salisbury.
> The King and Queen deeply regret the loss you and the Army have sustained by the death of your husband in the service of his country. Their Majesties truly sympathise with you in your sorrow.
> PRIVATE SECRETARY.

Walter Dawes was killed in action at the Battle of Ciply, south-west of Mons, one of the many engagements fought during the retreat in the first stages of the war. Though the date of death is given as Saturday 23 August 1914, the War Diary states he was killed during shelling on 24 August 1914. The 1st Battalion's trenches had been continuously bombarded by German shells throughout the day, one of these shells being responsible for killing Dawes and three other men along with about twenty wounded. During this action the horse of the 1st Battalion Wiltshire Regiment's commanding officer was shot from under him. The Wiltshires were forced to withdraw to St Wass with the Germans in what was described as 'leisurely pursuit'.

Dawes is buried in Nouvelles Communal Cemetery, Belgium, with eight other casualties from the First World War.

L/Cpl George Green   *1st Battalion Wiltshire Regiment*
Service No.:   8747
Place of birth: Norton Sub Hamdon, Somerset   Home country: England
Date of death: 24/08/14   Cause of death: Killed in action
War cemetery: St Symphorien Military Cemetery, Belgium
Theatre of war: Belgium
Next of kin: Mrs Green (mother)
Address: 91 Winchester Street, Salisbury, Wiltshire

Another casualty of the action at Ciply on Monday 24 August 1914 was L/Cpl George Green. Mrs Green received the official news that her son had been killed in action during the bombardment of the Wiltshires' trenches on that day. He is buried in St Symphorien Military

British troops moving into action in the early part of the war; the stiff outline of their forage caps can be clearly seen. The wire from their caps was soon removed to present a softer outline and less of a target to snipers in the trenches. The first steel helmets would not be issued until 1915.

Cemetery, Belgium, which is believed to contain the first and last Commonwealth soldiers to be killed during the First World War.

Sapper Edward John Ezard		*B Signal Company Royal Engineers*	
Service No.:	12135	Age:	31
Place of birth:	Manchester, Lancashire	Home country:	England
Date of death:	24/08/14	Cause of death:	Died of wounds
Memorial:	Salisbury, Wiltshire		
War cemetery:	Bavay Communal Cemetery, France		
Theatre of war:	France		
Next of kin:	Priscilla Ezard (wife); Mr & Mrs J. Ezard, of Manchester (parents)		
Address:	32 Newton Cottage, The Friary, Salisbury, Wiltshire		

Edward Ezard died in hospital and it was presumed from wounds received at the front. No details were given in a communication which Mrs Ezard received from Chatham on Saturday, 29 August 1914, to the effect that her husband had died in hospital on the previous Monday. Edward Ezard was a Manchester man. He served in the South African War as a member of the Imperial Yeomanry.

Edward Ezard had lived in Salisbury for about three years, being engaged on the staff of the Post Office as a telegraph linesman. He left a widow, Priscilla (Davis) who he had married in Yeovil during 1909, and two children aged five years and one year. He is buried in Bavy Communal Cemetery, France, along with twelve other casualties from the First World War.

26 August 1914 – The Battle of Le Cateau, France
6 September 1914 – First Battle of the Marne, France
9 September 1914 – Battle of Fere Champenoise, France

A Soldier
of the
KING.

AFTER the War every man who has served will command his Country's gratitude. He will be looked up to and *respected* because he answered his country's call.

The Regiments at the Front are covering themselves with Glory.

Field-Marshal Sir John French wrote in an Order of the day,

"It is an Honour to belong to such an Army."

Every fit man from 19 to 38 is eligible for this great honour. Friends can join in a body, and serve together in the same regiment.

Rapid Promotion.

There is rapid promotion for intelligence and zeal. Hundreds who enlisted as private soldiers have already become officers because of their merits and courage, and thousands have reached non-commissioned rank.

Enlist To-day.

At any Post Office you can obtain the address of the nearest Recruiting Office. **Enter your name to-day on the Nation's Roll of Honour and do your part.**

GOD SAVE THE KING.

Above: *A British machine-gun crew watching and waiting to go into action before trench lines were established.*

Left: *This recruiting advert appeared in 1914 at the start of the war. The age range for recruits, of nineteen to thirty-eight years, was varied throughout the war with the result that in 1918 eighteen year olds were legally sent into action. Rapid promotion was almost a guarantee with the losses during the war; if you survived there was a strong chance you would be promoted as an experienced soldier.*

Pte Sidney Charles Allen		1st Battalion Dorsetshire Regiment	
Service No.:	6143	Age:	32
Place of birth:	Lytchett Minster, Dorset	Home country:	England
Date of death:	09/09/14	Cause of death:	Killed in action
War cemetery:	Montreuil Aux Lions British Cemetery, France		
Theatre of war:	France		
Next of kin:	Florence G. Allen (wife); Frederick & Olive Allen (parents)		
Adresses:	Waterloo, Poole, Dorset		
	4 George Street, Salisbury		

The 1st Battalion Dorset Regiment were stationed in Belfast, Ireland, in 1914 and at the outbreak of the war were sent to France joining the 5th Division. After the long retreat from Mons the British Expeditionary Force regrouped and at the request of the French Gen. Joffre, attacked the Germans at the Battle of the Marne. On Wednesday 9 September 1914, Sidney Allen was killed in action when the British were re-crossing the river.

Pte Allen left a widow, Florence, who lived in Poole, Dorset. His parents were given more sorrowful news in November 1914 when another son Frederick James Allen was killed in action while also serving with the 1st Battalion Dorset Regiment.

14 SEPTEMBER 1914 – FIRST BATTLE OF THE AISNE, FRANCE

Pte Alfred George Stickland   *1st Battalion Wiltshire Regiment*

Service No.:	9083	Age:	19
Place of birth:	Hinton Marshall, Dorset	Home country:	England
Date of death:	16/09/14	Cause of death:	Died of wounds
Memorial:	Salisbury, Wiltshire		
War cemetery:	La Ferte Sous Jouarre Memorial, France		
Theatre of war:	France		
Next of kin:	Walter John Stickland (father)		
Address:	The Railway Inn, Southampton Road, Salisbury, Wiltshire		

After the Battle of the Marne, the British Expeditionary Force pursed the retreating German army and the next major engagement at the Aisne river came to be known as the Battle of the Aisne. The battle was fought between Friday 11 September and Tuesday 15 September and it is likely that Pte Strickland was wounded on the last day of the battle when the 1st Battalion Wiltshire Regiment were at Vailly, France, where their positions were shelled by the Germans and the Wiltshires sustained several casualties.

Walter Stickland is remembered on the La Ferte Sous Jouarre Memorial, France, with 3,740 officers and men of the British Expeditionary Force who died in August, September and the early part of October of 1914 and who have no known grave.

Pte John Francis Freeston   *1st Battalion Wiltshire Regiment*

Service No.:	6085	Age:	30
Place of birth:	Harnham, Wiltshire	Home country:	England
Date of death:	22/09/14	Cause of death:	Killed in action
Memorial:	Salisbury, Wiltshire		
War cemetery:	Vailly British Cemetery		
Theatre of war:	France		
Next of kin:	Agnes Violet M. Freeston (wife); Walter James & Eva Laura Freeston (parents)		
Address:	West Harnham, Wiltshire		
	Old Street, Harnham, Salisbury, Wiltshire		

The death of Pte Francis Freeston, killed in action, was recorded on 22 September 1914. He was thirty years of age and was attached to the 1st Battalion Wiltshire Regiment. He left a widow and three young children.

Freeston was the eldest son of Walter James and Eva Laura Freeston and had married Agnes Violet M. Adams in Salisbury during 1910. He was another casualty of the Battle of Aisne and the War Diary tells of much hardship as the battalion had been in the line for nine days with little rest. Pte Freeston is buried in Vailly British Cemetery, France, with around 350 other casualties who died in this area in the First World War.

25 SEPTEMBER 1914 – THE BATTLE OF ALBERT, FRANCE

Pte Ernest Alfred Heath   *1st Battalion Royal West Surrey Regiment*

Service No.:	9093	Age:	33
Place of birth:	Aldershot, Hampshire	Home country:	England

Date of death: 26/09/14   Cause of death: Died of wounds
Memorial: Salisbury, Wiltshire
War cemetery: City of Paris Cemetery, France
Theatre of war: France
Next of kin: Quartermaster Sgt Alfred & Annie Maria Heath (parents)
Address: 2 Queens Road, Salisbury, Wiltshire

Mr A. Heath recieved news of the death of his son, Ernest, from injuries sustained in the war. Pte Heath, who was in the 1st (Queen's) Royal West Surrey Regiment, died in Paris on 1 October from injuries occasioned by a bullet wound to the neck on 19 September. He was educated at St Thomas' School and had been in the Army for nine years.

Pte Heath was wounded in one of the actions on the Aisne. Interestingly, according to regimental records it was believed he died on Saturday 26 September, but his parents received the news of his death on 1 October.

Shoeing Smith Cpl Thomas James Gascoigne   *70th Battery Royal Field Artillery*
Service No.:   35790   Age: 27
Place of birth: Croydon, Surrey   Home country: England
Date of death: 30/09/14   Cause of death: Died of wounds
Memorial: Salisbury, Wiltshire
War cemetery: St Nazaire Toutes Aides Cemetery, France
Theatre of war: France
Next of kin: Edith Ellen Gascoigne (wife); Tom & Sarah Gascoigne (parents)
Addresses: 31 Argyle Road, Ealing, London
                  54 Barnard Street, Salisbury, Wiltshire

Cpl Gascoigne was killed during the September fighting around the Aisne and according to information given to his parents, their eldest son died of wounds at the front on Thursday 1 October 1914, although this conflicts with the official records.

1 OCTOBER 1914 – THE FIRST BATTLE OF ARRAS, FRANCE

A wounded soldier of the Wiltshires told of his experiences during the opening stages of the war:

> A crowd of Germans came running at us while we were at grub one day and a German officer called out in English 'hands up'. We had no time to get our rifles, but we gave them our 'dukes' instead. You'll never find a 'White Hope' out of Germany. One of our fellows could tackle and beat any three Germans with the fists. The beggars were so surprised by our method of fighting that many actually dropped their arms and ran. Our fellows like a hand-to-hand 'scrap' but they hardly ever get it. The Germans have such splendid artillery, and so much of it, that we can seldom get up to them, but when we do they simply fly from us.
>
> We had a bayonet charge at the Oise, where the Germans attempted the same thing. It was the first time we had seen them about to use the bayonet and, as they were more than us, we thought we were in the 'pickle.' We also advanced with bayonets fixed, but when the Germans were within 30 yards of us and saw our steel, they simply turned and fled.

Above, left: *British soldiers preparing a meal behind the firing line in France.*

Above, right: *George Findlay's grave in Salisbury.*

19 OCTOBER 1914 – THE FIRST BATTLE OF YPRES, BELGIUM

Pte George Duncan Findlay   *10th Battalion Royal Welsh Fusiliers*

Service No.:	12958	Home country:	Scotland
Date of death:	20/10/14	Cause of death:	Died
War cemetery:	Salisbury London Road Cemetery, England		
Theatre of war:	Home		
Next of kin:	James & Lillias Duncan Findlay (parents)		
Address:	38 Esslemont Avenue, Aberdeen		

George Findlay volunteered for service with the 10th Battalion Royal Welsh Fusiliers in September 1914 for the duration of the war. During the early months of the war, Pte Findlay's battalion had many difficulties in obtaining kit because of the number of men who had joined up for service. This resulted in many variations in uniform from khaki, to red and blue, and a shortage of cap badges which led to regimental buttons being used in their place. Findlay died, most likely of illness, on Tuesday 20 October 1914 at one of the hospitals in the Salisbury area. His unit were probably training on Salisbury Plain.

Sgt Wilfred Ralph Crockett   *1st Battalion Duke of Cornwall's Light Infantry*

Service No.:	8982	Age:	26
Place of birth:	Salisbury, Wiltshire	Home country:	England
Date of death:	21/10/14	Cause of death:	Killed in action
Memorial:	Salisbury, Wiltshire		
War cemetery:	Le Touret Memorial, France		
Theatre of war:	France		
Next of kin:	Edwin & Jane Crockett (parents)		
Address:	Salisbury, Wiltshire		

Wilfred Crockett was killed in action during fighting at the Battle of La Bassée and he is remembered on Le Touret Memorial for men who died in this area of France and have no known grave.

Pte George Hawkins   *1st Battalion Duke of Cornwall's Light Infantry*

Service No.:   8226   Age: 27
Place of birth: Shrewton, Wiltshire   Home country: England
Date of death: 21/10/14   Cause of death: Killed in action
Memorial: Salisbury, Wiltshire
War Cemetery: Le Touret Memorial, France
Theatre of war: France
Next of kin: George & Caroline Hawkins (parents)
Address: 21 Trinity Street, Salisbury, Wiltshire

Another casualty of the Battle of La Bassée, George Hawkins was killed on Wednesday 21 October 1914 and is also remembered on Le Touret Memorial. His brother, William Charles Hawkins, was killed in Egypt in 1917.

Pte Reginald William Liversidge   *1st Battalion Dorsetshire Regiment*

Service No.:   9315   Age: 22
Place of birth: Salisbury, Wiltshire   Home country: England
Date of death: 22/10/14   Cause of death: Killed in action
Memorial: Salisbury, Wiltshire
War cemetery: Le Touret Memorial, France
Theatre of war: France
Next of kin: George & the late Ellen Liversidge (parents)
Address: 55 Culver Street, Salisbury, Wiltshire

On 22 October 1914, Reginald Liversidge was killed in action in the La Bassée/Armentières battles. He is remembered on the Le Touret Memorial with 13,375 men who were killed in this area of France and have no known grave.

Pte Charles Cropp   *2nd Battalion Wiltshire Regiment*

Service No.:   03/165   Age: 31
Place of birth: Salisbury, Wiltshire   Home country: England
Date of death: 24/10/14   Cause of death: Killed in action
Memorial: Salisbury, Wiltshire
War cemetery: Ypres Menin Gate Memorial, Belgium
Theatre of war: Belgium
Next of kin: The late George & Ann Cropp (parents)
Address: 3 Meadow Cottages, Harnham, Salisbury, Wiltshire

The Battle of Langemarck began at about 5.30 a.m. on Saturday 24 October 1914 at Beselare, Belgium, when the Germans attacked the Wiltshires' trenches and the enemy were driven back with heavy casualties. The attacks continued and, after two hours, hundreds of dead and dying Germans were lying before the Wiltshires' defences. Around the time the Germans broke the British line, the trenches had been vacated by the Wiltshires. All that remained were about thirty non-commissioned officers and men, for by this time the rest of the battalion had been killed or the majority captured. A corporal and some other men formed a rearguard action and protected the battalion ambulances.

Special mention on this day was made about medical officers and stretcher bearers, who for the final three days and nights were continuously handling wounded or burying the dead. Charles Cropp was killed in action during the fighting that took place at Langemarck, Belgium; he is remembered on the Ypres Menin Gate Memorial and has no known grave.

Pte Frederick William Young		*2nd Battalion Wiltshire Regiment*	
Service No.:	8177	Age:	24
Place of birth:	Fisherton Anger, Wiltshire	Home country:	England
Date of death:	24/10/14	Cause of death:	Killed in action
Memorial:	Salisbury, Wiltshire		
War cemetery:	Ypres Menin Gate, Belgium		
Theatre of war:	Belgium		
Next of kin:	George Harry & Rosina Young (parents)		
Address:	21 Sidney Street, Salisbury, Wiltshire		

Frederick Young was killed in action on Saturday 24 October 1914 at Langemarck, Belguim (see Charles Cropp). He is remembered on the Menin Gate Memorial at the City of Ypres, a memorial to soldiers who died in Belgium during the First World War and have no known grave.

Pte William King		*1st Battalion Wiltshire Regiment*	
Service No.:	6932	Age:	31
Place of birth:	Tisbury, Wiltshire	Home country:	England
Date of death:	25/10/14	Cause of death:	Killed in action
Memorial:	Salisbury, Wiltshire		
War cemetery:	Le Touret Memorial, France		
Theatre of war:	France		
Next of kin:	Edward & Martha King (parents)		
Address:	Odstock, Salisbury, Wiltshire		

On Sunday 25 October the 1st Battalion Wiltshire Regiment were in trenches in the Neuve Chapelle area of the front. For most of the day the area was shelled by the Germans, which destroyed nearly all the buildings in the vicinity and resulted in the Wiltshires suffering thirty-seven killed and forty-two wounded.

William King is remembered on the Le Touret Memorial, France, with 13,375 other men who fell in this area before September 1915 and have no known grave.

Pte Albert John Gray		*5th Dragoon Guards*	
Service No.:	5211	Age:	30
Place of birth:	Wishford, Wiltshire	Home country:	England
Date of death:	30/10/14	Cause of death:	Killed in action
Memorial:	Salisbury, Wiltshire		
War cemetery:	Ypres Menin Gate Memorial, Belgium		
Theatre of war:	First Battle of Ypres, Belgium		
Next of kin:	Ebeneezer & Mary J. Gray (parents)		
Address:	Wishford, Wiltshire		

Albert Gray was killed during the First Battle of Ypres, probably in the Gheluvelt area where the 5th Dragoon Guards, a cavalry regiment, were fighting dismounted as infantry. This was due to the shortage of infantry available towards the end of 1914. He has no known grave and is remembered on the Ypres Menin Gate Memorial, Belgium.

Above: *Members of the 1st Battalion Wiltshire Regiment, in trenches, Belgium, during 1914.*

Right: *Members of the 1st Battalion Wiltshire Regiment, in the trenches near Kemmel, Belgium, November 1914.*

Pte Horace Frank Brown Dredge   *1st Battalion Wiltshire Regiment*
Service No.:   7978   Age: 23
Place of birth: Salisbury, Wiltshire   Home country: England
Date of death: 30/10/14   Cause of death: Died of wounds
War cemetery: Pont Du Hem Military Cemetery, La Gorgue, France
Theatre of war: France
Next of kin: Olive Dredge (mother)
Address: Salisbury, Wiltshire

Horace Dredge was probably wounded on Thursday 29 October 1914 at Pont Logy in Northern France, where the 1st Wiltshires suffered approximately 300 casualties.

    He is buried in the Pont Du Hem Military Cemetery La Gorgue, France, which is situated on the main road from La Bassee to Estaires, France; the cemetery was originally an apple orchard.

Pte Thomas Trubridge   *1st Battalion Wiltshire Regiment*
Service No.:   7046   Age: 29
Place of birth: Fisherton, Salisbury, Wiltshire   Home country: England
Date of death: 31/10/14   Cause of death: Killed in action
Memorial: Salisbury, Wiltshire
War cemetery: Le Touret Memorial, France
Theatre of war: France
Next of kin: Elsie Alice Beck (formally Trubridge) (wife); William & Jane Trubridge (parents)
Addresses: 1 West End Road Wilton Road, Salisbury, Wiltshire
                  Fisherton Anger, Salisbury, Wiltshire

There is no record of casualties for the 1st Battalion Wiltshire Regiment on Saturday 31 October 1914. This may have been because Thomas Trubridge was actually missing and was killed in the days leading up to 31 October 1917. His body was never recovered and he is remembered on the Le Touret Memorial. His brother, Lionel Cecil Trubridge, was killed in action in 1918.

Pte Frederick James Allen   *1st Battalion Dorsetshire Regiment*

Service No.:   03/7809   Age: 39
Place of birth: Canford, Dorset   Home country: England
Date of death: 06/11/14   Cause of death: Killed in action
Memorial: Salisbury, Wiltshire
War cemetery: Ypres Menin Gate Memorial, Belgium
Theatre of war: Belgium
Next of kin: Frederick & Olive Allen (parents)
Address: 4 George Street, Salisbury, Wiltshire

Pte Allen was killed in action on Friday 6 November 1914 during the First Battle of Ypres. He is remembered upon the Ypres Menin Gate Memorial and has no known grave. His brother Sydney Allen died on 9 September 1914, also serving with the 1st Battalion Dorsetshire Regiment.

7 NOVEMBER 1914 – BRITISH FORCES LAND IN THE PERSIAN GULF TO PROTECT BRITISH OIL INTERESTS

Guardsman Leonard Walter Oram Head   *2nd Battalion Grenadier Guards*

Service No.:   16315   Age: 19
Place of birth: Salisbury, Wiltshire.   Home country: England
Date of death: 07/11/14   Cause of death: Killed in action
Memorial: Salisbury, Wiltshire
War cemetery: Ypres Menin Gate Memorial, Belgium
Theatre of war: Belgium
Next of kin: William Henry & Louise Wootton (formerly Head) (parents)
Address: 17 Spring Place, Endless Street, Salisbury, Wiltshire

Guardsman Head was killed in action on Saturday 7 November 1914 during the First Battle of Ypres; he has no known grave and is remembered on the Ypres Menin Gate Memorial, Belgium.

Lt William Augustus Portman Foster   *1st Battalion South Staffordshire Regiment*

Place of birth: Hardingham, Norfolk   Home country: England   Age: 27
Date of death: 11/11/14   Cause of death: Died of wounds
Memorial: Salisbury, Wiltshire
War cemetery: Niederzwehren Cemetery, Germany
Theatre of war: Germany
Next of kin: Col. Sir William Yorke & Lady Foster (parents)
Address: Ascot Lodge, Ascot, Berkshire

The 1st Battalion South Staffordshire Regiment was part of the 7th Division, known as the Immortal 7th after fighting the Germans to a standstill at the First Battle of Ypres in 1914. The division suffered many casualties and was not considered an effective fighting force again until February 1915.

William Foster was educated at Wellington School and was a graduate of the Royal Military College, Sandhurst. He was captured and died of wounds as a prisoner of war.

He is today buried in Niederzwehren Cemetery, Germany. The cemetery was first used in 1915 and it is likely that his remains were moved to this location from the original place of burial.

Sgt William Edward Walley Blencowe — 1st Battalion Wiltshire Regiment

Service No.:	4352	Age:	36
Place of birth:	Devizes, Wiltshire.	Home country:	England
Date of death:	16/11/14	Cause of death:	Killed in action
Memorial:	Salisbury, Wiltshire		
War cemetery:	Ypres Menin Gate Memorial, Belgium		
Theatre of war:	Belgium		
Next of kin:	Mabel M. Blencowe (wife); Harry & Emily Margaret Blencowe (parents)		
Address:	Winton, 48 Coombe Road, Salisbury, Wiltshire		

On Monday 16 November 1914 the 1st Battalion Wiltshire Regiment was in trenches at Hooge, east of Ypres, Belgium. Sgt Blencowe was killed, along with two other members of the battalion, by heavy German shelling. His body was never recovered and he is remembered on the Ypres Menin Gate Memorial, Belgium.

Pte William Henry Smith — 1st Battalion Wiltshire Regiment

Service No.:	7387	Age:	24
Place of birth:	Wishford, Wiltshire	Home country:	England
Date of death:	17/11/14	Cause of death:	Killed in action
War cemetery:	Ypres Menin Gate, Belgium		
Theatre of war:	Belgium		
Next of kin:	William & Rose Smith (parents)		
Address:	Fisherton Anger, Salisbury, Wiltshire		

On Tuesday 17 November 1914 Pte Smith was serving with the 1st Battalion Wiltshire Regiment at Hooge, east of Ypres. At 9 a.m. the Wiltshires' trenches were shelled by the Germans and an enemy attack followed at about 10.30 a.m. By noon, 150 Germans had occupied the advanced trenches and about ten minutes later D Company of the Wiltshire Regiment executed a bayonet charge, driving the enemy from the trenches, killing about fifty Germans and wounding many others. The Wiltshires, taking residence in the recaptured advance trenches, were then heavily shelled by the Germans.

It is almost certain that Pte Smith was killed during this attack. It is likely he would have originally been buried close to the scene of his death and the grave then lost in subsequent fighting.

William is remembered on the Ypres Menin Gate Memorial, Belgium.

Guardsman Reginald Sheppard — 3rd Battalion Coldstream Guards

Service No.:	6124	Age:	26
Place of birth:	Salisbury, Wiltshire.	Home country:	England
Date of death:	20/11/14	Cause of death:	Killed in action
Memorial:	Salisbury, Wiltshire		
War cemetery:	Ypres Menin Gate Memorial, Belgium		
Theatre of war:	Belgium		
Next of kin:	Thomas & Martha Sheppard (parents)		
Address:	Salisbury, Wiltshire		

Guardsman Sheppard was killed in action in fighting to the east of Ypres on Friday 20 November 1914. He is remembered on the Ypres Menin Gate Memorial with 54,343 other men who died in the area during the First World War and have no known grave.

On Saturday 1 December 1914, Pte A.H. Spencer wrote to his parents:

Have they got any of the Belgium refugees at Salisbury? If so you can tell the people around that they gave nearly everything they could to us when we were on the retreat; so that it won't do the people at home any harm to put their hands in their pockets for them. I hope for the Belgiums' sake this war won't last very long. It is not nearly as bad for us as it is for them. We always get plenty of good food and warm blankets. We have just been given a new blanket each for the winter.

Pte Harry Batt		*2nd Battalion Border Regiment*	
Service No.:	8218	Age:	28
Place of birth:	Great Cheverell, Wiltshire	Home country:	England
Date of death:	05/12/14	Cause of death:	Killed in action
Memorial:	Salisbury, Wiltshire		
War cemetery:	Zandvoorde British Cemetery, Belgium		
Theatre of war:	Belgium		
Next of kin:	John & Annie Batt (parents)		
Address:	6 Spring Place Endless Street, Salisbury, Wiltshire		

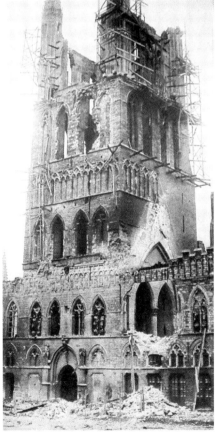

Above: *The cloth hall and tower at Ieper (Ypres) today, which has been restored to its pre-First World War glory.*

Right: *The tower of the cloth hall at Ypres, Belgium. During the early stages of the war it was a prominent target for German gunners, who shelled the town continuously throughout the war.*

Belgian refugees escaping from the advancing Germans.

The 2nd Battalion Border Regiment was part of the 7th Division, the Immortal 7th, which were decimated during the First Battle of Ypres.

Harry Batt is buried in Zandvoorde British Cemetery, Belgium. It lies south-east of the town of Ypres on the Menin Road. The cemetery was created after the Armistice and remains were brought in from the surrounding cemeteries and battlefields. Many of the casualties died during the desperate fighting round Zantvoorde, Zillebeke and Gheluvelt.

18 DECEMBER 1914 – BATTLE OF GIVENCHY, BELGIUM

Capt. Malcolm A.R. Bell   *54th Sikhs Frontier Force, Indian Army*
Place of birth: Edinburgh, Scotland   Home country: India   Age: 33
Date of death: 20/12/14   Cause of death: Killed in action
War cemetery: Le Touret Military Cemetery, Richebourg L Avoue, France
Theatre of war: France
Next of kin: The late Mr & Mrs Russell Bell (parents)
Address: The Close, Salisbury, Wiltshire

News reached Salisbury, just before Christmas 1914, that Malcolm Bell had been killed in action on Tuesday 22 December 1914 although official records state that he died on Sunday 20 December. His father, the late Mr Russell Bell, had been Advocate Sheriff Substitute of Stirlingshire and his mother was a resident of The Close, Salisbury.

Bell was attached to the 58th Rifles Frontier Force, Indian Army, and is buried in Le Touret Military Cemetery, Richebourg L. Avoue, near Bethune, France.

25 DECEMBER 1914 – UNOFFICIAL CHRISTMAS TRUCE

2

1915 - The War that should have been over by Christmas

Sapper L.H. Fooks, of 49 Cowmeadow Road, Salisbury, wrote to his parents in January 1915:

I am in a place writing this letter 150 yards from the Germans, in a nice, cosy, little dugout with my instrument. I am in communication with Brigade Headquarters, which are 2½ miles from here. You cannot imagine the condition of the trenches – liquid mud up over our knees, and we have to sleep in these wet muddy clothes. Still we are quite happy, although we are experiencing terrible times. It is the cause we are fighting for, and the troops are very determined to wipe the Germans out. There is a terrible lot of sniping going on. One needs to be very careful or they get you. These snipers have their rifles fixed on a certain object, and immediately anyone passes that object they 'snipe.' At the present time I am operator to the Jocks (Argyle and Sutherland Highlanders). They are a pleasant lot, and are singing as I write. They wear kilts, and the Germans call them 'The ladies from hell'.

Sapper Fooks survived the war.

Rifleman William Oliver Chapman   *2nd Battalion Kings Royal Rifle Corps*

Service No.:	11978	Age:	18
Place of birth:	Sandown, Isle of Wight.	Home country:	England
Date of death:	10/01/15	Cause of death:	Killed in action
Memorial:	Salisbury, Wiltshire		
War cemetery:	Le Touret Memorial, France		
Theatre of war:	France		
Next of kin:	Walter H. & Louise M. Chapman (parents)		
Address:	91 Culver Street, Salisbury, Wiltshire		

Rifleman Chapman, known as Oliver, died in northern France aged eighteen in 1915. Young men had to be eighteen to join the Army and nineteen to serve overseas or, if younger, have a letter from their parents to agree to them serving overseas. He is remembered on Le Touret Memorial with 13,374 other casualties who died prior to September 1915 and have no known grave.

Pte Albert Edward Mortimer   *2nd Battalion Wiltshire Regiment*

Service No.:	7979	Age:	27
Place of birth:	Salisbury, Wiltshire	Home country:	England
Date of death:	15/01/15	Cause of death:	Killed in action
Memorial:	Salisbury, Wiltshire		
War cemetery:	Rue David Military Cemetery, Fleuxbaix, France		
Theatre of war:	France		
Next of kin:	Edward & Eliza A. Mortimer (parents)		
Address:	St Edmund, Salisbury, Wiltshire		

At the time of his death Albert Mortimer was serving in the trenches at Pont de la Justice, France. After heavy rain the trenches had about 4ft of water in them and pumps which were employed to drain the trenches could not keep up with the amount of water filling them. This gives an idea of the conditions that had to be endured at this time in the trenches. Albert was killed in action on Friday 15 January 1915 and is buried in Rue David Military Cemetery, Fleuxbaix, France.

Gunner Ernest Walter Ellery   *22nd Reserve Battery Royal Field Artillery*

Service No.:	14683	Age:	18
Place of birth:	Britford, Wiltshire.	Home country:	England
Date of death:	30/01/15		
War cemetery:	East Harnham All Saints Churchyard, England		
Theatre of war:	Home		
Next of kin:	William Walter & Emily A. Ellery (parents)		
Address:	Beaulieu, Downton Road, Salisbury, Wiltshire		

The funeral of Gunner Ernest W. Ellery, RFA, who died in Woolwich Hospital at the age of eighteen, took place at East Harnham on Friday 6 February 1915 and he was accorded military honours. Ernest had been employed in the gardens at the Bishop's Palace but joined the Royal Field Artillery in September 1914. Ellery was taken ill and had to undergo an operation. His death at such an early age was deeply regretted by all who knew him. The funeral service took place at East Harnham Church and the interment in the cemetery was conducted by Revd G. Hill and Revd T.J. Woodall. The coffin was conveyed on a gun carriage provided by the RFA Bulford, and a firing party from the Southern Command Headquarters also attended. Amongst the floral tributes was a wreath from the Bishop of Salisbury.

L/Cpl Cecil George Sandbrook Rawlings   *12th Battalion London Regiment, The Rangers*

Service No.:	1784	Age:	20
Place of birth:	Salisbury, Wiltshire.	Home country:	England
Date of death:	15/02/15	Cause of death:	Killed in action
Memorial:	Salisbury, Wiltshire		
War cemetery:	Sanctuary Wood Cemetery, Belgium		
Theatre of war:	Belgium		
Next of kin:	George & Ida Rawlings (parents)		

On Monday 15 February 1915, L/Cpl Rawlings, the eldest and dearly loved son of George and Ida Rawlings, was killed in action in the Zillebeke area, to the east of Ypres, and he is buried in Sanctuary Wood Cemetery, Belgium.

Pte Joseph Tiffin   *8th Service Battalion, Border Regiment*

Service No.:	15829	Age:	28
Place of birth:	Cockermouth, Cumberland	Home country:	England
Date of death:	22/02/15		
War cemetery:	Salisbury (Devizes Road) Cemetery, Wiltshire		
Theatre of war:	Home		
Next of kin:	William N. & Ada Tiffin (parents)		
Address:	6 Derwent Street, Cockermouth, Cumberland		

Joseph Tiffin joined the 8th Battalion the Border Regiment as a volunteer in September 1914 after the call made by Lord Kitchener. These volunteers were known as Kitchener's Army and the term service means that he joined for a fixed term service, for the duration of the war. His

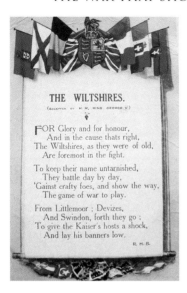

A patriotic postcard designed to encourage men of Wiltshire to enlist and fight for right against crafty foes – the Kaiser and the German people.

regiment were likely to have been in training on Salisbury Plain and he died in the Salisbury area and is buried in Salisbury (Devizes Road) Cemetery, Wiltshire. One of the issues faced by the borough council at the time was deciding who was responsible for the cost of burials of servicemen in Salisbury.

Gunner Harry Edgar Randolph Jackson   1st Division Ammunition Column Canadian Field Artillery

Service No.:	44001	Age:	21
Place of birth:	Leicester, Leicestershire	Home country:	Canada
Date of death:	08/03/15		
War cemetery:	Salisbury London Road Cemetery, England		
Theatre of war:	Home		
Next of kin:	Charles T. & Annie M. Jackson (parents)		
Address:	32 Marlborough Road, Leicester, Leicestershire		

Harry Jackson had taken the oath and joined the Canadian Overseas Expeditionary Force in September 1914, after a call to arms had gone out to the British Empire to supply men to fight against the Germans. Prior to the start of the First World War many young men had left Great Britain for a new life in Australia and Canada and joined the dominion forces to fight for the Empire. Many were drawn by sense of duty, while others joined for the free ticket home to England; many thought was the war would be over by Christmas and it would be a chance to see relatives and then return to Canada.

Gunner Jackson was a book keeper but had a year of service in the Territorial Army as a signaller. He died in the Salisbury area and is buried in Salisbury London Road Cemetery, England.

10 MARCH 1915 – THE BATTLE OF NEUVE CHAPELLE

Neuve Chapelle first came to prominence for the people of Salisbury in newspaper reports and letters concerning the British Expeditionary Forces eastward advance to the north of Le Bassée in October 1914. The fighting toward the end of October 1914 had been described as murderous and had forced the British out of the village of Neuve Chapelle.

Neuve Chapelle was, like many other villages in this part of French Flanders, an unimportant collection of houses and small farms, scattered about a junction of country roads with a church at its centre. It was really quite a small place, but owing to the universal tendency of all these villages to straggle, with each house apparently built without any reference to neighbours, it covered considerable ground. On the western side of the village there were some detached houses of a better class, surrounded by enclosures and orchards bounded by tall hedgerows. The ground all round is completely flat and, except in the open space which extends round the village and beyond the enclosures, the view was restricted by the hedges and pollard trees.

After the fighting of 1914 – and the advances and retreats – a static line of entrenched positions stretched from the North Sea to Switzerland. Sir John French, the commander of the British Forces, was under pressure to regain the confidence of his French allies and to break out of the trenches and return to a more mobile war. The battle began on 10 March 1915.

In April 1915, after the battle from the west, all that could be seen of the place was a few ruined, crumbling red-brick houses, nearly all roofless, and in their midst a tall, white, shapeless mass which represented the church. The ground between the Le Bassée road and the village was an expanse of pasture and arable land seamed with trenches. The original configuration of the German first line was hard to trace in many places, for the ground had been so furrowed and pitted by shells. All that remained were confused mounds, which represented the former parapets, and hollows representing the trenches and dugouts. Calico sand bags, articles of equipment, the remains of food, ammunition, Pickelhauben helmets and Jagers' shakos could all be seen strewn along the abandoned defences. In many areas the original trenches had been reversed by the British attacking troops, who had prepared them against counter-attack by the Germans. The ground, in places, appeared to be powdered with a bright yellow fungus growth, and the stagnant water in the older shell craters were covered in scum of the same hue. This was due to the lyddite from the British high explosive shells.

In the orchard close to the church the fruit trees were nearly all torn about, while one large oak, 4ft in diameter, was broken in half about a yard above the roots. The ground was strewn with branches and pitted with craters, the older ones being full of water. The ditches which in the water-logged country, were dug around the houses and enclosures had their banks blown in. One result was that the water had overflowed into various hollows of the ground, forming large pools and patches of bog.

The appearance of the village itself looked as though an earthquake had wrought havoc, for the place resembled a huge rubbish heap; it was almost impossible to distinguish the streets

Far left: *Joseph Tiffin, a volunteer from Cockermouth.*

Left: *Harry Jackson returning from Canada.*

amongst the rubble and bricks which had been hurled across and obliterated them. Portions of houses were still standing, but these were few and far between, and were dangerous to enter due to the peril of falling tiles and tottering walls.

In the churchyard the dead trees had been uprooted, only to be buried again under masonry which had fallen from the church, and crosses from the heads of tombs lay scattered in all directions. The sole thing in the cemetery that had escaped damage was a wooden crucifix standing erect amid the medley of overturned graves. There was another large crucifix still standing at the crossroads at the north end of the village, where at the time British soldiers entered a dead German was lying at its foot.

Collected together at different points behind the British line were the graves of many of the British soldiers. In some places the dead had been buried where they fell, either singly or in little groups; in others there are regular cemeteries. All the graves had been carefully made, a wooden cross having been erected over each, with the name and regiment of the dead marked on it. Many had been turfed and had flowers placed on them.

Pte Thomas Williams		_2nd Battalion Wiltshire Regiment_	
Service No.:	7651	Age:	27
Place of birth:	Salisbury, Wiltshire	Home country:	England
Date of death:	11/03/15	Cause of death:	Killed in action
Memorial:	Salisbury, Wiltshire		
War cemetery:	Le Touret Memorial, France		
Theatre of war:	Neuve Chapelle, France		
Next of kin:	Thomas & Emma Williams (parents)		
Address:	Salisbury, Wiltshire		

Pte Williams was killed on Thursday 11 March 1915 in the trenches at Neuve Chappelle, where the 2nd Battalion, Wiltshire Regiment, were opposite the German position of the Quadrilateral. During the day the Wiltshires were continuously showered by bullets and shell fire. Williams is remembered on the Le Touret Memorial, France, and has no known grave.

Pte Albert George Victor Crook		_2nd Battalion Wiltshire Regiment_	
Service No.:	10412	Age:	17
Place of birth:	Fisherton, Wiltshire	Home country:	England
Date of death:	12/03/15	Cause of death:	Killed in action
Memorial:	Salisbury, Wiltshire		
War cemetery:	Le Touret Memorial, France		
Theatre of war:	Neuve Chapelle, France		
Next of kin:	The late Albert Crook & Elizabeth Frampton (formerly Crook) (parents)		
Address:	65 Windsor Street, Salisbury, Wiltshire		

Albert Crook was an under-age soldier and had probably volunteered in September 1914 and was sent to the 2nd Battalion Wiltshire Regiment as a replacement for the heavy losses that had been suffered at the front.

On Friday 12 March 1915, around 5.30 a.m., the rations were just arriving when the Germans carried out a bomb attack on the Wiltshires' trenches. There was some chaos but D Company easily stopped the attack going into the second line and, with C Company, attacked the Germans and made good progress. Eventually they were driven back by heavy machine-gun fire. The British then counter-attacked, retaking the lost trenches. At the end of the day, 350 German prisoners had been taken. Pte Crook and around fifty members of the 2nd Battalion Wiltshire Regiment were killed in the assault. He is remembered on the Le Touret Memorial and has no known grave.

Pte Lewis Joseph Daniels   *2nd Battalion Wiltshire Regiment*

Service No.:	8468	Age:	26
Place of birth:	Salisbury, Wiltshire	Home country:	England
Date of death:	12/03/15	Cause of death:	Killed in action
Memorial:	Salisbury, Wiltshire		
War cemetery:	Le Touret Memorial, France		
Theatre of war:	Neuve Chapelle, France		
Next of kin:	Ellen Daniels (mother)		
Address:	27 Salt Lane, Salisbury, Wiltshire		

Lewis Daniels was another casualty of Neuve Chapelle on Friday 12 March 1915. He has no known grave and is remembered on Le Touret Memorial.

Pte Arthur Frederick Randell   *1st Battalion Wiltshire Regiment*

Service No.:	8493	Age:	26
Place of birth:	East Harnham, Wiltshire	Home country:	England
Date of death:	11/03/15		
Memorial:	Salisbury, Wiltshire		
War cemetery:	Berlin South Western Cemetery, Germany		
Theatre of war:	Germany		
Next of kin:	Fred & Catherine J. Randell (parents)		
Address:	St Edmund, Salisbury, Wiltshire		

Pte Randell, known as Fred, was probably captured by the Germans in the fighting of 1914. He would have been transported to the eastern part of Germany and died on Thursday 11 March 1915. A likely cause of death was disease.

Pte Evans of Salisbury was captured after being wounded and was lucky to be freed as a wounded combatant with 200 other injured soldiers, who were exchanged for German prisoners. However, he tells us in the Salisbury Journal of 1915 that British soldiers were subject to 'German discipline', accompanied by a good deal of bullying on the part of his captors, as well as scanty food. The worst time he had was just after capture, when they were stripped and searched for no apparent reason except hatred of the English. On the journey into Germany, the prisoners travelled in cattle trucks, and evidently word of their arrival was sent to the different places along the line, for at every station they came to a crowd of Germans who applied opprobrious epithets to them.

Pte Evans characterised the treatment of the prisoners by the Germans as bad, and said the French had a fine time compared to the British, who had to undergo a lot of bullying. The food which they were supplied was poor, consisting for the most of soups made of a kind of pickled cabbage, pickled French beans and horse beans, in which they occasionally discovered a piece of meat floating. Rice was the best food they received.

Prisoners spent their time employed on a number of farms in the neighbourhood, and others were set to do labouring work in connection with the building of barracks near their camp. The prisoners who worked on the farms were granted pay at the rate of 3*d* per day. Pte Randell's remains were transferred to Berlin South Western Cemetery, Germany, in the early 1920s.

Capt. Sir Edward Hamilton Westrow Hulse   *2nd Battalion Scots Guards*

Date of death:	12/03/15	Age	25
Memorials:	Salisbury, Wiltshire	Cause of death:	Killed in action
	Salisbury Cathedral, Breamore Church, Hampshire		

War cemetery: Rue David Military Cemetery Fleuxbaix
Theatre of war: France
Next of kin: The late Sir Edward Henry & Hon. Lady Edith Maud Hulse
Address: Breamore House, Breamore, Wiltshire

On Tuesday 16 March 1915 the sad news reached Lady Hulse, Capt. Hulse's mother, and when it became known throughout Salisbury and a wider district, profound regret was caused by the knowledge that the war had claimed another victim, a gallant officer of such high promise.

The deepest sympathy was felt for Lady Hulse and other members of the family, which had long been connected by political and social ties with the city and its neighbourhood. The deceased officer's father, Sir Edward Henry Hulse, who died in South Africa in 1903, was Member of Parliament for Salisbury from 1886 to 1897. His work for the Conservative Party in the city was continued after his death by Lady Hulse and at the last election, the late Capt. Hulse also took a prominent part in furthering the interests of the party.

Hulse was the seventh baronet. Born in 1889, he was the only son of the late Sir Edward Henry Hulse and Lady Hulse. He was educated at Eton and at Balliol College, Oxford. His coming of age, on 31 August 1910, was the occasion of festivities at Breamore House and Edward took the opportunity to testify to the affection he had for the family home for every stick, stone and lug, as he put it and his determination to do his duty, as far as in him lay, to all those who were connected with the estate of which he was the owner. Evidence of the esteem with which Edward was held was shown to some extent by the number of recipient gifts from relatives and personal friends being augmented by those from tenants, employees and cottagers on the estates at Breamore and Hall Barn, Beaconsfield, Buckinghamshire, and from members of the Fordingbridge Unionist Club. Shortly afterwards, the Unionists of Salisbury and members of the Primrose League took the opportunity of expressing their appreciation of the political services rendered by present and past members of the family, and their good wishes for the future career of Edward Hulse. The presentation was made by Mr W.M. Hammick, as chairman of the Salisbury Unionist Association, who headed the deputation to Breamore House. After serving as a lieutenant in the Hampshire Yeomanry, Hulse was gazetted to the Scotts Guards in February 1912, becoming a lieutenant in March 1913. After serving abroad with his regiment he returned to England and went out with the 1st Battalion Scotts Guards at the beginning of the war. Later, he was transferred to the 2nd Battalion. During the early days of the campaign his health broke down through hardships

Wiltshire Regiment prisoners of war in Germany during 1915.

Above: *Breamore House, near Salisbury, the home of Sir Edward Hulse.*

Left: *Sir Edward Hulse (left), photographed in the trenches during the Christmas truce of 1914, with Captain Warner, brother of John Warner, who contested the Salisbury seat in the 1910 General Election.*

incidental to trench warfare, but even then his indomitable courage and determination were apparent and he would not give up until he was helpless and had to be lifted out of the trenches. His mother proceeded to France, and remained with her son until his recovery, when he returned to the trenches. That he rendered valuable service at the front can be no doubt. In a despatch published on 17 February 1915, Sir John French specially mentioned Hulse for his distinguished conduct in the field. Sir John French wrote: 'On the night of 26/27 November a small party of the 2nd Scots Guards under Lt Sir E.H.W. Hulse, Bart. rushed the trenches opposite the 20th Brigade, and after pouring heavy fire into them returned with useful information as to the strength of the Germans and the position of machine guns.' Edward was promoted to temporary captain and this was published on 27 February 1915.

Edward Hulse was the second grandson of Lord Burnham who had fallen in the First World War. Lt W.B.W. Lawson, Scots Guards, son of Col. the Honourable William Lawson DSO (late of the Scots Guards, and now commanding the Royal Bucks Hussars Reserve Regiment) having been killed in action at Boesinghe on 22 October 1914. Mr Charles Westrow Hulse, uncle of Edward, was killed in action at Braklaagate, South Africa, on 4 June 1901. The successor to the baronetcy was Sir Edward Hulse's uncle Mr Hamilton John Hulse, of Sandle Manor, Fordingbridge.

A friend wrote in the *Times*:

In the death of Sir Edward Hulse, who was killed in action on Sunday 14 March 1915 , the Scots Guards sustain a serious loss. Although he only joined the regiment in 1912 and had no opportunity before the war to show his considerable military gifts, he came to the notice of his superior officers in the very earliest stages of the campaign as an officer of unusual capacity. His instinct for war and love even for the hardships of his profession made him conspicuous even in the gallant band of the Scots Guards. And it was with real satisfaction that his brother officers learned of his mention in dispatches and of his rapid promotion. Hulse's letters home, which were only shown to a privileged few, were remarkable for their graphic and simple style and their expression of a soldier's thought. His intense keenness showed in every line of them, and were a true picture of the writer's personality. His friends and comrades will never forget Hulse's unwavering cheerfulness through all the difficulties of the most arduous campaign ever fought by the British army, and they will never cease to deplore his untimely loss.

In November 1915, two memorials, a marble tablet and a stained-glass window, were dedicated to Edward Hulse at Breamore Church. 'To the dear and honoured memory of the late Capt. Sir Edward Hamilton Westrow Hulse, 7th Baronet of Breamore House. 2nd Battalion Scots Guards, born 31 August 1889, killed at the battle of Neuve Chapelle, 12 March 1915.' This plaque was erected by his mother.

One of Capt. Hulse's letters described the famous Christmas truce of 1914 during which he met German soldiers in No Man's Land and exchanged gifts. He also negotiated the burial of British soldiers whose bodies had been lying in No Man's Land from previous attacks. He was killed at Neuve Chapelle while going to the aid of his Commanding Officer.

Pte James Smith		*1st Battalion Wiltshire Regiment*
Service No.:	11001	
Place of birth:	Brighton, Sussex:	Home country: England
Date of death:	12/03/15	Cause of death: Killed in action
Memorial:	Salisbury, Wiltshire	
War cemetery:	Ypres Menin Gate Memorial, Belgium	
Theatre of war:	Belgium	

On Friday 12 March 1915, while to the south the Battle of Neuve Chapelle was progressing, the 1st Battalion Wiltshire Regiment were in Belgium near Kemmel, in the trenches preparing to attack the German-held position of Spanbroek Molen. The morning was dull and misty and the British Artillery bombardment had to be delayed. At about 2.30 p.m. the mist cleared and the bombardment began and continued for an hour and forty minutes. At the end of the bombardment it appeared that the German trenches were still intact. A Company of the 1st Battalion Wiltshire Regiment rushed forward and encountered heavy rifle and machine-gun fire from the German trenches. Only a few small groups reached the German wire 200 yards away. B Company then attacked, but got no further than 50 yards before they too were stopped by the same murderous fire. B Company tried to crawl forward but could not get very far and at about 5 p.m. began to fall back, taking many casualties in the process. The remainder of the survivors of A and B Companies made their way back to the British lines under the cover of darkness.

Pte Smith was one of thirty-three men killed during the attack. He has no known grave and is remembered on the Ypres Menin Gate Memorial, Belgium.

Pte George Gray		*No.1 Heavy Transport Depot Company Royal Army Service Corps*
Service No.:	T/15089	Age: 33
Place of birth:	Salisbury, Wiltshire	Home country: England
Date of death:	21/03/15	Cause of death: Died of illness
Memorial:	Salisbury, Wiltshire	
War cemetery:	Salisbury London Road Cemetery, England	
Theatre of war:	Home	
Next of kin:	Annie Laura Gray (wife); Jesse & Ellen Gray (parents)	
Addresses:	59 The Friary, Salisbury, Wiltshire	
	Milford, Salisbury, Wiltshire	

The funeral of Driver George Gray, of the Army Service Corps, whose death occurred at his home in the Friary on Sunday 21 March 1915, after a painful illness, took place at the London Road Cemetery on the afternoon of 25 March 1915 with military honours.

Above: *War Memorial to the Fallen at Breamore Church, near Salisbury.*

Right: *Stained-glass window dedicated to Sir Edward Hulse by his mother.*

Far left: *George Gray, who died of illness in Salisbury.*

Left: *William Campbell died in a motor-car accident at Broken Cross near Salisbury. When he enlisted, Campbell described himself as a 'Gentleman'.*

He was employed as one of the city postmen and on the outbreak of war was called up for service as a reservist. He served on the continent for some time, and was invalided home in November 1914. He left a widow and five children.

The coffin was borne on a gun carriage provided by the Army Service Corps at Bulford, while a firing party from the Southern Command Headquarters attended. The Salisbury Post Office was represented at the funeral by the postmaster (Mr A. Williams), the inspector (Mr S. Young), the assistant inspector (Mr E. Eyres) and about thirty postmen. The service was conducted by Revd J. Wellington, and concluded with the *Last Post*, sounded by a bugler, and the firing of a volley over the grave.

Driver William Constantine Campbell   *1st Division Ammunition Park Canadian Army Service Corps*

Service No.:	37048		Age:	27
Place of birth:	Simcoe, Canada		Home country:	Canada
Date of death:	26/03/15		Cause of death:	Accidental
War cemetery:	Salisbury London Road Cemetery, England			
Theatre of war:	Home			
Next of kin:	Robert Albert & Alice Campbell (parents)			
Address:	Toronto, Ontario			

A motor-car accident, resulting in the death of Cpl William Campbell, of the Canadian Divisional Ammunition Park, occurred on the afternoon of Friday 26 March 1915 on the Winterbourne Road, near Salisbury, at a spot known as Broken Cross, where the road crossed the London and South Western Railway line.

The deceased, who was driving a Ford car containing two officers as passengers, successfully negotiated one turn in the road, but while taking a second turn the motor car for some unknown reason apparently turned turtle. William's head was caught between the car door and the road and pinned to the ground, and sustained injuries to such an extent that he died almost immediately.

William was born on 23 June 1889 and when he had joined the Canadian Army in September 1914 he described his occupation as 'a gentleman'.

Pte Frederick Massey		*1st Battalion Wiltshire Regiment*	
Service No.:	8145	Age:	22
Place of birth:	Salisbury, Wiltshire.	Home country:	England
Date of death:	30/03/15	Cause of death:	Killed in action
Memorial:	Salisbury, Wiltshire		
War cemetery:	Voormezeele Enclosure No.3, Belgium		
Theatre of war:	Belgium		
Next of kin:	Edward & Annie Massey (parents)		
Address:	St Martin, Salisbury, Wiltshire.		

On Saturday 1 May 1915 news came from the War Office of the death of Pte Frederick Massey, of the 2nd Battalion Wiltshire Regiment, on Tuesday 30 March 1915. The first intimation of his death was received by his mother, Mrs Massey, of 38 Rampart Road, on 2 April 1915, from his brother, who was serving in the same regiment. Mrs Massey had five sons – four serving with the colours, one with the 1st Wilts, two with the 2nd Wilts (Expeditionary Forces) and one with the 4th Wilts, who was in India. Three of her sons were ex-members of the St Martin's Church Lads Brigade.

Frederick Massey was actually with the 1st Battalion Wiltshire Regiment and he died on 29 March 1915 at Vormezeele, Belgium. The War Diary states: 'A quiet day, one man killed and one man wounded.' Frederick's brother Sidney died of wounds in 1917 while serving with the 2nd Battalion Wiltshire regiment.

Gunner Willie Manks		*42nd Brigade Royal Field Artillery*	
Service No.:	24469	Age:	35
Place of birth:	Halifax, Yorkshire	Home country:	England
Date of death:	31/03/15		
War cemetery:	Netley Military Cemetery, England		
Theatre of war:	Home		
Next of kin:	Annie Manks (wife)		
Address:	City Chambers, Catherine Street, Salisbury, Wiltshire		

Annie Manks's beloved husband Willie died on Wednesday 31 March 1915 at the Royal Victoria Hospital, Netley, in Hampshire. They had been married since the spring of 1910.

Pte David Reat Smith		*Royal Army Pay Corps*	
Service No.:	1462	Age:	35
Place of birth:	Chelsea, Middlesex	Home Country:	England
Date of death:	10/04/15		
War cemetery:	Salisbury (Devizes Road) Cemetery, Wiltshire		
Theatre of war:	Home		

Far left: David Reat Smith worked at Southern Command Headquarters.

Middle: Edward Curtain, who died in Salisbury Infirmary.

Right: John Mates was forty-seven years old when he enlisted but told the army he was just forty-one.

Next of kin: Rose Isabel Smith (wife); David Reat Smith & Emily Smith (parents)
Address: 13 Chichester Street, Pimlico, London

Pte Smith died, most likely of illness, on Saturday 10 April 1915 and is buried in Salisbury (Devizes Road) Cemetery, Wiltshire.

Pte Edward Daniel Curtain   *2nd Gen. Hospital Canadian Army Medical Corps*

Service No.:   34593   Age: 21
Place of birth: Toronto, Canada.   Home country: Canada
Date of death: 11/04/15
War cemetery: Salisbury (Devizes Road) Cemetery, Wiltshire
Theatre of war: Home
Next of kin: Daniel & Violetta Curtin (parents)
Address: Talbot Street, London, Ontario

The funeral of Pte Edward Curtain, of the Canadian Army Medical Corps, No.2 Gen. Hospital, who died in Salisbury Infirmary, took place with military honours at the Devizes Road Cemetery on Wednesday 14 April 1915. Prior to the interment a short service took place at the Roman Catholic Church by Father Mather, who officiated at the graveside. A number of men from Pte Curtain's corps acted as bearers, and at the conclusion of the ceremony three volleys were fired over the grave by a firing party from the Southern Command Headquarters, under Sgt Cullen, and the *Last Post* was sounded. Among those present were Col. Rogers of the Canadian detachment, Mr C.H. Harris, assistant commandant of the British Red Cross, Capt. Gillespie the staff captain, and Lt Sparks, orderly officer. The funeral arrangements were carried out by Messrs E.J. Harrison & Co. of the High Street.

   Edward Curtain was born on 23 November 1893 and by the time he volunteered for overseas duty in September 1914 he had served three years in the Medical Corps as a driver.

Cpl John A Mates   *2nd Battalion Eastern Ontario Regiment Canadian Army*

Service No.:   7818   Age: 48
Place of birth: Bromley, Kent   Home country: Canada
Date of death: 15/04/15
War cemetery: Salisbury (Devizes Road) Cemetery, Wiltshire
Theatre of war: Home

Next of kin: Sarah E. Mates (wife); Edward & Sarah Mates (parents)
Addresses: 105 Schofield Avenue, Brockville, Ontario
                 Upper Norwood, Surrey

Cpl Mates was born on Boxing Day 1867, in Bromley, Kent. He was a carpenter and emigrated with his wife and children to Canada prior to the First World War. Mates volunteered on 22 September 1914 and it is interesting to note he lied about his age. He told the Army he was forty-one but his actual age was forty-seven years old.

THE CAPTURE OF HILL 60

On the evening of 17 April 1915 an attack was made on the enemy's trenches on Hill 60, a commanding point lying on the north side of the Ypres-Comines railway, about 2½ miles south-east of Ypres. This spot was frequently the scene of action; heavy fighting had occurred between 14–17 February 1915, during which the summit of the hill was in the enemy's hands throughout. The British attack began at 7 p.m. on 17 April 1915, when heavily charged mines were fired under the German position, blowing up a length of trench with some 150 men manning it, who nearly all perished. Then, within a few minutes, British Infantry rushed the craters in the enemy's line and gained possession of the some 250-yards' length of the latter. So suddenly was the assault carried out that the British troops met with hardly any resistance, and sustained few casualties whilst securing fifteen prisoners, amongst whom were two officers. The Germans shortly afterwards opened heavy fire on the section gained and kept it up throughout the night, but the British held firm, working hard to strengthen the ground they had won and beating off several counter-attacks.

Shortly before seven on Sunday morning the Germans made their real reply with a determined effort. The Germans assaulted in force, coming in close formations, and hand-to-hand fighting continued for some time. At this juncture, invaluable service was rendered by some British motor-machine guns, which were rushed to the front, and opened fire on the masses coming forward, while the British artillery raked the German ranks with shrapnel.

The counter-attack was beaten off with heavy loss to the Germans, who, as usual, showed no inclination to accept defeat. Throughout the whole of 18 April 1915, German troops continued to be hurled against the British trenches and once, towards evening, some of the Germans obtained a footing on the southern edge of the crest. It was only a momentary advantage, however, for at 6 p.m. the British infantry charged with bayonet, dislodged the Germans from their foothold and secured the whole position. An hour later, the hill was held in strength by the British. The British casualties, as to be expected from the nature of the fighting were heavy, but the German losses were greater.

Canadian troops training on Salisbury Plain.

Lt Hugh Arthur Grenville Malet　　　　　　*A Company 2nd Battalion King's Own Scottish Borderers*

Place of birth:	India	Home country:	England	Age: 23
Date of death:	18/04/15	Cause of death:	Killed in action	
Memorial:	Salisbury, Wiltshire			
War cemetery:	Ypres Menin Gate Memorial, Belgium			
Theatre of war:	Belgium			
Next of kin:	Allan A.G. & Elizabeth Malet (parents)			
Address:	The Butts, Harrow-on-the-Hill, Middlesex			

Lt Malet was killed on Sunday 18 April 1915 during the fighting on Hill 60. He has no known grave and is remembered on the Ypres Menin Gate Memorial.

On Thursday 22 April 1915, The Second Battle of Ypres began and the Germans used chlorine gas against British Forces at Langemarck. A lieutenant serving in the Dorset Regiment wrote an account of his first experience of asphyxiating gas:

> I expect you have heard how the Germans on this Hill 60 played us the dirtiest trick that any British regiment has had to put up with. The Canadians did not have it like we did, they had it from 400 to 500 yards away, whereas our trenches are, at most, 40 yards from the Germans. I saw more of the affair than anyone else, so I can tell you exactly what happened. At about seven o'clock I came out of my dug out and saw a hose sticking over the German parapet, which was starting to spout out a thick yellow cloud with a tinge of green in it. The gas came out with a hiss that you could hear quite plainly. I at once shouted to my men to put on respirators (bits of flannel), then I got mine and went and warned the captain, who did not yet have his respirator on. The Huns began a terrible bombardment, not so much at us but at our supports and our dressing station.
>
> Now, either they had miscalculated the direction of the wind or else it had changed, for the gas did not come directly toward us, but went slantwise then, with our trench being so close, the gas went into part of the German trenches as well as into ours. They bolted from theirs when they got a wiff of the filthy stuff, a few of our men staggered away down the hill, some got into a wood behind it and died there, as the ground was low and the gas followed them, others only got as far as the mine head and communication trenches. The company in support on my left moved up into the firing line, as did also half of my platoon. Consequently, I was left with a few men to do all the rescue work. My men were splendid; they all came with me into the gas, except the ones I ordered to stay behind, and we must have saved scores of lives. The men in most cases were lying insensible in the bottom of the trenches, and quite a number were in the mine head, which was the worst possible place. The best place after the first rush of gas was the firing line, being the highest point.
>
> I was the only officer not in the firing line, and I should think quite 200 men passed through my hands, some died with me and some died on the way down. The battalion had, I believe, 337 casualties. I can't understand how it was I was not knocked out; it must have been the work I had to do. I was simply mad with rage, seeing strong men drop to the ground and die in this way. They were in agonies. I had to argue with many of them as to whether they were dead or not. Why we got it so bad was because of the closeness of our tenches to the Germans, and this affair does away with the idea that it is not deadly. I saw two men staggering over in a field in our rear last night, and when I went to look for them this morning they were both dead. Altogether, I suppose 100 or 120 men and two or three officers are dead or will die of the stuff. I am absolutely sickened. Clean killing is at least comprehensible, but this murder by slow agony, it absolutely knocks me. The whole civilised world ought to rise up and exterminate those swine across the hill.

3

GALLIPOLI

On Sunday 25 April 1915, British forces were landed on the Gallipoli Peninsula, the British and French Navies had been attempting to force a passage through the Dardanelles Narrows with a view to put pressure on Germany's allies, the Ottoman Empire, to aid Russia.

The ships were stopped by mines and the Turkish Forts that dominated the Dardanelles. A plan was conceived to land British, Commonwealth and French troops on the Gallipoli Peninsula, to capture the forts and march north to Constantinople, thus knocking the German allies out of the war and relieve pressure on Russia.

28 APRIL 1915 – FIRST BATTLE OF KRITHIA, GALLIPOLI, TURKEY

Pte Joseph Bolwell   *Royal Marine Light Infantry, Portsmouth Battalion, Royal Naval Division*

Service No.:	PO/14785	Age:	25
Place of birth:	East Harnham, Wiltshire	Home country:	England
Date of death:	01/05/15	Cause of death:	Died of wounds
Memorial:	Salisbury, Wiltshire		
War cemetery:	Portsmouth Naval Memorial, England		
Theatre of war:	At sea		
Next of kin:	Joseph John & Alice Louise Bolwell (parents)		
Address:	12 Harnham Road, Salisbury, Wiltshire		

On 15 May 1915 Alice Bolwell, of 12 Harnham Road, Salisbury, received an intimation that her son, Joseph, who was serving in the Portsmouth Battalion with the Royal Marine Brigade of the Royal Naval Division, had died on 5 May 1915 from wounds received in action near the Dardanelles.

Pte Bolwell's official date of death is Saturday 1 May and he was probably buried at sea, but the wounds he received that caused his death were inflicted at Gallipoli.

Pte Frank Newton Cooke   *A Company 4th Battalion Australian Infantry, Australian Imperial Force*

Service No.:	649	Age:	27
Place of birth:	Piddletrenthide, Dorset	Home country:	Australia
Date of death:	01/05/15	Cause of death:	Killed in action
War cemetery:	Lone Pine Memorial, Turkey		
Theatre of war:	Gallipoli		
Next of kin:	Newton & Leonora Cooke		
Address:	West Harnham, Harnham, Wiltshire		

Frank Cooke, who had been a printer, volunteered for service with Australian Imperial Force on 27 August 1914. He was part of the Australian & New Zealand Forces which landed on Gallipoli in late April 1915 in the beachhead that became known as Anzac Cove. He was killed on Saturday 1 May while attacking an area called Lone Pine, which lies in the southern part of the Anzac area. It was a strategically important plateau held by the Turkish Forces.

Frank Cooke had emigrated to Australia prior to the First World War and enlisted at Albury, New South Wales. He was the eldest son of Newton and Leonora Cooke and is remembered on Lone Pine Memorial with 4,900 men of the Anzac Corps; he was originally buried in what was called Shrapnel Valley, Gallipoli, but the grave location was lost. His personnel effects were sent to his parents, consisted of a pocket book.

Pte Frederick Arthur Newton		*Princess Patricia's Canadian Light Infantry, No.2 Company, Eastern Ontario Regiment*	
Service No.:	567	Age:	19
Date of death:	04/05/15	Cause of death:	Killed in action
Place of birth:	Salisbury, Wiltshire	Home country:	Canada
Memorial:	Salisbury, Wiltshire		
War cemetery:	Ypres Menin Gate Memorial, Belgium		
Theatre of war:	Belgium		
Next of kin:	Frederick & Emma Newton (parents)		
Address:	22 East Street Fisherton, Salisbury, Wiltshire		

Fred Newton had enlisted on 12 August 1914, at Edmonton, Alberta. On 4 May 1915, the Germans opened an intense bombardment of the Frezenberg Ridge, east of the town of Ypres. It is likely Fred was killed during this bombardment and is remembered on the Ypres Menin Gate Memorial, with 54,343 other men who have no known grave and fell in the area known as the Ypres Salient.

---

6 MAY 1915 – SECOND BATTLE OF KRITHIA, GALLIPOLI, TURKEY
ON 20 MAY 1915, RMS LUSITANIA WAS SUNK BY THE U-20 OFF THE SOUTHERN COAST OF IRELAND.

Pte Albert George Kimber		*1st Battalion Monmouthshire Regiment*	
Service No.:	2277	Age:	21
Place of birth:	Newport, Monmouthshire	Home country:	Wales
Date of death:	08/05/15	Cause of death:	Killed in action
War cemetery:	Ypres Menin Gate Memorial, Belgium		
Theatre of war:	Belgium		
Next of kin:	Albert William & Bessie Kimber		
Address:	14 Rugby Road, Newport, Monaghan		

Albert Kimber was the only son of Albert William and Bessie Kimber, he had been living in Salisbury prior to the First World War. He was killed at Frezenburg during the Second Battle of Ypres on Sunday 8 May 1915 and it is likely he died just to the south of Cheddar Villa, north-east of the town of Ypres. By 9 May 1915 the brigade that the Monmouthshire Regiment belonged to had been decimated. A brigade was made up of four battalions and numbered approximately 4,000 men. After 9 May the 84th Brigade numbered around 1,400 men.

Sgt Edward Major		*B Company 2nd Battalion Gloucestershire Regiment*	
Service No.:	7053	Age:	29
Place of birth:	Salisbury, Wiltshire.	Home country:	England

Date of death: 09/05/15   Cause of death: Killed in action
Memorial: Salisbury, Wiltshire
War cemetery: Bedford House Cemetery, Belgium
Theatre of war: Belgium
Next of kin: Edward & Elizabeth Major (parents)
Address: 7 Sidney Street, Salisbury, Wiltshire

Edward Major was a casualty of the Second Battle of Ypres. He was killed in action at
Frezenburg on Monday 9 May 1915.

9 MAY 1915 – THE BATTLE OF AUBERS RIDGE, FRANCE

Sgt Albert George William Jones   *Royal Army Service Corps*
Service No.:   S/20944   Age: 29
Date of death: 10/05/15   Cause of death: Died of illness
Home country: England
Memorial: Salisbury, Wiltshire
War cemetery: Salisbury London Road Cemetery, England
Theatre of war: Home
Next of kin: Maj. & Mrs O.G. Jones (parents)
Address: 33 Castle Road, Salisbury, Wiltshire

Albert was the youngest son of Maj. and Mrs O.G. Jones and died most likely of illness at one
of the hospitals in the Salisbury area on Tuesday 10 May 1915.

15 MAY 1915 – BATTLE OF FESTUBERT, BELGIUM

L/Cpl William Benjamin Powney   *1st Battalion Royal Berkshire Regiment*
Service No.:   5779   Age: 41
Place of birth: Salisbury, Wiltshire   Home country: England
Date of death: 16/05/15   Cause of death: Died of wounds
Memorial: Salisbury, Wiltshire
War cemetery: Bethune Town Cemetery, France
Theatre of war: France
Next of kin: The late Joseph & Mary Ann Martha Powney (parents)
Address: Salisbury, Wiltshire

On 15 May 1915 the 1st Battalion Royal Berkshire Regiment were preparing for an attack
at Richbourg l'Avoue, France. William Powney was wounded, either in the trenches waiting
for the attack during a German counter bombardment or during the storming of the enemy
trenches. The 1st Berkshires suffered over 400 casualties during the course of the attack.

L/Cpl Powney was the second son of the late Joseph and Mary Ann Martha Powney of
Salisbury and the brother of Joseph Powney of Silver Street, Salisbury. He is buried at Bethune
Town Cemetery, France, which was the location of 33rd Casualty-Clearing Station, where he
was probably evacuated after being wounded.

Cpl Robert John Smith   *3rd Battalion Worcestershire Regiment*

Service No.:   11484   Age: 25

Place of birth: Belbroughton, Worcestershire   Home country: England

Date of death: 28/05/15   Cause of death: Died of wounds

War Cemetery: Salisbury London Road Cemetery, England

Next of kin: Annie E. Smith (wife); Thomas & Kate J. Smith (parents)

Addresses: Belbroughton, Worcestershire

                Belbroughton, Worcestershire

Robert John Smith, known as John, was serving with the 3rd Battalion Worcestershire Regiment and it is likely he was wounded during the fighting at Bellewaarde in mid-June when the Worcestors suffered around 300 casualties.

    Cpl Smith was probably evacuated to one of the military hospitals in the Salisbury area after being wounded on the continent and was buried locally after his death.

4 JUNE 1915 – THIRD BATTLE OF KRITHIA, GALLIPOLI, TURKEY

Pte Fred Crouch   *1st Battalion Wiltshire Regiment*

Service No.:   7588   Age: 30

Place of birth: Idminston, Wiltshire   Home country: England

Date of death: 06/06/15   Cause of death: Killed in action

Memorial: Salisbury, Wiltshire

War cemetery: Ypres Menin Gate, Belgium.

Theatre of war: Belgium

Next of kin: James & Emily Crouch (parents)

Address: Salisbury, Wiltshire.

On Sunday 6 June 1915 the 1st Battalion Wiltshire Regiment were in the trenches at Hooge in Belgium. Pte Crouch was killed by artillery fire from a Minen werfer, which was a large trench mortar that fired a shell about the size of a small dustbin. These shells were fired high in the air and could be seen falling and it was possible to dodge them. However, on this day the Germans were using two Minen werfers, one heavy and one medium sized. The enemy fired twenty-one shots before they were silenced by the British artillery.

Right: The Commonwealth War Grave Commission headstone for R. John Smith.

Middle: The original private memorial of Robert John Smith, known as John.

Far right: William Cain, who died due to illness.

Two men were killed and twenty wounded; one of these was Fred Crouch, who is remembered on the Ypres Menin Gate Memorial and has no known grave.

Pte William Charles Cain   *12th Battalion Middlesex Regiment*
Service No.:	2573	Age:	23
Place of birth:	Hampstead, Middlesex	Home country:	England
Date of death:	11/06/15		
War cemetery:	Salisbury (Devizes Road) Cemetery, Wiltshire		
Theatre of war:	Home		
Next of kin:	Mary A. Cain (mother)		
Address:	Hampstead, London		

William Cain volunteered in September 1914 when the regiment was formed in at Mill Hill Middlesex and moved with them to Salisbury Plain between 4–12 May 1915. It is almost certain that Cain had been training on Salisbury Plain and died of illness at one of the local hospitals.

Driver William Warner Lassetter   *59th Field Company Royal Engineers*
Service No.:	12586	Age:	34
Place of birth:	Bournemouth, Hampshire	Home country:	England
Date of death:	14/06/15	Cause of death:	Died of illness
War cemetery:	Eastry Churchyard, England		
Theatre of war:	Home		
Next of kin:	Mrs Naish (mother)		
Address:	7 Pennyfarthing Street, Salisbury, Wiltshire		

William Lassetter was the only son of Mrs Naish of Pennyfarthing Street, Salisbury, and the grandson of the late Thomas Spearing of Quidhampton. Prior to the war he had been a milkman. He died on Monday 14 June 1915 at the Isolation Hospital Eastry, Sandwich, Kent, of typhoid fever following an injury received in France.

L/Cpl Ishmael Newbury   *2nd Battalion Yorkshire Regiment*
Service No.:	9353	Age:	29
Place of birth:	Stockton, Wiltshire	Home country:	England
Date of death:	15/06/15	Cause of death:	Killed in action
Memorial:	Salisbury, Wiltshire		
War cemetery:	Le Touret Memorial, France		
Theatre of war:	France		
Next of kin:	George & Ruth Newbury (parents)		
Address:	41 Scotts Lane, Salisbury, Wiltshire		

Ishmael Newbury was killed in action at the Second Action of Givenchy on Tuesday 15 June 1915. The attack was a complete failure, the Germans were able to occupy their trenches while the British bombardment was still in progress and had little effect on the enemy defenders. The 2nd Battalion Yorkshire Regiment and the 2nd Battalion Wiltshire Regiment were cut down by rifle and machine-gun fire as they crossed No Man's Land. 120 members of the 2nd Battalion Yorkshire Regiment were killed on 15 June 1915, one of whom was Ishmael Newbury, who is remembered on the Le Touret Memorial and has no known grave.

Pte James Newman   *2nd Battalion Wiltshire Regiment*
Service No.:	10564	Age:	22

Place of birth: Fisherton, Wiltshire   Home country: England
Date of death: 15/06/15   Cause of death: Killed in action
Memorial: Salisbury, Wiltshire
War cemetery: Le Touret Memorial, France
Theatre of war: France
Next of kin: George & Maria Newman (parents)
Address: Fisherton Anger, Salisbury, Wiltshire

The 2nd Battalion Wiltshire Regiment also took part in the Second Action of Givenchy on Tuesday 15 June 1915. As the Wiltshires crossed No Man's Land they were met by murderous rifle and machine-gun fire. The Wiltshires only managed to get to a point 50 yards from the German line. James Newman was one of seventy-two members of the regiment to be killed on that day and he is remembered on the Le Touret Memorial and has no known grave. It is noted in the Wiltshire's War Diary that the Germans used incendiary bullets and sniped at the wounded in No Man's Land.

Cpl Sidney William Jack Pitman   *2nd Battalion Wiltshire Regiment*
Service No.:   10363   Age: 19
Place of birth: Salisbury, Wiltshire   Home country: England
Date of death: 15/06/15   Cause of death: Killed in action
Memorial: Salisbury, Wiltshire
War cemetery: Le Touret Memorial, France
Theatre of war: France
Next of kin: Mr & Mrs Pitman (parents)
Address: 39 Rampart Road, Salisbury, Wiltshire

News was received in July 1915 from the War Office of the death in action of Cpl S.W.J. Pitman, known as Jack, of 39 Rampart Road, Salisbury, serving with the 3rd Wilts Regiment. He had joined the Army in the early part of September 1914, and having had only a few weeks' training, was sent to France at the end of October 1914. He had been in the trenches on Christmas Day and taken part when English and German soldiers exchanged greetings. Suffering from frozen feet, he was sent home in January 1915, having survived several fierce engagements without being wounded. Jack had only returned to the front in May 1915 when he was killed on 15 June 1915, dying within a few minutes of being struck by shrapnel. In a letter to Jack Pitman's mother, the commanding officer writes of him as a very brave corporal, who was leading a section against the German trenches at Givenchy when he was struck down.

Cpl Pitman, who was only nineteen, was well known in Salisbury, his good nature and ready wit making him many friends. He was a former member of the St Martin's CLB, and was an under-gardener employed by Mr C.H.E. Chubb prior to enlisting. Jack originally joined the 3rd Reserve Battalion but was transferred to the 2nd Battalion as a replacement.

Cpl Frank Reginald Safe   *1st Battalion Wiltshire Regiment*
Service No.:   5815   Age: 32
Place of birth: Harnham, Wiltshire   Home country: England
Date of death: 16/06/15   Cause of death: Killed in action
Memorial: Salisbury, Wiltshire
War Cemetery: Ypres Menin Gate Memorial
Theatre of war: Belgium
Next of kin: Mrs Martin
Address: Salisbury, Wiltshire

Frank Safe was killed in what was described as a minor operation, the first attack at Bellewaarde, a lake at Hooge in Belgium. In the early hours of the morning of Wednesday 16 June, the Wiltshires attacked taking the German trench. By 6 a.m. the British had advanced to within 50 yards of Hooge village. At 9 a.m. the Germans advanced down communication trenches and a fierce fight took place with bomb and bullet. After about one and a half hours the Wiltshires' supply of grenades was exhausted and the Germans succeeded forcing the British troops back down the trench. The Wiltshires suffered heavy casualties and were forced to retreat in the open suffering more casualties and then attempted a counter-attack which failed. The area where the British retreated was subjected to a heavy German bombardment which included gas shells.

Frank is remembered on the Ypres Menin Gate Memorial, Belgium, and has no known grave.

Pte Thomas Brady   *10th Battalion Black Watch*
Service No.:   S/5774   Age: 29
Place of birth: Glasgow, Lanarkshire   Home country: Scotland
Date of death: 21/06/15
War cemetery: Salisbury (Devizes Road) Cemetery, Wiltshire
Theatre of war: Home

Thomas Brady volunteered in September 1914 joining the 10th Service Battalion The Black Watch, who were at Perth. During the early stages of the war service battalions had little or no equipment. Civilian clothing was worn and battalions wore coloured cloth patches for identification. He died on Monday 21 June 1915 of illness after coming to Salisbury Plain with the 26th Division for training.

30 JUNE 1915 – ALLIED CASUALTIES AT GALLIPOLI REACH 42,434

Pte Herbert John Meigh   *Royal Army Service Corps 26th Division Field Bakery*
Service No.:   S4/070272   Age: 27
Place of birth: Ashton, Warwickshire   Home country: England
Date of death: 06/07/15
War cemetery: Salisbury (Devizes Road) Cemetery, Wiltshire
Theatre of war: Home
Next of kin: Walter & Sarah Meigh (parents)
Address: 215 Bloomsbury Street, Nechells, Birmingham, Warwickshire

The 26th Division had been training on Salisbury Plain in the summer of 1915. Herbert Meigh was attached to the field bakery which fed the division. He died of illness on Tuesday 6 July 1915.

25 JULY 1915 – NASRIYA IN MESPOTAMIA IS CAPTURED BY BRITISH TROOPS
30 JULY 1915 – GERMANS ATTACK WITH FLAME-THROWERS AT HOOGE, BELGIUM

Driver Arthur Mitchell   *Royal Army Service Corps 202nd Heavy Transport Company*
Service No.:   T4/035573   Age: 45
Place of birth: Kidderminster, Worcestershire Home country: England

Far left: *Thomas Brady from Glasgow, who died due to illness.*

Middle: *John Meigh, like thousands of other soldiers in First World War, died due to illness.*

Left: *Arthur Buckle volunteered for service in 1914.*

Date of death: 06/08/15
War cemetery: Salisbury London Road Cemetery, England
Theatre of war: Home
Next of kin: Lavinia Mitchell (wife); Henry & Jane Mitchell (parents)
Addresses: St Martin, Herefordshire
                 Kidderminster, Worcestershire

The funeral of Arthur Mitchell of the 202nd Company, ASC, stationed at Sutton Veny, who died at Salisbury Red Cross Hospital on Thursday 6 August 1915, took place at London Road Cemetery on the afternoon of 9 August 1915. He was held in high esteem by the officers and men of the company, and the service was attended by Capt. Maclear, the officer commanding the company and fifty non-commissioned officers and men, in addition to a firing party under Sgt Littleley. Mr C.H. Harris, the assistant commandant, represented the Salisbury Men's Detachment, British Red Cross Hospital, and followed the coffin, which was covered by a Union Jack, six of the deceased's comrades acting as bearers, to the cemetery where the interment was conducted by Revd J. Wellington, who was a member of the Salisbury Detachment British Red Cross Society.

Among the mourners was Arthur Mitchell's mother, who lived at Kidderminster. Beautiful wreaths were sent by Capt. Maclear, the non-commissioned officers and men of the 202nd Company ASC, the 203rd Company ASC and the officers of the 26th Divisional Train.

6 AUGUST 1915 – BATTLE OF SARI BAIR AND LANDINGS AT SUVLA BAY AND ACHI BABA, GALLIPOLI, TURKEY

Pte Arthur Bloy Buckle   *8th Battalion Duke of Cornwall's Light Infantry*
Service No.:   17844   Age: 33
Place of birth: Islington, London   Home country: England
Date of death: 07/08/15   Cause of death: Died of illness
War cemetery: Salisbury (Devizes Road) Cemetery, Wiltshire
Theatre of war: Home
Next of kin: Alfred George & Hannah Buckle (parents)
Address: 58 Maury Road, Stoke Newington, London

The 8th Service Battalion Duke of Cornwall's Light Infantry was part of the 26th Division who came to Salisbury Plain for training in summer 1915. Arthur volunteered for service in September 1914, when the 8th Service Battalion Duke of Cornwall's Light Infantry were formed at Bodmin.

In January 1916 a report in the local paper lead with the headline '5TH WILTS ALMOST ANNIHILATED'. It referred to Sir Ian Hamilton, who had been the commander of the Gallipoli Peninsula Operations, with dispatches describing the events of 6–10 August 1915 when a great attack had taken place from the Anzac area.

The aims were to break out of Anzac and isolate the bulk of the Turkish forces on the peninsula from Constantinople and to gain a commanding position for the artillery to cut off the Turkish Army with sea traffic. The 5th Wiltshire Regiment were part of the left covering column and were to march northwards along the beach and seize a hill called Damakjelik Bair some 1,400 yards north of Table Top. This would enable 9th Corps to be aided as it landed south of Nibrunei Point while protecting the flank of the other assaulting columns.

During the main attack, a hill Chunuk Bair had been taken and on the night of 9/10 August 1915, the 5th Battalion Wiltshire Regiment and the 6th Loyal North Lancashire Regiment were chosen to hold this position. The Loyal North Lancashires arrived first and their commanding officer, even though it was dark, recognised how dangerously the trenches were sited. He at once ordered that observation posts were dug on the actual crest of the hill.

The Wiltshires were delayed by the rough terrain of the intricate country. They did not reach the position until 4 a.m. The War Diary disagrees with this time, stating the Wiltshires arrived at 3 a.m. and laying the blame on a New Zealand officer who was their guide. When the Wiltshires arrived they were told to lie down in what was believed, erroneously, to be a covered and safe position.

At daybreak on 10 August, the Turks delivered a grand attack from the line Chunuk Bair Hill Q against the Wiltshires and the Loyal North Lancashires, already weakened in numbers by previous fighting. First the British were shelled and then, at 5.30 a.m., were assaulted by a huge column, consisting of a division plus a regiment and three battalions. The Loyal North Lancashire Regiment were overwhelmed in their shallow trenches by the sheer weight of the Turkish attack while the Wilts Regiment were caught out in the open and literally almost annihilated. The War Diary for the Wiltshire Regiment states the Turks attacked fifteen minutes after machine guns opened fire at 4.30 a.m. It also gives an indication of how desperate the British were to escape from the fighting. During the fierce fighting, Lt-Col. J. Carden commanding the 5th Wiltshire's was killed. Another account is given from Capt. (then Lt) Bush who was honoured for his conspicuous service during the Gallipoli campaign. According to the despatches, the Wiltshires and another regiment had a whole division of Turks and two other Battalions against them on 10 August 1915. The enemy opened fire on them at dawn with terrible results. Those who could retired down a narrow gully, only to come under fire from more machine guns and here, with the two remaining senior officers being killed, Lt Bush found himself left in command. Immediately, with the help of two sergeants, Lt Bush rallied the men and lined them against the side of the gully just out of reach of the machine guns. He went up and across the gully, finding a fairly practicable, though terribly steep, way up, got the men across by twos and threes, and led them to a place of safety under the top of the cliffs. Leaving them with the two remaining subalterns with orders not to move till after dark, if he did not return, and then to make their way to the beach. Lt Bush went across the open, under rifle and machine-gun fire about 300 yards, finally reaching a New Zealand trench. From there he was passed down to headquarters and was able to pass word along the line to look out for the men as they came in after dark. A party was sent out to clear the bottom of the gully; about 150 to 200 men came in that night. Lt Bush was invalided home about ten days afterwards, with dysentery.

Some of the men of the 5th Wiltshire's lay hidden and survived the attack returning to their unit as late as 26 August 1914. Almost 150 members of the 5th Wiltshire's were killed on 10 August 1915, the majority have no known grave and are remembered on Helles Memorial.

Pte Frederick Hamilton Bates   *5th Battalion Wiltshire Regiment*

Service No.:	9743	Age:	34
Place of birth:	Salisbury, Wiltshire	Home country:	England
Date of death:	10/08/15	Cause of death:	Killed in action
Memorial:	Salisbury, Wiltshire		
War cemetery:	Helles Memorial, Turkey		
Theatre of war:	Gallipoli		
Next of kin:	Frederick Thomas Burrough & Mary Bates		
Address:	Salisbury, Wiltshire		

Frederick Bates was killed in action on Tuesday 10 August 1915 at Damakjelik Bair, Gallipoli. He is remembered on Helles Memorial, Gallipoli, and has no known grave.

Pte Charles Cobb   *5th Battalion Wiltshire Regiment*

Service No.:	9314	Age:	18
Place of birth:	Salisbury, Wiltshire	Home country:	England
Date of death:	10/08/15	Cause of death:	Killed in action
Memorial:	Salisbury, Wiltshire		
War cemetery:	Helles Memorial, Turkey		
Theatre of war:	Gallipoli		
Next of kin:	Ellen Elizabeth Cobb (mother)		
Address:	105 Culver Street, Salisbury, Wiltshire		

Eighteen years old and under-age, Charles Cobb was killed in action at Damakjelik Bair, Gallipoli. He is remembered on Helles Memorial, Gallipoli, and has no known grave.

Lt Alfred James Hinxman   *5th Battalion Wiltshire Regiment*

Place of birth:	Devizes, Wiltshire	Home country:	England	Age: 21
Date of death:	10/08/15	Cause of death:	Killed in action	
Memorial:	Salisbury, Wiltshire			
War cemetery:	Helles Memorial, Turkey			
Theatre of war:	Gallipoli			
Next of kin:	Alfred & Emma A. Hinxman (parents)			
Address:	146 Fisherton Street, Salisbury, Wiltshire			

Information Wanted 5th Wiltshire Regiment

Will any of the Officers, NCOs, or men of the 5th Battalion Wiltshire Regiment, having seen Lt A.J. Hinxman after 5 o'clock on Tuesday morning, the 10 August, in Gallipoli, kindly communicate with Mrs Hinxman, 146, Fisherton Street, Salisbury. Lt Hinxman is reported missing since the 10 August

Many of the men involved in the disaster on Tuesday 10 August were first reported missing as we can see from the advert which was placed in a local paper, above. Lt Hinxman was, however, killed in action at Damakjelik Bair, Gallipoli. He is remembered on Helles Memorial, Gallipoli and has no known grave.

Pte Albert Edward Humphries   *5th Battalion Wiltshire Regiment*

Service No.:	9334	Age:	23

Place of birth: Alsford, Hampshire   Home country: England
Date of death: 10/08/15   Cause of death: Killed in action
Memorial: Salisbury, Wiltshire
War cemetery: Helles Memorial, Turkey
Theatre of war: Gallipoli
Next of kin: Albert Edward & Elizabeth Humphries (parents)
Address: 37 Highfield Road, Salisbury, Wiltshire

Albert Humphries was killed in action on Tuesday 10 August 1918 at Damakjelik Bair, Gallipoli. He is remembered on Helles Memorial, Gallipoli, and has no known grave.

Pte Charles James Sewell   *5th Battalion Wiltshire Regiment*
Service No.:   9788   Age: 23
Place of birth: Gosport, Hampshire   Home country: England
Date of death: 10/08/15   Cause of death: Killed in action
Memorial: Salisbury, Wiltshire
War cemetery: Helles Memorial, Turkey
Theatre of war: Gallipoli

Charles Sewell was killed in action on Tuesday 10 August 1918 at Damakjelik Bair, Gallipoli. He is remembered on Helles Memorial, Gallipoli, and has no known grave.

Pte William Wells   *5th Battalion Wiltshire Regiment*
Service No.:   9556
Place of birth: Huntsbourne, Hampshire   Home country: England
Date of death: 10/08/15   Cause of death: Killed in action
Memorial: Salisbury, Wiltshire
War cemetery: Helles Memorial, Turkey
Theatre of war: Gallipoli

William Wells was killed in action on Tuesday 10 August 1918 at Damakjelik Bair, Gallipoli. He is remembered on Helles Memorial, Gallipoli, and has no known grave.

Pte Albert William Jeans   *6th Battalion Leinster Regiment*
Service No.:   1061   Age: 28
Place of birth: Salisbury, Wiltshire   Home country: England
Date of death: 10/08/15   Cause of death: Killed in action
Memorial: Salisbury, Wiltshire
War cemetery: Helles Memorial, Turkey
Theatre of war: Gallipoli
Next of kin: Edith Emma Jeans (wife); George & Fanny Jeans (parents)
Addresses: Lower Woodford, Wiltshire
                  110 Milford Hill, Salisbury

Albert Jeans volunteered in September 1914. He originally enlisted in the Wiltshire Regiment but because the call for volunteers had been so successful, the Wiltshire Regiments were full, many volunteers from Wiltshire then found themselves in other regiments such as the Leinster part of the 29th Brigade of the 10th Irish Division.

Albert was killed during fighting at Sari Bair on Tuesday 10 August 1915; he is remembered on Helles Memorial and has no known grave.

L/Cpl James Cull   *Military Police, Military Foot Police*

Service No.:   P/1936   Age: 35
Place of birth: Gussage, Dorset   Home country: England
Date of death: 10/08/15
Memorial: Salisbury, Wiltshire
War cemetery: Salisbury London Road Cemetery, England
Theatre of war: Home
Next of kin: Joseph & Harriet L. Cull (parents)
Addresses: Elm Grove Road, Salisbury
                     Gussage All Saints, Dorset

The death of James Cull occurred at Aldershot on Tuesday 10 August 1915 of the Military Foot Police, who prior to the outbreak of war was a member of the Salisbury City Police Force. James Cull was a native of Gussage, Dorset, and went through the South African War in the Grenadier Guards, receiving the medal for the campaign. In March 1903 he joined the City Police Force. His career in the city was marked by his plucky action in stopping a runaway horse on Christmas Eve 1912, when, attached to a cart, it bolted down Fisherton Street towards the Butcher Row, which was crowded at the time. At the risk of his own life, he dashed at the animal's head, and undoubtedly prevented an accident which would have been attended with disastrous results. His conduct received official recognition in January 1913, when at the sitting City Petty Sessions the mayor presented the constable with a watch. Promotion followed on 23 January, when Cull was made a first class constable. He was a good all-round cricketer and a highly respected member in the force, becoming familiar to residents as one of the police who undertook mounted duty.

In September 1914 he left Salisbury to act as a drill instructor, with the rank of sergeant, at the depot of the Wiltshire Regiment at Devizes, and he transferred to the Military Foot Police at Aldershot. He was taken ill suddenly on 5 August, and died on 10 August. His funeral was held on 14 August, his coffin was placed on a wheeled bier and covered with a Union Jack. It was followed by family mourners and a long procession which included many members of the City Police Force and special constables and members of the military from the Foot Police.

He was thirty-five and left a widow and one little boy.

Pte William Henry John Fry   *5th Battalion Wiltshire Regiment*

Service No.:   9336   Age: 17
Place of birth: Marlborough, Wiltshire   Home country: England
Date of death: 14/08/15   Cause of death: Died of wounds
Memorial: Salisbury, Wiltshire
War cemetery: Helles Memorial, Turkey
Theatre of war: Gallipoli
Next of kin: Harry & Mary Fry (parents)
Address: 53 Paynes Hill, Salisbury, Wiltshire

William was just seventeen, and as such under-age, when he volunteered for service. After training he embarked for the Mediterranean and Gallipoli in June 1915. He died of wounds received on Tuesday 10 August 1915 at Damakjelik Bair, Gallipoli. He is remembered on Helles Memorial, Gallipoli, and has no known grave.

21 AUGUST 1915 – ANZAC ATTACK AT ANAFARTA, SUVLA BAY AND THE START OF THE BATTLE OF SCIMITAR HILL, GALLIPOLI

Above: *4th Battalion Wiltshire Regiment in India.*

Right: *James Cull of the Military Foot Police.*

In a letter to his mother, Pte Frank Tanner, an old Bishop Wordsworld schoolboy who was serving as stretcher bearer with New Zealand forces in Gallipoli, gives us a taste of August 1915:

> Our dressing station and bivouacs are just at the back of the trenches. We are quite safe there. They pass the word back when anyone is hurt, and it does not take us long to get there. It is very awkward getting the badly wounded out, at night especially, but you take all things as they come. They say, 'Never mind, old chap, you are doing your best for me I know'; and sometimes they apologise for groaning. The other night one of the 2nd Company's sergeants got a glancing wound across the skull. He would not be carried to the dressing station, and it was a job to get him out on a stretcher to go down the hill, although after he had gone the doctor did not give him much chance.
>
> We will be going back to the rest gully again on Monday. We do not get many casualties here unless we have to do any charging, then the 'SBs' (stretcher bearers) have a busy time. I was in the trenches yesterday looking over through a periscope, watching a cruiser bombing some Turkish trenches. The Turks are very close, but keep well down. I had a good view of the country, but could not see one. They have great trenches, line after line of them.

Frank Tanner survived the war.

Pte Harry Sheldrake   *2nd Battalion Wiltshire Regiment*

Service No.:   18739   Age: 37
Place of birth: Salisbury, Wiltshire   Home country: England
Date of death: 23/08/15   Cause of death: Died of wounds
Memorial: Salisbury, Wiltshire
War cemetery: Gorre British & Indian Cemetery, France
Theatre of war: France
Next of kin: George & Eliza Jane Sheldrake (parents)
Address: Salisbury, Wiltshire

It is likely that Harry Sheldrake died from wounds received on Friday 20 August 1915 in the trenches at Festubert. The War Diary states, 'All quiet nothing of importance to report. One killed and six wounded by shell fire.' He is buried in Gorre British & Indian Cemetery, France.

> *31 AUGUST 1915 – THE ALLIES LOSSES IN GALLIPOLI DURING AUGUST NUMBER 40,000 SOLDIERS, FROM DEATH DUE TO FIGHTING OR THROUGH DYSENTERY AND OTHER DISEASES*

Pte Frederick Arthur Horton   *5th Battalion Wiltshire Regiment*

Service No.:   9348   Age: 20
Place of birth: Salisbury, Wiltshire: Home country: England
Date of death: 02/09/15   Cause of death: Died of wounds
Memorial: Salisbury, Wiltshire
War cemetery: Helles Memorial, Turkey
Theatre of war: Gallipoli
Next of kin: Caroline Horton (mother)
Address: 32 Rollestone Street, Salisbury, Wiltshire

Fredrick Horton, known as Fred, had volunteered in September 1915 and died of wounds at Gallipoli. He was either buried at sea from one of the hospital ships or his grave was lost. He is remembered on the Helles Memorial.

Cpl Edward Graham   *Royal Army Service Corps*

Service No.:   MS/2378   Age: 33
Date of death: 03/09/15   Cause of death: Accidental
Place of birth: Fisherton, Wiltshire   Home country: England
Memorial: Salisbury, Wiltshire
War cemetery: St Albans Cemetery, England
Theatre of war: Home
Next of kin: Annie Graham (wife)
Address: 28 Coldharbour Lane, Salisbury Wilts

Cpl Edward Graham, of the Army Service Corps, Mechanical Transport, whose home was at 28 Coldharbour Lane, Salisbury, died in St Albans on Friday 3 September 1915. Edward, who left a widow and five young children, had been in France twice, and had returned home wounded. While on duty as a despatch rider, the sparking plug of his machine flew out and his clothes caught fire. He was severely burnt and died in hospital. The funeral was conducted at St Albans with full military honours, and among the floral tributes were wreaths from St Paul's Conservative Club and his civilian friends in Salisbury.

The official date of death was Friday 3 September while unofficially it was thought he died on Monday 6 September. This gives a very good indication of how communication sometimes broke down during the First World War.

Stoker 1st Class Sidney Emm   *Royal Navy HMS* Dahlia

Service No.:	144882	Age:	21
Place of birth:	Portsea, Hampshire	Home country:	England
Date of death:	04/09/15		
Memorial:	Salisbury, Wiltshire		
War cemetery:	Rosskeen Parish Churchyard Extension or Burial Ground, Scotland		
Theatre of war:	Home		
Next of kin:	Sidney & Lillian Emm (parents)		
Address:	Salisbury, Wiltshire		

It is likely that Sidney Emm died at the nearby naval base and was buried at Rossken Churchyard, Scotland.

Pte Stanley John Swayne   *02/4th Battalion Wiltshire Regiment*

Service No.:	2607	Age:	21
Place of birth:	Salisbury, Wiltshire	Home country:	England
Date of death:	20/09/15	Cause of death:	Died of illness
Memorial:	Salisbury, Wiltshire		
War cemetery:	Kirkee 1914–18 Memorial, India		
Theatre of war:	India		
Next of kin:	Thomas & Fanny Swayne (parents)		
Address:	1 Waverley Place, Gigant Street, Salisbury, Wiltshire		

Stanley Swayne was the younger son of Thomas and Fanny Swayne of Salisbury. After volunteering in 1914 he left for India in December 1914 to replace regular troops who had been stationed in India at the start of the war. He died of illness, at Poona, India, on 20 September 1915.

Pte Harry Victor Beaven   *1st Battalion Wiltshire Regiment*

Service No.:	9175	Age:	33
Place of birth:	Salisbury, Wiltshire	Home country:	England
Date of death:	23/09/15	Cause of death:	Killed in action
Memorial:	Salisbury, Wiltshire		
War cemetery:	Ypres Menin Gate, Belgium		
Theatre of war:	Belgium		
Next of kin:	Mrs Beaven (wife); William & Mary Anne Beaven (parents)		
Addresses:	Salisbury		
	St Martin, Salisbury, Wiltshire		

Harry Beaven was killed in action on Thursday 23 September 1915, during a bombardment by the Germans. The Wiltshires were billeted at Ypres in cellars and were employed on working parties – digging trenches and carrying food and ammunition during the nights. During the day they rested; however, it was difficult to sleep because of the continuous shelling by the British and the Germans. The men were feeling the strain due to the lack of sleep.

Beaven was one of four of the Wiltshires who died on Thursday 23 September; he is remembered on the Ypres Menin Gate Memorial and has no known grave.

4

LOOS

This was to be the biggest British offensive to date in the First World War and involved six divisions. It was the first time that poison gas was used by the British and the battle began on 25 September. Gas was released early on the morning of 25 September and in some places hung where it had been released. Though the battle was successful, heavy casualties were inflicted on the British and Commonwealth Forces.

2nd-Lt John Harold Clark *3rd Battalion Wiltshire Regiment*

Place of birth:	Salisbury, Wiltshire	Home country: England Age: 24
Date of death:	25/09/15	Cause of death: Killed in action
Memorial:	Salisbury, Wiltshire	
War cemetery:	Loos Memorial, France	
Theatre of war:	Loos, France	
Next of kin:	J. William Clark JP & Gertrude S. Clark JP (parents)	
Address:	The Canal, Salisbury, Wiltshire	

Early in October 1915 the news of the death in action of 2nd-Lt John Harold Clark, 2nd Wiltshire Regiment, the only son of Mr and Mrs J.W. Clark, of the Canal, Salisbury, was received with deep regret by his many friends, of whom he was held in high esteem. 2nd-Lt Clark, who was killed on the Western Front towards the end of September, was educated at Cleveland House School, Salisbury and Lewisham College, Weston-super-Mare, and was twenty-four years of age.

Before he was twenty-one he had risked his life three times to save others. On one of these occasions he pluckily saved the life of a miner at Redruth. He spent two years in Australia engaging in farming pursuits. Whilst in Australia he was a member of the Australian Defence Force. He returned to England about six months before the outbreak of war, on account of ill health. When war broke out Clark was anxious to discharge his duty to his country by personal service, and accordingly enlisted in the Royal Wiltshire Yeomanry as a trooper. He was subsequently granted a commission in the 3rd Battalion Wiltshire Regiment, and was then attached to the 2nd Battalion Wiltshire Regiment. He proceeded to France early in September 1915.

He was killed on the opening day of the Battle of Loos and is remembered on the Loos Memorial with over 20,000 soldiers who died in the area during the First World War and have no known grave.

Pte Frank Thomas Anscombe *8th Battalion Devonshire Regiment*

Service No.:	15946	Age: 18
Place of birth:	Salisbury, Wiltshire	Home country: England
Date of death:	25/09/15	Cause of death: Killed in action
Memorial:	Salisbury, Wiltshire	
War cemetery:	Loos Memorial, France	
Theatre of war:	Loos, France	
Next of kin:	Arthur Edwin & Marian Anscombe (parents)	
Address:	17 Meeching Road, Newhaven, Sussex	

Frank Anscombe was seventeen when he volunteered in August 1914; he was the younger son of Arthur Edwin and Marian Anscombe, who had lived in Salisbury prior to the First World War. He was killed in action on the opening day of the Battle of Loos, along with nearly 300 other members of the 8th Battalion Devonshire Regiment. He is remembered on the Loos memorial and has no known grave.

Pte Albert Edward Burbage	*2nd Battalion Wiltshire Regiment*
Service No.: 03/9983	Age: 18
Place of birth: St Martin, Wiltshire	Home country: England
Date of death: 25/09/15	Cause of death: Killed in action
Memorial: Salisbury, Wiltshire	
War cemetery: Loos Memorial, France	
Theatre of war: Loos, France	
Next of kin: Charles William & Sarah Burbage	
Address: 26 Trinity Street, Salisbury, Wiltshire	

Albert Burbage was officially under-age to serve overseas but was killed in action on the first day of the Battle of Loos on Sunday 25 September 1915 along with thirty comrades from the 2nd Battalion Wiltshire Regiment. Albert's brother George Sidney B. Burbage was to be killed in action in Mesopotamia in 1917.

Pte Hedley Giles Sainsbury	*2nd Battalion Wiltshire Regiment*
Service No.: 8034	Age: 25
Place of birth: Salisbury, Wiltshire	Home country: England
Date of death: 25/09/15	Cause of death: Killed in action
Memorials: Salisbury, Wiltshire	
Salisbury United Methodists Memorial & St Martin's Church Memorial	
War cemetery: Cabaret Rouge British Cemetery, Souchez, France	
Theatre of war: France	
Next of kin: George & Ada Sainsbury (parents)	
Address: 7 Green Croft, Salisbury, Wiltshire	

Hedley Sainsbury was killed in action on the first day of the Battle of Loos near Vermelles, France. The 2nd Wiltshires had suffered heavy losses during the advance and it is likely he was buried where he fell and his remains were brought to Cabaret Rouge British Cemetery at the end of the war. Pte Sainsbury was the brother of Frederick Murray Sainsbury who would be killed in action during September 1916.

L/Cpl Charles Palmer	*1st Battalion Wiltshire Regiment*
Service No.: 11108	Age: 29
Place of birth: Salisbury, Wiltshire	Home country: England
Date of death: 25/09/15	Cause of death: Killed in action
Memorial: Salisbury, Wiltshire	
War cemetery: Ypres Menin Gate Memorial, Belgium	
Theatre of war: Belgium	
Next of kin: John & Sarah Palmer (parents)	
Address: Salisbury, Wiltshire	

While the Battle of Loos was raging to the south a number of diversionary attacks took place to the north and in Belgium. Charles Palmer was killed in action in one of these attacks at Hooge,

Above: *Arthur Card, who died of his wounds at Basra, Iraq.*

Right: *After the initial rush to enlist in the army recruiting levels levelled off and then started to fall. With the increase in casualties, more men were needed and in 1915 the Derby Scheme was introduced. Men would register for service but they would not be called up until needed. The Derby Scheme was only a partial success and, with an increased need for more men, conscription was introduced in 1916.*

The ROLL *of* HONOUR

IS *YOUR* NAME on a ROLL of HONOUR ?

IF YOUR NAME goes down on your firm's Roll of Honour, it also goes on that mighty Scroll which records the names of all who have rallied round the Flag.

There is room for your name on the Roll of Honour.

Ask your employer to keep your position open for you. Tell him that you are going to the help of the Empire. Every patriotic employer is assisting his men to enlist, and he'll do the right thing by you.

Tell him NOW—

Your King and Country Want you——TO-DAY.

At any Post Office you can obtain the address of the nearest Recruiting Officer.

GOD SAVE THE KING.

on the Bellewarde Ridge, east of the town of Ypres. The attack was opened by the explosion of two large mines which had been dug under the German frontline and filled with explosives. At the end of the fighting the action was known as the second attack on Bellewarde.

Charles is remembered on the Ypres Menin Gate Memorial and has no known grave.

Pte Frederick William Stokes	2nd Battalion Wiltshire Regiment
Service No.: 5972	Age: 30
Place of birth: Stratford Castle, Wiltshire	Home country: England
Date of death: 26/09/15	Cause of death: Killed in action

Memorials: Salisbury, Wiltshire
Dews Road Primitive Methodist Memorial
War cemetery: Loos Memorial, France
Theatre of war: France, Loos
Next of kin: Henry & Jane Stokes (parents)
Address: Clarendon Park, Alderbury, Wiltshire

Pte Stokes was killed in action on Monday 26 September 1915 on the second day of the Battle of Loos. Around thirty members of the 2nd Wiltshire's died on the same day, including their commanding officer Lt-Col. B.H. Leatham. Frederick is remembered on Loos Memorial and has no known grave.

Sgt Walter Taylor Habgood		*7th Battalion Seaforth Highlanders*	
Service No.:	S/3204	Age:	32
Place of birth:	Southampton, Hampshire	Home country:	England
Date of death:	27/09/15	Cause of death:	Died of wounds
War cemetery:	Lilliers Communal Cemetery, France		
Theatre of war:	France		
Next of kin:	Walter Thomas & Mary Habgood (parents)		

Sgt Habgood had obviously lived locally for a time after his birth because his parents considered him as a native of Salisbury. He had volunteered at the start of the war. He was wounded while doing his duty in fighting on 25 September on the first day of the battle of Loos. He died of wounds at a casualty-clearing station at Lilliers, France, and was interred in the communal cemetery on Tuesday 27 September 1915.

27 September 1915 – British Guards Division Capture Hill 70 at Loos, France

L/Cpl William Fletcher		*1st Battalion Coldstream Guards*	
Service No.:	7146	Age:	30
Place of birth:	Salisbury, Wiltshire	Home country:	England
Date of death:	28/09/15	Cause of death:	Killed in action
Memorials:	Salisbury, Wiltshire		
	St Paul's Church Memorial		
War Cemetery	Loos Memorial, France		
Theatre of war:	France, Loos		
Next of kin:	Ada Victoria Lodge (formerly Fletcher); William & Mary Anne Beaven (parents)		
Addresses:	3 James Street, Salisbury, Wiltshire		
	St Martin, Salisbury		

In the summer of 1913 William Fletcher married Ada Victoria Doel at St Martin's Church, Salisbury, not knowing a little over one year later the First World War would start. Just over two years later, William Fletcher would be dead. He was killed in action on Tuesday 28 September 1915 during the latter stages of the Battle of Loos and has no known grave. In 1919 his brother, Francis James Fletcher, and his wife's brother, Joseph Henry Doel, also became victims of the conflict.

Sgt Albert Edward Card		*01/4th Battalion Wiltshire Regiment*	
Service No.:	34	Age:	24
Place of birth:	Salisbury, Wiltshire	Home country:	England
Date of death:	30/09/15	Cause of death:	Died of wounds
Memorials:	Salisbury, Wiltshire		
	St Thomas Church Memorial & Bishop Wordsworth's School Memorial		
War cemetery:	Basra Memorial, Iraq		
Theatre of war:	Mesopotamia		
Next of kin:	Frank Edward & Beatrice Annie Card (parents)		
Address:	15 Harnham Road, Salisbury		

On Tuesday 12 October 1915 Frank Card received letters of condolence from the Viceroy of India and Maj. H.H. Willis, commanding the 1/4th Wilts Regiment, informing him of the death of his son, Albert. Sgt Card died from wounds received in action in Mesopotamia while serving with the Persian Gulf Expeditionary Force.

The letter from the Viceroy read:

> Viceregal Lodge, Simla
> 11 October, 1915
> The King-Emperor commands me to assure you of the true sympathy of his Imperial Majesty and the Queen-Empress in your sorrow.
> HARDINGE OF RENSHURST
> Viceroy of India.

Maj. Willis forwarded the letter of the Viceroy, and added:

> At the time on behalf of all ranks of the 1/4th Wiltshire Regiment, I beg to tender you our heartfelt sympathy in the loss you have sustained, and assure you that we are all truly grieved at losing such a good comrade from our ranks. Speaking personally, it was my privilege to know your son very well, and I always considered him one of the most efficient and conscientious sergeants in the battalion, and he was invariably cheery and kept his men on good terms with themselves; consequently he was both respected and loved by all.

Sgt Card was known to a large circle of friends in Salisbury by whom his death was deeply felt. He was one of the first men to join the 4th Wiltshire Battalion when it was raised as part of the Territorial Force and was an enthusiastic member. At one time he had been attached to the signalling section attached to the battalion. In 1906 he entered the office of Messrs Fletcher & Fletcher, chartered accountants, and was with them when the 4th Wiltshire Battalion mobilised at the beginning of the war. He proceeded with his battalion to India, and while stationed at Delhi it fell to his lot to be the first territorial NCO to mount guard at the Viceroy's Lodge.

Early in May 1915, Albert was chosen by Lord Radnor as the sergeant to accompany the draft sent to Mesopotamia to complete the establishment of the Dorset Regiment. A regimental send-off was arranged for the party who were entertained to a dinner and a concert, and Sgt Card received the gift of a case of pipes from his company.

He was the eldest son of Mr and Mrs Card, and died from wounds received in action in Mesopotamia on Thursday 30 September 1915, during the first advance on Baghdad. Sgt Card is remembered on the Basra Memorial, Iraq, with 40,657 members of the Commonwealth force who died between 1914 and 1921 in Mesopotamia and have no known grave.

---

5 OCTOBER 1915 – A BRITISH AND FRENCH FORCE LANDS AT SALONIKA, GREECE, TO SUPPORT SERBIA
TUESDAY 12 OCTOBER 1915 – ENGLISH NURSE EDITH CAVELL WAS SHOT BY THE GERMANS FOR HELPING BRITISH PRISONERS OF WAR TO ESCAPE FROM BELGIUM INTO HOLLAND.

Cpl Edwin James Witt		*1st Labour Battalion Royal Engineers*	
Service No.:	110788	Age:	52
Place of birth:	Salisbury, Wiltshire	Home country:	England

Right: *The harbour at Salonika.*

Below: *A postcard of the death of Edith Cavell, executed by the Germans. It is interesting to note Edith Cavell is portrayed in white for good, while the dastardly German is portrayed in black for evil, part of the propaganda war that was in operation on both sides.*

Date of death: 07/11/15
Memorial: Salisbury, Wiltshire
War cemetery: Sailly Sur La Lys Canadian Cemetery, France
Theatre of war: France
Next of kin: Emily Witt (wife)
Address: St Edmund, Salisbury, Wiltshire

Royal Engineers' labour battalions were employed digging trenches, repairing roads and general carrying of stores. Edwin Witt, at fifty-two years of age, can be described as an old soldier. He died either from illness or natural causes on Sunday 7 November 1915.

22 NOVEMBER 1915 – BATTLE OF CTESIPHON, MESOPOTAMIA

L/Cpl Alfred Edward V. Beck   *02/4th Battalion Wiltshire Regiment Service*
Service No.:   3160   Age: 22
Place of birth: Fisherton, Wiltshire   Home country: England

Date of death: 22/11/15   Cause of death: Killed in action
Memorials: Salisbury, Wiltshire
                 St Paul's Church Memorial
War cemetery: Basra Memorial, Iraq
Theatre of war: Mesopotamia
Next of kin: Henry & Ellen Beck (parents)
Address: Fisherton Anger, Salisbury, Wiltshire

L/Cpl Beck, known as Edward, was killed in action on Monday 22 November 1915 at the Battle of Sulaiman Pak (the ancient Ctesiphon), Mesopotamia, which is about 20 miles south of Baghdad in modern-day Iraq. He is remembered on the Basra Memorial and has no known grave.

> ## 5 DECEMBER 1915 – BRITISH FORCE IN KUT ARE SURROUNDED BY TURKISH TROOPS
> ## – 8 DECEMBER 1915 – EVACUATION OF GALLIPOLI BEGINS

Pte Henry Bowey   *5th Battalion Wiltshire Regiment*
Service No.:   19191   Age: 31
Place of birth: Salisbury, Wiltshire Home country: England
Date of death: 22/12/15   Memorial: Salisbury, Wiltshire
                 St Paul's Church Memorial
War cemetery: Alexandria Chatby Military and War Memorial Cemetery, Egypt
Theatre of war: Gallipoli
Next of kin: Bessie Bowey (wife); Henry & Henrietta Bowey (parents)
Addresses: 3 Finchley Road, Wilton Road, Salisbury, Wiltshire
                 Fisherton Anger, Salisbury

Henry Bowey was one of the thousands of troops to be afflicted with illness while serving on the Gallipoli Peninsula during the campaign. He was evacuated to the hospital at Alexandria where he died on Wednesday 22 December 1915.

Pte Frank Gatford   *11th Battalion Royal Fusiliers*
Service No.:   7852   Age: 19
Place of birth: Salisbury, Wiltshire Home country: England
Date of death: 22/12/15   Cause of death: Died of wounds
Memorials: Salisbury, Wiltshire
                 St Mark's Church Memorial
War cemetery: Corbie Communal Cemetery, France
Theatre of war: France
Next of kin: Mr & Mrs H. Gatford (parents)
Address: Holmewood, 69 Castle Road, Salisbury, Wiltshire

Frank Gatford had originally volunteered for the Middlesex Regiment in 1914 but was transferred to the 11th Battalion Royal Fusiliers, landing in France during May 1915. He died of wounds on 22 December at one of the casualty-clearing stations, Corbie, which lies east of Amiens, and was buried in the Corbie Communal Cemetery.

Driver William White   *Royal Field Artillery 32nd Division Ammunition Column*
Service No.:   102237

Date of death: 03/01/16
War cemetery: Salisbury (Devizes Road) Cemetery, Wiltshire
Theatre of war: Home

The 32nd Division had arrived at Codford for training on Salisbury Plain in August 1915. William White died of illness on Monday 3 January 1916 at one of the local hospitals.

4 JANUARY 1916 – THE BATTLE OF SHEIK SA'AD, MESOPOTAMIA – AN ATTEMPT TO RELIEVE THE BRITISH GARRISON IN KUT

Pte Albert Edward Brown   *5th Battalion Wiltshire Regiment*
Service No.:   9450   Age: 19
Place of birth: Fisherton, Wiltshire   Home country: England
Date of death: 06/01/16   Cause of death: Killed in action
Memorials: Salisbury, Wiltshire
                   St Paul's Church Memorial
War cemetery: Helles Memorial, Turkey
Theatre of war: Gallipoli
Next of kin: John & Alice Mary Brown (parents)
Address: 1 Brandon Cottages, Highfield Road, Salisbury, Wiltshire

In December 1915 the withdrawal of British and Commonwealth forces from Gallipoli commenced after the campaign had been acknowledged as a disaster. Albert Brown was the only member of the 5th Battalion Wilts Regiment to be killed during the final evacuation. The successful extraction of forces from Gallipoli is probably regarded as one of the campaign's few successes and was carried out with very few casualties. Pte Brown was killed in action on Thursday 6 January 1916 and was probably felled by a high-explosive shell at Gully Beach, Cape Helles, Gallipoli.

9 JANUARY 1916 – GALLIPOLI EVACUATION COMPLETED

William White, another who died due to illness.

Pte George Albert Sennett   *5th Battalion Connaught Rangers*

Service No.:   9603   Age: 27
Place of birth: Salisbury, Wiltshire   Home country: England
Date of death: 17/01/16   Cause of death: Died of wounds
Memorials: Salisbury, Wiltshire
                 St Martin's Church Memorial & Salisbury United Methodists Memorial
War cemetery: Dorian Memorial, Greece
Theatre of war: Salonika
Next of kin: Alfred & Laura Ann Sennett (parents)
Address: Joiners Hall, St Ann Street, Salisbury, Wiltshire

In October 1915 a British and French force landed at Salonika in Greece at the request of the Greek prime minister, originally it was planned that they would support the Serbs, who were in conflict with the Bulgarians, but the force arrived too late and the Serbs had been beaten. It was decided that the force would remain in Salonika for future operations. During the Salonika campaign, for every casualty of battle, three died from disease.

Pte Sennett had volunteered to join the 5th Battalion Connaught Rangers in 1914 and his battalion was sent to Gallipoli in 1915. After the evacuation of the peninsula the Connaughts were sent to Salonika. George died of wounds on Monday 17 January 1916 and is remembered on Dorian Memorial, Greece, and has no known grave.

Sapper Frederick William Mayor   *2nd Reserve Battalion Royal Engineers*

Service No.:   140635   Home country: England   Age: 21
Place of birth: Salisbury, Wiltshire   Date of death: 18/01/16
Memorials: Salisbury, Wiltshire
                 Bishop Wordsworth's School Memorial
War cemetery: Salisbury London Road Cemetery, England
Theatre of war: Home
Next of kin: William J. & Rhoda Mayor (parents)
Address: Fern Bank, Wyndham Road, Salisbury

Frederick was the only son of William and Rhoda Mayor of Salisbury. He died of illness on 18 January 1916 at the Alexandra Hospital, Wigmore, Chatham, Kent.

Pte Arthur Reginald Cannings   *D Company 5th Battalion Wiltshire Regiment*

Service No.:   31990   Age: 19
Place of birth: Donhead, Wiltshire   Home country: England
Date of death: 21/01/16   Cause of death: Died of wounds
Memorial: Salisbury, Wiltshire
War cemetery: Amara War Cemetery, Iraq
Theatre of war: Mesopotamia
Next of kin: Charles & Fanny Cannings (parents)
Address: 24 Scots Lane, Salisbury, Wiltshire

It is likely that Arthur was attached to the Dorset Regiment in Mesopotamia where he died of wounds on Friday 21 January 1916 in the hospital centre at Amara, Iraq.

ON *24 JANUARY 1916* THE MILITARY SERVICE ACT IS PASSED IN PARLIAMENT.
CONSCRIPTION WILL COMMENCE IN MAY *1916.*

Brig.-Gen. George Benjamin Hodson   *Gen. Staff Commanding 33rd Infantry Brigade*

Place of birth:	Baugalove, India	Home country: India	Age: 52
Date of death:	25/01/16	Cause of death: Died of wounds	
Decorations:	CB DSO		
War cemetery:	Pieta Military Cemetery, Malta		
Next of kin:	Dorothy Clara Hodson (wife)		
Address:	Holly Cottage, Knockholt, Kent		

In February 1916 the news of the death from wounds at Malta, on Tuesday 25 January of Brig.-Gen. G.B. Hodson who, prior to proceeding on active service, was attached to the Southern Command Headquarters, and resided in the Close, Salisbury. Brig.-Gen. George Benjamin Hodson, 7th Madras Native Infantry Regiment, had a distinguished record of service in Egypt, Burma, India and Nigeria, and, at the time of receiving the wounds from which he died, was serving on the brigade staff of the Mediterranean Expeditionary Force. He was born in October 1863 and entered service in May 1882, when he was gazetted to the South Staffordshire Regiment, from which he transferred to the Oxfordshire Light Infantry in 1884. The same year he entered the Indian Army, in which he reached the rank of lieutenant-colonel in November 1905. Brevet rank of colonel was given to him in November 1909 and this was made substantive in January 1911. He was employed with the Aro Expedition in Southern Nigeria in 1901, and in November 1912, he was appointed AQMG on the Indian Staff. In the October of previous year he was gazetted to the command of a Brigade. Gen. Hodson had seen a great deal of active service. He was part of the Egyptian Expedition of 1882 and received the medal and bronze star, while after the Burmese campaign (1885–87) he was mentioned in despatches, and earned the Burma Medal with clasp. He won another clasp for the Hazara Expedition in 1891, and for service on the North West Frontier (1897–88) he was again mentioned in despatches and received the medal with clasp. The Aro Expedition (Southern Nigeria) of 1902 brought him further mention in despatches and the medal with clasp, in addition to which he won the DSO. Gen. Hodson, who was made a CB in 1911, married Dorothy Clara in 1910, daughter of Mr William Murray of Clanricarde Gardens, Bayswater.

Malta was a hospital and convalescent centre from spring 1915, George Hodson died of his wounds on 25 January 1916 and is buried in Pieta Military Cemetery.

Pte Charles Frederick Bunsell   *D Company 2nd Battalion Wiltshire Regiment*

Service No.:	03/9959	Age:	21
Place of birth:	Fisherton, Wiltshire	Home country:	England
Date of death:	4 February 1916	Cause of death:	Died of wounds
Memorials:	Salisbury, Wiltshire		
	St Martin's Church Memorial		
War cemetery:	Corbie Communal Cemetery, France		
Theatre of war:	France		
Next of kin:	George & Elizabeth Jane Bunsell (parents)		
Address:	6 Park Terrace, Friary, Salisbury, Wiltshire		

In mid-February 1916 news was received in Salisbury of the death of Charles Bunsell who had been serving with the Wiltshire Regiment. He was one of three sons born to George and Elizabeth Bunsell of the Friary, and served with His Majesty's Forces. Early in 1915 Bunsell had suffered from frostbite that was contracted in the trenches. His parents had received very sympathetic letters from the nurse in charge of the hospital and the chaplain, who stated Charles's wounds were numerous and were caused by shrapnel.

It is likely Charles received the wounds on Friday 28 January 1916 during a heavy bombardment when the Wiltshires were in the trenches at Carnoy, France.

Pte Alfred Thomas Sturgess		*3rd Battalion Wiltshire Regiment*
Service No.:	5416	Age:	35
Place of birth:	Salisbury, Wiltshire	Home country: England
Date of death:	18 February 1916	
Memorial:	Salisbury, Wiltshire	
War cemetery:	Salisbury London Road Cemetery, England	
Theatre of war:	Home	
Next of kin:	William J. & Annie Sturgess (parents)	
Address:	St Thomas, Salisbury, Wiltshire	

Alfred Sturgess died on Friday 18 February 1918, probably of illness and is buried in Salisbury London Road Cemetery.

L/Cpl Sidney Caleb Cox		*1st Battalion Manchester Regiment*
Service No.:	1843	Age:	24
Place of birth:	Fisherton, Wiltshire	Home country: England
Date of death:	8 March 1916	Cause of death: Killed in action
Memorials:	Salisbury, Wiltshire	
	St Paul's Church Memorial	
War cemetery:	Basra Memorial, Iraq	
Theatre of war:	Mesopotamia	
Next of kin:	Caleb & Eliza Beatrice Cox (parents)	
Address:	5 West End Road, Wilton Road, Salisbury, Wiltshire	

After marching throughout the night the British and Commonwealth infantry arrived in front of the Turkish defences of Dujaila Redoubt, about 7 miles from Kut, in Iraq. Patrols were sent out and found that the Turkish defences were only lightly manned and that the redoubt was empty. The plan had been to precede the attack with an artillery bombardment. However, the artillery had not yet reached the agreed assembly point. Some guns arrived at 7 a.m. but the majority did not arrive until 10 a.m. By this time the element of surprise had been lost. This delay allowed the Turks to re-occupy and strengthen their defences.

Alfred Sturgess, who died due to illness.

The infantry then launched a direct assault – the Manchesters were in front of the 2nd Rajputs of the Indian Army and were immediately exposed to heavy shelling from the Turks. An eyewitness reports that the British and Indian troops were 'knocked over like nine pins from shrapnel.' By the time the Manchesters and Rajputs reached the redoubt they were in disarray and the Manchesters had been reduced to around 100 men and the Rajputs about 50.

The Turks fled from the trenches, but then counter-attacked and the Manchesters and Rajputs were forced to retire. The 166 members of the 1st Battalion Manchester Regiment were killed in the attack and one of them was Sidney Cox. He is remembered on the Basra Memorial, Iraq, and he has no known grave.

L/Cpl Brian Moray Williams		*D Company 19th Battalion Royal Fusiliers*	
Service No.:	3614	Age:	20
Place of birth:	Fisherton, Wiltshire	Home country:	England
Date of death:	29 March 1916		
Memorials:	Salisbury, Wiltshire		
	Choir School Memorial		
War cemetery:	Longuenesse St Omer Souvenir Cemetery, France		
Theatre of war:	France		
Next of kin:	Alfred Ernest & Mary Elizabeth Williams (parents)		
Address:	73 Harnham Road, Salisbury, Wiltshire		

L/Cpl Williams was the only son of A. Ernest Williams of Salisbury and was killed on active service on 29 March 1916. Brian, who was educated at Salisbury Choristers' School and Haileybury College, enlisted at the outbreak of the war and joined the Public Schools Corps on its formation. He had been on active service since the beginning of November 1915. In March 1916 he was recommended for a commission, and was on the point of coming home for training when he was killed. He was only twenty years of age.

Sapper Charles Harry Robinson		*90th Field Company Royal Engineers*	
Service No.:	144595	Age:	37
Place of birth:	Salisbury, Wiltshire	Home country:	England
Date of death:	04/04/16	Cause of death:	Died of wounds
Memorials:	Salisbury, Wiltshire		
	St Paul's Church Memorial, St Martin's Church of Memorial		
War cemetery:	London Rifle Brigade Cemetery, Belgium		
Theatre of war:	Belgium		
Next of kin:	Mrs Robinson (wife); Thomas & Helen Robinson (parents)		
Address:	Salisbury, Wiltshire		

Charles Robinson had originally joined the Royal Garrison Artillery but was transferred to the Royal Engineers. He married his wife in Wilton in 1904 but lived in Salisbury prior to the great war. He died of his wounds on Tuesday 4 April 1916 and is buried in a cemetery near Ploegsteert, south of Ypres – called Plog Street by the British troops – in Belgium.

5 APRIL 1916 – FIRST BATTLE OF KUT

L/Cpl Frank Augustus Butler		*5th Battalion Wiltshire Regiment*	
Service No.:	18018	Age:	37

Place of birth:	St Peter Port, Guernsey	Home country:	Channel Islands
Date of death:	05/04/16	Cause of death:	Killed in action
Memorial:	Salisbury, Wiltshire		
War cemetery:	Amara War Cemetery, Iraq		
Theatre of war:	Mesopotamia		
Next of kin:	Henrietta Butler (wife)		

Frank Butler was killed on Wednesday 5 April 1915 during an attack on Turkish positions at Falahiyeh, Mespotamia, while trying to relieve the British at the city of Kut. British and Commonwealth forces suffered 2,000 casualties inflicted by the Turks on this day at Hanna and Falahiyeh, in modern-day Iraq.

Cpl Philip Owen   *5th Battalion Wiltshire Regiment*

Service No.:	9918	Age:	28
Place of birth:	Salisbury, Wiltshire	Home country:	England
Date of death:	05/04/16	Cause of death:	Killed in action
Memorial:	Salisbury, Wiltshire		
War cemetery:	Basra Memorial, Iraq		
Theatre of war:	Mesopotamia		
Next of kin:	James & Sarah Owen (parents)		
Address:	Salisbury, Wiltshire		

On Wednesday 5 April 1916 the 5th Battalion Wiltshire Regiment were in action at Falahiyeh, Mesopotamia. The Wiltshires were the leading battalion of the brigade and captured the Turkish frontline trenches without difficulty, taking twelve Turkish prisoners in the process.

At 9 a.m. the Wiltshires continued to advance but came under heavy rifle and machine-gun fire from the Turks in Falahiyeh, which was some 2 miles ahead. The advance was continued to about 800 yards from the Turks, where the Wiltshires dug in. At dusk the British withdrew one mile to their bivouac position by the river Tigris. During the fighting the Wiltshires suffered seventeen killed, 150 wounded and a further seventeen missing in action.

Philip Owen was one of the casualties killed in action during the attack on Falahiyeh; he is remembered on the Basra Memorial and has no known grave.

Pte Alfred Arthur Vicary   *5th Battalion Wiltshire Regiment*

Service No.:	19545	Age:	18
Place of birth:	Teignmouth, Devon	Home country:	England
Date of death:	07/04/16	Cause of death:	Died of wounds
Memorial:	Salisbury, Wiltshire		
War cemetery:	Basra Memorial, Iraq		
Theatre of war:	Mesopotamia		
Next of kin:	Susan Vicary (mother)		

Alfred Vicary was under-age at eighteen when he died of his wounds on Friday 7 April 1916. It is likely that the wounds were received during the attack on Turkish positions at Falahiyeh; he is remembered on the Basra Memorial but has no known grave.

Pte Reginald Stone   *5th Battalion Wiltshire Regiment*

Service No.:	21192	Age:	19
Place of birth:	Gussage St Michael, Dorset	Home country:	England
Date of death:	09/04/16	Cause of death:	Killed in action

Memorials: Salisbury, Wiltshire
                  St Mark's Church Memorial
War cemetery: Basra Memorial, Iraq
Theatre of war: Mesopotamia
Next of kin: James & Ellen Stone (parents)
Address: Stoford Hill, Wishford, Salisbury, Wiltshire

On 9 April 1916, while still attempting to relieve the city of Kut, the 5th Battalion Wiltshire Regiment were advancing on the Turkish position of Sannaiyat, Mesopotamia. There was some confusion when the Wiltshires came under fire in the dark and they lost direction, eventually digging in 650 yards from the Turks. During the next twenty-four hours many of the men who had advanced too far returned to the Wiltshires' position, many wounded crawled in and many were collected. Two soldiers 18077 Pte J.H. Nelson and 9842 Pte W.G. Price, were recommended for the Distinguished Conduct Medal for displaying conspicuous gallantry and devotion to duty in collecting wounded and evacuating the casualties of the Wiltshires. During the action there were twenty-three killed, 163 wounded and forty-two missing in action.

One of those killed in action was nineteen-year-old Reginald Stone, who is remembered on Basra Memorial and has no known grave.

Pte Walter John Tucker		5th Battalion Wiltshire Regiment	
Service No.:	20582	Age:	20
Place of birth:	Salisbury, Wiltshire	Home country:	England
Date of death:	09/04/16	Cause of death:	Killed in action
Memorial:	Salisbury, Wiltshire		
War cemetery:	Basra Memorial, Iraq		
Theatre of war:	Mesopotamia		
Next of kin:	Richard & Jane Tucker (parents)		
Address:	37 Church Street, Salisbury, Wiltshire		

During the actions that took place on 9 April 1916 the Turks inflicted over 2,000 casualties on the British and Commonwealth forces.

Twenty-year-old Walter Tucker was killed in action at Sannaiyat, Mesopotamia. He is remembered on Basra Memorial and has no known grave.

L/Cpl Leslie James Maskett Webb		5th Battalion Wiltshire Regiment	
Service No.:	20841	Age:	18
Place of birth:	Salisbury, Wiltshire	Home country:	England
Date of death:	09/04/16	Cause of death:	Killed in action
Memorials:	Salisbury, Wiltshire		
	St Thomas Church Memorial		
War cemetery:	Basra Memorial, Iraq		
Theatre of war:	Mesopotamia		
Next of kin:	Gideon & Ellen Webb (parents)		
Address:	St Thomas, Salisbury, Wiltshire		

At eighteen, Leslie was an under-age soldier and was killed in action at Sannaiyat, Mesopotamia on Sunday 9 April 1916. He is remembered on Basra Memorial and has no known grave.

Pte Henry James Witt		5th Battalion Wiltshire Regiment	
Service No.:	19154	Age:	35

Place of birth: Woodford, Wiltshire   Home country: England
Date of death: 09/04/16   Cause of death: Killed in action
UK memorial: Salisbury, Wiltshire
                  St Paul's Church Memorial
War cemetery: Basra Memorial, Iraq
Theatre of war: Mesopotamia
Next of kin: Harriet Witt (wife); John & Mary A. Witt (parents)
Addresses: 7 Meron Row, Devizes Road, Salisbury, Wiltshire
                  Woodford, Wiltshire

Henry James was killed in action at Sannaiyat, Mesopotamia, on Sunday 9 April 1916. He is remembered on Basra Memorial and has no known grave.

Pte Gilbert Aplin   *5th Battalion Wiltshire Regiment*
Service No.:   20887   Age: 20
Place of birth: Bemerton, Wiltshire   Home country: England
Date of death: 13/04/16   Cause of death: Died of wounds
Memorials: Salisbury, Wiltshire
                  St Mark's Church Memorial and Dews Road Primitive Methodist Memorial
War cemetery: Basra Memorial, Iraq
Theatre of war: Mesopotamia
Next of kin: Henry & Emma Ann Aplin (parents)
Address: 45 North Street, Wilton, Wiltshire

It is likely that twenty-year-old Gilbert Aplin died of wounds received at Sannaiyat, Mesopotamia on 9 April 1916. He is remembered on Basra Memorial and has no known grave.

Pte Joseph Tyler   *5th Battalion Wiltshire Regiment*
Service No.:   20989   Age: 22
Place of birth: Fisherton, Wiltshire   Home country: England
Date of death: 18/04/16   Cause of death: Killed in action
Memorials: Salisbury, Wiltshire
                  St Paul's Church Memorial
War cemetery: Basra Memorial, Iraq
Theatre of war: Mesopotamia
Next of kin: Miss B.M. Tyler (sister)
Address: 6 James Street, Salisbury, Wiltshire

Joseph Tyler was one of twelve men killed in action on Tuesday 18 April 1916, during a Turkish attack on the 5th Wiltshires' positions at Bait Aisa, Mesopotamia. He is remembered on Basra Memorial and has no known grave.

Pte John Davis   *5th Battalion Wiltshire Regiment*
Service No.:   18939   Age: 18
Place of birth: Woodford, Wiltshire   Home country: England
Date of death: 19/04/16   Cause of death: Killed in action
Memorial: Salisbury, Wiltshire
War cemetery: Basra Memorial, Iraq
Theatre of war: Mesopotamia

Next of kin: Charles & Elizabeth Davis (parents)
Address: Avonhurst, Durrington, Wiltshire

John Davis was an under-age soldier and was killed in action on Wednesday 19 April 1916 at Bait Aisa, Mesopotamia, along with four other members of the battalion. He is remembered on Basra Memorial and has no known grave.

Pte Albert 'Bert' Sherlock   *5th Battalion Wiltshire Regiment*
Service No.:   20742   Age: 24
Place of birth: Salisbury, Wiltshire Home country: England
Date of death: 25/04/16   Cause of death: Died of wounds
Memorial: Salisbury, Wiltshire
War cemetery: Basra War Cemetery, Iraq
Theatre of war: Mesopotamia
Next of kin: William & Kate Sherlock (parents)
Address: St Martin, Salisbury, Wiltshire

Albert Sherlock died from wounds received in the fighting to relieve the city of Kut on 25 April 1916. Four days later the British and Commonwealth forces at Kut surrendered to the Turks.

29 APRIL 1916 – BRITISH FORCES IN KUT EL AMARA SURRENDER TO THE TURKS

Pte Reginald Frank Gordon Bush   *8th Battalion Royal West Kent Regiment*
Service No.:   G/2877   Age: 19
Place of birth: Salisbury, Wiltshire Home country: England
Date of death: 05/05/16   Cause of death: Died of wounds
Memorial: Salisbury, Wiltshire
War cemetery: Dranoutre Military Cemetery, Belgium
Theatre of war: Belgium
Next of kin: Frank & Kate Bush (parents)
Address: Endless Street, Salisbury, Wiltshire

Frank Bush died of his wounds on Friday 5 May 1916 and is buried in Dranoutre Military Cemetery, Belgium. On 30 April 1916, the 24th Division, of which he was a member, was sent to the Wulverhem sector of the front at Ypres and subjected to a large-scale gas attack by the Germans.

Pte William Frank Wise   *Royal Dublin Fusiliers*
Service No.:   15217   Age: 31
Place of birth: Netheravon, Wiltshire Home country: England
Date of death: 06/05/16
Memorial: Salisbury, Wiltshire
War cemetery: Salisbury (Devizes Road) Cemetery, Wiltshire
Theatre of war: Home
Next of kin: Florence May Wise (wife); Isaac & Millicent Wise (parents)
Addresses: 2 Meadow Road, Salisbury, Wiltshire
                 Netheravon, Wiltshire

Above: *British troops marched across the desert into captivity by the Turks.*

Left: *William Wise, who died in Salisbury.*

William Wise, who married Florence May Thorne in Salisbury during 1910, died at Salisbury on Saturday 6 May 1916.

Pte John Hopgood   *02/4th Battalion Wiltshire Regiment*

Service No.:	201338	Age:	20
Place of birth:	Fisherton, Salisbury, Wiltshire	Home country:	England
Date of death:	9/05/16		
Memorials:	Salisbury, Wiltshire		
	St Paul's Church Memorial		
War cemetery:	Basra Memorial, Iraq		
Theatre of war:	Mesopotamia		
Next of kin:	Frederick & Mary Selina Hopgood		
Address:	20 East Street, Salisbury, Wiltshire		

A year after the end of the war in November 1919, Frederick and Mary Hopgood discovered the fate of their eldest son John, who had been a member of the roughly 10,000-strong garrison at Kut that was surrendered to the Turks on 29 April 1915. They believed he was a prisoner of the Turks and hoped that he would be returned at the war's end. John Hopgood died on Tuesday 9 May 1916 at Shamran, Meopatamia, as the garrison of Kut were marched north through the desert.

John Hopgood, who was only twenty years old, is remembered on the Basra Memorial, Iraq, and has no known grave.

Pte Alfred Ernest Hart   *2nd Battalion Wiltshire Regiment*

Service No.:	3/122	Age:	23
Place of birth:	Salisbury, Wiltshire	Home country:	England
Date of death:	27/05/16	Cause of death:	Killed in action
Memorial:	Salisbury, Wiltshire		
War cemetery:	Carnoy Military Cemetery, France		
Theatre of war:	France		
Next of kin:	Arthur & Agnes Hart (parents)		
Address:	Culver Street, Salisbury, Wiltshire		

Alfred Hart was killed in action in the trenches at Carnoy, France, on Saturday 27 May 1916. The War Diary for the day simply states: 'still in trenches, quiet day.'

5

JUTLAND

On 31 May 1916 the only major naval battle of the First World War began and was to become known as the Battle of Jutland. It took place off the north-west coast of Denmark. The battle ended on 1 June 1916 and both the British and the German navies claimed victory. Though the British lost more ships, the German fleet returned to port and remained there for the rest of the war.

A number of Salisbury men lost their lives in the battle and the shock that was felt in the city was also felt in towns and cities throughout Great Britain.

Ordinary Seaman Kenneth Alder   *Royal Navy HMS* Indefatigable
Service No.:   J/32882   Age: 18
Place of birth: Salisbury, Wiltshire   Home country: England
Date of death: 31/05/16   Cause of death: Died
Memorials: Salisbury, Wiltshire
                  St Martin's Church Memorial
War cemetery: Plymouth Naval Memorial, England
Theatre of war: At sea, Jutland
Next of kin: Isaac John & Flora Thirza Alder (parents)
Address: 24 St Martin's, Church Street, Salisbury, Wiltshire

Kenneth Alder was drowned on Wednesday 31 May 1916 while serving on HMS *Indefatigable*, only two of the 1,019 crew survived. Just after 5 a.m. *Indefatigable* was hit and a cloud of smoke rose twice as high as her masts; though shells had pierced the ship's armour without exploding, shortly afterwards they detonated causing flame and smoke to appear from the hull and debris was hurled 200ft in the air. The *Indefatigable* rolled over and sank. Kenneth Alder is remembered on the Plymouth Naval Memorial, commemorating those members of the Royal Navy who have no known grave.

Petty Officer Stoker Percy Beck   *Royal Navy HMS* Invincible
Service No.:   302836   Age: 32
Place of birth: Salisbury, Wiltshire   Home country: England
Date of death: 31/05/16   Cause of death: Killed in action
Memorials: Salisbury, Wiltshire
                  St Paul's Church Memorial
War cemetery: Portsmouth Naval Memorial, England
Theatre of war: At sea, Jutland
Next of kin: William & Elizabeth Beck (parents)
Address: 2 West End Road, Wilton Road, Salisbury, Wiltshire

Petty Officer Stoker Percy Beck would have worked in the engine room in the bowls of the ship. At 7.31 a.m. the HMS *Invincible*, which was Admiral Hood's flagship, was hit by a salvo of shells and blew up; only six survivors were picked up from her 1,021 crew.

Percy is remembered on the Portsmouth Naval Memorial, commemorating those members of the Royal Navy who have no known grave.

Pte Fred Hibberd   *Royal Marine Light Infantry HMS* Invincible
Service No.:   PO/16713   Age: 20
Place of birth: Salisbury, Wiltshire   Home country: England
Date of death: 31/05/16   Cause of death: Drowned
Memorials: Salisbury, Wiltshire
                   St Paul's Church Memorial
War cemetery: Portsmouth Naval Memorial, England
Theatre of war: At sea, Jutland
Next of kin: Fred & Ellen Hibberd (parents)
Address: 15 Kingsland Road, Salisbury, Wiltshire

Early in June 1916, Fred and Ellen Hibberd received the news of the death of their son Fred on HMS *Invincible* at the battle of Jutland. Fred Sr, who was employed by the Salisbury Corporation, was a national reservist and had four other sons: Sgt H.C. Hibberd, serving with the Royal Marine Light Infantry; Gunner Albert Edwin Hibberd, serving with the Royal Marine Artillery; William Hibberd, serving with the Hampshire Regiment; and Frank Hibberd with the Territorials. He also had a son-in-law, William Bullock, serving with the Royal Horse Artillery. Much sympathy was felt for the Hibberds who were considered a very patriotic family. Fred Jr was killed in the sinking of HMS *Invincible* and is remembered on the Portsmouth Naval Memorial, commemorating those members of the Royal Navy who have no known grave.

Engine Room Artificer 4th Class   *Royal Navy HMS* Black Prince
John Reginald George
Service No.:   M/11769   Age: 25
Place of birth: Salisbury, Wiltshire   Home country: England
Date of death: 31/05/16   Cause of death: Killed in action
Memorials: Salisbury, Wiltshire
                   St Paul's Church Memorial and Dews Road Primitive Methodist Memorial
War cemetery: Portsmouth Naval Memorial
Theatre of war: At sea, Jutland
Next of kin: Emily George (mother)
Address: 15 Uverdale Road, King's Road, Chelsea, London

John George worked in the engine room of the HMS *Black Prince*, which during the night of Wednesday 31 May 1916 lost touch with the British Fleet. She steamed in the dark toward what she thought were British battleships. Upon arrival she was immediately illuminated by the search lights of ships from the German Fleet. After being raked by German shells and torpedoes the *Black Prince* blew up with the loss of all of the 857 crew. John George is remembered on the Portsmouth Naval Memorial, commemorating those members of the Royal Navy who have no known grave.

Pte Henry George Elliott   *Royal Marine Light Infantry HMS* Black Prince
Service No.:   PO/17171   Age: 19
Place of birth: Salisbury, Wiltshire   Home country: England
Date of death: 31/05/16   Cause of death: Killed in action
Memorial: Salisbury, Wiltshire
War cemetery: Portsmouth Naval Memorial, England
Theatre of war: At sea, Jutland
Next of kin: George & Harriett Elliott (parents)
Address: 18 Exeter Terrace, Salisbury, Wiltshire

Nineteen-year-old Pte Elliott, known as George, was member of the Royal Marine Light Infantry attached to HMS *Black Prince*. He is remembered on the Portsmouth Naval Memorial, commemorating those members of the Royal Navy who have no known grave.

Able Seaman Walter Edmund George   *Royal Navy HMS* Barham
Service No.:   J/22161   Age: 20
Place of birth: Salisbury, Wiltshire   Home country: England
Date of death: 31/05/16
Memorials: Salisbury, Wiltshire
                St Paul's Church Memorial
War cemetery: Portsmouth Naval Memorial, England
Theatre of war: At sea, Jutland
Next of kin: James & Annie George
Address: 13 Hartington Road, Devizes Road, Salisbury, Wiltshire

Walter George was one of twenty-six members of the crew of HMS *Barham* to be killed during the Battle of Jutland. He is remembered on the Portsmouth Naval Memorial, commemorating those members of the Royal Navy who have no known grave.

L/Cpl Henry George Head   *Royal Marine Light Infantry HMS* Queen Mary
Service No.:   PO/16317   Age: 23
Place of birth: Salisbury, Wiltshire   Home country: England
Date of death: 31/05/16   Cause of death: Killed in action
Memorial: Salisbury, Wiltshire
War cemetery: Portsmouth Naval Memorial, England
Theatre of war: At sea, Jutland
Next of kin: William H. & Louise Head (parents)
Address: Milford, Salisbury, Wiltshire

L/Cpl Henry Head was a member of the Royal Marine contingent attached to the HMS *Queen Mary*. At about 5.30 a.m. on Wednesday 31 May 1916 the Germans concentrated fire at the *Queen Mary* and after a huge explosion she was broken in two and the roofs of the turrets were hurled 100ft in the air. All that remained of the *Queen Mary* was a gigantic column of smoke and eight survivors from her crew of 1,274.

    Henry Head is remembered on the Portsmouth Naval Memorial, commemorating those members of the Royal Navy who have no known grave.

Able Seaman Harry Daniel West   *Royal Navy HMS* Queen Mary
Service No.:   J/22146   Age: 20
Place of birth: Fisherton, Wiltshire   Home country: England
Date of death: 31/05/16   Cause of death: Killed in action
Memorials: Salisbury, Wiltshire
                St Paul's Church Memorial
War cemetery: Portsmouth Naval Memorial, England
Theatre of war: At sea, Jutland
Next of kin: Mr H. & Lily A. West (parents)
Address: 108 Devizes Road, Salisbury, Wiltshire

Harry West was a crew member of the HMS *Queen Mary*, remembered on the Portsmouth Naval Memorial, commemorating those members of the Royal Navy who have no known grave.

Leading Seaman Henry Gordon Blackburn   *Royal Navy HMS* Queen Mary

Service No.:	228808	Age:	29
Date of death:	31/05/16	Cause of death:	Killed in action

War cemetery: Portsmouth Naval Memorial, England
Theatre of war: At sea, Jutland
Next of kin: Lilian Marian Blackburn (wife)
Address: 4 Friary Lane, Salisbury, Wiltshire

Henry Blackburn was a leading gunner on HMS *Queen Mary*, but he is not recorded on the Salisbury War Memorial despite living there before the war. He is remembered on the Portsmouth Naval Memorial, commemorating those members of the Royal Navy who have no known grave.

2 JUNE 1916 – THIRD BATTLE OF YPRES, BELGIUM

Pte Norman Froud Weston   *1st Battalion Saskatchewan Regiment Canadian Infantry*

Service No.:	108602	Age:	27
Place of birth:	Salisbury, Wiltshire	Home country:	Canada
Date of death:	02/06/16	Cause of death:	Killed in action
Memorial:	Salisbury, Wiltshire		

War cemetery: Ypres Menin Gate Memorial, Belgium
Theatre of war: Belgium
Next of kin: The late Arthur Henry & Elizabeth Anne Weston (parents)
Address: Salisbury, Wiltshire

Norman Weston volunteered to serve in the Canadian Army during 1914. He had previous military experience and joined the 1st Canadian Mounted Rifles. He was the youngest son of Mr and Mrs Weston and was a native of Salisbury. On 2 June 1916 the 1st Canadian Mounted Rifles were in trenches at Hill 62, near Sanctuary Wood, which is south-east of the town of Ypres. At 8.30 a.m. the Germans started a bombardment which broke like thunder over the Canadian trenches. By 1.15 p.m. the 1st Canadian Mounted Rifles had suffered 367 casualties.

   Norman Weston was killed in action during the fighting on Friday 2 June 1916 and is remembered on the Ypres Menin Gate Memorial. His brother, Leopold George Weston, who was a member of the Canadian Field Artillery would be killed in September 1918.

5 JUNE 1916 – LORD KITCHENER DIES AFTER HMS HAMPSHIRE SINKS AFTER HITTING A MINE

Capt. James Hannay Stewart McClure   *16th Battalion Manitoba Regiment*

Place of birth:	Greenock, Scotland	Home country:	Canada	Age: 30
Date of death:	17/06/16	Cause of death:	Died of illness	

War cemetery: Salisbury London Road Cemetery, England
Next of kin: James McCure (father)
Address: Greenock, Scotland

Above: *Inscription to James McClure's memory.*

Right: *Private memorial of Capt. James McClure paid for by subscription from his friends in Salisbury.*

The members of the Canadian Surplus Baggage Depot, stationed at Salisbury, had lost more than one of their number through death, and on Saturday 17 June, Capt. J.H.S. McClure of the Canadian Expeditionary Force, succumbed in Salisbury Infirmary to acute pneumonia. Capt. McClure had been invalided from France prior to being detailed for duty at the Surplus Baggage Depot. He was buried at the London Road Cemetery with full military honours.

In 1918, friends of James McClure, decided to erect a monument at the London Road Cemetery, where he was buried. Mr F. Sutton informed the subscribers that the memorial had been erected. On the plinth supporting the cross, the following is inscribed:

Remembrance

James Hannay Stewart McClure, Captain, 16th Batt., Canadian Regiment. Born in Greenock, 23 December, 1876. Died at Salisbury, 17 June 1916.

At the call of the Motherland he patriotically came to take his part in the Empire's Great War for right against wrong, and laid down his life for that sacred cause.

Erected by friends in England, who honoured his memory.

6

THE SOMME

Pte Alfred Wells　　　　　　　　　　　*2nd Battalion Wiltshire Regiment*

Service No.:	10876	Age:	26
Place of birth:	Newport, Isle of Wight	Home country:	England
Date of death:	28/06/16	Cause of death:	Killed in action
Memorial:	Salisbury, Wiltshire		

War cemetery:　Cerisy Gailly Military Cemetery, France
Theatre of war:　The Somme, France
Next of kin:　William & Laura Wells (parents)
Address:　62 St Edmund's, Church Street, Salisbury, Wiltshire

On Wednesday 28 June 1916, the 2nd Battalion Wiltshire Regiment were in trenches south-west of Albert on the Somme front in France. The bombardment prior to the Battle of the Somme was working towards its peak, and the German artillery was retaliating weakly. Final preparations were being made for the attack. 2nd-Lts Badgely and Martin led reconnaissance patrols out into No Man's Land to a part of the enemy trenches known as 'Loop Sap'. When they arrived at the hostile trench they were attacked by grenades thrown from the enemy's frontline and the patrol found that the Germans were holding the trenches in force. One man was wounded, likely to have been Alfred Wells, and the patrol had great difficulty bringing in the wounded man who later died. Alfred was buried close to the front and his remains were later moved to Cerisy Gailly Military Cemetery, France. He was one of the first soldiers from Salisbury to die in the Battle of the Somme.

On 1 July 1916, the first day of the Somme offensive, the British suffered 58,000 casualties. These were the heaviest losses ever suffered by the British Army on a single day during any war. Of those to fall, over 19,000 were killed.

Rifleman Victor George Besant　　　　　　*1st Battalion Rifle Brigade*

Service No.:	S/11630	Age:	18
Place of birth:	Andover, Hampshire	Home country:	England
Date of death:	01/07/16	Cause of death:	Killed in action
Memorial:	Salisbury, Wiltshire		

War cemetery:　Thiepval Memorial, France
Theatre of war:　The Somme, France
Next of kin:　Herbert & Ellen Bennett (parents)
Address:　16 The Croft, London Road, Salisbury, Wiltshire

Victor Besant had originally joined the 9th Lancers, but on Saturday 1 July 1916 he found himself a member of the 1st Battalion Rifle Brigade, in trenches south-west of the village of Serre, France. He was one of the first to go over the top in the 'big push' but by the end of the day he and over 150 other men of the 1st Rifle Brigade were dead. He is remembered on the Thiepval Memorial, France, with over 72,000 men who have no known grave. He was an under-age soldier.

Pte William Harry Bush

Service No.:	13584
Place of birth:	Milford, Wiltshire
Date of death:	01/07/16
Memorials:	Salisbury, Wiltshire
	St Mark's Memorial
War cemetery:	Thiepval Memorial, France
Theatre of war:	The Somme, France
Next of kin:	Harry & Ellen Bush (parents)
Address:	6 Wain a Long Road, Salisbury, Wiltshire

101st Company Infantry Machine Gun Corps

Age:	26
Home country:	England
Cause of death:	Killed in action

William Bush had originally joined the Wiltshire Regiment and had transferred to the Machine Gun Corps. The 101st Company was attached to the 34th Division which attacked the German line near the village of Ovilliers le Boisselle. He was killed in action on Saturday 1 July 1916. He is remembered on the Thiepval Memorial, France, and has no known grave.

Pte Frederick Charles Giddings

Service No.:	15251
Place of birth:	West Lavington, Wiltshire
Date of death:	01/07/16
Memorials:	Salisbury, Wiltshire
	St Mark's Church Memorial
War cemetery:	Thiepval Memorial, France
Theatre of war:	The Somme, France
Next of kin:	James & Mary A. Giddings

2nd Battalion Royal Dublin Fusiliers

Age:	24
Home country:	England
Cause of death:	Killed in action

Frederick Giddings had originally joined the Wiltshire Regiment, but, probably just after enlisting, transferred to the 2nd Battalion Royal Dublin Fusiliers. On 1 July 1916, he was preparing for the forthcoming attack in the trenches south-west of the town of Serre.

At 9.30 a.m. an order to halt the attack was not received by the 2nd Battalion Royal Dublin Fusiliers. As they rose from the trenches they were fired upon from the German positions at Ridge Redoubt and Beaumont Hamel. Frederick Giddings was one of over fifty men that died. He is remembered on the Thiepval Memorial, France, and has no known grave.

Sgt Stanley Glover

Service No.:	6883
Place of birth:	Yeovil, Somerset
Date of death:	02/07/16
Memorials:	Salisbury, Wiltshire
	St Paul's Church Memorial
War cemetery:	Thiepval Memorial, France
Theatre of war:	The Somme, France
Next of kin:	Florence M. Glover (wife); John & Charlotte Glover
Addresses:	Salisbury, Wiltshire
	Fisherton Anger, Salisbury, Wiltshire

6th Battalion Wiltshire Regiment

Age:	32
Home country:	England
Cause of death:	Killed in action

On the morning of Sunday 2 July 1916, Stanley Glover would have been preparing to take part in an attack. He may have written a letter to his wife Florence, who he had married at Salisbury in 1913. At 4 p.m. the Wiltshires advanced in open order and attacked the German frontline trenches just south of La Boiselle. Two lines of enemy trenches were taken and the casualties were thirty-eight killed, 242 wounded and thirty-five missing in action.

Stanley Glover, who was one of the thirty-eight men killed, is remembered on the Thiepval Memorial and has no known grave.

Lt Ronald Henry Spinney		*2nd Battalion Coldstream Guards*		
Place of birth:	Salisbury, Wiltshire	Home country:	England	Age: 28
Date of death:	02/07/16	Cause of death:	Died of wounds	
War cemetery:	Lijssenthoek Military Cemetery, Belgium			
Theatre of war:	Belgium			
Next of kin:	Absalom George & Jane Charlotte Spinney (parents)			
Address:	Marmora Road, Honor Oak, London			

On Sunday 2 July 1916, Ronald Henry Spinney, of the 2nd Battalion Coldstream Guards, died of the wounds he received the previous week. Lt Spinney was the son of Mr and Mrs A.G. Spinney of Marmora Road, Honor Oak, London, and was born in 1887. Lt Spinney was educated at the Modern School under Mr Bentley, and later went on to Salisbury School, having won a Chafyn Grove scholarship. He was a man of great ability, with a very strong personality, and a fine all-round sportsman. He was popular with all who knew him, and had a large circle of friends. In Salisbury he was articled to his uncle, the late Mr William Trethowan of Messrs Nodder & Trethowan, solicitors. He obtained his articles at the age of twenty-one, but soon after was appointed to a responsible position in a commercial enterprise in Java. In Java he held a very important and lucrative position, but came home intending to enlist as a private in the guards. The company, however, in which he served in Java treated him with great liberality. He returned to enlist in the Army, joining the Artists Rifles in March 1915. The following June he was gazetted a second-lieutenant in the Coldstream Guards and became lieutenant after going to the front. Two of Lt Spinney's brothers had seen active service and had attained the rank of lieutenant, while a third was on home service.

2nd-Lt Siegfried Thomas Hinkley		*C Company 6th Battalion East Kent Regiment*		
Place of birth:	India	Home country:	India	Age: 19
Date of death:	03/07/16	Cause of death:	Killed in action	
Memorials:	Salisbury, Wiltshire			
	St Mark's Memorial			
War cemetery:	Ovillers Military Cemetery, France			
Theatre of war:	The Somme, France			
Next of kin:	Revd William & Mrs Hinkley (parents)			
Address:	Anantapur, South India			

2nd-Lt Siegfried T. Hinkley, East Kent Regiment, was the only son of Revd and Mrs William Hinkley of Anantapur, South India, and of Salisbury, and was killed on Monday 3 July 1916 aged nineteen. He was educated at Packwood Haugh and Trent College, where he had been a member of the school OTC for years. He was gazetted from the Inns of Court OTC to the Buffs in the summer of 1915. His commanding officer wrote:

> I saw your son start off gallantly leading his men, but while getting through our wire he received a bullet through his thigh and fell. He refused to stop, calling out 'come on boys, I won't stop for this,' and pushed on. He was killed between the first and second German lines.

Siegfried Hinkley was taking part in an attack on Ovilliers, France, which commenced at 3.15 a.m. By 9 a.m. the attack was reported as a total failure and cost the 12th Division 2,400 casualties.

Pte Albert John Andrews   *1st Battalion Wiltshire Regiment*

Service No.:   22291
Place of birth: Salisbury, Wiltshire   Home country: England
Date of death: 05/07/16   Cause of death: Killed in action
Memorial: Salisbury, Wiltshire
War cemetery: Thiepval Memorial, France
Theatre of war: The Somme, France

Albert Andrews embarked for France on 24 May 1915 and on Wednesday 5 July 1916 he was with the 1st Battalion Wiltshire Regiment preparing to attack at Hindenburg Trench. The Wiltshires had moved into an old enemy trench and with a view to advancing against the enemy's strongly held second line, which formed part of the Leipzig Redoubt. After a thirty-second intense artillery and Stokes mortar bombardment, the first wave attacked under heavy enemy machine-gun fire. Although they reached their objective, they were insufficient in number to withstand the heavy German counter-attack, which followed immediately, and were compelled to withdraw. The second wave then attacked, after the trench had been cleared of Germans, all dugouts were bombed immediately and then took in hand the consolidation of the position gained.

The War Diary states: 'The men in this attack were magnificent, all showing the greatest coolness and initiative.'

On 7 July 1916 Albert Andrews was listed as missing. In July 1917 news was received to the effect that Albert was regarded – for official purposes – to have died on 5 July 1916. He is remembered on the Thiepval Memorial and has no known grave.

Sgt William Frank Welsh   *1st Battalion Wiltshire Regiment*

Service No.:   9005   Age: 22
Place of birth: Rodborne, Wiltshire   Home country: England
Date of death: 06/07/16   Cause of death: Killed in action
Memorials: Salisbury, Wiltshire
                  St Martin's Church Memorial
War cemetery: Lonsdale Cemetery, Authuile, France
Theatre of war: The Somme, France
Next of kin: William & Sarah Anne Welsh (parents)
Address: 103 Culver Street, Salisbury, Wiltshire

William Welsh was killed in action in the trenches at Leipzig Salient on Thursday 6 July 1916. The Germans attacked throughout the day with artillery and bombing raids. It is likely that Welsh was killed during this action.

Pte Walter John Sanger   *1st Battalion Wiltshire Regiment*

Service No.:   6954   Age: 28
Place of birth: Tisbury, Wiltshire   Home country: England
Date of death: 07/07/16   Cause of death: Killed in action
Memorials: Salisbury, Wiltshire
                  St Martin's Church Memorial
War cemetery: A.I.F. Burial Ground, Flers, France
Theatre of war: The Somme, France
Next of kin: Mrs Sanger (wife); William & Maria Sanger (parents)
Addresses: The Friary, Salisbury, Wiltshire
                  Tisbury

On Friday 7 July 1916 the 1st Battalion Wiltshire Regiment were in the trenches at the Leipzig Salient, planning to make another attack on the strongest part of the Leipzig Redoubt. At 1.15 a.m. the Germans attempted to rush a trench held by the Wiltshires; the attack was beaten off, but further attacks carried on until dawn.

At 9.30 a.m. the attack commenced, after half a minute of intense bombardment by British artillery and Stokes mortars, the British snipers crawled in shell holes in No Man's Land and fired thirty rounds of steel-nosed bullets at the German machine guns, which were put out of action. The Wiltshires advanced, they reached the enemy trench parapet though the Germans were not surprised, the German trench was successfully captured.

At 1 p.m. the Germans counter-attacked but were repulsed and for the remains of the day the Wiltshires were subjected to a terrific high-explosive bombardment. Walter Sanger was killed in action on Friday 7 July 1916 and is buried in the Australian Imperial Force Burial Ground at Flers, France.

Pte Alfred Henry Wisdom		*6th Battalion Wiltshire Regiment*	
Service No.:	9345	Age:	18
Place of birth:	Fisherton, Wiltshire	Home country:	Wiltshire
Date of death:	07/07/16	Cause of death:	Killed in action
Memorials:	Salisbury, Wiltshire		
	St Paul's Church Memorial		
War cemetery:	Serre Road, Cemetery No.2, France		
Theatre of war:	The Somme, France		
Next of kin:	John & Fanny Wisdom		
Address:	34 Meadow Road, Salisbury		

On 12 August 1914, sixteen-year-old Alfred Wisdom volunteered for service with the 6th Battalion Wiltshire Regiment. Two years later, on Friday 7 July 1916, eighteen-year-old Alfred found himself in the old German frontline near La Boisselle. It is likely he was killed by a sniper during the afternoon.

Pte William Farr		*2nd Battalion Wiltshire Regiment*	
Service No.:	9184	Age:	19
Place of birth:	Donhead, Wiltshire	Home country:	England
Date of death:	08/07/16	Cause of death:	Killed in action
Memorial:	Salisbury, Wiltshire		
War cemetery:	Thiepval Memorial, France		
Theatre of war:	The Somme, France		
Next of kin:	William & Elizabeth Roberts (uncle and aunt)		
Address:	Bowerchalke, Wiltshire		

On 1 August 1914, William volunteered for service with the 2nd Battalion Wiltshire Regiment. On Saturday 8 July 1916 it is likely William was killed in action in the area of Bernafy Wood or Trones Wood, the Somme during actions carried out that day. Nineteen-year-old William is remembered on the Thiepval Memorial, Somme, France, and has no known grave.

Capt. Francis Dodgson		*8th Battalion Yorkshire Regiment*			
Place of birth:	Hampstead, London	Home country:	England	Age:	27
Date of death:	10/07/16	Cause of death:	Killed in action		
Memorial:	Salisbury, Wiltshire				
War cemetery:	Serre Road, Cemetery No.2, France				

Theatre of war: The Somme, France
Next of kin: The late Henley F. Dodgson & Helen Hamilton Fulton (parents)
Address: The Close, Salisbury, Wiltshire

Francis Dodgson, of the 8th Battalion Yorkshire Regiment, was the son of the late Mr H. Dodgson of Bovingdon, Hertfordshire, and Mrs Hamilton Fulton of the Close, Salisbury. He was reported missing on Monday 10 July 1916 and, in early August 1916, was officially reported killed in action. His commanding officer wrote to his mother as follows:

> It is with the deepest sympathy that I write to you to say that I fear there is now no doubt whatever that your son was killed on advance on Contalmaison. The ground that we advanced over was quite open, and the Battalion did magnificently, led by your son and Capt. Thomson. The advance was without cover, and advantage was taken of the numerous trenches and shell holes, and your son was evidently killed and completely buried in one of the trenches or shell holes, for we found no trace. He died gloriously, leading his men, and he lies with many others of his Company, in the torn and shell-swept valley just south-west of Contalmaison.

Dodgson had been educated at Marlborough College and Trinity College, Cambridge. His remains were recovered and he is buried at Serre Road Cemetery No. 2, Somme, France. His brother, Guy Dodgson, died of wounds three days after the Armistice was declared in 1918.

Pte John Thresher   *2nd Battalion Devonshire Regiment*
Service No.:   8688   Age: 25
Place of birth: Taunton, Somerset   Home country: England
Date of death: 13/07/16   Cause of death: Died of wounds
War cemetery: Salisbury (Devizes Road) Cemetery, Wiltshire
Theatre of war: Home.
Next of kin: James & Elizabeth Thresher (parents)
Address: Taunton, Somerset

On the afternoon of Monday 17 July 1916, the funeral took place, with military honours, of John Thresher of the Devons, who died at the Salisbury Infirmary on 13 July from wounds received in action during the British advance in France. This was the first death to occur among the many wounded soldiers received at the local hospitals, a fact which spoke well of the efficiency of local Red Cross work. Thresher, who had been twice wounded in action, came from a fighting family, and has several relations serving in the forces. A firing party was supplied through the courtesy of the officer commanding the 8th City of London Battalion (Post Office Rifles) and the bearers were supplied by Maj. Watts, of the Canadian Baggage Depot of Salisbury. The interment was conducted at Devizes Road Cemetery, by Revd W.C. Procter. Among those present at the graveside were Sgt-Maj. Seldon, representing the deceased soldier's regiment, Assistant Commandant C.H. Harris, representing the Salisbury Men's Detachment, VAD and a number of wounded soldiers from the infirmary. At the conclusion of the ceremony three volleys were fired over the grave and the *Last Post* was sounded.

It is likely that Thresher was wounded on 1 July, the first day of the Battle of the Somme, when the Devons attacked Mash Valley, near Pozieres, France.

Pte Edgar Percy Rousell   *1st Battalion Middlesex Regiment*
Service No.:   G/10923   Age: 20
Place of birth: Salisbury, Wiltshire   Home country: England
Date of death: 15/07/16   Cause of death: Killed in action

Above left: *John Thresher died of his wound received in France.*

Above right: *British burials in France.*

Memorials: Salisbury, Wiltshire
                St Martin's Church Memorial
War cemetery: Thiepval Memorial, France
Theatre of war: The Somme, France
Next of kin: William J. Rousell
Address: 66 St Mark's Road, Salisbury, Wiltshire

Edgar Roussell was killed in action on Saturday 15 July 1916, south-east of Pozieres, Somme. The 1st Battalion Middlesex Regiment began an attack at 9 a.m. as soon as they left Bazentin-le-Petit, they were shelled and machine gunned. By 5 p.m. the attack had been abandoned. Edgar Roussell is remembered on the Thiepval Memorial and has no known grave.

Able Seaman Henry Richard T. Woolford   *Royal Navy HMS* Alert
Service No.:   207406   Age: 34
Place of birth: Portsea, Hampshire   Home country: England
Date of death: 15/07/16
Memorials: Salisbury, Wiltshire
                St Paul's Church Memorial
War cemetery: Baghdad North Gate War Cemetery, Iraq
Theatre of war: Mesopotamia
Next of kin: Kate Woolford (wife)
Address: 10 Russell Road, Salisbury, Wiltshire

Henry Woolford had married his wife Kate in summer 1906 in Portsmouth but in the summer of 1916 he found himself as part of the river flotilla on the River Tigris in Mesopotamia. He died somewhere along the route of the river and his remains were exhumed and buried at Baghdad North Gate War Cemetery, Iraq, after the war.

Pte Ernest Edward Whitlock   *02/6th Battalion Gloucestershire Regiment*
Service No.:   4071   Age: 37
Place of birth: Salisbury, Wiltshire   Home country: England
Date of death: 19/07/16   Cause of death: Killed in action

Memorial:	Salisbury, Wiltshire
War cemetery:	Laventie Military Cemetery, La Gorgue, France
Theatre of war:	The Somme, France
Next of kin:	George Whitlock (grandfather)
Address:	49 College Street, Salisbury, Wiltshire

Ernest Whitlock, known as Jock, was killed in action on Wednesday 19 July 1916 while attacking Fromelles. He lies in Laventie Military Cemetery, La Gorgue, France, with over sixty members of the 2/6th Battalion Gloucestershire Regiment, who also died on that day.

Pte William James Crotty   *5th Battalion Wiltshire Regiment*

Service No.:	20911	Age:	21
Place of birth:	Crockerton, Wiltshire	Home country:	England
Date of death:	29/07/16	Cause of death:	Died of wounds
Memorial:	Salisbury, Wiltshire		
War cemetery:	Kirkee 1914-18 Memorial, India		
Theatre of war:	Mesopotamia		
Next of kin:	Sidney A. & Alice Crotty (parents)		
Address:	8 Trinity Hospital, Trinity Street, Salisbury, Wiltshire		

During the campaign in Mesopotamia, wounded soldiers were evacuated by ship to India. William Crotty died of his wounds in India on Saturday 29 July 1916. It is probable he died in Calaba Hospital, Bombay, India.

Capt. William Bramwell Pepper   *3rd Siege Battery Royal Garrison Artillery*

Place of birth:	Salisbury, Wiltshire	Home country:	England	Age:	32
Date of death:	04/08/16	Cause of death:	Died of wounds		
Memorials:	Salisbury, Wiltshire				
	St Martin's memorial				
War cemetery:	Dantzig Alley British Cemetery, Mametz, France				
Theatre of war:	The Somme, France				
Next of kin:	The late Col. George Nicholson & Emma Pepper (parents)				
Address:	Milford Hill, Salisbury, Wiltshire				

Capt. W.B. Pepper, Royal Garrison Artillery, died of his wounds on Friday 4 August 1916. He was the youngest son of the late Lt-Col. Pepper of Milford Hill, Salisbury, and formerly of Lissinisky King's Company, Ireland. Educated at Weymouth College, he joined the militia at the outbreak of the South African War at the age of sixteen, serving as a temporary officer at Plymouth. He was gazetted to the Royal Garrison Artillery in 1902 and after serving for some years in the Channel Islands and Bermuda, he exchanged into a mounted battery in India. At the outbreak of the First World War he was adjutant to the Antrim Special Reserve Royal Garrison Artillery. In August 1915, he joined another brigade as adjutant, and proceeded with them to Egypt, being transferred to France in April 1916. He was wounded by a shell on 4 August on his way to the trenches, and died shortly after, at the age of thirty-two.

His commanding officer wrote: 'We are all very much cut up about it. He was a great favourite with us, and such a good officer too.' His Commanding Officer of the Royal Artillery, County Antrim, wrote:

Capt. Pepper was closely associated with me in the work here for over a year, and during that time I came to know him intimately, and to admire and appreciate his sterling qualities. No commanding officer could have a better or more capable adjutant. He was so very thorough in everything he undertook, so loyal and devoted to his work, and to those whom he served.

Your son was eminently suited for staff work, and I repeatedly urged him to put forth all his energies in that direction. Now all my hopes of him are as nothing, and I have to mourn the loss of a gallant gentleman and good friend. He never forgot me as so many do when they leave the regiment, and it only seems a week since he came to see how we are all doing. Perhaps you will think it strange when I tell you that I knew immediately your son was struck down, for in some strange psychological way it was conveyed to me in such a vivid dream that I told both my wife and Mr Donkin, my present adjutant, that Capt. Pepper was either killed or wounded.

Pte Robert William Webb   *2nd Battalion Wiltshire Regiment*

Service No.:	22271	Age:	19
Place of birth:	Salisbury, Wiltshire	Home country:	England
Date of death:	05/08/16	Cause of death:	Died of wounds
Memorial:	Salisbury, Wiltshire		
War cemetery:	Abbeville Communal Cemetery Extension, France		
Theatre of war:	The Somme, France		
Next of kin:	Charlotte Mary Ann Webb (mother)		
Address:	Upper Mill, Bishopstone, Wiltshire		

Robert William Webb died of wounds on Saturday 5 August 1916, at one of the hospitals based at Abbeville, France. It is likely he received the wounds in action at the Somme in July 1916.

Sapper Francis Newton Talbot *13th Division Signal Company Royal Engineers*

Service No.:	66957	Age:	19
Place of birth:	Winterslow, Wiltshire	Home country:	England
Date of death:	06/08/16	Cause of death:	Heat exhaustion
Memorials:	Salisbury, Wiltshire		
	St Mark's Church Memorial		
War cemetery:	Amara War Cemetery, Iraq		
Theatre of war:	Mesopotamia		
Next of kin:	Albert Sidney & Emma Talbot (parents)		
Address:	60 St Mark's Road, Salisbury, Wiltshire		

Francis Talbot was the only son of Albert and Emma Talbot; he died in Mesopotamia from the effects of the heat. He is buried at Amara War Cemetery, Iraq.

Capt. Eric Noel Player   *8th Battalion Yorkshire Regiment*

Place of birth:	Winlaton, Durham	Home country: England	Age:	28
Date of death:	06/08/16	Cause of death: Killed in action		
War cemetery:	Becourt Military Cemetery, Becordel Becourt, France			
Theatre of war:	The Somme, France			
Next of kin:	Charles E. & Maria L. Player (parents)			
Address:	Osborne House, Clevedon, Somerset			

Capt. Eric Player was a student of the Salisbury Theological College; he took his degree at Cambridge and came to Salisbury in July 1914. Soon after, he volunteered for service in the Army. He received a commission as a second-lieutenant in the East Yorkshire Regiment, and attained the rank of captain. He fell on Sunday 6 August 1916 at the Somme, while leading a successful attack.

Cpl William James Clare   *1st Battalion Liverpool Regiment*
Service No.:   23748   Age: 25
Place of birth: Rock Ferry, Cheshire   Home country: England
Date of death: 08/08/16   Cause of death: Killed in action
Memorial: Salisbury Choir School Memorial
War cemetery: Delville Wood Cemetery, Longueval, France
Theatre of war: The Somme, France
Next of kin: Joseph & Helen Clare (parents)
Address: 15 Wye Street Rock Ferry, Liverpool, Cheshire

Cpl Clare was killed in action on Tuesday 8 August 1916, during an attack on Waterlot Farm, Guillemont, during the second month of the battle of the Somme. He is remembered in Salisbury on the Choir School Memorial.

2nd-Lt Basil Austin Gummer   *9th Battalion Liverpool Regiment*
Place of birth: Salisbury, Wiltshire   Home country: England   Age: 29
Date of death: 12/08/16   Cause of death: Killed in action
Memorials: Salisbury, Wiltshire
                   St Mark's Church Memorial
War cemetery: Thiepval Memorial, France
Theatre of war: The Somme, France
Next of kin: Henry B. Oakley & Mary Emily Gummer (parents)
Address: 3 Swaynes Close, Salisbury, Wiltshire

2nd-Lt Basil Austin Gummer, of 'The Kings' (Liverpool Regiment), was killed in action in France on 12 August 1916 and was the third son of Mr and Mrs Oakley Gummer of Salisbury. He was a member of the staff of Lloyds Bank, Frome, and was previously in Portsmouth for six years. Whilst at Portsmouth he was closely associated with the work of St Michael's Church, where he was server, sidesman, a member of the church council and secretary of the debating society. He also took an active part in the management of the boys' and young men's clubs, and conducted a dramatic society in Southsea. He joined the Artists' Rifles that October, having undergone an operation in the spring to render himself fit, and was gazetted to his regiment on 1 June 1916. He went to France on Saturday 1 July 1916.

His colonel wrote:

Your son was killed whilst gallantly leading his platoon in an attack on the German trenches. Although he had been with us only just over four weeks, I had formed a high opinion of his capabilities. He had envinced a great keeness in his work, and was very popular with his fellow officers and the men of his platoon.

The honorary secretary of the St John Freewill Offering, Frome, a post held by Lt Gummer until leaving Frome, wrote conveying sympathy to the family for their loss and added:

We greatly appreciated the work he had done for this scheme and for the church at which he so regularly worshipped. We deeply regret that in his keeness to serve his country in this great crisis it has fallen to his lot to make this supreme sacrifice of giving his life, so full of promise, for the sake of his Motherland.

It is likely Lt Gummer was killed during at attack south of Guillemont, Somme, at 5.15 p.m. on Saturday 12 August 1916. He is remembered on the Thiepval Memorial and has no known grave.

2nd-Cpl Ernest Frank Viney   *23rd Field Company Royal Engineers*

Service No.:	42638	Age:	26
Place of birth:	Salisbury, Wiltshire	Home country:	England
Date of death:	14/08/16	Cause of death:	Killed in action
Memorials:	Salisbury, Wiltshire		
	Bishop Wordsworth's School Memorial		
War cemetery:	Thiepval Memorial, France		
Theatre of war:	The Somme, France		
Next of kin:	Walter C. & Sarah A. Viney (parents)		
Address:	St Edmunds, Salisbury, Wiltshire		

2nd-Cpl Viney was killed in action on Monday 14 August 1916 in the area of Switch Line, east of Pozieres, Somme. He is remembered on the Thiepval Memorial and has no known grave.

Leading Seaman Francis Henry Jolliffe   *Royal Navy HM Submarine E4*

Service No.:	219416	Age:	32
Place of birth:	Salisbury, Wiltshire	Home country:	England
Date of death:	15/08/16	Cause of death:	Lost at sea
Memorials:	Salisbury, Wiltshire		
	St Martin's Church Memorial		
War cemetery:	Shotley St Mary Churchyard, Suffolk, England		
Theatre of war:	Home		
Next of kin:	Frederick William & Eliza Jane Jolliffe (parents)		
Address:	8 Park Terrace, The Friary, Salisbury, Wiltshire		

On Tuesday 15 August 1916 Francis Jolliffe was on board HM Submarine E4, which was taking part in an exercise in the North Sea, when she collided with another Submarine E41. A Royal Navy ship, HMS *Fairdrake*, had been monitoring the exercise and reached the stricken vessels in less than two minutes. There were no survivors from the E4, although both submarines were salvaged and returned to service.

Pte William John Brock   *7th Battalion Northamptonshire Regiment*

Service No.:	20729	Age:	39
Place of birth:	Salisbury, Wiltshire	Home country:	England
Date of death:	18/08/16	Cause of death:	Killed in action
Memorial:	Salisbury, Wiltshire		
War cemetery:	Thiepval Memorial, France		
Theatre of war:	The Somme, France		
Next of kin:	Ada F. Brock (wife); John & Mary Brock (parents)		
Addresses:	St Sepulchre, Northampton, Northamptonshire		
	St Martin, Salisbury, Wiltshire		

William Brock was killed in action near the quarry, east of Trones Wood, west of Guillemont, on Friday 18 August 1916. As the 7th Battalion Northamptonshire Regiment attacked they were halted by German machine guns. William Brock is likely to have fallen in this manoeuvre. He is remembered on the Thiepval Memorial, and has no known grave.

L/Cpl Henry Charles Scutt   *01/4th Battalion Wiltshire Regiment*

Service No.:	200098	Age:	27

Place of birth: Dorset   Home country: England
Date of death: 18/08/16   Cause of death: Died of illness
Memorial: Salisbury, Wiltshire
War cemetery: Baghdad North Gate War Cemetery, Iraq
Theatre of war: Mesopotamia

Henry Scutt was probably one of the 1/4th Battalion Wiltshire Regiment who had been part of the garrison of Kut that surrendered on 29 April 1916. He died of illness as a prisoner of war on Friday 18 August 1916. His remains were brought into Baghdad North Gate War Cemetery at the end of the war.

Pte William Gaisford   *01/7th Battalion Royal Warwickshire Regiment*
Service No.:   2516   Age: 25
Place of birth: Fisherton, Wiltshire   Home country: England
Date of death: 20/08/16   Cause of death: Killed in action
Memorials: Salisbury, Wiltshire
                 St Paul's Church Memorial
War cemetery: Thiepval Memorial, France
Theatre of war: The Somme, France
Next of kin: Charles & Letitia Gaisford (parents)
Address: 5 South Front Dews Road, Salisbury, Wiltshire

On 18 August 1916 the 1/7th Battalion Royal Warwickshire Regiment made a successful attack on the Hindenburg Trench and Nab Valley, South of Thiepval, near Authuille Wood. Pte Gaisford was killed in action on Sunday 20 August 1916 when he was one of only two members of his regiment killed on that day, probably by shell fire or a sniper. He is remembered on Thiepval Memorial and has no known grave.

Pte William Ralph Mould   *5th Battalion Royal Berkshire Regiment*
Service No.:   23679   Age: 19
Place of birth: Salisbury, Wiltshire   Home country: England
Date of death: 20/08/16   Cause of death: Died of wounds
Memorials: Salisbury, Wiltshire
                 Salisbury United Methodists
War cemetery: St Sever Cemetery Extension, Rouen, France
Theatre of war: France
Next of kin: George & Rosa Mould (parents)
Address: 17 Rolleston Street, Salisbury, Wiltshire

Nineteen-year-old William Mould died of wounds at one of the hospitals in the Rouen area. He had probably been evacuated from the fighting at the Somme, where on 8 August 1916 the 5th Battalion Royal Berkshire Regiment were in action at Ration Trench, which was situated between Thiepval and Pozieres. An extract from the regimental War Diary gives an understanding of life under close attack:

> The enemy employed *flammenwerfer* (flame thrower) and under cover of the smoke got into the trench. After hand-to-hand fighting they were driven out and beyond the barricade. At 5.30 a.m. they repeated the attack and this time succeeded in getting into the trench and compelling our men to withdraw down the trench. A fresh barricade was erected about 50 yards from the old one and the enemy were checked there.

The net result of the four attacks was that the enemy gained about 50 yards of trench with great loss of life. Casualties of six officers and 128 other ranks.

Maj. William Neville Pitt	*2nd Battalion Lincolnshire Regiment*
Date of death: 20/08/16	Cause of death: Died of wounds
Memorials: Salisbury, Wiltshire	
St Martin's Church Memorial	
War cemetery: Chocques Military Cemetery, France	
Theatre of war: The Somme, France	
Next of kin: Col. William Pitt	
Address: Fairseat House, Fairseat, Seven Oaks, Kent	

By August 1916, Salisbury Theological College had lost two of its students. William Neville Pitt had already served as a captain in the Lincolnshire Regiment when he joined the college in 1910. On the outbreak of the war he rejoined his regiment, and later was promoted to major. He died as a result of a severe wound on Sunday 20 August, leaving a widow and two infant sons.

It is likely William Pitt died of wounds received on 1 July 1916 when the 2nd Battalion Lincolnshire Regiment attacked up Mash Valley, toward Pozieres.

Pte Cecil Jack Wort	*01/8th Battalion Royal Warwickshire Regiment*
Service No.: 5288	Age: 19
Place of birth: Tisbury, Wiltshire	Home country: England
Date of death: 20/08/16	Cause of death: Killed in action
Memorials: Salisbury, Wiltshire	
St Mark's Church Memorial	
War cemetery: Thiepval Memorial, France	
Theatre of war: The Somme, France	
Next of kin: Samuel & Ellen Wort (parents)	
Address: 8A Hamilton Road, Salisbury, Wiltshire	

Cecil Wort was killed in action on Sunday 20 August 1916 in the area of the Nab, south of Thiepval. He was one of four members of his regiment killed on that day. He is remembered on Thiepval Memorial and has no known grave.

L/Cpl Frederick Short	*1st Battalion Wiltshire Regiment*
Service No.: 7722	Age: 27
Place of birth: Salisbury, Wiltshire	Home country: England
Date of death: 20/08/16	Cause of death: Killed in action
Memorials: Salisbury, Wiltshire	
St Paul's & St Martin's Church Memorials	
War cemetery: Blighty Valley Cemetery, Authuile Wood, France	
Theatre of war: The Somme, France	
Next of kin: Harry & Emily Short (parents)	
Address: The Close, Salisbury, Wiltshire	

Blighty Valley Cemetery, Authuile Wood, is near the mouth of Nab Valley, south of Thiepval. On Sunday 20 August 1916 Frederick Short was the only member of the 1st Battalion Wiltshire Regiment to be killed, while in trenches at the Leipzig Salient. The War Diary for the regiment that day states that it was moderately quiet and the weather fine and clear. The frontline was shelled by the Germans, and thus, it is likely L/Cpl Short was killed during the German bombardment.

Pte Frank William Dredge | *1st Battalion Wiltshire Regiment*

Service No.:	24142
Place of birth:	Salisbury, Wiltshire
Date of death:	22/08/16
Memorial:	Salisbury, Wiltshire
War cemetery:	Thiepval Memorial, France
Theatre of war:	The Somme, France
Next of kin:	James & Ellen Dredge (parents)
Address:	Salisbury, Wiltshire

Age:	36
Home country:	England
Cause of death:	Killed in action

On Tuesday 22 August 1916 Frank Dredge was with his regiment in the trenches at Leipzig Salient preparing for attack on the Lemburg trench in order to strengthen their hold on the salient.

The attack was made at one minute past six, with the Wiltshires advancing behind a artillery barrage. The attack was successful and the trench was captured. The Germans shelled the Wiltshires' trenches throughout the night. It is likely Frank Dredge was killed during the shelling. He is remembered on the Thiepval Memorial and has no known grave. The 1st Battalion Wiltshire Regiment suffered about ninety casualties but Pte Dredge was the only soldier to die on this day.

Lt Col. Joseph Francis Mary Kelly | *Royal Army Medical Corps*

Home country:	Ireland
Date of death:	22/08/16
War cemetery:	Salisbury London Road Cemetery, England
Theatre of war:	Home
Next of kin:	Mrs Kelly (wife); Late Mr Bernard Michael & Mrs Kelly (parents)
Address:	Shannon View, Athlone, Ireland

Age:	47
Cause of death:	Died of illness

Lt-Col. Joseph Francis Kelly, MB, RAMC, died at the nursing home in Salisbury, on Sunday 22 August 1916 aged forty-seven. Lt-Col. Kelly had come to live in Salisbury, in connection with his duties at the Southern Command Headquarters. His death cut short a career of distinction. Born in 1869, he was the son of the late Mr Bernard Michael Kelly, of Shannon View, Athlone, Ireland. In 1895 he went out with the Chittral Relief Expedition. He served through the whole of the Boer War, and entered Ladysmith with Gen. Buller, receiving the South African Medal. He married a daughter of Dr Mitchell, and in 1904 was promoted to the rank of major. During the First World War he served on the continent, but subsequently was at the landing at Suvla Bay. He remained in Gallipoli until the end of the campaign, and while there contracted poisoning. Later, however, he was placed in sole charge of the Medical Board in Egypt. Afterwards he was sent again to France. After twice being mentioned in despatches for his work in various theatres of war he came home on sick leave, and spent some time in Brighton. Three or four weeks later he was passed as fit for home service only and was posted to the Southern Command. His death at Salisbury followed a brief illness.

The body was conveyed to St Osmund's Church on the evening of 24 August 1916, and a Requiem Mass was said on Friday morning. The funeral took place with military honours in the afternoon, the first portion being held at the church. The family mourners were Mrs Kelly (widow), Miss C. Kelly (sister), Mr John Kelly (brother), Dr Mitchell (father-in-law), Maj. Adye Curran and Maj. Murray (cousins). Among those present at the church and graveside were Surgeon-Gen. Birrell, MB, Surgeon-Gen. Lloyd and Mrs Lloyd, Mrs Dodd, Col. Webb, Capt. Sheedy, Lt Traill, Lt Williams, Lt Newey, Lt Ramsbottom, Lt C.D. Day and Cpl Kenwick, in charge of a detachment from Lt-Col. Kelly's branch of the RAMC stationed at Salisbury. Col. Dodd was unable to be present through illness.

A detachment from the 3rd London Regiment, Royal Fusiliers, fired three volleys over the grave and the regimental buglers sounded the *Last Post*. The coffin bore the inscription:

JOSEPH FRANCIS KELLY
Lt-Colonel, RAMC
Died 22 August, 1916
Aged 47 years

Pte Frederick Stevens		*1st Battalion Wiltshire Regiment*	
Service No.:	14214	Age:	25
Place of birth:	Tisbury, Wiltshire	Home country:	England
Date of death:	23/08/16	Cause of death:	Killed in action
War cemetery:	AIF Burial Ground, Flers, France		
Theatre of war:	The Somme, France		
Next of kin	Elsie A. Stevens (wife); Sydney & Sarah Stevens (parents)		
Address:	Bee Farm, Old Castle, Salisbury, Wiltshire		

Frederick Stevens was killed in action on Wednesday 23 August 1914 at the Leipzig Salient, south of Thiepval. He was killed during intermittent German shelling, along with six comrades from his regiment.

Pte Ernest Frank House		*C Company 1st Battalion Wiltshire Regiment*	
Service No.:	22113	Age:	19
Place of birth:	Salisbury, Wiltshire	Home country:	England
Date of death:	24/08/16	Cause of death:	Killed in action
Memorial:	Salisbury, Wiltshire		
War cemetery:	Thiepval Memorial, France		
Theatre of war:	The Somme, France		
Next of kin:	Ellen Pitman (mother)		
Address:	46 Clifton Road, Salisbury, Wiltshire		

Nineteen-year-old Ernest Pitman was killed in action during attacks on the Hindenburg Trench, near the Leipzig Salient, south of Thiepval village, on Thursday 24 August 1916. Pitman was in C Company, which was chosen to stay in support while A, B and D Companies carried out the attack. It is likely he was killed either from German shelling or snipers, which were both prevalent during the attack. The 1st Battalion Wiltshire Regiment had over 300 casualties and Pitman was one of those killed. He is remembered on the Thiepval Memorial and has no known grave.

Pte Frederick Clarence Scott		*14th Service Battalion Gloucestershire Regiment*	
Service No.:	25640	Age:	26
Place of birth:	Wardour, Wiltshire	Home country:	England
Date of death:	24/08/16	Cause of death:	Killed in action
Memorials:	Salisbury, Wiltshire		
	St Paul's Church Memorial		
War cemetery:	Thiepval Memorial, France		
Theatre of war:	The Somme, France		
Next of kin:	Edwin & Annie Scott (parents)		

When Frederick Scott volunteered for service in 1914 it is likely he was rejected for being under height. In April 1915 the 14th Service Battalion Gloucestershire Regiment was formed at Bristol, by the Citizens Recruiting Committee, as a Bantam Battalion. These battalions were composed entirely of men who were under regulation size but otherwise fit for service.

On the night of 22/23 August 1916, Frederick Scott's division took over Angle Wood from the French Army. It is probable that Frederick was killed in action in this area on Thursday 24 August 1916. He is remembered on the Thiepval Memorial and has no known grave.

Gunner Edward James Goff   *40th Battery 26th Brigade Royal Field Artillery*

Service No.:	69557	Age:	19
Place of birth:	Camberwell, Middlesex	Home country:	England
Date of death:	27/08/16	Cause of death:	Killed in action
Memorials:	Salisbury, Wiltshire		
	St Paul's Church Memorial		
War cemetery:	Gordon Dump Cemetery, Ovillers La Boisselle, France		
Theatre of war:	The Somme, France		
Next of kin:	Edward & Emily Goff (parents)		
Address:	The Cottage, Ashley Manor, Kings Somborne, Hampshire		

A Royal Field Artillery Brigade in the First World War consisted of approximately 750 to 800 men and about twenty officers, with either 18lb field guns or 4.5in howitzers. Nineteen-year-old Gunner Goff was killed near La Boisselle, on Sunday 27 August 1916. It is likely he died during German shelling of his battery. He is buried in Gordon Dump Cemetery, Ovillers La Boisselle, France.

Pte William John Blake   *1st Battalion Duke of Cornwall's Light Infantry*

Service No.:	27400		
Place of birth:	Salisbury, Wiltshire	Home country:	England
Date of death:	03/09/16	Cause of death:	Killed in action
Memorial:	Salisbury, Wiltshire		
War cemetery:	Thiepval Memorial, France		
Theatre of war:	The Somme, France		

William Blake was killed in action on Sunday 3 September 1916 during the Somme campaign at the Battle of Guillemont. The attack commenced at noon with the 1st Battalion Duke of Cornwall's Light Infantry attacking from the south and at 2.50 p.m. had advanced to Wedge Wood, about 750 yards south-east of the centre of Guillemont.

Pte Blake is remembered on the Thiepval Memorial and has no known grave.

L/Cpl Edgar Robert Foakes   *7th Battalion Royal Dublin Fusiliers*

Service No.:	24007	Age:	23
Place of birth:	Maddington, Wiltshire	Home country:	England
Date of death:	03/09/16	Cause of death:	Killed in action
Memorials:	Salisbury, Wiltshire		
	St Martin's Church Memorial		
War cemetery:	Struma Military Cemetery, Greece		
Theatre of war:	Balkans		
Next of kin:	Charles & Elizabeth Foakes		
Address:	5 Park Terrace, The Friary, Salisbury, Wiltshire		

Edgar Foakes had originally volunteered for service with the Duke of Cornwall's Light Infantry but was transferred to the 7th Battalion Royal Dublin Fusiliers. In July 1915 his battalion embarked for Gallipoli where they remained until the end of September 1915, when orders were received to prepare for service in Macedonia. Edgar Foakes was killed in action, on Sunday 3 September 1916 near the Struma River, on the Greek-Bulgarian border, while fighting the Bulgarians. He would have fought alongside Russians, Italians and Serbs, who formed an allied force in this theatre of war.

Pte Frederick Murray Sainsbury   *1st Battalion Wiltshire Regiment*
Service No.:   11004   Age: 23
Place of birth: Salisbury, Wiltshire   Home country: England
Date of death: 3/09/16   Cause of death: Killed in action
Memorials: Salisbury, Wiltshire
               St Martin's Church Memorial & Salisbury United Methodists Memorial
War cemetery: Thiepval Memorial, France
Theatre of war: The Somme, France
Next of kin: George & Eda Sainsbury (parents)
Address: 7 Green Croft, Salisbury, Wiltshire

At about 5.10 a.m. on 2 September 1916, the 1st Battalion Wiltshire Regiment were preparing for an attack, with the objective being a number of enemy trenches in the vicinity of the Leipzig Salient. During a British bombardment of the German positions the Wiltshires advanced to about 50 yards from their objective. As soon as they left the protection of their trenches, they were met by heavy 'whizz-bang' fire and machine-gun fire from either flank. D Company got into the enemy trench, but were wiped out when the British barrage did not lift in time.

Only one company managed to hold a part of the German trench and the other companies were forced to retire, the attack was a failure.

Frederick Sainsbury and eighteen other members of the 1st Battalion died on Sunday 3 September 1916; he is remembered on the Thiepval Memorial and has no known grave.

His brother, Hedley Giles Sainsbury, had died in France a year earlier in September 1915.

15 SEPTEMBER 1916 – FIRST USE OF THE BRITISH SECRET WEAPON THE 'TANK' – GREAT ADVANCES MADE AND A TANK DROVE DOWN THE MAIN STREET OF FLERS

Pte Bertie Francis Andrews   *338th Company Royal Army Service Corps*
Service No.:   M2/18152   Age: 32
Place of birth: Salisbury, Wiltshire   Home country: England
Date of death: 15/09/16   Cause of death: Died of illness
Memorial: Salisbury, Wiltshire
War cemetery: Mikra British Cemetery, Kalamaria, Greece
Theatre of war: Balkans
Next of kin: Catherine Mary Andrews (wife); Sydney & Sarah Stevens (parents)
Address: 44 St Edmunds, Church Street, Salisbury, Wiltshire

During the campaign in the Balkans for every casualty sustained in fighting, three died from diseases such as influenza, dysentery or malaria. Bertie Andrews died on Friday 15 September 1916 more than likely from one of these diseases. He is buried in Mikra British Cemetery, Greece.

Lt John Philip Morton Carpenter   *Royal Field Artillery*
Place of birth: Salisbury, Wiltshire   Home country: England   Age: 23

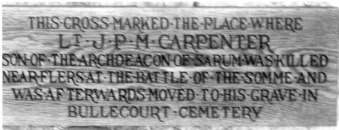

Top: *A British tank goes into action.*

Above and right: *This cross marked the place where John Carpenter was killed nears Flers, France. It can now be seen in the cloisters at Salisbury Cathedral, along with the plaque.*

Date of death: 15/09/16   Cause of death: Killed in action
Memorials: Salisbury, Wiltshire
                   Choir School Memorial
War cemetery: Bulls Road Cemetery, Flers, France
Theatre of war: The Somme, France
Next of kin: Marjorie Clare Carpenter (wife); Archdeacon Harry W. & Annie S.
                   Carpenter
Addresses: The Hall, Salisbury
                   North Canonry, The Close, Salisbury, Wiltshire

On 16 September 1916, news reached Salisbury of the death of Lt John Philip Morton, Royal Field Artillery, youngest surviving son of the Archdeacon of Sarum and Mrs Carpenter, of the Close, Salisbury. He had been killed in action in France on Friday 15 September 1916.

He was born on 4 August 1893, and was educated at Marlborough and Lancing. He had intended to take up farming and was for a time the pupil of Mr John Harding at Odstock, and later he was with Mr W.P. Hayter, of Compton Pauncefote. At both places he endeared himself to all who knew him. On the outbreak of war he enlisted in the Public Schools' Battalion, and shortly after obtained a temporary commission in the 5th Wilts Regiment. He was seriously wounded in the landing at Sulva Bay in August of 1915, and was in hospital for some time in Malta, and then was invalided home to Longford Castle, where he remained until convalescent. He was transferred to the Royal Field Artillery and after completing his training, went to France. An excellent officer, he won the high regard of both the officers and men of his battery.

On 15 September 1916, during the advance, it is believed he was instantaneously killed by a shell. In December 1915 he married Marjorie Clare, elder daughter of Dr. W. W. Ord and Mrs Ord, of The Hall, Salisbury. Among the many letters of condolence received by Archdeacon and Mrs Carpenter was one from the committee of the Salisbury branch of the QMNG, and one from the Mayor of Salisbury, who wrote: 'On behalf of the citizens of Salisbury please accept my most sincere sympathy in this, your great sorrow. Our feelings are beyond words.' A memorial service was held at Salisbury Cathedral on 15 September 1916 at 2.15 p.m. The first part of the service was taken by the Dean and the latter by the Bishop. Lt Carpenter's elder brother was in India with his regiment, while his four brothers-in-law, who were on service, were also prevented from being present.

A telegram was received by Mrs Carpenter from the King and Queen expressing their Majesties' sympathy with her in her bereavement. In a letter received by Mrs Carpenter, Capt. M. de Burgh, an officer of the late Lt Carpenter's battery, who was invalided home some weeks before, wrote:

> I am writing to offer my deepest sympathy at the loss of your son. I thought you would like to know how greatly I, and I know the battery, will feel his loss. He came to me as my senior subaltern, just before leaving England in May, and was my most valued officer. He will be a loss to the battery indeed. He worked very hard and was a great help to me out in France. I cannot tell you any more about him, as I left the battery before they went down to the Somme. I expect you will hear all that from his new battery commander.

The new commander, Maj. Stopford, was also killed on the day that Lt Carpenter met his death.

Cpl Alfred Firmston Williams		*49th Alberta Regiment Canadian Infantry*	
Service No.:	100884	Age:	27
Place of birth:	Shrewsbury, Shropshire	Home country:	Canada
Date of death:	15/09/16	Cause of death:	Killed in action
Memorials:	Salisbury, Wiltshire		
	St Mark's Church Memorial		
War cemetery:	Vimy Memorial, France		
Theatre of war:	France		
Next of kin:	Alfred & Annie S. Williams (parents)		
Address:	8 Marlborough Road, Salisbury, Wiltshire		

Alfred Williams volunteered for service with the Canadian infantry on 15 July 1915, as part of the Canadian 2nd Division which was formed in England that year. Just over a year later he found himself near the village of Courcellette, about 2 miles east of Thiepval. Aided by a tank, the Canadians pushed the Germans out of the nearby sugar factory and captured the village. Pte Williams, who had been a farmer, was the second son of Alfred and Annie Williams. His, father Alfred Sr was Postmaster of Salisbury. He died on Friday 15 September 1916 and is remembered on Vimy Memorial for Canadians who fought during the First World War; he has no known grave.

L/Sgt Arthur Reginald Weeks		*3rd Battalion Coldstream Guards*	
Service No.:	8266	Age:	25
Place of birth:	St Edmunds, Salisbury, Wiltshire	Home country:	England
Date of death:	16/09/16	Cause of death:	Killed in action
Memorial:	Salisbury, Wiltshire		
War cemetery:	Thiepval Memorial, France		
Theatre of war:	The Somme, France		
Next of kin:	Job & Emily H. Weeks (parents)		
Address:	St Edmund, Salisbury, Wiltshire		

L/Sgt Weeks was killed in action on Saturday 16 September 1916 during the advance on Flers. The Guards Division were advancing from Trones Wood to the north of Flers. Arthur Weeks was one of 139 members of the Coldstream Guards who died on that day. He is remembered on the Thieval Memorial and has no known grave.

Stoker 1st Class Edmund James Leaver   *Royal Navy HMS* Dalhousie

Service No.:	K/9437
Place of birth:	Salisbury, Wiltshire
Date of death:	18/09/16
Memorial:	Salisbury, Wiltshire
War cemetery:	Basra Memorial, Iraq
Theatre of war:	Mesopotamia
Next of kin:	Edward & Edith Leaver (parents)
Address:	St Thomas, Salisbury, Wiltshire

Age: 27
Home country: England
Cause of death: Died of illness

HMS *Dalhousie* was an armed merchant ship that was based in Abadanin, modern-day Iraq. He died on Monday 18 September 1916, most probably from disease. He is remembered on the Basra Memorial and has no known grave.

Lt Edward Wyndam Tennant   *4th Battalion Grenadier Guards*

Place of birth:	Stockton, Wiltshire
Date of death:	22/09/16
Memorials:	Salisbury, Wiltshire
	Salisbury Cathedral Pte Memorial
War Cemetery:	Guillemont Road Cemetery, Guillemont, France
Theatre of war:	The Somme, France
Next of kin:	Edward Priaux, 1st Baron Glenconner, & Lady Glenconner (parents)

Home country: England   Age: 19
Cause of death: Killed in action

In late September 1916 news reached Lord and Lady Glenconner of the death of their eldest son, the Hon. E. Wyndham Tennant, who had been killed in action on Friday 22 September 1916, at the age of nineteen. Lt Tennant, Grenadier Guards, was educated at West Downs and Winchester. He joined the Army at the outbreak of war, and went to the front in August 1915. In his letter to his mother, dated just before going into action, he wrote:

> This is written in case anything happens to me, for I should like you to have just a little message from my own hand. Your love for me and my love for you have made my whole life one of the happiest there has ever been. This is a great day for me. 'High heart, high speech, high deeds, mid-honouring eyes' God bless you and give you peace.

Lt Tennant had been well known to inhabitants of Salisbury ever since his father, then Sir Edward Tennant, came before the burgesses as a candidate for Parliamentary honours, and afterwards as MP for the city, and his career, which promised to be a brilliant one, was watched with interest. As a boy he accompanied his parents to many political and social gatherings in Salisbury and South Wiltshire, and by his charm of manner made many friends, as did other members of the family. The next heir, the Hon. Christopher Tennant, was serving in the Navy.

A memorial service was held in October 1916 at St Margaret's, Westminster (the House of Commons Church) in hour of Lt Tennant, who was the nephew of Prime Minister and Mrs Asquith. The bereaved parents and many other members of the family were present. Cabinet ministers and other representatives of both Houses of Parliament attended, and the Colonel commanding the Grenadier Guards, with many of his fellow officers, represented the regiment.

Far left: *Bim Tennant.*

Left: *Bim Tennant's memorial in Salisbury Cathedral.*

The service, conducted by the Rector Canon Carnegie, was brief and simple, but not the less impressive on that account. It opened on a note of triumph, referred as little as such a service could to the bitterness of death, and ended with the *Hallelujah Chorus*.

A feature of the service was the handing, on arrival, to each member of the congregation, a brochure with an excellent inset portrait of the late officer in khaki and containing a reprint of a letter sent home by him on 20 September, two days before he fell. It reads as follows:

Tonight we go up to the last trenches we were in, and tomorrow or the next day go over the top. Our brigade has suffered less than either of the other two brigades in Friday's biff of the 15th, so we shall be in the forefront of this battle. I am full of hope and trust, and I pray that I may be worthy of my fighting ancestors: the one I know best is Sir Henry Wyndham, whose bust is in the hall at 44 Belgrave Square, and there is another picture of him on the stairs at 34 Queen Anne's Gate.

We shall probably attack over about 1200 yards, but we shall have such artillery support as will probably smash the line we are going for and even if the artillery doesn't come up to our hopes (which is very unlikely), the spirit of the Brigade of Guards will carry all resistance before it.

O darling Moth'. the pride of being in so great a regiment! The thought that all the old men 'late Grenadier Guards' who sit in London clubs are thinking and hoping about what we are doing here now!

I have never been prouder of anything, except your love for me, than I am of being a Grenadier. That line of Harry's rings through my mind, 'High hear, high speech, high deeds mid-honouring eyes.'

I went to a service on the side of a hill this morning, and I took the Holy Communion afterwards, which always seems to help one along doesn't it?

I slept like a top last night and dreamed that someone I know very well, but I can't remember who it was, came and told me how much I had grown. I feel rather like saying, 'if it be possible let this cup pass from me' but the triumphant finish, 'nevertheless, not what I will, but what thou willest' steels my heart, and send me into battle with a heart of triple bronze.

I always carry four photos of you when I go into action, one in my note case, two in that little leather book and one around my neck. And I have kept my medal of the Blessed Virgin. Brutus farewell to Cassius sounds in my heart. 'If not, farewell; and if we meet again we shall smile'. Your love for me and my love for you have made my life one of the happiest that has ever been.

This is a great day for me.

God bless you and give you peace.

Now all my blessings go with you always, and with all we love.

Eternal love from BIM.

On the flyleaf was a quotation from this letter followed by an appropriate exert from Macbeth which has reference to the death of Siward's son with 'his hurts before'. The document also included the following quotation:

> We are troubled on every side, yet not distressed; we are perplexed, but not in despair. Persecuted, but not forsaken; cast down, but not destroyed. For which cause we faint not; but though the outward man perish, yet the inward man is renewed day by day.

Col. Wyndham, Lady Glenconner's brother, was away in Scotland on military duty, and thus could not attend the Westminster service.

Bim was one of the war poets; he wrote the poems, *Home Thoughts of Laventie* and *Reincarnation*. He was killed by a German sniper near the village of Les Bouefs, France.

L/Sgt Henry Simeon Burton		*1st Battalion Wiltshire Regiment*	
Service No.:	6951	Age:	31
Place of birth:	Salisbury, Wiltshire	Home country:	England
Date of death:	23/09/16	Cause of death:	Died of wounds
Memorial:	Salisbury, Wiltshire		
War cemetery:	Tenby St Mary Church Cemetery, Wales		
Theatre of war:	Home		
Next of kin:	Mrs Burton (wife); Cornelius E. & Martha Burton (parents)		
Address:es	Pembroke, Wales		
	St Edmund, Salisbury, Wiltshire		

Henry Burton married his wife in 1907; he died of his wounds, probably received in fighting on the Somme, on Saturday 23 September 1916.

Pte John Gatford		*12th Battalion Middlesex Regiment*	
Service No.:	G/2839	Age:	22
Place of birth:	East Grinstead, Sussex	Home country:	England
Date of death:	26/09/16	Cause of death:	Killed in action
Memorial:	Salisbury, Wiltshire		
	St Mark's Church Memorial		
War cemetery:	Thiepval Memorial, France		
Theatre of war:	The Somme, France		
Next of kin:	Henry & Eliza Gatford (parents)		
Address:	Holme Wood, Castle Road, Salisbury		

On Tuesday 26 September 1916 the 12th Battalion Middlesex Regiment attacked Thiepval village. The Middlesexes met little opposition until they were held up by machine-gun fire from the chateau on the edge of Thiepval, a tank arrived and ended all German resistance in the village.

John Gatford was in the machine-gun section of the 12th Battalion Middlesex Regiment and was reported missing on 26 September 1916. Just before Christmas 1916 the official news reached Henry and Eliza Gatford, in Salisbury, that Gatford had been killed in action. He is remembered on Thiepval Memorial and has no known grave.

Pte Thomas Read		*6th Battalion Dorsetshire Regiment*	
Service No.:	14412	Age:	19
Place of birth:	Northam, Hampshire	Home country:	England

Date of death: 27/09/16   Cause of death: Died of wounds
Memorial: Salisbury, Wiltshire
War cemetery: Salisbury London Road Cemetery, England
Theatre of war: Home
Next of kin: Thomas & Rose Read (parents)
Address: 22 Scots Lane, Salisbury, Wiltshire

Nineteen-year-old Pte Read volunteered for service in September 1914 after Kitchener's call for more men. He was most likely wounded during the Somme and evacuated to England. He died from the wounds, on Wednesday 27 September 1916, in a hospital in London and is buried in Salisbury London Road Cemetery, England.

Gunner Herbert Thomas Geater   *C Battery 177th Brigade Royal Field Artillery*
Service No.:   31222   Age: 22
Place of birth: Darsham, Suffolk   Home country: England
Date of death: 27/09/16   Cause of death: Died of illness
War cemetery: Salisbury (Devizes Road) Cemetery, Wiltshire
Theatre of war: Home
Next of kin: Albert & Eliza Geater (parents)
Address: Mill Hill Farm, Darsham, Suffolk

On the morning of Wednesday 27 September 1916, Herbert Geater died in Salisbury Infirmary. He had been in France since January 1916, the youngest son of Mr and Mrs Geater, of Mill House Farm, Darsham, Ipswich, who had two other sons serving in the Army. Herbert was invalided home from the front at the beginning of September suffering from an acute disease, to which he quickly succumbed. The funeral took place with full military honours at the Devizes Road Cemetery the following Saturday. The cortége, forming an impressive procession, was headed by a cross borne by Pte Richardson, a wounded soldier, after whom followed the officiating clergyman, Revd H.C. Bush, followed by the firing party and gun carriage bearing the coffin covered with a Union Jack. Six soldiers acted as pall bearers. The coffin was of unpolished oak with plain brass furniture and bore the inscription: 'Herbert Thomas Geater, died September 27th 1916, aged 22 years'.

   The chief mourners were the deceased's father and mother. Assistant Commandant C.H. Harris represented the local Red Cross Society and a large number of wounded soldiers also followed. At the conclusion of the committal three volleys were fired over the grave by the firing party, composed of men of the 6th London Regiment, and the Bugler sounded the *Last Post*.

Pte William Richard Whitehead   *1st Battalion Wiltshire Regiment*
Service No.:   18074   Age: 24
Place of birth: Alhampton, Somerset   Home country: England
Date of death: 03/10/16   Cause of death: Died of wounds.
Memorial: Salisbury, Wiltshire
War cemetery: Regina Trench Cemetery, Grandcourt, France
Theatre of war: The Somme, France
Next of kin: F.D. Whitehead (wife); George & Rosa Whitehead (parents)
Address: 167 Franciscan Road, Tooting Common, London

Pte Whitehead died of his wounds on Tuesday 3 October 1916 during the actions around Stuff Redoubt, north-west of the village of Courcelette. He is buried in Regina Trench Cemetery, which is named after a German defensive trench. Stuff Redoubt was a defensive position situated on that trench.

Pte Lionel William Bushrod   *15th Service Battalion Hampshire Regiment*

Service No.:	22548	Age:	25
Place of birth:	Dorchester, Dorset	Home country:	England
Date of death:	06/10/16	Cause of death:	Killed in action
Memorial:	Salisbury, Wiltshire		
War cemetery:	Thiepval Memorial, France		
Theatre of war:	The Somme, France		
Next of kin:	William & Kezia Bushrod (parents)		
Address:	Fisherton Anger, Salisbury, Wiltshire		

The 15th Battalion Hampshire Regiment was raised by the mayor of Portsmouth on 5 April 1915, a response to Kitchener's 1915 appeal. They embarked for France in May 1916. The regiment's first taste of action was at the Battle of the Somme. Lionel was killed in action on Friday 6 October 1916, north of Courcelette. His regiment were preparing to take part in the attacks that took place on the Transloy Ridges. He is remembered on the Thiepval Memorial and has no known grave.

L/Cpl Ernest Leonard Holcombe   *18th Battalion Kings Royal Rifle Corps*

Service No.:	C/8004	Age:	23
Place of birth:	Hinton Charterhouse, Somerset	Home country:	England
Date of death:	10/10/16	Cause of death:	Killed in action
Memorials:	Salisbury, Wiltshire		
	St Mark's Church Memorial		
War cemetery:	Thiepval Memorial, France		
Theatre of war:	The Somme, France		
Next of kin:	Edward & Kate Holcombe (parents)		

Ernest Holcombe volunteered in June 1915 and the 18th Battalion Kings Royal Rifle Corps embarked for France in May 1916. His first experience of war would have been at the Battle of the Somme. Killed on Tuesday 10 October 1916, just north of the town of Flers during the attacks on the Transloy Ridges, he is remembered on Thiepval Memorial and has no known grave.

Pte Herbert Frederick Taylor   *1st Garrison Battalion Royal Berkshire Regiment*

Service No.:	31675	Home country	England	Age:	31
Date of death:	11/10/16	Cause of death:	Suicide		

Far left: *Thomas Read, who died of wounds received on the battlefield.*

Left: *The grave of Herbert Taylor.*

War cemetery: Salisbury (Devizes Road) Cemetery, Wiltshire
Theatre of war: Home
Next of kin: Samuel Parsons Taylor
Address: Spottiswoode, London

A distressing tragedy occurred in Salisbury at about midnight on Tuesday 10 October 1916 when a soldier, after attempting to commit a murder, took his own life.

The parties directly concerned were an orderly employed at military offices in Salisbury – Herbert Taylor, whose home was in Tottenham, London – and a girl named Jessie Bolwell, a daughter of Mrs Bolwell, of 17 Avon Terrace, Salisbury. The two had been acquainted for some six months. It appears to have been the custom of Taylor to take the girl home to her mother's house in the evening and then to escort her to the house of a Mrs Handford, where she slept.

On Tuesday evening, Taylor, Miss Bolwell and her mother had been to a party at a neighbour's house, and it was somewhere about midnight when, after having returned home, Herbert Taylor and the girl finally left for Mrs Handford's house.

The tragedy followed in a very short space of time. From the facts which were subsequently ascertained, it seems that Pte Talyor, just before arrival at their destination, suddenly drew a razor and made a desperate attempt to cut his companion's throat. He succeeded in inflicting two wounds, and then turned the instrument upon himself, drawing it across his own throat no less than six times, and causing frightful injuries. Herbert then made his way towards the river, and his dead body was subsequently found in the water near Black Well. The girl was taken to the Salisbury Infirmary, where she recovered from her wounds.

An inquest was held at the council chamber on the morning of 12 October 1916 by the City Coroner, Mr Buchanan Smith. Mr J.S. Rambridge was chosen foreman of the jury.

Samuel Parson Taylor, a compositor on the employ of Messrs Eyre & Spottiswoode, London, and reading at Tottenham, said the deceased was his son. He was a single man of thirty-one years of age. Prior to the war he lived at home, and was employed by the same firm as the witness, as a labourer. He joined the Army about six weeks after the commencement of the war. He had been home three times since joining, the last occasion being in February. He always appeared to be well and had had no serious illness. He had written to his mother to say he had not felt so well since he had been in Salisbury, and thought at one time that he would have to go back to his place. He had also written to his brother complaining of pains in the head and dizziness, and they were surprised that he had not mentioned it to them at home. The witness supposed, however, that he did not want to cause his mother any more worry, because they had two sons at the front as it was.

Sgt Spires, Somerset Light Infantry, stationed at the Southern Command Office, Salisbury, said that he was in charge of the cycle orderlies. The deceased had been at the office as cycle orderly since 4 March 1916. He then belonged to the Duke of Cornwall's Light Infantry, and after about a fortnight was transferred to the home service garrison battalion of the Royal Berkshire Regiment. Witness last saw him alive at one o'clock on 10 October and he then appeared to be in his usual health. He had never made any complaint of not feeling well. Deceased and other orderlies were warned to attend a medical examination on the Wednesday. He was in Class C. On Wednesday morning, witness visited the city mortuary in Salt Lane and there identified the body of the deceased.

Mrs Annie Bolwell, widow, of 17 Avon Terrace, said that she had three children, the eldest of whom, Jessie Evelyn May, was twenty years of age. Since Mr Handford, of 1 Meadow-view, Avon Terrace, had joined the Army, the witness's daughter, Jessie, had been sleeping at the house to keep Mrs Handford and her daughter company. The deceased, Herbert Taylor, lodged at 53 Clifton Road, with a Mrs Jefferys and had kept company with witness's daughter for about six months. He had been in the habit of going out with her daughter in the evening and bringing her home, coming into the house also to wish witness good night. He then accompanied her daughter to 1 Meadow View, at the bottom of Avon Terrace.

On Tuesday 10 October 1916., Mr Beck, a cousin, living at 55 Clifton Road, invited her daughter and herself to a small party which was being given on the occasion of one of his daughters becoming engaged to a soldier. After they had been there a few minutes the deceased came in, and they all had supper together. The deceased seemed bright and cheerful. He had a glass of beer to drink. The three of them left Mr Beck's house at about twelve o'clock, and Taylor was at that time quite normal and perfectly sober. They all went into witness's house and remained there about ten minutes. Deceased asked witness if she was tired, to which she replied in the affirmative, and he then said 'Come along, Jessie' upon which they both left the house, as witness supposed, for Meadow View as usual. About five minutes afterwards witness heard a scream, and her daughter rushed into the house, with the words 'Oh Mother, Taylor has been and cut my throat.' She was bleeding profusely from the face and neck, the witness laid her on the couch and attended to her. Her clothing was saturated with blood. She asked her where the deceased was, and she replied 'I don't know,' while to her query as to why he had done it she returned a similar answer. In the meantime the police and Mr Armitage had been sent for. Mr Armitage, who arrived shortly afterwards, attended her and ordered her removal to the infirmary, whither she was immediately taken. Her daughter suffered from rheumatism, and was in consequence obliged to give up her situation as a domestic servant in December last. She was under medical treatment by Mr W. Gordon, and had been ordered to the infirmary. She had not the full use of her right arm, and since 28 December last had been employed at the milk factory, Devizes Road. This was the only work she had done since that time.

The Coroner: 'Have you ever heard the deceased threaten to commit suicide?'
Witness: 'No, I have not.'
'Did the deceased and your daughter always appear to be perfectly happy?'
'Yes.'
'Have you ever heard that they have ever had a cross word?'
'No I have not.'

Alfred Henry Beck, stoker, in the employ of the Salisbury Gas Company, living at 55 Clifton Road, said that on the 10 October he invited several people, including Mrs and Miss Bolwell, to a party given at his house on account of one of his daughters being engaged to marry a soldier. The deceased also came. The proceedings commenced between nine and ten o'clock.

The deceased, Herbert Taylor, and Jessie Bolwell appeared to be enjoying themselves, and deceased took part in the dancing and singing. He had two glasses of beer to drink during his supper.

The Coroner: 'Was he quite normal and perfectly sober?'
Witness: 'Yes.'

Proceeding, witness said that Mrs and Miss Bolwell and the deceased left at about midnight, and the party broke up at about 12.30 a.m. At that time his son was standing outside the house, and suddenly said that he had heard someone shout 'Murder!' His son ran down the street and returned with the news that 'Taylor had cut Jessie's throat.'

In answer to the foreman, witness said the deceased was quite sober.

Mr J. Armitage, of Endless Street, said that on Wednesday morning he examined the body of the deceased. He found six wounds in the throat, five of them insignificant, and one very serious.

The Coroner: 'Were the injuries in your opinion sufficient to cause death?'
Witness: 'Yes.'

Charles Henry Poole, stoker, in the employ of Salisbury Gas Co., said he was also invited to the party already referred to. He left at about midnight, and proceeded to his house at 33 Clifton Road, while Mrs Bolwell and her daughter and the deceased went towards Avon Terrace. Taylor was sober. Shortly afterwards he heard screams, and eventually saw the girl, Jessie, lying on the sofa in her home with her face cut. She said that Taylor had done the deed when they were inside the gate. In company with Pte Goddard, witness went to the spot. They noticed blood marks on the galvanised iron and a blood-stained razor was also found lying nearby, which was handed to PC Toogood.

Salisbury Journal 1916

Pte Harry Taylor   *5th Battalion Royal Berkshire Regiment*
Service No.:   23579
Place of birth: Salisbury, Wiltshire   Home country: England
Date of death: 14/10/16   Cause of death: Killed in action
Memorial: Salisbury, Wiltshire
War cemetery: Bulls Road Cemetery, Flers, France.
Theatre of war: The Somme, France

Harry Taylor had originally joined the Somerset Light Infantry but he was killed in action with three comrades from the 5th Battalion Royal Berkshire Regiment, probably by German shelling, on Saturday 14 October 1916 in Smoke Trench, near Gueudecourt, Somme.

2nd-Lt Eric Wallace Ware   *3rd Battalion Wiltshire Regiment*
Place of birth: Salisbury, Wiltshire   Home country: England   Age: 20
Date of death: 18/10/16   Cause of death: Killed in action
Memorials: Salisbury, Wiltshire
                      St Martin's Church Memorial
War cemetery: Caterpillar Valley Cemetery, Longueval, France
Theatre of war: The Somme, France
Next of kin: Hubert Gale & Sarah Margaret Ware (parents)
Address: Milford, Salisbury, Wiltshire

Mr and Mrs H.G. Ware of Milford House, Salisbury, were informed that their second son, 2nd-Lt Eric W. Ware, of the Wiltshire Regiment, had been wounded and missing since 18 October 1916. News was received by Mr Ware from the War Office on Wednesday 1 November 1916, with an intimation that a further report would be sent when received. 2nd-Lt Ware was educated at Salisbury School and St Edward's School, Oxford. At the outbreak of war he was in the Wiltshire Yeomanry and was granted a commission in the Wiltshire Regiment in December 1914. He was invalided from active service, but went back to the front in spring 1916. He was twenty years old and of fine physique, a good all-round sportsman always popular with his regiment. He earned the high opinion of his commanding officer, and did such good work that he was placed in command of a company. The following letter was received from the officer commanding the regiment:

Dear Mr Ware
It is with the utmost sorrow and sympathy I write to tell you what I know as to how your son came to be reported wounded and missing.

My battalion attacked the enemy's position at 3.40 a.m. on the morning of the 18 October. Your son was in command of D Company, and was in the first wave of the attack. D. Company's runner reported to me that your son was wounded both in the neck and stomach. The runner placed him in a shell hole with another wounded officer, as it was impossible to get him back at the time, and, owing to the nature of his wounds, your son stood a better chance of being left where he was.

It was mainly owing to your son's great courage in rallying his men, after he had already been wounded, to make a second charge, that our men got into the enemy's trenches. Unfortunately we were unable to retain the position, and it was therefore impossible to discover what became of your son. If there is any question you would like answered I shall be glad to do my best to answer it.

I am sorry I have been unable to write before, but my battalion only came up out of the trenches on the twenty-second, and since then my time has been fully occupied.

May I add that there are many here who sincerely regret the loss of a friend, as your son was most popular with officers and men alike.

In the first week of December 1916, Lt Ware's orderly and one of the runners of the battalion, wrote to Lt Ware's Father, Mr H.G. Ware. The man, a native of Wilsford, placed Lt Ware in a critical condition in a shell hole with another officer. The wounds were such that Lt Ware must have died while unconscious shortly after the runner left. Further news other than from this unofficial source it is considered is out of the question as the ground was afterwards re-captured by the Germans.

Eric Ware was killed in action on Wednesday 18 October 1916; he is buried in Caterpillar Valley Cemetery Longueval, south of Bapaume, France.

Cpl Albert Charles Massey   *21st Company Infantry Machine Gun Corps*

Service No.:	21549	Age:	27
Place of birth:	Fisherton, Wiltshire	Home country:	England
Date of death:	21/10/16	Cause of death:	Killed in action
Memorials:	Salisbury, Wiltshire		
	St Paul's Church Memorial and Dews Road Primative Methodist Memorial		
War cemetery:	Thiepval Memorial, France		
Theatre of war:	The Somme, France		
Next of kin:	Albert & Bessie Massey (parents)		
Address:	Fisherton, Salisbury, Wiltshire		

Albert Massey had originally joined the Wiltshire Regiment but transferred to the Machine Gun Corps which was created on 14 October 1915. He was killed in action, on Saturday 21 October 1916 during the Battle of Transloy Ridges, most likely in the area of Bayonet Trench, located to the north of Flers. He is remembered on Thiepval Memorial and has no known grave.

Pte Alfred Leopold Burrough   *24th Battalion Royal Fusiliers*

Service No.:	G/24769	Age:	24
Place of birth:	Salisbury, Wiltshire	Home country:	England
Date of death:	24/10/16	Cause of death:	Killed in action
Memorial:	Salisbury, Wiltshire		
War cemetery:	Euston Road Cemetery, Colincamps, France		
Theatre of war:	The Somme, France		
Next of kin:	Alfred & Alice S. Burrough (parents)		
Address:	63 Park Street, Salisbury, Wiltshire		

Alfred Burrough volunteered for service in the 24th Service Battalion, known as the 2nd Sportsman's. He was killed in action on Thursday 24 October 1916, when his regiment were in action north of Les Boeufs. Remembered on the Thiepval Memorial, he has no known grave.

Able Seaman Leslie Arthur Claridge	*Royal Navy HMS* Flirt
Service No.: J/17581	Age: 19
Place of birth: Wilton, Wiltshire	Home country: England
Date of death: 26/10/16	Cause of death: Killed in action
Memorials: Salisbury, Wiltshire	
St Paul's Church Memorial & St Mark's Church Memorial	
War cemetery: Portsmouth Naval Memorial, England	
Theatre of war: At sea	
Next of kin: James H.C. & Emily Claridge (parents)	
Address: Milford, Salisbury, Wiltshire	

Twelve German destroyers broke through the Dover Barrage, which was a minefield, and sunk seven of the attendant trawlers and drifters. HMS *Flirt* went to investigate and mistook the German ships for friendly destroyers returning to Dover. *Flirt* stopped to rescue the survivors of the trawlers and drifters. Moments after she put on her searchlight, a torpedo struck her amidships and she sank immediately with the loss of nearly all the crew.

Nineteen-year-old Leslie Claridge was killed while serving on HMS *Flirt*. He is remembered on the Portsmouth Naval Memorial and has no known grave.

Pte Arthur Edward Chambers	*4th Battalion Central Ontario Regiment*
	Canadian Infantry
Service No.: 22004	Age: 28
Place of birth: Salisbury, Wiltshire	Home country: Canada
Date of death: 28/10/16	Cause of death: Died of illness
Memorial: Salisbury, Wiltshire in St Martin's Church Memorial	
War cemetery: Salisbury London Road Cemetery, England	
Theatre of war: Home	
Next of kin: John & Sarah Chambers (parents)	
Address: 92 Gigant Street, Salisbury, Wiltshire	

The death of Pte Arthur Edward Chambers occurred at the Chatham Military Hospital, on Saturday 28 October 1916. Pte Chambers was part of the 1st Canadian Division and son of Mr John Chambers, of 92 Gigant Street, Salisbury. The deceased, who was only twenty-nine years of age, left England in 1911 and took up a homestead in Canada. Upon the outbreak of war he came to England with the 1st Canadian Contingent. He went to France in February of the following year and, after nineteen months fighting, was wounded by shrapnel on 13 September 1916. He was ultimately taken to the Chatham Military Hospital, where following an operation, pneumonia set in and this was the immediate cause of death.

Prior to leaving Salisbury, Pte Chambers was a member of the St Martin's Church Choir, the St Martin's Church Lads Brigade, and the St Martin's Men's Bible Class, and he was held in high esteem throughout the parish.

The funeral took place at the London Road Cemetery on Wednesday afternoon, with full military honours, and the proceedings were organised by Maj. Watts and members of the Canadian Surplus Baggage Depot. The coffin, covered with the Union Jack, upon which was placed the deceased belt, bayonet and hat, was mounted upon a gun carriage, accompanied by a firing party supplied from the depot. Six of the deceased's old comrades who were themselves wounded, acted as bearers. The officers present were Maj. Watts and Capt. Mitchell. The first part of an impressive ceremony was held at St Martin's Church, in the presence of a considerable congregation. The cortege then proceeded to the London Road Cemetery. The first part of the service at the Graveside was taken by Revd L.A.H. Isaac, and the committal sentences were pronounced by Revd I.G. Cameron. The *Last Post* was sounded, and three volleys fired over the grave.

2nd-Lt Bertram T Collier   *31st Northumberland Fusiliers attached to the*
                                              25th Northumberland Fusiliers (Tyneside Irish)
Place of birth: Johannesburg, South Africa   Home country: England   Age: 19
Date of death: 05/11/16   Cause of death: Died of wounds
War cemetery: Trois Arbres Cemetery, Steenwerck, France
Theatre of war: The Somme, France
Next of kin: Tom George & Annie Collier
Address: Ikaya Wentworth Avenue, Bournemouth, Dorset

Bertram Collier was the younger son of Tom and Annie Collier who had lived in Salisbury prior to the First World War. He died of wounds at the 2nd Australian casualty-clearingstation, in the village of Steenwerck on Sunday 5 November 1916. He most likely received the wounds in actions around Flers in October 1916.

L/Cpl Charles William Brookson   *Royal Army Pay Corps*
Service No.:   4566   Age: 38
Place of birth: Beddington, Surrey   Home country: England
Date of death: 09/11/16   Cause of death: Died of illness
War cemetery: East Harnham All Saints Churchyard, England
Theatre of war: Home
Next of kin: Esther Brookson (wife); William & Emma Brookson of Surrey (parents)
Address: Bognor Cottage, Brize Norton, Oxfordshire

The death of L/Cpl Brookson occurred on Thursday 9 November 1916, at the Salisbury Infirmary, after a painful illness. Brookson had been stationed at the Southern Command, Salisbury. L/Cpl Brookson was with the West Kent Volunteers for ten years and was invalided home from South Africa during the Boer War. He returned to the scene of the action in the Army Medical Corps, and while on service contracted injuries which ultimately caused his death. He had been a schoolmaster in Canada, and tried to join the Canadian Expeditionary Force. Refused on account of the state of his health he sailed to England, and joined the Army Pay Corps.

His funeral took place at East Harnham Church on the afternoon of 13 November 1916. A procession, headed by the cross borne by Pte Kinner, walked from the infirmary to the church, and the coffin, draped with a Union Jack, was drawn on a gun carriage. A large party of the Army Pay Corps, under Lt Hepburn, and a number of the wounded from the infirmary, also followed. The service was conducted by Revd G. Hill, assisted by Revd H. Cromwell Bush. A firing party was supplied by the Queen Victoria Rangers. Every man of the party had been wounded once or more while fighting abroad. Wreaths were sent from the headquarters' staff, the Army Pay Corps, and relatives and friends of the deceased.

Pte Alfred Blake   *2nd Battalion Royal Marine Light Infantry*
                                                 Royal Naval Division
Service No.:   PO/13216   Age: 30
Place of birth: Salisbury, Wiltshire   Home country: England

Far left: *Charles Brookson, who died of illness.*

Left: *Private memorial to Charles Sanctuary at St Mark's Church, Salisbury.*

		Cause of death:	Killed in action
Date of death:	13/11/16		
Memorial:	Salisbury, Wiltshire		
War cemetery:	Ancre British Cemetery, Beamont Hamel, France		
Theatre of war:	The Somme, France		
Next of kin:	George & Elizabeth Blake (parents)		
Address:	9 Guilder Lane, Salisbury, Wiltshire		

Pte Blake was killed in action on Monday 13 November 1916 on the first day of the Battle of Ancre, during the latter stages of the Somme Campaign. At 3 a.m. the marines crawled out into No Man's Land and they got close to the Germans' barbed wire; then at 6 a.m. they attacked towards Beuamont Hamel. Alfred Blake was the third son of George and Elizabeth Blake.

Pte Hercules Hopkins   *3rd Battalion Coldstream Guards*

Service No.:	3303	Age:	35
Place of birth:	Buckland Newton, Dorset	Home country:	England
Date of death:	14/11/16	Cause of death:	Killed in action
Memorials:	Salisbury, Wiltshire		
	St Paul's Church Memorial		
War cemetery:	Guards Cemetery, Lesboeufs, France		
Theatre of war:	The Somme, France		
Next of kin:	Harriet Pamela Hopkins (wife); Hillary & Eliza Hopkins		
Addresses:	Salisbury		
	Buckland Newton, Dorset		

Hercules Hopkins was killed in action on Tuesday 14 November 1916 during the final stages of the Battle of the Somme. He was the only member of his regiment killed on this day, which indicates he may have fallen victim to a sniper or shell fire. It is likely he died locally and his remains were brought up to the cemetery.

Capt. Charles Lloyd Sanctuary   *8th Battalion Suffolk Regiment*

Place of birth:	Dorchester, Dorset	Age:	28
Decorations:	Military Cross	Home country:	England
Date of death:	15/11/16	Cause of death:	Died of wounds
Memorial:	Salisbury, Wiltshire		
	St Thomas Church Memorial		
War cemetery:	Boulogne Eastern Cemetery, France		

Theatre of war: France
Next of kin: Charles Lloyd & Evangeline Hopgood Sanctuary (parents)
Address: Frampton Vicarage, Frampton, Dorset

Capt. Charles Lloyd Sanctuary, MC, died in hospital in France of wounds received in action on 28 September 1916. Capt. Sanctuary was the eldest son of Revd C. Lloyd Sanctuary, Canon of Salisbury, and Mrs Sanctuary, and was twenty-eight. Educated at St Edmund's School, Hindhead, at Marlborough College and at the City and Guilds (Engineering) College, he joined the Inns of Court OTC on the outbreak of war and received a commission in the Suffolk Regiment in September 1914. He made it to the front for July 1915 and was with his battalion until he was wounded. He was signalling officer until his promotion to captain in the spring of 1916. He saw much fighting on the Somme.

An announcement for the award of the Military Cross to Capt. Sanctuary in the official record reads: 'Single-handed he attacked twelve of the enemy, and captured nine prisoners. He has displayed great courage and determination throughout the operations.'

18 NOVEMBER 1916 – THE END OF THE BATTLE OF THE SOMME

The British sustained 420,000 casualties; the French 200,000 casualties; the Germans an estimated 500,000 casualties.

Sgt George Mullins   *7th Battalion Royal Fusiliers*
Service No.: L/6205   Age: 34
Date of death: 22/11/16   Cause of death: Died of wounds
Home country: England
War cemetery: Salisbury London Road Cemetery
Theatre of war: Home
Next of kin: James & Frances Louisa Mullins (parents)
Address: 11 Blondel Street, Battersea, London

Sgt Mullins, of the Royal Fusiliers, died at the Red Cross Hospital, Salisbury, on Wednesday 22 November 1916 as the result of wounds received in action. He was thirty-four years old and came from fighting stock. He had served nineteen years, and both his father and grandfather

Right:
*Thiepval
Memorial,
Somme, France.*

Far right:
George Mullins.

had been in the Army. Three brothers were with the forces. Full military honours were accorded at the funeral, which took place at the London Road Cemetery. The coffin was borne on a gun carriage and carried into the cemetery by six sergeants of the 8th (Reserve) Battalion, London Regiment. A firing party of thirty men under an officer was provided by the same regiment. After the interment three volleys were fired over the grave, and buglers sounded the *Last Post.*

Capt. George Alec Parker   *60th Squadron Royal Flying Corps*
Place of birth: Salisbury, Wiltshire   Home country: England   Age: 23
Date of death: 27/11/16   Cause of death: Killed in action
Decorations: Distinguished Service Order & Military Cross
Memorials: Salisbury, Wiltshire
                         St Thomas Church Memorial & Choir School Memorial
War cemetery: Arras Flying Services Memorial, France
Theatre of war: France
Next of kin: Lewis Jacques Parker & Emily Parker (parents)
Address: Castle Street, Salisbury, Wiltshire

Mr and Mrs L.J. Parker of Castle Street, Salisbury, received notification in 1916 from the War Office on the evening of Thursday 30 November that their son, Flight-Commander G.A. Parker (Northamptonshire Regiment), RFC, had been missing since 27 November 1916. The telegram added that this did not necessarily mean Flight-Commander Parker was wounded or killed. Unfortunately this was indeed the case.

   His commanding officer wrote:

He always did most excellent work both as observer and pilot. I have not met a better officer. It is not possible to say definitely what his fate was, though from the way the machine went down it looked as if he was hit. He may, however, be alive, and a prisoner. In that case you may be sure that he will be well looked after as the Germans are known to treat English aviators properly. I have just heard that he has been awarded both the DSO, and the Military Cross, for some exploits of his during the last three weeks. The pity is that the news has only just come through, and that he did not know about it this morning when he went up. If I hear anything further I will write immediately, but you will probably get definite news sooner than we shall.

The many fiends of Mr and Mrs Parker joined in the hope that they may soon have reassuring news of the gallant officer. Unfortunately, news arrived that Alec Parker was killed in action on Monday 27 November 1916. He is remembered on the Arras Flying Memorial and has no known grave. Alec Parker's brother, Tom Geoffrey Milsome Parker, was to die in November 1918.

Sapper Rupert Eustace Akers   *108th Field Company Royal Engineers*
Service No.:   65784   Age: 26
Place of birth: Surbiton, Surrey   Home country: England
Date of death: 28/11/16   Cause of death: Killed in action
Memorials: Salisbury, Wiltshire
                         St Mark's Church Memorial
War cemetery: Dorian Memorial, Greece
Theatre of war: Salonika
Next of kin: Rupert & Jane Mary Akers (parents)
Address: Stockbridge, Hampshire

Rupert Akers, known as Eusty, was the eldest son of Rupert and Jane Akers. He volunteered for service with the Royal Engineers and in September 1915 they embarked for Salonika. He was killed in action, most likely by shelling from the Bulgarian artillery, on Tuesday 28 November 1916.

Rupert Akers is remembered on Dorian Memorial and has no known grave.

Cpl Percy Edwin Victor Briant	*Royal Army Service Corps*	
Service No.:	T/1514	Age:	24
Place of birth:	Salisbury, Wiltshire	Home country:	England
Date of death:	28/11/16	Cause of death:	Died of illness
War cemetery:	Bournemouth East Cemetery, England		
Theatre of war:	Home		
Next of kin:	The late Sidney & Sarah Jane Briant (parents)		
Address:	Bournemouth, Dorset		

Percy Briant, a native of Salisbury, was the youngest son of Sidney and Jane Briant, who had lived in Salisbury prior to the war. He had originally joined the Hampshire Regiment, but transferred to the Royal Army Service Corps, probably because he had a useful skill, such as driving. He died of illness at a hospital in Christchurch on Tuesday 28 November 1916.

Sapper Ernest Cassey	*134th Field Company Royal Engineers*	
Service No.:	145557	Age:	29
Place of birth:	Salisbury, Wiltshire	Home country:	England
Date of death:	16/12/16	Cause of death:	Died of illness
War cemetery:	Wimereux Communal Cemetery, France		
Theatre of war:	France		
Next of kin:	Mrs E. Cassey (wife); Thomas & Martha Cassey (parents)		
Addresses:	5 Gardener Street, Brighton, Sussex		
	5 Gardener Street, Brighton, Sussex		

Sapper Cassey joined the Army in August 1915. He was the youngest son of the Late Thomas and Martha Cassey, who had lived in Salisbury prior to the war. Ernest was a native of Salisbury and died on Saturday 16 December at Wimereux, an important hospital centre during the First World War.

Driver David Herbert Squires	*3rd Artillery Reserve Brigade 13th Reserve Battery Royal Field Artillery*	
Service No.:	28754	Age:	33
Place of birth:	Bristol	Home country:	England
Date of death:	16/12/16	Cause of death:	Died of illness
War cemetery:	West Harnham St George Churchyard, England		
Theatre of war:	Home		
Next of kin:	Annie Squires (wife)		
Address:	6 The Cottages, West Harnham, Harnham, Wiltshire		

The death of Driver Squires occurred in Salisbury Infirmary on Saturday 16 December 1916 after a short illness. Driver Squires, who had been in the Army thirteen years, was invalided from the front some time ago, and at the time of his death was in the employ of Col. Sir William Foster. The funeral took place with full military honours on Wednesday afternoon at West Harnham Church, the officiating clergy being Revd G. Hill, Revd H.C. Bush and the

Private memorial to Harold Tozer, who died in an aircraft accident. The memorial has been moved adjacent to the church wall at East Harnham.

Infirmary Chaplain Revd E. Glanfield. After the interment a firing party under Lt D. Graham, of the London Regiment, fired three volleys, and the buglers sounded the *Last Post*. Among those present besides the deceased's widow and relatives was Col. Sir William Foster.

2nd-Cpl Harold Percy Tozer   *Royal Flying Corps*
Place of birth: Lambeth, London   Home country: England Age: 25
Date of death: 16/12/16
War cemetery: East Harnham All Saints Churchyard, England
Theatre of war: Home
Next of kin: Henry James & Agnes Emma Tozer (parents)
Address: 31 Lansdowne Gardens, Clapham, London

A fatality occurred at the Netheravon Aerodrome on the afternoon of Saturday 16 December 1916, 2nd-Lt H.R. Tozer, Durham Light Infantry, attached to a Reserve Squadron, RFC being instantaneously killed through the slide slipping of a Maurice Farman Biplane. The deceased, whose home is at 31 Laburnham Gorve, Clapham, was twenty-five years of age.

An inquest was held on the afternoon of Monday 18 December 1918 before Mr F.A.P. Sylvester, coroner for mid-Wiltshire.

2nd-Lt Wild, RFC, said the deceased went up at 1.45 p.m. in a Maurice Farman machine, which was an ordinary biplane for a pupil to use. When about 100ft up, the right wing dropped and the machine side slipped. It was good flying weather, and witness had just previously been up in the same machine. This was the deceased officer's third solo flight. The witness thought the cause of the accident may have been that the rudder was not used as it should have been under the circumstances. The witness was 400 yards away when the accident occurred, and went to the spot where the machine fell. Tozer was quite dead.

Sgt Davis, RFC, said he examined and tested the engine of the machine on 15 December. It ran nicely and with full power.

First A.M. Jackson, RFC, a rigger attached to the squadron, stated that he inspected and overhauled the machine on the Friday. It was in proper order for flying and was practically new.

Capt. Moore, RAMC, said he medically examined the deceased when he came to Netheravon. He was quite sound. It was customary to examine all pupils on arrival. He examined the body after death and found the principle injury was fracture of the skull. Death was instantaneous.

The coroner, in summing up, expressed his deep sympathy with the relatives of the deceased, and he was sure the jury would like to join him in that expression. It was exceptionally sad in the case of a young fellow coming as Lt Tozer did, from civilian life to serve his country. The jury returned a verdict of accidental death.

Harold Tozer , who was a nephew of Mr S.C. Tozer of Harnham, was buried at Harnham on 21 December 1916. The service was attended by relatives, officers of the Royal Flying Corps and a detachment of men from Netheravon.

Pte Bertrum Frederick Ernest Jerrard		*36th Battalion Australian Infantry Australian Imperial Force*	
Service No.:	1145	Home country: Australia	Age: 20
Date of death:	22/12/16	Cause of death: Died of wounds	
Memorials:	Salisbury, Wiltshire		
	St Mark's Church Memorial		
War Cemetery:	Bailleul Communal Cemetery Extension, Nord, France		
Theatre of war:	France		
Next of kin:	Cecelia Frances Jerrard (mother)		
Address:	62 Park Street, London Road, Salisbury, Wiltshire		

Twenty-year-old Bertram Jerrard, a native of Salisbury, had enlisted in the Australian Army in January 1916 and in May that year he embarked for England on a ship called the Beltana, arriving at Devenport, on 9 July 1916. He proceeded to France upon leaving Southampton on 22 November 1916. On 19 December 1916, while undertaking a bombing practice, he was accidentally injured when a mills grenade thrown by a Pte Keown fell short. Bertram received wounds to his chest, neck (perforated trachea) and right wrist. He died at 11.50 p.m. on Friday 22 December 1916, at 8th Casualty-Clearing Station.

A letter of condolence was sent to Cecelia Jerrard and later Bertram's personnel effects followed: identity disc; dictionary; wallet; prayer book; fountain pen; three coins; handkerchief; card; French book; photographs; button; metal pencil case and eight stamps were sent to his mother.

In 1917 Cecelia Jerrard made a pension claim for her dead son Bertram. It would appear that the Australian War Pensions Office received information that Cecelia Jerrard was not Bertram's natural mother. Cecelia Jerrard was interviewed by the Salisbury Police, it was found that she had made an arrangement with a pregnant woman called Johns, to take the child and bring him up as her own. When the child was born, Cecelia Jerrard registered the birth and declared herself as the mother. She also stated that soon after the birth the woman Johns was married and she had no idea of her whereabouts.

Sgt Henry Palmer		*1st Battalion Wiltshire Regiment*	
Service No.:	10358	Age:	22
Place of birth:	St Lukes, London	Home country: England	
Date of death:	23/12/16	Cause of death: Died of wounds	
Memorial:	Salisbury, Wiltshire		
	Wilsford, Wiltshire, St Martin's Church Memorial		
War cemetery:	Boulogne Eastern Cemetery, France		
Theatre of war:	France		
Next of kin:	John & Mary Ann Palmer (parents)		
Address:	Ivy Cottage, Southampton Road, Salisbury, Wiltshire		

Henry Palmer, known as Harry, died of his wounds on Saturday 23 December 1916 at Boulogne, France. During the First World War, Boulogne was a main hospital centre and it is most likely that Palmer received wounds during the Battle of the Somme, which officially ended in the latter part of November.

7

1917

Cpl Arthur Cudmore   *4th Labour Battalion Royal Engineers*

Service No.:	115908	Age:	53
Place of birth:	Dolton, Devon	Home country:	England
Date of death:	04/01/17	Cause of death:	Died of wounds

War cemetery: Salisbury (Devizes Road) Cemetery, Wiltshire
Theatre of war: Home
Next of kin: Christopher Cudmore (father)
Address: Dolton, Devon

The death of Cpl A. Cudmore, Labour Battalion, RE, occurred on 4 January 1917, at the Salisbury Infirmary. The deceased, who held four medals for previous service, had served eighteen years in the Army and was invalided from France the previous November. The funeral took place at the Devizes Road Cemetery with full military honours, the procession headed by a cross being carried by Cpl W. Wiles of the 9th Royal Sussex Regiment (a wounded soldier from the infirmary), after whom followed the officiating clergy, the Infirmary Chaplain Revd E. Glanfield, Revd H. Cromwell Bush, and a firing party of men of the Lincoln Regiment. The pall bearers were six Canadians from the local surplus-baggage depot. The coffin, borne on a gun carriage and covered with the Union Jack, was followed by the deceased's widow and daughter. After the committal was performed the firing party fired three volleys over the grave and the bugler sounded the *Last Post*.

Pte Walter Musselwhite   *5th Battalion Suffolk Regiment*

Service No.:	5834	Age:	34
Place of birth:	Salisbury, Wiltshire	Home country:	England
Date of death:	11/01/17	Cause of death:	Died of wounds

Memorials: Salisbury, Wiltshire
            St Paul's Church Memorial & St Martin's Church Memorial
War cemetery: Ypres Reservoir Cemetery, Belgium
Theatre of war: Belgium
Next of kin: Frances Musselwhite (wife); Edward & Elizabeth Musselwhite (parents)
Address: 13 Meadow Cottages Friary, Salisbury, Wiltshire

Walter Musselwhite originally joined the 5th Battalion Suffolk Regiment but transferred to the 53rd Company The Labour Corps. The Labour Corps was employed for everything from digging trenches, dugouts, to burying the dead or repairing roads. He died of his wounds on 11 January 1917. The British at Ypres held an area known as a salient, an area that was a bulge in the frontline. This gave the Germans an opportunity to shell or snipe at the British from three sides. It is likely Walter was wounded by shelling on the salient while he was at work.

Pte James Kiddle   *5th Battalion Wiltshire Regiment*

Service No.:	21150	Age:	27
Place of birth:	Britford, Wiltshire	Home country:	England
Date of death:	16/01/17	Cause of death:	Died of wounds

Memorials: Salisbury, Wiltshire
                    St Paul's Church Memorial
War cemetery: Amara War Cemetery, Iraq
Theatre of war: Mesopotamia
Next of kin: David & Elizabeth Kiddle (parents)
Address: 10 Avon Terrace, Fisherton, Salisbury, Wiltshire

James Kiddle died of his wounds on 16 January 1917 at the hospital centre in Amara, now in modern-day Iraq. It is likely he was wounded in the fighting around Kut al Amara.

Pte Alfred Stephen Drake   *5th Battalion Wiltshire Regiment*
Service No.:   21151
Place of birth: Chillington, Somerset   Home country: England
Date of death: 18/01/17   Cause of death: Killed in action
Memorial: Salisbury, Wiltshire
War cemetery: Amara War Cemetery, Iraq
Theatre of war: Mesopotamia

Alfred Drake was killed in Queen Trench near Kut al Amara on 18 January 1917. It is likely he was killed by 'friendly fire' when two British shells burst short of their targets.

Cdr Edward Tyrrell Inman   *Royal Navy HMS* Simoom
Place of birth: Salisbury, Wiltshire   Home country: England   Age: 38
Date of death: 23/01/17   Cause of death: Killed in action
War cemetery: Chatham Naval Memorial, England
Theatre of war: At sea
Next of kin: Canon Edward & Eleanora M. Inman (parents)
Address: Parkstone, Dorset

Above: *Arthur Cudmore, who was from Devon but is remembered on the Salisbury Memorial.*

Right: *Burials in the desert.*

Commander Inman was killed in action on the North Sea during 23 January 1917. His ship, a destroyer, HMS *Simoom*, was part of the Harwich Force, which included six light cruisers and eighteen destroyers. The action took place off the Schouwen light vessel. The German Destroyer S50 torpedoed HMS *Simoom*. After the action, the ship was too badly damaged to return to port and was scuttled. Edward Inman is remembered on the Chatham Naval Memorial, England.

Pte William Lowne Smith		*5th Battalion Wiltshire Regiment*	
Service No.:	22536	Age:	35
Place of birth:	Framlingham, Suffolk	Home country: England	
Date of death:	25/01/17	Cause of death: Killed in action	
Memorials:	Salisbury, Wiltshire		
	St Martin's Church Memorial		
War cemetery:	Amara War Cemetery, Iraq		
Theatre of war:	Mesopotamia		
Next of kin:	Emily Morehen (formerly Smith) (wife); Henry & Sophia Smith (parents)		
Address:	99 Culver Street, Salisbury, Wiltshire		

On 25 January 1917 the British Forces in Mesopotamia were preparing to attack the Hai Salient, about 50 miles north-west of Amara, in modern-day Iraq. At about 9.42 a.m. the 5th Battalion Wiltshire Regiment was advancing toward the Turkish trenches, under the cover of an intense bombardment. The Turkish trenches were strongly held but, with the aid of the artillery, the Wiltshires succeeded and captured the Turkish frontline. By this time the Turks artillery was replying, with great effect. The Wiltshires' bombing parties, armed with grenades, worked their way along the Turkish communication trenches. Once again aided by the British artillery, further trenches were captured along with nearly 100 prisoners and arms. The Wiltshire casualties for the action were thirty-five killed and 114 wounded. Messages of congratulations were received from Army Corps, divisional and brigade commanders. The Regiment during the assault displayed great dash and conducted itself in a most gallant manner. This was the more praiseworthy in view of the fact that only eleven officers of the battalion were allowed to go into action, the remainder being held in reserve. Several cases of gallantry were specially noted for reward and in two cases immediate rewards have been granted by the Army commander – No.25978 Pte Cook H. Distinguished Conduct Medal and No.9255 L/Cpl Barclay S.G. Military Medal.

Wiltshires' War Diary

William Smith was killed in action during the attack on 25 January 1917 at Hai Salient. He is buried in Amara War Cemetery, Iraq.

Driver Charles Hazel Beaven		*Base Detail Royal Engineers*	
Service No.:	173546	Age:	26
Place of birth:	Salisbury, Wiltshire	Home country: England	
Date of death:	01/02/17	Cause of death: Died of illness	
Memorial:	Salisbury, Wiltshire		
War cemetery:	Salonika Lembet Road Military Cemetery, Greece		
Theatre of war:	Salonika		
Next of kin:	Mabel Etta Beaven (wife)		
Address:	Whaddon, Wiltshire		

Charles Beaven died on 1 February 1917, at one of the hospitals based in the town of Thessalonika, Greece. The town was the base of the British forces in Salonika. For every man who died in action in Salonika, three died of disease and it is likely this fate befell Driver Beaven.

Pte Sidney Martin   *1st Battalion Wiltshire Regiment*
Service No.:   19045   Age: 32
Place of birth: Salisbury, Wiltshire   Home country: England
Date of death: 17/02/17   Cause of death: Killed in action
Memorials: Salisbury, Wiltshire
                 St Paul's Church Memorial
War cemetery: Berks Cemetery Extension, Belgium
Theatre of war: France
Next of kin: Agnes Mabel Martin (wife); Charles & Maria Martin (parents)
Addresses: 12 Macklin Road, Salisbury, Wiltshire
                 St Edmund, Salisbury

Sidney Martin married Agnes Mabel Clarke in Salisbury in the spring of 1909. Little did they know that just five years in the future Great Britain would be involved in the First World War. By February 1917 the 1st Battalion Wiltshire Regiment had left the flat plains of the Somme and were in northern France, at le Romarin, on the French-Belgium border just south of Ploegsteert.

Above: *British troops in the Balkans.*

Right: *This cross marked the grave where Frederick Burges fell in France. It now hangs in St Mark's Church, Salisbury.*

On 17 February 1917 Sidney Martin, a member of the 1st Battalion Wiltshire Regiment, was preparing for a raid on German positions at Factory Farm. The raid commenced at 10.40 a.m. and all objectives were seized except for Factory Farm. The purpose of these raids was to keep the enemy alert and to identify the opposing enemy regiments. In this raid no identification was made, however, about twenty Germans were killed and two prisoners were taken. Six members of the Wiltshire Regiment were killed in this action, probably by German machine-gun fire as the party was returning to the British trenches. One of the British casualties was Sidney Martin and he is buried in Berks Cemetery Extension, near Ploegsteert.

Pte Albert James Baugh		*No.1 Section Auxiliary Horse Transport Depot*
		Royal Army Service Corps
Service No.:	S2/14703	Age: 27
Place of birth:	Salisbury, Wiltshire	Home country: England
Date of death:	19/02/17	Cause of death: Died of illness
Memorials:	Salisbury, Wiltshire	
	St Martin's Church Memorial	
War cemetery:	Abbeville Communal Cemetery Extension, France	
Theatre of war:	France	
Next of kin:	Sidney & Delsey Baugh (parents)	
Address:	St Martin, Salisbury, Wiltshire	

Albert James Baugh, known as James, died on 19 February 1917, most likely of illness in the hospital centre of Abbeville, northern France. Pte Baugh was probably based in the area, which was the headquarters of the Commonwealth lines of communication.

Pte Henry Tucker		*5th Battalion Wiltshire Regiment*
Service No.:	32265	Age: 29
Place of birth:	Glastonbury, Somerset	Home country: England
Date of death:	21/02/17	Cause of death: Killed in action
Memorials:	Salisbury, Wiltshire	
	St Paul's Church Memorial	
War cemetery:	Basra Memorial, Iraq	
Theatre of war:	Mesopotamia	
Next of kin:	Mrs J. Coombs (sister)	
Address:	54 Hill Head, Glastonbury, Somerset	

Henry Tucker originally joined Somerset Light Infantry, but transferred to the 5th Battalion Wiltshire Regiment. On 20 February 1917 the Wiltshires were in Mesopotamia, on their way to Shumran, Iraq, near the Liquorice Factory. The Wiltshires, by way of a diversion, were trying to convince the Turks that the British were about to cross the river at the site of the Liquorice Factory. It would appear that the ruse worked, diverting a Turkish battalion and many machine guns to defeat the fictional attack. During this time, there was a great deal of sniping by the Turks from the direction of Kut. It is likely that Pte Tucker was killed in action, shot by one of these snipers.

He is remembered on Basra memorial and has no known grave.

25 FEBRUARY 1917 – KUT EL AMARA IS RE-OCCUPIED BY THE BRITISH

Pte Maurice George Edward Watts   *5th Battalion Wiltshire Regiment*

Service No.:	22792	Age:	24
Place of birth:	Hawkesbury, Gloucestershire	Home country:	England
Date of death:	01/03/17	Cause of death:	Died of wounds
Memorials:	Salisbury, Wiltshire		
	St Paul's Church Memorial		
War cemetery:	Amara War Cemetery, Iraq		
Theatre of war:	Mesopotamia		
Next of kin:	John M. & Lucy A. Watts (parents)		

Maurice died of his wounds on 1 March 1917 at one of the medical units in the Amara area. It is almost certain he was wounded in action as the 5th Battalion Wiltshire Regiment fought their way towards Kut.

L/Cpl Frederick William Burges   *20th Battalion Australian Infantry Australian Imperial Force*

Service No.:	5297	Age:	24
Place of birth:	Boyton, Wiltshire	Home country:	England
Date of death:	01/03/17	Cause of death:	Died of wounds
Memorials:	Salisbury, Wiltshire		
	Bishop Wordsworths School Memorial & St Thomas Church Memorial		
War cemetery:	Contalmaison Chateau Cemetery, France		
Theatre of war:	France		
Next of kin:	The late Frederick Ford & Edith Ford Burges (parents)		
Address:	12 Churchfields, Salisbury, Wiltshire		

L/Cpl Burges was one of the British young men who set off for the new world prior to the First World War. He enlisted in the Australian Imperial Force on 16 February 1916 and his trade prior to joining the Army was farming. In August 1916 he embarked from Sydney as part of the 14th Reinforcement Battalion and arrived in England at Plymouth in October 1916. In November he probably visited his mother when he was posted to Rollstone Camp near Shrewton. Just before Christmas 1916 he arrived in France and was sent to Etaples, which was a battlefield training school in northern France. Soldiers were always glad to leave because of the manner in which they were treated by the Etaples Camp training staff known as 'canaries'. Towards the end of January he was sent to the frontline.

On 1 March 1917 L/Cpl Burges was wounded in the legs and lung by shell fire, he was evacuated to the 5th Australian Field Ambulance, but succumbed to his wounds on the same day. On 20 April 1917, Frederick's mother, Edith Burges, received his personal effects which consisted of a photo case; whistle; lanyard; knife; diary; metal mirror in case; roll book; small photograph case; wallet; metal wristwatch and correspondence. A little later a further package was received containing: a book called *Where Is It?* and two pairs of spectacles in their case (one pair damaged). In January 1918 Edith Burges received the following letter from the Australian Base Records Office:

18 January 1918
Dear Madam,
With reference to the report of the regrettable loss of your son, the late No. 5297 L/Cpl Burges, 20th Battalion, I am now in receipt of advice which shows that he died at 5th Australian Field Ambulance, on 1 March 1917, of wounds received in action, and was buried of Contamaison, France, the Rev. F.T. Clerverdon officiating.

These additional details are furnished by direction, it being the policy of the department, to forward all information received in the connection with the death of members of the Australian Imperial Force.

Yours faithfully

Officer i/c Base Records

> *11 MARCH 1917 – BAGHDAD IS CAPTURED BY THE BRITISH – 15 MARCH 1917 – RUSSIAN TSAR NICHOLAS II ABDICATES FOLLOWING THE START OF THE RUSSIAN REVOLUTION; 18 MARCH 1918 – GERMANS RETIRE TO THE HINDENBURG LINE*

Pte Edward Bright   *Royal Wiltshire Yeomanry*

Service No.:	320748	Age:	20
Place of birth:	Ford, Wiltshire	Home country:	England
Date of death:	20/03/17	Cause of death:	Died of wounds

Memorials: Salisbury, Wiltshire
                        St Thomas Memorial

War Cemetery: Perrone Road Cemetery, Maricourt, France

Theatre of war: France

Next of kin: Eli & Elizabeth Bright (parents)

Address: St Thomas, Salisbury, Wiltshire

Pte Bright was a member of the Wiltshire Yeomanry, which was a Territorial Calvary Force. He died of his wounds on 20 March 1917 near Maricourt. At the start of the Battle of the Somme in 1916, Maricourt had been the point where the British and French trench lines met.

Pte Leslie Eneas Phillimore   *01/8th Battalion Royal Warwickshire Regiment*

Service No.:	307226	Age:	29
Place of birth:	Salisbury, Wiltshire	Home country:	England
Date of death:	22/03/17	Cause of death:	Died of wounds

Memorial: Salisbury, Wiltshire

War cemetery: St Sever Cemetery Extension, Rouen, France

Theatre of war: France

Next of kin: Eleanor Jane Phillimore (wife); William & Bertha Philimore (parents)

Addresses: 6 Florence Road, Parkstone, Dorset
                        Salisbury

In the winter of 1910 Leslie married Eleanor Jane Rose in Salisbury, about six and a half years later he was dead and she was a widow. The 1/8th Battalion the Royal Warwickshire Regiment were one of the battalions raised as a result of Kitcheners Appeal, and after the battle of the Somme, where many of the men who died were from Pals battalions, men who came from the same town and the grief hit the whole town or village or street on the same day. It is likely that Leslie was either recruited via the Derby Scheme, or through conscription. Leslie died of wounds on Thursday 22 March 1917, at one of the hospitals in the Rouen area.

2nd-Lt Philip Sellers   *Royal Flying Corps*

Home country:	England	Age:	19
Date of death:	23/03/17	Cause of death:	Accidental death

Philip Sellers died in an aircraft collision near Pewsey, Wiltshire.

War cemetery: Salisbury (Devizes Road) Cemetery, Wiltshire
Theatre of war: Home

Nineteen-year-old Philip Sellers originally joined the 2nd Battalion Worcester Regiment, but transferred to the Royal Flying Corps. On 23 March 1917, Lt Alfred Long of Bath, and 2nd-Lt Philip Sellers, of Malvern, had been ordered to practice 'fighting'. One aircraft played the part of the enemy, which would fly slowly waiting to be attacked, while the other was the attacker. It would appear that the aircraft that in this case the attacker made an error and collided into the other aircraft causing them both to crash. Both pilots were killed in the accident which happened in the Pewsey area.

25 MARCH 1917 – BATTLE OF JEBEL HAMRIN

Pte George Sidney B. Burbage　　　　　　*2nd Battalion Devonshire Regiment*

Service No.:	8395	Age: 28
Place of birth:	Salisbury, Wiltshire	Home country: England
Date of death:	25/03/17	Cause of death: Killed in action
Memorials:	Salisbury, Wiltshire	
	St Martin's Church Memorial	
War cemetery:	Basra Memorial, Iraq	
Theatre of war:	Mesopotamia	
Next of kin:	Charles William & Sarah Burbage (parents)	
Address:	26 Trinity Street, Salisbury, Wiltshire	

Records state that George Burbage served with the 2nd Battalion Devonshire Regiment, but in 1917 the 2nd Battalion was in France and Burbage was fighting in the Middle East. Therefore, Pte Burbage was probably serving with the 1/4th Battalion which was in Mesopotamia. He was killed in action on 25 March 1917, in what was called the Maude Offensive, named after the British commander of that name. George is remembered on the Basra Memorial and has no known grave, his brother, Albert Edward Burbage, was killed at the Battle of Loos in September 1915.

26 MARCH 1917 – THE FIRST BATTLE OF GAZA

Pte Henry J. Batt   *2nd Battalion Leinster Regiment*
Service No.:   5395   Age: 26
Place of birth: Bath, Somerset   Home country: England
Date of death: 01/04/17   Cause of death: Killed in action
Memorial: Salisbury, Wiltshire
War cemetery: Aix Noulette Communal Cemetery Extension, France
Theatre of war: France

Henry Batt had originally enlisted in the Dorsetshire Regiment but was transferred to the 2nd Battalion Leinster Regiment. He was killed in action on 1 April 1917 and is buried in Aix Noulette Communal Cemetery Extension, France.

2nd-Lt Osmund Bartle Wordsworth   *21st Company Machine Gun Corps*
Home country: England   Age: 29
Date of death: 02/04/17   Cause of death: Killed in action
Memorial: Salisbury, Wiltshire
War cemetery: Arras Memorial, France
Theatre of war: France
Next of kin: Revd Christopher Wordsworth & Mary Reeve Wordsworth (parents)
Address: St Nicholas, Salisbury, Wiltshire

Osmund Bartle Wordsworth, youngest son of the Sub-Dean of Salisbury, was killed in action 'sniped through the heart' in a village in France on 2 April 1917. A second-lieutenant in a machine-gun company, he led his team into position, helped consolidate the right wing, saw the men with his first gun into shelter, and was struck while proceeding to visit his other guns, having refused his men's offer to risk their lives instead. A scholar of Winchester and Trinity College, Cambridge, he took a first class degree in both parts of the Classical Tripos and was employed at Selwyn College and Trinity College, Toronto, in university education. On returning from Canada, he escaped drowning when the RMS *Lusitania* was torpedoed, his life being saved that he might sacrifice it 'for his men and for his sense of duty'. He is remembered on the Arras Memorial and has no known grave.

Pte Frederick Crutcher   *2nd Battalion Leinster Regiment*
Service No.:   5375   Age: 31
Place of birth: Salisbury, Wiltshire   Home country: England
Date of death: 02/04/17   Cause of death: Died of wounds
Memorials: Salisbury, Wiltshire
                   St Martin's Church Memorial
War cemetery: Chocques Military Cemetery, France
Theatre of war: France
Next of kin: Mena Mary Crutcher (wife); Alf & Elizabeth Crutcher (parents)
Addresses: 45 North Street, Wilton, Wiltshire
                   Trinity Street, Salisbury

Frederick Crutcher, known as Fred, married Mena Mary Stokes in 1913. He had originally joined the Dorsetshire Regiment, but was transferred to the 2nd Battalion Leinster Regiment. He was the third son of Alf and Elizabeth Crutcher and died of his wounds on

2 April 1917 at No.1 Casualty-Clearing Station, which was based at the village of Chocques, France.

Pte Arthur Lionel Chappell   *6th Company Royal Army Ordinance Corps*
Service No.:   022675   Age: 36
Place of birth: Keynsham, Somerset   Home country: England
Date of death: 03/04/17   Cause of death: Died of wounds
Memorial: Salisbury, Wiltshire
War cemetery: Southampton Old Cemetery, England
Theatre of war: Home
Next of kin: Edith Francis Chappell (wife); Edwin & Annie Chappell (parents)
Addresses: North Wood Castle Road, Salisbury, Wiltshire
                 Western-super-Mare, Somerset

The funeral of the late Mr Arthur Chappell, Army Ordnance Corps, honorary secretary for the Salisbury and District Branch UKCTA took place at Southampton Cemetery on the morning of 10 April 1917. The mourners were Mrs Chappell, widow, Mr Ernest Chappell and Mr Chappell of York (brothers), Miss Chappell (sister), Mr Ivens (father-in-law), Miss Wells and Mr Walter Drew. The coffin was covered with the Union Jack, and among the wreaths sent was one from the local branch of the UKCTA, 'in affectionate remembrance of a valued friend and brother,' tied with the colours of the Association. Mr Chappell, who was thirty-six, and prior to joining the Army was resident in Castle Road, was held in the highest esteem as a man of irreproachable character. He entered the service of Titley & Son upon leaving school, and was in their employ continuously for almost twenty years, the last ten or eleven years having been spent as their traveller. At the time of his death he was actually in office as honorary secretary for the local branch of the UKCTA, having been re-elected in his absence on military service, though the duties were being carried on by Mr Ryder, as acting honorary secretary. To this office Mr Chappell devoted himself with the keeness that he displayed in anything he undertook. What he undertook to do he did thoroughly and efficiently. As soon as the call for military service came he responded , and was first with the Worcesters then the Hampshires, and finally with the AOC, in which he was serving when invalided from France. He leaves a widow and one infant daughter, with whom, and with his aged father and mother, who live at Weston-super-Mare, much sympathy is expressed.

6 APRIL 1917 – THE UNITED STATES DECLARES WAR ON GERMANY

8

ARRAS

The Nivelle Offensive started on 9 April 1917, it was a joint action between the French and the British. The British attack took place around Arras.

L/Cpl Harry Bell   *2nd Battalion Wiltshire Regiment*
Service No.:   7076   Age: 29
Place of birth: Fisherton, Wiltshire   Home country: England
Date of death: 09/04/17   Cause of death: Killed in action
Memorials: Salisbury, Wiltshire
                   St Paul's Church Memorial
War cemetery: Arras Memorial, France
Theatre of war: Arras, France
Next of kin: Elizabeth Bell (wife); Late Frederick & Bessie Bell (parents)
Addresses: 115 Devizes Road, Salisbury, Wiltshire
                   3 Gas Lane, Salisbury, Wiltshire

On 9 April 1917 the 2nd Battalion Wiltshire Regiment were preparing to make attacks on the German Hindenburg Line, their first objective a mill on the Henin-Neuville Vitasse Road, south-west of Arras. At 1.30 a.m. the Wiltshires attacked, but met considerable resistance from the German defenders, who it was later discovered numbered about 120 men and two machine guns. The Wiltshires were forced to retire with thirty-seven casualties. The main British attack started at 5.30 a.m. The 2nd Battalion Wiltshire Regiment attacked at 11.38 a.m. and were met by heavy shelling from the Germans, causing many casualties before the objective could be seen. When the Wiltshires arrived at the German wire it was found to be uncut and British troops took cover in shell holes in front of the German line, but were eventually forced to retire. All that was left of the 2nd Battalion was about ninety men. Total casualties for the second attack were 342, L/Cpl Bell was killed in action on the battlefield and is remembered on the Arras memorial and has no known grave.

L/Cpl William Charles Burrough   *2nd Battalion Wiltshire Regiment*
Service No.:   8360   Age: 28
Place of birth: Eddington, Somerset   Home country: England
Date of death: 09/04/17   Cause of death: Killed in action
Memorial: Salisbury, Wiltshire
War cemetery: Wancourt British Cemetery, France
Theatre of war: Arras, France
Next of kin: Flossie V. Burrough (wife); William & Kate Burrough (parents)
Addresses: 35 Scots Lane, Salisbury, Wiltshire
                   Eddington, Somerset

William Burrough was killed in action on 9 April 1917 on the first day of the Battle of Arras. He was killed as the 2nd Battalion Wiltshire Regiment attacked the Hindenburg Line (as described for Harry Bell). During the attack 130 members of the 2nd Wiltshires were killed.

The ruins of the Hôtel de Ville, Arras, France.

A fallen British soldier.

Pte Harry Victor White   *2nd Battalion Wiltshire Regiment*

Service No.:	9177	Age:	20
Place of birth:	Harnham, Wiltshire	Home country:	England
Date of death:	09/04/17	Cause of death:	Killed in action
Memorial:	Salisbury, Wiltshire		
War cemetery:	Arras Memorial, France		
Theatre of war:	France		
Next of kin:	Charles & Eliza White (parents)		
Address:	11 Exeter Terrace, Exeter Street, Salisbury, Wiltshire		

Twenty-year-old Harry White was killed in action on 9 April 1917 on the first day of the Battle of Arras. He was killed as the 2nd Battalion Wiltshire Regiment attacked the Hindenburg Line.

Cpl Thomas George Marchant   *10th Hussars*

Service No.:	1935	Age:	28
Place of birth:	Salisbury, Wiltshire	Home country:	England
Date of death:	11/04/17	Cause of death:	Killed in action
Memorials:	Salisbury, Wiltshire		
	St Mark's Church Memorial		
War cemetery:	Arras Memorial, France		
Theatre of war:	France, Arras		
Next of kin:	Thomas & Janet Marchant (parents)		
Address:	St Thomas, Salisbury, Wiltshire		

Thomas Marchant was killed in action on 11 April 1917, the third day of the battle of Arras. It is likely he was killed during the capture of Monchy-le-Preux, a village to the east of Arras. He is remembered on the Arras Memorial and has no known grave.

Pte Ernest Samuel Batchelor   *3rd Dragoon Guards*

Service No.:	4685	Age:	32
Place of birth:	Downton, Wiltshire	Home country:	England
Date of death:	11/04/17	Cause of death:	Killed in action
Memorial:	Salisbury, Wiltshire		
War cemetery:	Arras Memorial, France		
Theatre of war:	France		
Next of kin:	George F. & Jane Batchelor (parents)		
Address:	Downton, Wiltshire		

Ernest Batchelor was another victim of the Battle of Arras, he was killed in action on 11 April 1917, the third day of the battle. He is remembered on the Arras Memorial and has no known grave.

2nd-Lt Joseph Plumbtre Gilbert   *4th Battalion Hampshire Regiment*

Place of birth:	Allerton, Somerset	Home country: England	Age:	31
Date of death:	11/04/17	Cause of death:	Killed in action	
War cemetery:	Chili Trench Cemetery Gavrelle, France			
Theatre of war:	France, Arras			
Next of kin:	Revd Joseph & Emmeline Gilbert (parents)			
Address:	Chacewater, Cornwall			

Joseph Gilbert was the eldest son of Revd Joseph and Emmeline Gilbert. Revd Joseph Gilbert was vicar of Chancewater, Cornwall. Prior to the war 2nd-Lt Gilbert was employed by Lloyds Bank, Salisbury, and was well known in the city. He was killed in action on 11 April 1917, the third day of the offensive at Arras. He was killed north-east of Arras near the Douai Road, most probably during an attack on, or near, Chili Trench, which gave its name to the cemetery where he is buried.

Pte Harry Shergold   *6th Battalion Wiltshire Regiment*

Service No.:	23683	Age:	18
Place of birth:	Salisbury, Wiltshire	Home country:	England
Date of death:	11/04/17	Cause of death:	Died of wounds
Memorial:	Salisbury, Wiltshire		
War cemetery:	Bailleul Communal Cemetery Extension, Nord, France		
Theatre of war:	France		
Next of kin:	Pte Henry & Mary Shergold (parents)		
Address:	Bedwin Street, Salisbury, Wiltshire		

Eighteen-year-old Harry Shergold died of his wounds that were most likely received during the Battle of Arras during 11 April 1917 at a casualty-clearing station based at Bailleul, France.

Pte Bertie James Fiander   *2nd Battalion Wiltshire Regiment*

Service No.:	22296	Age:	21
Place of birth:	Salisbury, Wiltshire	Home country:	England
Date of death:	12/04/17	Cause of death:	Died of wounds
Memorials:	Salisbury, Wiltshire		
	St Paul's Church Memorial and Dews Road Primitive Methodist Memorial		
War cemetery:	Warlincourt Halte British Cemetery, Saulty, France		
Theatre of war:	Arras, France		
Next of kin:	Tom & Annie Fiander (parents)		
Address:	2 James Street, Fisherton, Salisbury, Wiltshire		

It is likely Pte Fiander died of the wounds he received in action that took place on the first day of the Arras offensive. He died at one of the casualty-clearing stations based at Warlincourt village.

Able Seaman Frank Albert Hibberd   *Hawke Battalion Royal Naval Division Royal Naval Voluteer Reserve*

Service No.:	R/511	Age:	31
Place of birth:	Salisbury. Wiltshire:	Home country:	England
Date of death:	18/04/17	Cause of death:	Killed in action
Memorial:	Salisbury, Wiltshire		
War cemetery:	Arras Memorial, France		
Theatre of war:	Arras, France		
Next of kin:	Emma A. Lynn (formerly Hibberd) (wife); George J. & Anna Hibberd (parents)		
Addresses:	23 Nursery Road, Salisbury, Wiltshire		
	St Edmund, Salisbury, Wiltshire		

Frank Hibberd married Emma Frances A. Burnett at the start of 1910 and seven years later was in the trenches east of Arras. He was a member of the Royal Naval Reserve, Royal Naval Division, which fought as infantry during the First World War. He was killed in action on 18 April 1917, probably preparing for the second stage of the Battle of Arras. He is remembered on the Arras Memorial and has no known grave. His brother, Gilbert Charles Hibberd, died in October 1918.

19 APRIL 1917 – SECOND BATTLE OF GAZA

Pte Hugh Gordon Sutton   *11/8th Battalion Hampshire Regiment*

Service No.:	331402	Age:	23
Place of birth:	Fisherton, Wiltshire	Home country:	England
Date of death:	19/04/17	Cause of death:	Killed in action
Memorials:	Salisbury, Wiltshire		
	St Paul's Church Memorial		
War cemetery:	Jerusalem War Cemetery, Israel		
Theatre of war:	Palestine		
Next of kin:	Arthur John Sutton (father)		
Address:	17 North Street, Fisherton, Salisbury, Wiltshire		

Pte Sutton had originally joined the Wiltshire Regiment but was transferred to the 1/8th Battalion the Hampshire Regiment. He was killed in action on 19 April 1917 during the final day of the Second Battle of Gaza, Palestine. At this time Gaza was a strongly defended part of the Turkish defence line.

20 APRIL 1917 – BRITISH FORCES OCCUPY SAMARRAH, 60 MILES NORTH OF BAGHDAD

Pte William Arthur Grace   *7th Battalion Wiltshire Regiment*

Service No.:	25623	Age:	28
Place of birth:	Dublin, Ireland	Home country:	England
Date of death:	24/04/17	Cause of death:	Killed in action
Memorials:	Salisbury, Wiltshire		
	St Paul's Church Memorial		
War cemetery:	Dorian Military Cemetery, Greece		
Theatre of war:	Salonika		
Next of kin:	Ada Louisa Grace (wife)		
Address:	Bodenham, Wiltshire		

In August 1918 news reached Salisbury that Pte William Grace of the Wiltshire Regiment had been reported missing on 24 April 1917, and was presumed to have been killed in action. For twelve years he had been in the employ of Messrs Brown, the Canal, Salisbury, and joined the County Regiment early in 1916. Mrs Grace, who lived at Bodenham, received a letter from an officer of the company in which her husband served stating:

> I fear my news can only be of a negative character. Your husband went over the top with the company on the night of 24/25 April, but did not return after the assault, nor was he found by our subsequent search parties. I am afraid, therefore, he must have been killed when we were held

up by the Bulgar wire, or got through and was killed in the enemy trenches. We have received names of very few who were taken prisoners by the enemy on this occasion, but unfortunately your husband's name does not occur. Your husband, 'Gracie', as he was known to us all, was in my platoon before I took over the company, and was most popular with us all, being always eager and willing to do his job and give anybody all the assistance that in his power lay. His comrades all mourn a good soldier gone to his rest. Permit me, madam, to offer you, on behalf of his comrades and myself, our profound condolence and sympathy in your bereavement.

Sgt Ernest Higgs	*A Company 7th Battalion Wiltshire Regiment*	
Service No.:	03/482	Age: 45
Place of birth:	Burghfield, Berkshire	Home country: England
Date of death:	24/04/17	Cause of death: Killed in action
Memorials:	Salisbury, Wiltshire	
	St Thomas Memorial	
War cemetery:	Dorian Memorial, Greece	
Theatre of war:	Salonika	
Next of kin:	Annie Higgs (wife); David & Jane Higgs (parents)	
Addresses:	Orleigh Hill, Crest Road, Parkstone, Dorset	
	Burghfield, Reading	

In April 1919 a letter brought the news of the death of Sgt Ernest Higgs, who was custodian at the Church House, Salisbury, and came into contact with a very wide circle of people and was greatly esteemed. Early in the war Sgt Higgs rejoined the Wiltshire Regiment and served with the 7th Battalion in Salonika, after a short period in France. On 24 April 1917, he was reported as 'missing' but it was not until a stray letter arrived from the front was it known that he sacrificed his life so splendidly in volunteering to lead an attack on the Bulgarian trenches and died at the moment of victory. As a member of the CEMS, he did much useful work in the City.

Deepest sympathy was expressed with Mrs Higgs, who had borne the anxiety of many months of suspense with hopefulness, and was then faced with the sad fact of the death of her husband. Sgt Higgs had met Annie Hayter when they were in service; she was a lady's maid and he was a footman. He married Annie at the start of 1903 in Salisbury. Ernest had served on the North-West Frontier of India (1897–98) and in the South African Campaign with the Rifle Brigade. He is remembered on the Dorian Memorial and has no known grave.

Pte Ernest Edward Rowe	*16th Battalion Middlesex Regiment*	
Service No.:	G/40315	Age: 30
Place of birth:	Steeple Langford, Wiltshire	Home country: England
Date of death:	24/04/17	Cause of death: Killed in action
War cemetery:	Arras Memorial, France	
Theatre of war:	Arras, France	
Next of kin:	Alice Mabel Rowe (wife); Mrs T. Pearce (sister)	
Addresses:	69 Elphick Road, New Haven, Sussex	
	Spire View, Harnham, Wiltshire	

In mid-May 1917, news was received by Mrs T. Pearce, Spire View, Harnham, of the death of her brother, Pte Ernest Rowe, who was killed on 25 April in France. Pte Rowe, who was a native of West Harnham, was well known in the district. He worked in a business establishment at Salisbury for many years, and then at Winchester. Latterly he had been in business for himself at Newhaven. Pte Rowe joined the Middlesex Regiment in March 1916. He left a wife and one son. Much sympathy was felt for Mrs Rowe and Mrs Pearce in their bereavement. In writing to his wife, the chaplain of the regiment said: 'Pte Rowe was very popular with the officers and men of the regiment and his death was felt by all.'

Pte Harry Alfred Stone   *D Company 7th Battalion Wiltshire Regiment*
Service No.:   18609   Age: 22
Place of birth: Salisbury, Wiltshire   Home country: England
Date of death: 25/04/17   Cause of death: Killed in action
Memorial: Salisbury, Wiltshire
War cemetery: Dorian Memorial, Greece
Theatre of war: Salonika
Next of kin: Albert & Selina Stone (parents)
Address: Salisbury, Wiltshire

In April 1917 the British forces in Salonika, Greece, attacked Bulgarian lines near Lake Dorian. Harry Stone was in D Company, 7th Battalion Wiltshire Regiment; they attacked the Bulgarian trenches under cover of a British artillery barrage which had cut the first line of the enemy barbed wire. When they arrived at the second line of barbed wire and were held up due to it still being almost intact, the Bulgarian trenches were heavily manned and the enemy made great use of hand grenades, causing many casualties and forcing D Company to retire.

Harry Stone was intially listed as missing in the casualty return though later he was officially reported killed in action on 25 April 1917. He is remembered on the Dorian Memorial, Greece, and has no known grave.

Pte Raymond Walter Welch   *2nd Battalion Wiltshire Regiment*
Service No.:   33231
Place of birth: Bourton, Dorset   Home country: England
Date of death: 25/04/17   Cause of death: Killed in action
Memorials: Salisbury, Wiltshire
                   St Paul's Church Memorial
War cemetery: Arras Memorial, France
Theatre of war: Arras, France
Next of kin: Arthur & Maria Welch (parents)

After the second stage of the offensive at Arras, the 2nd Battalion Wiltshire Regiment were consolidating and strengthening their positions to the east of Arras. Raymond Welch was killed in action on 25 April 1917, most likely as a result of shell fire, as the Wiltshires trenches were shelled throughout the day by the Germans. He is remembered on the Arras Memorial, France, and has no known grave.

Sapper Edward John Besent   *249th Field Company Royal Engineers*
Service No.:   208809   Age: 28
Place of birth: Blandford, Dorset   Home country: England
Date of death: 28/04/17   Cause of death: Died of wounds
Memorials: Salisbury, Wiltshire
                   Bishop Wordsworth's School Memorial & St Thomas Church Memorial
War cemetery: Aubigny Communal Cemetery Extension, France
Theatre of war: France
Next of kin: The late Edward & Mary C.A. Besent (parents)
Address: 56 Endless Street, Salisbury, Wiltshire

In May 1917 news reached Salisbury that Sapper Edward John Besent, Royal Engineers, Royal Naval Division, had died of his wounds on 28 April 1917. He was the elder son of the late Mr Edward Besent of Berwick St James, and of Mrs Besent, 56 Endless Street, Salisbury. He was educated at the Bishop's School, and for ten years was engaged at the office of Messrs Lemon & Blizzard, Engineers. He successfully passed examinations for the Surveyor's Institute, and had done much survey work while on active service in Gallipoli, Salonika and France, where he was seriously wounded by a shell bursting on the top of the dug-out. Sapper Besent died the following day at the casualty-clearing station. He had a younger brother serving in France with the Yeomanry.

Pte Sidney Charles Laurence		*1st Battalion Royal Marine Light Infantry*
		Royal Naval Division
Service No.:	PO/1745(S)	Age:	27
Place of birth:	Salisbury, Wiltshire	Home country:	England
Date of death:	28/04/17	Cause of death:	Killed in action
Memorials:	Salisbury, Wiltshire		
	Baptist Church Memorial		
War cemetery:	Arras Memorial, France		
Theatre of war:	Arras, France		
Next of kin:	Sidney & Annie Lawrence (parents)		
Address:	St Edmund, Salisbury, Wiltshire		

On 23 April 1917 the Royal Naval Division captured German-held Gavrelle, north-east of Arras. Sidney Laurence was killed in action on 28 April 1917, most likely in the Gavrelle area. He is remembered on the Arras Memorial and has no known grave.

Pte George Robert Rowe		*1st Battalion Royal Marine Light Infantry*
		Royal Naval Division
Service No.:	PO/16412	Age:	24
Place of birth:	Salisbury, Wiltshire	Home country:	England
Date of death:	28/04/17	Cause of death:	Killed in action
Memorial:	Salisbury, Wiltshire		
War cemetery:	Arras Memorial, France		
Theatre of war:	Arras, France		
Next of kin:	Mr & Mrs Rowe (parents)		
Address:	87 Gigant Street, Salisbury, Wiltshire		

George Rowe was killed in action on 28 April 1917 most likely in the Gavrelle area. He is remembered on the Arras Memorial and has no known grave.

Rifleman Reginald Claude Hawkins		*16th Battalion Kings Royal Rifle Corps*
Service No.:	R/18944	Age:	24
Place of birth:	Salisbury, Wiltshire	Home country:	England
Date of death:	29 April 1917	Cause of death:	Died of wounds
Memorials:	Salisbury, Wiltshire		
	St Mark's Church Memorial		
War cemetery:	Mont Huon Military Cemetery, Le Treport, France		
Theatre of war:	France		
Next of kin:	George Henry & Sarah Ann Hawkins (parents)		
Address:	St Mark's Road, Salisbury, Wiltshire		

Reginald Hawkins was the fifth son of Henry and Sarah Ann Hawkins and it is likely he was wounded in the second part of the Arras offensive, between 23/24 April 1917. He died of his wounds at one of the Canadian General Hospitals based at Le Treport, France, on 29 April 1917.

Col. Frank Albert Symons　　　　　　　*Royal Army Medical Corps ADMS (9th Div.)*
Place of birth:　Halifax, Nova Scotia, Canada　Home country: England　Age: 48
Date of death:　30/04/17　　　　　　　　Cause of death: Killed in action
War cemetery:　St Nicholas British Cemetery, France
Theatre of war: France
Next of kin:　Dorothy Symons (wife)
Address:　　　The Close, Salisbury, Wiltshire

Col. Frank A. Symons, CMG, DSO, Assistant Director of Medical Services, was killed on 30 April 1917 while on his way to an advanced dressing station. He left England in August 1914, in command of a clearing hospital, and excepting a few days leave at intervals, had been abroad ever since. He was mentioned in Lord French's despatches and again later. In the first Honours List of the war he was awarded the DSO, and in the New Year Honours List of 1917 he was made a CMG. He served in the South African War, being present at the Relief of Ladysmith, including the action at Colenso. Col. Symons was a son of the late John Hughes Symons of Nova Scotia. In 1900 he married Dorothy, second daughter of the late Edmund Grove Bennett, of the Close, Salisbury, and left a widow and four daughters.

One of his brother officer's wrote:

He died at his post doing his duty, as always. He was a gallant officer, gifted above all of us, and a true friend who was universally beloved and respected. His place will be difficult to fill, and it is cruel that such a career as his should have been cut short by such a mischance. The coffin was draped with the Union Jack, and in brilliant sunshine this lovely first of May we buried him in the cemetery of St Nicholas to the accompaniment of the booming guns.

Another wrote:

The cross that marked the resting place of Frank Symons now hangs in the cloisters at Salisbury Cathedral.

Col. Symons was one of our most valued senior medical officers, and I regarded his judgement and opinion in difficult situations as likely to be soundest and most practical, and constantly I sought his advice. He was always a great favourite, and officers serving under him were always happy and confident in carrying out his orders. With a large number of officers, who were all old personal friends, assembled to do him the last honours, I attended his funeral this morning.

A memorial service for Col. Symons was held in Salisbury Cathedral at 2.15 p.m., 12 May 1917.

Pte Elliot Walter Grace   *9th Battalion Royal Fusiliers*

Service No.:	G/65229	Age:	24
Place of birth:	Fordingbridge, Hampshire	Home country:	England
Date of death:	07/05/17	Cause of death:	Died of wounds
Memorial:	St Mark's Church Memorial		
War cemetery:	Duisans British Cemetery, Etrun, France		
Theatre of war:	France		
Next of kin:	Walter J. & Alice Grace (parents)		
Address:	72 Bellevue Road, Salisbury, Wiltshire		

Elliot Grace was the third youngest son of Walter and Alice Grace and prior to the war he had been a member of B Division of the Metropolitan Police. Pte Grace had originally joined Royal West Kent Regiment. He was wounded, most likely on 3 May 1917, in the attack at Roeux, east of Arras. He died of wounds at 8th Casualty-Clearing Station, Duisans, France, on 7 May 1917.

Sgt John Lawrence Morey   *D Company 1st Battalion Honourable Artillery Company*

Service No.:	4249	Age:	24
Place of birth:	Stoke Newington, London	Home country:	England
Date of death:	08/05/17	Cause of death:	Died of wounds
Memorial:	St Thomas Memorial		
War cemetery:	Etaples Military Cemetery, France		
Theatre of war:	France		
Next of kin:	George Henry & Elizabeth Morey		
Address:	43 Catherine Street, Salisbury, Wiltshire		

In a letter to his parents, Sgt J.L. Morey, of Sniper's Platoon, recounted his experiences of the fighting and manoeuvres attending an attack in France during November 1916:

For some days previous to the attack, the platoon had been reconnoitring the ground we contemplated attacking, often waist deep in mud. We reported on the strength of the wire and the obstacles that were expected to stop us. The night before the attack we went up in battle order, and spent the night in assembly trenches. For two days there had been a continuous bombardment by all our available artillery, which ceased only when we went up. The whole attack was, of course, arranged to a settled timetable that everyone was acquainted with. Shortly before the appointed time we spread out ready to go over. At the exact second every battery and machine gun on the front seemed to open fire. The inferno cannot possibly be described. The artillery put up a barrage and over we clambered , keeping as close to the barrage as safe. The air was full of the roar of bursting shells and bullets, and it seemed a miracle that anyone could live a minute in it. The Boches, directly the first shot was fired, got every gun, rifle, and machine gun into action as fast as possible, as well as trench mortars, hand and rifle grenades. Above all only a few feet above our heads, sounded the continuous scream of our shells going over. Our artillery was marvellous. Shells were poured on the Huns like rain in a thunderstorm, and when we reached their trenches we found them literally non-existent. They had been blown clean out of the ground. Directly we advanced the Boches came pouring towards us with their hands up and crying 'Kamerad'. They were absolutely frightened to death and shaking with fear, and were never better pleased than to be taken as prisoners. They were finely built men, belonging to the finest regiment in the German army, but all the fight was knocked out of them, except their snipers, who lay in shell holes and sniped us after we had gone by. We routed them out one by one. The German infantry have no fight in them. It is simply their artillery and machine guns that save them, and even they are not equal now to the British. That first day we captured five or six lines of German trenches. The next day, before the Boches could counter-attack, we went over again and captured, in all, about twelve lines of trenches, many more prisoners, and a strongly fortified village. This we held, and then advanced some distance further. After about four nights without a wink of sleep or anything to eat, apart from iron rations, we were relieved, and went down. Our men did remarkably well, and advanced as though on parade, keeping a straight line, and moving steadily, perfectly unaffected by the opposing fire. Our casualties you will see in the papers in due course. The battlefield was in a frightful state, ploughed into a mass of shell holes and littered with fragments of shells and bits of barbed wire. I have obtained a good many souvenirs, both from the Boches we captured and from their wonderful dugouts, which are really underground palaces, often fitted with electric light and baths. After being relieved we had a week's march across France away from the line, and have arrived at a village, where we are nominally resting but in reality training and re-fitting for the line again.

In early May 1917, news reached Mr and Mrs C.H. Morey, of Catherine Street, that their son, Sgt John Lawrence Morey, Hon. Artillery Company, had been wounded in France, where he had been on service for about seventeen months. A shell burst so near to the sergeant that his face was scorched, and his arm and wrist were injured. He participated in the Somme fighting, and had more than one narrow escape. On one occasion a shell killed and injured nearly everyone in a group except himself. Sgt Morey was well known in Salisbury, having been educated at the Bishop's School and Modern School, before taking up a civil service appointment in London. On 7 May 1917 a message was received from the War Office stating that John was dangerously ill and in consequence, Mrs Morey proceeded to France to see him. A letter received from the War Office states that he died on 8 May 1917:

> In proud loving memory of our noble son Jack (John Lawrence) who was wounded in action April 24th 1917. Passed to his Higher Life May 8th 1917. He was youngest surviving son of George and Elizabeth Morey.

> No Hate was his no thirst for fame
> When forth to death by honour sent;
> Life beckoned sweet , the Great Call came,
> He knew his duty and he was sent.

Pte Ernest George Read   *9th Battalion Gloucestershire Regiment*

Service No.:	31843	Age:	20
Place of birth:	Salisbury, Wiltshire	Home country:	England
Date of death:	09/05/17	Cause of death:	Killed in action
Memorials:	Salisbury, Wiltshire		
	Bishop Wordsworth's School Memorial		
War cemetery:	Dorian Memorial, Greece		

Theatre of war: Salonika
Next of kin: George & Emma J.L. Read (parents)
Address: Glenwood, 75 Harnham Road, Salisbury, Wiltshire

In mid-July 1917 news of the supposed death of their eldest son, Pte E.G. Read, of the
Gloucesters, reached Mr and Mrs G. Read of Fitzgerald Dairy, West Harnham. Around the end
of May, information was received that Pte Read was reported missing on 9 May 1917, and a
cablegram was dispatched to his commanding officer, whose reply stated:

> Pte E.G. Read was in the forefront of the attack, and was hit before the objective was reached.
> It is fairly certain that he was killed outright, but it cannot be proved, as the body could not be
> brought in.

Pte Read, who was educated at Bishop's Wordsworth's School, joined the Wiltshire Yeomanry
in October 1915. He volunteered for active service, was sent to Salonika, and transferred to the
Gloucesters. For many years he was a member of the East Harnham choir, and a drummer in
the Harnham Fife and Drum Bands.

Sapper Alwyn Sidney Macey   *58th Signal Company Royal Engineers*
Service No.:   510393   Age: 22
Place of birth: Salisbury, Wiltshire   Home country: England
Date of death: 13/05/17   Cause of death: Killed in action
Memorials: Salisbury, Wiltshire
                  St Paul's Church Memorial & St Martin's Church Memorial
War cemetery: Arras Memorial, France
Theatre of war: Arras, France
Next of kin: Sidney & Ada Blanche Macey
Address: 70 York Road, Salisbury, Wiltshire

Alwyn Macey was killed in action on 13 May 1917, along with three other members of the
58th Signal Company Royal Engineers. It is likely they were killed by shell fire to the east
of Arras. All four are remembered on the Arras Memorial and have no known grave. His
brother, William Moncrieffe Macey, was killed in action just over a year later in France during
October 1918.

Pte Wilfred Louis Bradshaw   *177th Company Labour Corps*
Service No.:   105662   Age: 24
Place of birth: Chichester, Sussex   Home country: England
Date of death: 17/05/17   Cause of death: Died of illness
Memorials: Salisbury, Wiltshire
                  St Mark's Church Memorial
War cemetery: Warlincourt Halte British Cemetery, Saulty, France
Theatre of war: France
Next of kin: Marion H. Bradshaw (mother)
Address: 31 London Road, Salisbury, Wiltshire

Wilfred Bradshaw had originally joined the Devonshire Regiment but transferred to the
177th Company Labour Corps, he died, probably of illness, at one of the casualty-clearing
stations in Warlincourt Village. After the war in 1919 his mother inserted the following
memoriam:

In proud and ever loving memory of my good beloved boy who nobly gave his life for England in France, 17 May 1917.

'The Master called Him'
I cannot think my darling boy is gone
He lives all day all night I find him near
I feel his loving arms around me throw
His joyful laugh his happy voice I hear
Look where I will no face but his I see
How can I think my hero boy is dead
He lives because he gave his life for me
And life eternal crowns his fair young head
His warfare's o'er from earthy strife he's gone
To hear his Masters sweet gracious words
'Well done'

Inserted by his sorrowing lonely mother

Pte Alfred Conduit   *1st Battalion Wiltshire Regiment*
Service No.:   03/8277   Age: 40
Place of birth: Salisbury, Wiltshire   Home country: England
Date of death: 05/06/17   Cause of death: Killed in action
Memorial: Salisbury, Wiltshire
War cemetery: Wulverghem Lindenhoek Road, Military Cemetery, Belgium
Theatre of war: Belgium
Next of kin: George & Eliza Conduit (parents)
Address: St Edmunds, Salisbury, Wiltshire

On 4 June 1917 Alfred Conduit was serving with the 1st Battalion Wiltshire Regiment, who were preparing for a raid on the German trenches opposite the Wulverghem Sector, Belgium. They managed to penetrate into the German reserve line and the War Diary states: 'Unfortunately, none of the enemy were encountered and the trenches were found to be quite unoccupied.'

Pte Conduit and two other men were killed on the raid, either from German snipers on the flanks or from British shells falling short.

L/Cpl William Sutton   *6th Battalion Wiltshire Regiment*
Service No.:   8215   Age: 25
Place of birth: St Mark's, Salisbury, Wiltshire Home country: England
Date of death: 05/06/17   Cause of death: Killed in action
Decoration: Military Medal
Memorial: Salisbury, Wiltshire
War cemetery: Ypres Menin Gate Memorial, Belgium
Theatre of war: Belgium
Next of kin: Frank & Emma Sutton (parents)
Address: Salisbury, Wiltshire

William Sutton had won the Military Medal for Valour on a previous engagement. He was killed in action on 5 June 1917, while two companies of the Wiltshire Regiment were relieving the 9th Welsh Regiment. It is likely he was killed by German shell fire, and is remembered on the Ypres Menin Gate Memorial, Belgium. He has no known grave.

7 JUNE 1917 – THE BATTLE OF MESSINES, BELGIUM

Capt. Claude Romako a' Beckett Terrell   *15th Brigade Royal Horse Artillery*

Place of birth:	London
Date of death:	10/06/17
Decorations:	Military Cross
Memorial:	Private Memorial St Mark's Church
War cemetery:	Duisans British Cemetery, Etrun, France
Theatre of war:	France
Next of kin:	Arthur & Georgina a' Beckett Terrell (parents)
Address:	12 Fitz James Avenue, Kensington, London

Home country: England   Age: 33
Cause of death: Died of wounds

Notice was received in Salisbury of the death, from his wounds, of Acting-Capt. Claude Romako a' Becket Terrell on 10 June 1917. Capt. Terrell was the youngest son of Mr and Mrs Arthur a' Beckett Terrell of Fitz James Avenue, Barons' Court S.W. and a nephew of Mr Hamilton Fulton of The Close, Salisbury.

Claude Terrell died from wounds he had received a few days earlier at one of the casualty-clearing stations based in the area west of Arras.

Pte Albert Robinson   *6th Battalion Wiltshire Regiment*

Service No.:	31771
Place of birth:	Rotherhithe, Sussex
Date of death:	13/06/17
Memorial:	Salisbury, Wiltshire
War cemetery:	Ypres Menin Gate Memorial, Belgium
Theatre of war:	Belgium
Next of kin:	Elizabeth Annie Robinson (wife); George Robinson (father)
Addresses:	Sandle Heath, Salisbury, Wiltshire
	Powder Mills, Tonbridge, Kent

Age: 39
Home country: England
Cause of death: Killed in action

Albert Robinson was killed in action in the trenches at Oostterverne Wood, south of the town of Ypres, Belgium, on 13 June 1917. There had been heavy shelling by both sides during the day that Pte Robinson was killed. He is remembered on the Ypres Menin Gate Memorial, Belgium, and has no known grave.

Pte Charles William Andrews   *6th Battalion Wiltshire Regiment*

Service No.:	20774
Place of birth:	Deal, Kent
Date of death:	14/06/17
Memorial:	Salisbury, Wiltshire
War cemetery:	Oosttaverne Wood Cemetery, Belgium
Theatre of war:	Belgium
Next of kin:	Caleb & Sarah Andrews (uncle & aunt)
Address:	St Martin, Salisbury, Wiltshire

Age: 23
Home country: England
Cause of death: Killed in action

Charles Andrews was killed in action on 14 June 1917 at Oostterverne Wood, south of the town of Ypres. He was one of two men killed during a German attack during the evening of that day.

Far left: The cross that marked the resting place of Claude Romako a' Beckett Terrell in St Mark's Church, Salisbury.

Left: Private memorial of Arthur Johnson in Salisbury

Pte Arthur Brindley Johnson   *12th Battalion Suffolk Regiment*

Service No.:	41007	Age:	24
Place of birth:	Salisbury, Wiltshire	Home country:	England
Date of death:	16/06/17	Cause of death:	Died of wounds
Memorials:	Salisbury, Wiltshire		
	St Paul's Church Memorial		
War cemetery:	Fins New British Cemetery, Sorel Le Grand, France		
Theatre of war:	France		
Next of kin:	Stephen & Mary E. Johnson (parents)		
Address:	Fisherton Anger, Salisbury, Wiltshire		

Arthur Johnson died of his wounds on 16 June 1916 near the village Fins, south-west of the town of Cambrai. He was one of five of his regiment to die on that day.

Pte William Samuel Orchard   *10th Battalion Royal West Kent Regiment*

Service No.:	G/15484	Age:	30
Place of birth:	Salisbury, Wiltshire	Home country:	England
Date of death:	23/06/17	Cause of death:	Killed in action
Memorials:	Salisbury, Wiltshire		
	St Mark's Church Memorial		
War cemetery:	Ypres Menin Gate Memorial, Belgium		
Theatre of war:	Belgium		
Next of kin:	Susannah Rose Orchard (wife); William & Rosa Orchard (parents)		
Addresses:	41 Queen Street, Folkestone, Kent		
	100 Radnor Park Road, Folkestone, Kent		

In mid-July 1917 news reached Salisbury that Pte William Orchard of the Royal West Kent Regiment and a member of a well-known Salisbury family, had been killed in the recent fighting. Pte Orchard, who after leaving Salisbury lived in Folkestone, had been at the front for ten months. Describing the manner in which he met his death, a friend wrote:

> We had been carrying up rations to the frontline, and were almost back to our own support trenches when Fritz opened out a very heavy shell fire, catching us in the open, which I will add is very frequent now. A piece of shrapnel caught Will in the back of the head, but he could not have felt anything. We laid him out nicely, and he was taken down the next morning, being buried in a properly dug grave, with his cross and number on.

William's officers describe him as a thoroughly good and efficient soldier, and speaks of the regret felt by the whole company, officers and men alike, at this loss. Pte Orchard was thirty years of age and left a widow and two young children. His grave was lost in subsequent fighting and he is remembered on the Ypres Menin Gate.

Pte Gilbert Charles Green   *2nd Battalion Coldstream Guards*
Service No.:   18314   Age: 19
Place of birth: Salisbury, Wiltshire   Home country: England
Date of death: 10/07/17   Cause of death: Killed in action
War cemetery: Artillery Wood Cemetery, Belgium
Theatre of war: Belgium
Next of kin: Mrs Jane Green (mother)
Address: Tower House East Coombe Road, Salisbury, Wiltshire

Nineteen-year-old Gilbert Green was killed in action on 10 July 1917 at Boezinge, north of Ypres. It is likely that his remains were brought into the cemetery at the end of the war because Artillery Wood Cemetery was not begun until the end of July, when the Guards Division captured the wood during the Battle of Pilckem Ridge. In 1901 Gilbert Green, his mother and brother were paupers and residents in Salisbury Union Workhouse.

Gunner Henry Sidney Williams   *79th Siege Battery 67th Brigade Royal Garrison Artillery*
Service No.:   79526   Age: 34
Place of birth: Winterslow, Wiltshire   Home country: England
Date of death: 15/07/17   Cause of death: Killed in action
Memorial: Salisbury, Wiltshire
War cemetery: Bully Grenay Communal Cemetery, British Extension, France
Theatre of war: France
Next of kin: Alice Mary Clark (formerly Williams) (wife); Steven E. Williams (father)
Addresses: The Nook, Whalebone Grove, Chadwell Heath, Essex
              Winterslow, Wiltshire

Henry Williams was killed in action on 15 July 1917, near the town of Bully, north of Arras, probably as a result of a German artillery bombardment.

Pte Henry Giles Amor   *Royal Marine Light Infantry HMS* Tamar
Service No.:   PO/13143   Age: 30
Place of birth: Dewlish, Somerset   Home country: England
Date of death: 18/07/17   Cause of death: Died of wounds
Memorial: Salisbury, Wiltshire
War cemetery: Kranji War Cemetery, Singapore
Theatre of war: Singapore
Next of kin: Henry & Julia Amor (parents)
Address: 18 Milford Hill, Salisbury, Wiltshire

Amor was a member of the Royal Marines attached to HMS *Tamar*. He died in China (probably Singapore) from pneumonia on 18 July 1917. His brother William John died in May 1919.

Sgt James Musselwhite   *5th Battalion Wiltshire Regiment*
Service No.:   03/365   Age: 42
Place of birth: Salisbury, Wiltshire   Home country: England

Date of death: 19/07/17   Cause of death: Died of illness
Memorials: Salisbury, Wiltshire
                St Martin's Church Memorial
War cemetery: Baghdad North Gate War Cemetery, Iraq
Theatre of war: Mesopotamia
Next of kin: Edward & Elizabeth Musselwhite (parents)
Address: Salisbury, Wiltshire

Baghdad had fallen to Commonwealth forces in March 1917, but James Musselwhite died of illness or disease at one of the casualty-clearing stations based in the city on 19 July 1917.

Sapper Andrew John Clyde   *40th Division Signal Company Royal Engineers*
Service No.:   166167   Age: 41
Place of birth: Salisbury, Wiltshire   Home country: England
Date of death: 20/07/17   Cause of death: Accidental death
Memorial: Salisbury, Wiltshire
War cemetery: Fins New British Cemetery, Sorel Le Grand, France
Theatre of war: France
Next of kin: The late Josiah & Eliza Clyde (parents)
Address: 35 Wyndham Road, Salisbury, Wiltshire

Andrew Clyde was killed by 'friendly fire' near Fins, south-west of Cambrai on 20 July 1917.

Gunner James Francis Hope   *24th Reserve Battery Royal Field Artillery*
Service No.:   178836   Age: 24
Place of birth: Islington, London   Home country: England
Date of death: 22/07/17   Cause of death: Died of illness
War cemetery: Salisbury (London Road) Cemetery, England
Theatre of war: Home
Next of kin: James Hope (father)
Address: London

Gunner Hope died of illness at one of the hospitals in the Salisbury area on 22 July 1917.

Pte Ernest Robins   *24th Battalion Quebec Regiment Canadian Infantry*
Service No.:   749192   Age: 19
Place of birth: Salisbury, Wiltshire   Home country: England
Date of death: 23/07/17   Cause of death: Killed in action
War cemetery: Chocques Military Cemetery, France
Theatre of war: France
Next of kin: Ernest & Sarah J. Robins (parents)
Address: Winterbourne Gunner, Wiltshire

Nineteen-year-old Ernest Robins, a farmer, volunteered for service with the Canadian Victoria Rifles on 1 June 1916. At the time his father was serving with the British Expeditionary Force in France. He was killed in action in France on 23 July 1917.

Pte Edward Percy Lott Horne   *1st Battalion Somerset Light Infantry*
Service No.:   27932   Age: 19
Place of birth: Salisbury, Wiltshire   Home country: England

James Hope, who died of illness in Salisbury.

Date of death: 27/07/17   Cause of death: Killed in action
Memorials: Salisbury, Wiltshire
                  St Martin's Church Memorial
War cemetery: Feuchy Chapel British Cemetery, Wancourt, France
Theatre of war: France
Next of kin: Mary Horne (grandmother)
Address: 32 Meadows Cottages, Friary, Salisbury, Wiltshire

Edward Horne originally joined the Wiltshire Regiment but was transferred to the 1st Battalion Somerset Light Infantry. The nineteen year old was killed in action on 27 July 1917 while serving with his battalion, east of Arras.

Pte Leonard Wheeler   *8th Battalion Duke of Cornwall's Light Infantry*
Service No.:   34562   Age: 19
Place of birth: Salisbury, Wiltshire Home country: England
Date of death: 31/07/17   Cause of death: Died of illness
Memorial: Salisbury, Wiltshire
War cemetery: Sarigol Military Cemetery, Kriston Greece
Theatre of war: Balkans
Next of kin: Tom & Annie Wheeler (parents)
Address: 4 Bedwin Street, Salisbury, Wiltshire

Nineteen-year-old Leonard Wheeler died of disease on 31 July 1917 at the 21st Stationary Hospital, Sarigol, Greece.

9

PASCHENDAELE

On Tuesday 31 July 1917 the Third Battle of Ypres, also known as Paschendaele, commenced.

Pte Henry Joseph Harfitt   *2nd Battalion Irish Guards*
Service No.:   11302   Age: 35
Place of birth: Belfast, County Antrim   Home country: England
Date of death: 01/08/17   Cause of death: Died of wounds
Memorials: Salisbury, Wiltshire
                 Bishop Wordsworth's School Memorial
War cemetery: Canada Farm Cemetery, Belgium
Theatre of war: Belgium
Next of kin: The late Herbert & Louisa Harfitt (parents)
Address: Exeter Street, Salisbury, Wiltshire

Henry Harfitt was the third son of late Herbert and Louisa Harfitt. He died of wounds that were the result of an accident on Wednesday 1 August 1917 at Canada Farm, a farmhouse used as a dressing station, north-west of the town of Ypres.

Pte Sidney Hubert Uphill   *01/5th Battalion Durham Light Infantry*
Service No.:   201144   Age: 35
Place of birth: Salisbury, Wiltshire   Home country: England
Date of death: 09/08/17   Cause of death: Died of wounds
Memorials: Salisbury, Wiltshire
                 St Martin's Church Memorial
War cemetery: Tourcoing Pont Neuville Communal Cemetery, France
Theatre of war: France
Next of kin: Herbert & Harriet Uphill (parents)
Address: St Martin, Salisbury, Wiltshire

Sidney Uphill died from wounds as a prisoner of war on Thursday 9 August 1917 at Tourcoing, a northern suburb of Lille, France. He was probably captured during the Arras offensive.

Pte Harry Brown   *9th Battalion Royal Inniskilling Fusiliers*
Service No.:   43667   Age: 19
Place of birth: Salisbury, Wiltshire   Home country: England
Date of death: 10/08/17   Cause of death: Killed in action
Memorials: Salisbury, Wiltshire
                 St Martin's Church Memorial
War cemetery: New Irish Farm Cemetery, Belgium
Theatre of war: Belgium
Next of kin: George & Lucy A. Brown (parents)
Address: 45 Clarendon Road, Elm Grove, Salisbury, Wiltshire

Harry Brown had originally joined the Royal Fusiliers, but was transferred to the 9th Battalion Royal Inniskilling Fusiliers. He was killed in action on Friday 10 August 1917 along with ten other members of the battalion who died on this day.

Pte John Thomas Cook *1st Battalion Wiltshire Regiment*

Service No.:	26401	Age:	39
Place of birth:	Salisbury, Wiltshire	Home country:	England
Date of death:	11/08/17	Cause of death:	Killed in action
Memorials:	Salisbury, Wiltshire		
	St Martin's Church Memorial		
War cemetery:	Ypres Menin Gate Memorial, Belgium		
Theatre of war:	Belgium		
Next of kin:	Eva Cook (mother)		
Address:	The Close, Salisbury, Wiltshire		

John Cook was killed in action on Saturday 11 August 1917 as the 1st Battalion Wiltshire Regiment were strengthening the line between Bellewarde and Westhoek, east of Ypres on the Menin Road. He is remembered on the Ypres Menin Gate Memorial and has no known grave.

Cpl Herbert Arthur Rendell *5th Battalion Dorsetshire Regiment*

Service No.:	7878	Age:	31
Place of birth:	West Coker, Somerset	Home country:	England
Date of death:	16/08/17	Cause of death:	Died of wounds
Memorials:	Salisbury, Wiltshire		
	St Paul's Church Memorial		
War cemetery:	Bard Cottage Cemetery, Belgium		
Theatre of war:	Belgium		
Next of kin:	James & Emma Rendell (parents)		
Address:	15 York Road, Fisherton, Salisbury, Wiltshire		

Cpl Rendell, known as Arthur, died of his wounds on Thursday 16 August during the first day of the Battle of Langemark, north-east of Ypres. He was one of twenty-five men in his regiment to be killed on this day.

Pte Charles Alfred Tilley *07/8th Battalion Royal Inniskilling Fusiliers*

Service No.:	41754	Age:	19
Place of birth:	Fisherton, Wiltshire	Home country:	England
Date of death:	16/08/17	Cause of death:	Killed in action
Memorial:	Salisbury, Wiltshire		
War cemetery:	Tyne Cot Memorial, Belgium		
Theatre of war:	Belgium		
Next of kin:	John & Julia Tilley (parents)		
Address:	9 Farley Cottages, Friary, Salisbury, Wiltshire		

Nineteen-year-old Charles Tilley was killed in action on Thursday 16 August 1917, on the first day of the Battle of Langemark. Twenty-nine members of the 7/8th Battalion Royal Inniskilling Fusiliers died on the same day. He is remembered on the Tyne Cot Memorial, Belgium, which commemorates 34,874 men who have no known grave and died in the area during the First World War.

Capt. Felix George Buckley　　　　　　　　　*8th Battalion Northumberland Fusiliers*

Place of birth:　West Oystesmouth, Glamorgan　Home country:　England　Age:　22
Date of death:　17/08/17　Cause of death:　Died of wounds
Decorations:　Military Cross
War cemetery:　New Irish Farm Cemetery, Belgium
Theatre of war: Belgium
Next of kin:　Maj. Edmond D.H. & Ellen C. Buckley (parents)
Address:　New Hall, Salisbury, Wiltshire

Maj. Buckley, RA, and Mrs Buckley, of New Hall, Bodenham, received news of the loss of their younger son, Capt. Felix George Buckley, MC, of the Northumberland Fusiliers after he was wounded on 14 August 1917, but had refused to leave his battalion. He was wounded again, very severely, two days later and died a few hours afterwards, before reaching the dressing station.

　　Capt. Buckley, who was educated at Wellington College and Brasenose College, Oxford, obtained a commission in the Northumberland Fusiliers in August 1914. He was promoted to lieutenant a year later and in August 1916 became a captain. He served in Gallipoli from September 1915 until the evacuation, when he proceeded to the Suez Canal where he remained until July of 1916. His battalion was transferred to the Belgian front, where Capt. Buckley continued to render good service, and his bravery was recognised in June 1917, when he was awarded the Military Cross.

Pte Arthur Douglas Pile　　　　　　　　　*1st King Edwards Horse*

Service No.:　1084　Age:　21
Place of birth:　Salisbury, Wiltshire　Home country:　England
Date of death:　21/08/17　Cause of death:　Killed in action
War cemetery:　Divisional Collecting Post Cemetery and Extension, Belgium
Theatre of war: Belgium
Next of kin:　Richard & Beatrice Pile (parents)
Address:　Netton, Salisbury, Wiltshire

Arthur Pile was the second son of Richard and Beatrice Pile. He was killed in action at Ypres on Tuesday 28 August 1917.

Instructor Staff Sgt Leslie Vivian Hurle Bath　　　*83rd Brigade Headquarters Royal Field Artillery*

Service No.:　90189　Age:　25
Place of birth:　Salisbury, Wiltshire　Home country:　England
Date of death:　23/08/17　Cause of death:　Killed in action
Memorial:　Salisbury, Wiltshire
War cemetery:　The Huts Cemetery, Belgium
Theatre of war: Belgium
Next of kin:　Fred & Hannah H. Bath (parents)
Address:　Fisherton Anger, Salisbury, Wiltshire

On Thursday 23 August 1917, in Flanders, the death took place of Instructor Staff Sgt Leslie Vivien Hurle Bath, RFA, youngest son of Mr Fred Bath, architect of Salisbury. Bath was educated at Salisbury School, and was apprentice to Messrs Petter & Sons, engineers, of Yeovil, serving with them for four years until 1 May 1914. He remained in the Experimental Department until war broke out when, along with five others of the staff, he offered their services either for the Royal Flying Corps or Royal Engineers. Leslie Bath was accepted for the latter, and served on the East Coast until March 1915, when he, with another, was selected to go to Woolwich for gun training, afterwards passing with the full 100 marks, and was at once made Instructor Staff Sergeant. He subsequently went to France, having charge of two batteries of howitzers, remaining all through the fighting with only one short leave of absence until his untimely death. He was a clever engineer of great promise, and his death was regretted by a large circle of friends, both in Salisbury and Yeovil.

Pte Harry Jenkins

695th Mechanical Transport Company Royal Army Service Corps

Service No.:	M/303985	Age:	38
Place of birth:	Stratford Sub Castle, Wiltshire	Home country:	England
Date of death:	27/08/17		
Memorials:	Salisbury, Wiltshire		
	St Paul's Church Memorial		
War cemetery:	Basra War Cemetery, Iraq		
Theatre of war:	Mesopotamia		
Next of kin:	Emmeline Jenkins (wife); William & Martha Jenkins (parents)		
Address:	4 Sidney Street, Salisbury, Wiltshire		

Harry Jenkins was a member of the Mesopotamian Expeditionary Force, he died of illness or disease on Monday 27 August 1917. He is buried in Basra War Cemetery in modern-day Iraq.

Pte Robert John Huggins

7th Battalion Royal Inniskilling Fusiliers

Service No.:	41843	Age:	19
Place of birth:	Salisbury, Wiltshire	Home country:	England
Date of death:	03/09/17		
Memorials:	Salisbury, Wiltshire		
	St Martin's Church Memorial.		
War cemetery:	Hamburg Cemetery, Germany		
Theatre of war:	Germany, as a Prisoner of War		
Next of kin:	Francis & Emma Huggins (parents)		
Address:	Bemerton, Salisbury, Wiltshire		

Nineteen-year-old Robert Huggins had originally joined the Somerset Light Infantry, but had been transferred to the 7th Battalion Royal Inniskilling Fusiliers. He was probably captured by the Germans in the actions at Langemark in mid-August 1917. He died in captivity in Germany on Monday 3 September 1917 and is buried in Hamburg Cemetery.

Pte R. Verge of the Wiltshire Regiment wrote to a friend describing life as a prisoner of war in August 1915:

> You want to know a little of camp life in Germany. As I was only in the camp for three weeks I cannot tell you much. At six o'clock in the morning we got a cup of black coffee without sugar, and if we had any bread left we ate it. Every man had about six ounces of bread for twenty-four hours. At dinner time we got something – I really can't name it, but the Germans call it soup; and at night we got the same as at dinner time. Sometimes there was a little meat, but we could always tell when we were getting meat, as we could smell it as soon as it left the cook-house; so you can tell our prisoners lived badly. Will you believe me when I tell you that last winter our prisoners were eating potato peelings, and when it rained they used to hold there hands to catch the water, as they were so thirsty. I think the best thing's to send out are bread, any kind of tinned meat and cocoa. I think our prisoners receive all their parcels and money, but money takes a long time getting there. Food, of course, is all our prisoners look for.

I am sorry to say , not many of the men who were at Lyndhurst will return again, as we lost 600 on 24 October. I am always thinking of that dreadful day, and hope I shall never see such a day again. I saw plenty of men shot, and they didn't say a word against their task when they were dying . I think a soldier on the battlefield dies a splendid death. Of all the men I saw killed not one said a bad word. I expected to die, as I had nine bullet wounds. My left leg was blown off below the knee and I was treated very badly by the Germans. They picked me up, took me to a public house, and left me there for three days, and the only thing I had to live on was beer.

Pte Verge was exchanged for a wounded German soldiers and survived the war.

Pte Walter Charles Shergold		*1st Battalion Wiltshire Regiment*	
Service No.:	26141	Age:	33
Place of birth:	Bemerton, Wiltshire	Home country:	England
Date of death:	04/09/17	Cause of death:	Killed in action
Memorials:	Salisbury, Wiltshire		
	St Martin's Church Memorial		
War cemetery:	Menin Road South Military Cemetery		
Theatre of war:	Belgium		
Next of kin:	William Shergold (father)		
Address:	Homington, Wiltshire		

On Tuesday 4 September 1917 the 1st Battalion Wiltshire Regiment were in the reserve line near the dugouts at Zillebeke Lake, east of Ypres. During the morning, the Germans shelled the position with 8in howitzers, which caused three casualties. Walter Shergold was one of the men killed in action.

Gunner Harold Percival Morris		*Royal Marine Artillery Howitzer Brigade*	
Service No.:	RMA/1052(S)	Age:	26
Place of birth:	Shucknall, Herefordshire	Home country:	England
Date of death:	08/09/17	Cause of death:	Killed in action
Memorials:	Salisbury, Wiltshire		
	St Paul's Church Memorial		
War cemetery:	Dozinghem Military Cemetery, Belgium		
Theatre of war:	Belgium		
Next of kin:	The late Percy W. & the late Arabella M. Morris (parents)		
Address:	Shucknall Court, Shucknall, Herefordshire		

A report stated that Harold Morris was killed in action on 9 September 1917, although the official records state he was killed in action on Saturday 8 September 1917. He was the youngest son of the late Percy Morris of Shucknall Court, Hereford, grandson of the late Capt. W. Welsh RN and the dearly loved stepson of Mrs Percy Morris, Devizes Road, Salisbury.

Pte William James Burton		*02/1st Battalion Oxfordshire & Buckinghamshire Light Infantry*	
Service No.:	267162	Age:	28
Place of birth:	Salisbury, Wiltshire	Home country:	England
Date of death:	09/09/17	Cause of death:	Killed in action
Memorials:	Salisbury, Wiltshire		
	St Martin's Church Memorial		
War cemetery:	Tyne Cot Cemetery, Belgium		

Menin Road Cemetery.

Theatre of war: Belgium
Next of kin: Eliza Caroline Burton (wife); William James & Annie Burton (parents)
Addresses: 63 Rampart Road, Salisbury, Wiltshire
                 93 Gigant Street, Salisbury, Wiltshire

William Burton had originally joined the Wiltshire Regiment, but was transferred to the 2/1st Battalion Oxfordshire & Buckinghamshire Light Infantry. He was killed in action on Sunday 9 September 1917 and is remembered on the Tyne Cot Memorial, Belgium. Burton has no known grave.

Pte Sidney New Massey   *2nd Battalion Wiltshire Regiment*
Service No.:   6781   Age: 31
Place of birth: St Lukes, London   Home country: England
Date of death: 12/09/17   Cause of death: Died of wounds
Memorials: Salisbury, Wiltshire
                 St Martin's Church Memorial
War cemetery: Outterstreene Communal Cemetery Extension, Bailleul, France
Theatre of war: France
Next of kin: Edward & Annie Massey
Address: Rampart Road, Salisbury, Wiltshire

On 20 September 1917 a letter was received by Mrs Massey of Rampart Road from France. It informed her that her son, Sidney Massey, company stretcher bearer of the Wiltshire Regiment, was admitted to hospital on 11 September with severe wounds in the abdomen, to which he succumbed on Wednesday 12 September 1917. Pte Massey was one of the original British Expeditionary Force, leaving England with the Wiltshire Regiment for France in August 1914. He completed fourteen years with the colours in January 1916, and applied for time expired leave, which was granted in June 1917, when he was home for a month. During the early actions of the war he took part in all the hard work, being in the retreat from Mons, when the company stretcher bearers were praised by the officers of the regiment for their devotion to duty. In his Army career he served in India and South Africa, returning to England about twelve months before war was declared.

As a lad he joined the Wiltshire Militia and proceeded to St Helena, where he guarded Boer prisoners during the South African Campaign, for which he was awarded the King's Medal.

This was the second son Mrs Massey had lost during the war, her son Frederick Massey being killed in March 1915. Of her five sons, three were serving in France, one in Egypt and one in India.

Ordinary Seaman Ewart William Hill   *Royal Navy HMS* Stonecrop
Service No.:   J/68330   Age: 18

Place of birth: Salisbury, Wiltshire   Home country: England
Date of death: 18/09/17   Cause of death: Died of wounds
Memorials: Salisbury, Wiltshire
                    St Paul's Church Memorial and Dews Road Primitive Methodist Memorial
War cemetery: Portsmouth Naval Memorial England
Theatre of war: At sea
Next of kin: Thomas Charles & Louisa Ann Hill (parents)
Address: 3 High Field Road, Salisbury, Wiltshire

HMS *Stonecrop* was a British Q Ship, these ships were armed merchant ships which were used to lure German U-boats to point-blank range, at this time the British would uncover their guns and open fire on the unsuspecting submarines. On Monday 17 September 1917, the *Stonecrop* lured in the German submarine U-88, which had been responsible for the sinking of the passenger liner *Lusitania* in 1915. At 4.43 p.m. the U-88 was next to the Stonecrop and opened fire, the Q ship then uncovered her guns and returned fire sinking the German U-boat. It is likely eighteen-year-old Ewart Hill was wounded in this action and subsequently died. He is remembered on the Portsmouth Naval Memorial.

Ordinary Telegraphist Alfred Harold Orchard   *Royal Navy HMS* Contest
Service No.:   J/39825   Age: 18
Place of birth: Salisbury, Wiltshire   Home country: England
Date of death: 18/09/17   Cause of death: Died
Memorials: Salisbury, Wiltshire
                    St Mark's Memorial
War cemetery: Chatham Naval Memorial England
Theatre of war: At sea
Next of kin: William J. & Rosa Mary Orchard (parents)
Address: 100 Radnor Park Road, Folkestone, Kent

Wireless Operator Harold Orchard, youngest son of Mrs and Mrs Orchard of Folkestone, formerly of Salisbury, had been reported missing after the vessel on which he was serving had struck a mine. He had joined the Navy early in 1915, and had just come out of his boy's rating. He was in his eighteenth year. In June 1916 the eldest son of Mr and Mrs Orchard, Pte W. Orchard, Royal West Kents, was killed in action and in April 1918, another son, L/Cpl S. Ochard, having gained the Military Medal, would also be killed in action.

2nd-Lt Robert Henry Curtis   *10th Battalion Royal West Surrey Regiment*
Place of birth: Salisbury, Wiltshire   Home country: England   Age: 28
Date of death: 20/09/17   Cause of death: Killed in action
Memorials: Salisbury, Wiltshire
                    St Mark's Church Memorial
War cemetery: Tyne Cot Memorial, Belgium
Theatre of war: Belgium
Next of kin: The late William & Sarah Anne Curtis (parents)
Address: 3 New Street, Salisbury, Wiltshire

In October 1917, news was received of the death in action of 2nd-Lt Robert H. Curtis, younger and only surviving son of Mrs Curtis, New Street. He was educated at St Mark's School, Salisbury, and St Mark's Training College, Chelsea. When a pupil teacher at Sarum St Mark's, he passed first of all England in the Archbishop's examination in religious knowledge. A master at Tottenham Council School, Mr Curtis joined the Honourable Artillery Company, and served with them in France some months before getting his commission in the Royal West Surrey Regiment, where he had acted as signalling officer to his battalion. Robert is remembered on Tyne Cot Memorial and has no known grave.

Pte Percival Edward Rattue		*23rd Battalion Middlesex Regiment*	
Service No.:	TF/206179	Age:	25
Place of birth:	Salisbury, Wiltshire	Home country:	England
Date of death:	21/09/17	Cause of death:	Killed in action
Memorials:	Salisbury, Wiltshire		
	St Mark's Church Memorial		
War cemetery:	Tyne Cot Memorial, Belgium		
Theatre of war:	Belgium		
Next of kin:	Olive Henrietta Rattue (wife); William & Annie Rattue (parents)		
Addresses:	7 Fair View Road, Elm Grove, Salisbury, Wiltshire		
	Queen's Road, Salisbury		

Pte P.E. Rattue, Middlesex Regiment, second son of Mr and Mrs W. Rattue, of Queen's Road, husband of Olive, daughter of Mr & Mrs H. Walton, 7 Fair View Road, Salisbury, was killed in action on Friday 21 September 1917. Percival Rattue is remembered on Tyne Cot Memorial and has no known grave.

Pte Frederick Charles Nash		*7th Battalion Royal Inniskilling Fusiliers*	
Service No.:	41795	Age:	27
Place of birth:	Dogdean, Wiltshire	Home country:	England
Date of death:	23/09/17	Cause of death:	Died of wounds
Memorial:	Salisbury, Wiltshire		
War cemetery:	Boulogne Eastern Cemetery, France		
Theatre of war:	France		
Next of kin:	John & Ellen Nash (parents)		
Address:	Britford, Salisbury, Wiltshire		

Frederick Nash had originally joined the Somerset Light Infantry, but was transferred to the 7th Battalion Royal Inniskilling Fusiliers. It is likely he was wounded during the Battle of Langemarck or one of the following actions. He died of wounds at Boulogne, a hospital centre during the First World War, on Sunday 23 September 1917.

Pte Edward Frank Eyres		*215th Company Infantry Machine Gun Corps*	
Service No.:	64606	Age:	20
Place of birth:	Bemerton, Wiltshire	Home country:	England
Date of death:	24/09/17	Cause of death:	Died of wounds
Memorials:	Salisbury, Wiltshire		
	Bishop Wordsworth's School Memorial		
War cemetery:	Dozinghem Military Cemetery, Belgium		
Theatre of war:	Belgium		
Next of kin:	Frank & Fanny Eyres (parents)		
Address:	133 Devizes Road, Salisbury, Wiltshire		

In mid-October 1917, news was received by Mr and Mrs F. Eyres, of 133 Devizes Road, Salisbury, of the death of their eldest son Edward Frank Eyres, aged twenty, which occurred on Monday 24 September 1917 from wounds. Edward Eyres, was formally a sorting clerk and telegraphist in the Salisbury Post Office and enlisted in the Post Office Rifles in August 1916, and was subsequently transferred to the machine-gun section, in which he became a signaller. He was hit by an enemy sniper whilst delivering a message up the line and died an hour after admission to hospital. He had been in France for six months. He was educated at Bishop Wordsworth's School.

Maj. Roger Alvin Poore   *2nd Battalion Royal Welsh Fusiliers*

Place of birth:	Bath, Somerset	Home country: England	Age:	47
Date of death:	26/09/17	Cause of death: Killed in action		

Decorations: Distinguished Service Order
War cemetery: Poelcapelle British Cemetery, Belgium
Theatre of war: Belgium
Next of kin: Lorne Margery Poore (wife); Maj. Robert & Juliana Poore (parents)
Addresses: Fernyhurst, Rownhams, Hampshire
                    Old Lodge, Salisbury

In October 1917 news was received of the death in action on Wednesday 26 September 1917 of Maj. R.A. Poore while in command of a battalion of the Royal Welsh Fusiliers. Roger Poore was the third son of Maj. Robert Poore, late of the 8th Hussars, and Mrs Poore, late of Old Lodge, Salisbury, now living at Bournemouth.

Maj. Roger Alvin Poore had served twenty-four years in the Royal Wilts Yeomanry and commanded the 2nd Regiment Royal Wilts Yeomanry before being transferred to the Royal Welsh Fusiliers. He served all through the South African War with the Yorkshire Light Infantry (Mounted Infantry), was mentioned in despatches, awarded the DSO and held the Queens medal with seven clasps. The colonel of the Regiment, writing to Mrs Poore said:

> There is one thing that you will hear with pride and that is that the battalion under your husband's command behaved most gallantly in the action and has covered itself with glory. Your husband had endeared himself to everybody in the battalion, and his loss will be most acutely felt. He had helped and supported me most loyally; indeed, I do not know how I will get on without his wise advice. He was one of the most gallant gentlemen I have ever met.

Maj. Poore married Lorne Margery in 1913, daughter of the late Maj. R.W. Dennistoun, 64th Regiment of Foot and Mrs Despard, of Hamilton, Scotland, and leaves a widow and a son.

Poore was killed in Belgium with two other officers while in conversation when a German shell burst amongst them.

Pte Harry Osmond   *2nd Battalion Wiltshire Regiment*

Service No.:   24534   Age: 19
Place of birth: Fisherton, Wiltshire   Home country: England
Date of death: 28/09/17   Cause of death: Died of wounds
Memorials: Salisbury, Wiltshire
                    St Thomas Church Memorial
War cemetery: Outterstreene Communal Cemetery Extension, Bailleul, France
Theatre of war: France
Next of kin: William & Edith Osmond (parents)
Address: 13 Fisherton Street, Salisbury, Wiltshire

Mr and Mrs Osmund, of 13 Fisherton Street, received a wire from the War Office on Thursday 4 October 1917, intimating that their son, Pte Harry Osmund, a signaller in the Wiltshire Regiment, had died of wounds received in action. Pte Osmund, who was only nineteen years of age, joined the forces in March 1915, and had been in France for several months.

Pte William Richard John Janes		*1st Battalion Northumberland Fusiliers*	
Service No.:	46934	Age:	22
Place of birth:	Gosport, Hampshire	Home country:	England
Date of death:	28/09/17	Cause of death:	Died of wounds
War cemetery:	Tyne Cot Memorial, Belgium		
Theatre of war:	Belgium		
Next of kin:	John & Martha Janes (parents)		
Address:	10 Leonard Road, Forton, Gosport, Hampshire		

William Janes had originally joined the Hampshire Regiment, but was transferred to the 1st Battalion Northumberland Fusiliers. He died of his wounds on Friday 28 September 1918, most probably received in the actions at Polygon Wood, east of the town of Ypres, at the end of September 1917. William had lived in Salisbury up to the start of the war and he is remembered on the Tyne Cot Memorial, having no known grave.

Pte Harry William Stagg		*Devonshire Regiment 9th Service*	
Service No.:	291050	Age:	26
Place of birth:	Salisbury, Wiltshire	Home country:	England
Date of death:	06/10/17	Cause of death:	Killed in action
Memorials:	Salisbury, Wiltshire		
	St Martin's Church Memorial		
War cemetery:	Tyne Cot Memorial, Belgium		
Theatre of war:	Belgium		
Next of kin:	George & Lucy Stagg (parents)		
Address:	St Martin, Salisbury, Wiltshire		

Harry Stagg was killed in action on Saturday 6 October 1917 during fighting around Broodseinde, and Poelcapelle, east of the town of Ypres, Belgium. He is remembered on the Tyne Cot Memorial and has no known grave.

Lt James Cromwell Bush		*22 Squadron Royal Flying Corps*		
Place of birth:	Salisbury, Wiltshire	Home country:	England	Age: 26
Date of death:	07/10/17	Cause of death:	Killed in action	
Decorations:	Military Cross.			
Memorial:	Salisbury, Wiltshire			
	Choir School Memorial			
War cemetery:	Neuville En Ferrain Communal Cemetery, France			
Theatre of war:	France			
Next of kin:	Revd Herbert Cromwell Bush & Mabel A.H. Bush (parents)			
Address:	Wishford Rectory, Salisbury, Wiltshire			

On 20 October 1917, Lt J. Cromwell Bush, MC, of the Dorset Regiment and Royal Flying Corps was reported as missing from Sunday 7 October 1917. Two weeks later Revd H. Cromwell Bush, vicar of Seend, formerly of the Close, Salisbury, received an intimation from the War Office that a message had been dropped in our lines by a German aeroplane to say that his son Lt J.C. Bush,

MC, the Dorset Regiment and RFC is dead as well as his observer Lt Chapman. As both names are mentioned there seems to be no reason to doubt that this was true.

Lt J. Cromwell Bush was born in the Close, Salisbury, on 14 March 1891 and was educated at St Edward's School, Oxford where he was in the rowing IV and rugby 1st XV.

At the age of nineteen he went to Ceylon to tea-plant, and was invalided home. He went again to India and a second time was invalided home. At the outbreak of the war he obtained a commission in the Wiltshire Regiment, and went with them to the Dardanelles as machine-gun officer. He was one of the few survivors of Sulva Bay and was awarded the MC for his services. He was invalided home almost immediately and when he recovered went to Egypt as ADC to a brigadier general. After six months he volunteered for the RFC, came back to England to train, gaining his 'wings' in April 1917. He went to the front in May. He had been recommended for a flight of his own – he had shot down five Huns – and was constantly leading the patrols over the enemy lines. His grandfather was Gen. Reynell Taylor, CB, CSI the 'Bayard of the Punjab,' *sans peur et sans reproche,'* one of Lawrence of Arabia's men.

Pte Bertram John Gardner		*2nd Battalion Royal Warwickshire Regiment*	
Service No.:	306657	Age:	28
Place of birth:	Salisbury, Wiltshire	Home country:	England
Date of death:	09/10/17	Cause of death:	Killed in action
Memorials:	Salisbury, Wiltshire		
	St Martin's Church Memorial		
War cemetery:	Tyne Cot Memorial, Belgium		
Theatre of war:	Belgium		
Next of kin:	George & Naomi Ruth Gardner (parents)		
Address:	29 Meadow Cottages, Friary, Salisbury, Wiltshire		

Bertram Gardner was killed in the Battle of Poelcapelle, east of the town of Ypres, on Tuesday 9 October 1917. He is remembered on the Tyne Cot Memorial and has no known grave.

Pte Donald Horder		*B Company 26th Battalion Royal Fusiliers*	
Service No.:	19659	Age:	21
Place of birth:	Salisbury, Wiltshire	Home country:	England
Date of death:	09/10/17	Cause of death:	Died of wounds
Memorials:	Salisbury, Wiltshire		
	Bishop Wordsworth's School Memorial, St Martin's Church Memorial &		
	St Mark's Church Memorial		
War cemetery:	Godewaersvelde British Cemetery, France		
Theatre of war:	France		
Next of kin:	Harry Tom & Edith Maria Horder (parents)		
Address:	16 Queens Road, Salisbury, Wiltshire		

News was received in Salisbury, early in October 1917, that Pte Donald Horder, youngest son of Mr H.T. Horder, of 16 Queen's Road, was severely wounded in the fighting around Ypres on 29 September. This was the second time that Pte Horder had been wounded. Joining the Bankers Battalion of the Royal Fusiliers about two years previously, he was engaged on the Somme fighting in July of 1916 and in consequence of wounds was in hospital for five months at Eastborne. He recovered and had been home on leave Christmas 1916. After passing as a first-class signaller at Dover, he was again sent to France in May, and in the severe fighting at Ypres he received a serious wound in the right side, his ankle also being injured. On Tuesday 9 October 1917, Horder succumbed to the wounds he had received in action and died at a casualty-clearing station.

Pte Thomas Edwin Dunning　　　　*2nd Battalion West Riding Regiment*

Service No.:	26081	Age:	23
Place of birth:	Exeter, Devon	Home country: England
Date of death:	10/10/17	Cause of death: Killed in action
Memorial:	Salisbury, Wiltshire.	
War cemetery:	Cement House Cemetery, Belgium	
Theatre of war:	Belgium	
Next of kin:	Richard & Emma Dunning (parents)	
Address:	Salisbury, Wiltshire	

Thomas Dunning originally enlisted in the Royal Army Service Corps in 1915, but was transferred to the 2nd Battalion West Riding Regiment, he was killed in action on Wednesday 10 October 1917 in the vicinity of Poelcapelle, east of the town of Ypres, Belgium.

Pte Reginald Witt　　　　*6th Battalion Wiltshire Regiment*

Service No.:	203389	Age:	24
Place of birth:	Salisbury, Wiltshire	Home country: England
Date of death:	11/10/17	Cause of death: Died of wounds
Memorials:	Salisbury, Wiltshire	
	St Martin's Church Memorial	
War cemetery:	Duhallow ADS Cemetery, Belgium	
Theatre of war:	Belgium	
Next of kin:	Charles & Julia Witt (parents)	
Address:	52 St Ann Street, Salisbury, Wiltshire	

On Wednesday 10 October 1917, the 6th Battalion Wiltshire Regiment was in the frontline in Belgium, at a position known as Spoil Bank. Reginald Witt originally joined the Royal Wiltshire Yeomanry, which amalgamated with the 6th Battalion Wiltshire Regiment on 20 September 1917. He was wounded by German shelling and evacuated to the Duhallow advanced-dressing station north of the town of Ypres, Belgium, where he died on the following day.

Cpl Wifred Henry Scott　　　　*9th Trench Mortar Battery Royal Garrison Artillery*

Service No.:	35416	Age:	22
Place of birth:	Fisherton, Wiltshire	Home country: England
Date of death:	13/10/17	Cause of death: Killed in action
Decorations:	Military Medal	
Memorials:	Salisbury, Wiltshire	
	St Martin's Memorial	
War cemetery:	Tyne Cot Cemetery, Belgium	
Theatre of war:	Belgium.	
Next of kin:	Henry John & Eva May Scott	
Address:	Fisherton, Salisbury, Wiltshire.	

In August 1918, Henry & Eva Scott, of Rampart Road, Salisbury, received the Military Medal awarded to their son, the late Cpl Wilfred Scott, who was awarded the decoration in August 1917. He was killed in action on Saturday 13 October 1917, during the British offensive at Passchendaele, Belgium. Wilfred Scott is remembered on the Tyne Cot Memorial and has no known grave.

Pte Ernest Sidney Phillips　　　　*109th Company Labour Corps*

Service No.:	65168	Age:	30

Place of birth:	Salisbury, Wiltshire	Home country:	England
Date of death:	18/10/17	Cause of death:	Killed in action
Memorials:	Salisbury, Wiltshire		
	St Martin's Church Memorial		
War cemetery:	Artillery Wood Cemetery, Belgium		
Theatre of war:	Belgium		
Next of kin:	Arthur & Bessie Phillips (parents)		
Address:	18 St Anne Street, Salisbury, Wiltshire		

Ernest Phillips had originally joined the Gloucester Regiment, but transferred to 109th Company Labour Corps. He was killed in action, probably due to shell fire, on Thursday 18 October 1917, in the area of the village Boezinge, north of Ypres.

Pte Wilfred Gordon Anson   14th Battalion Gloucestershire Regiment

Service No.:	265915	Age:	27
Place of birth:	Littleover, Derbyshire	Home country:	England
Date of death:	22/10/17	Cause of death:	Killed in action
War cemetery:	Tyne Cot Cemetery, Belgium		
Theatre of war:	Belgium		
Next of kin:	Revd Harcourt S. & Edith Anson (parents)		
Address:	The Close, Salisbury, Wiltshire		

News of Mr Wilfred Gordon Anson's death was received in Salisbury in early November 1917. He was killed in action on Monday 22 October 1917. Wilfred Anson, who was twenty-seven years of age, enlisted in the Gloucesters soon after war broke out, and was wounded whilst serving with them. He went out again to France during September 1917. He was killed in the gallant advance made by his battalion against the enemy on 22 October. With a somewhat long military ancestry, he bore his part as a soldier manfully and courageously throughout. His late colonel, writing to his father, spoke in terms of high praise of his unassuming heroism. He is remembered on the Tyne Cot Memorial and has no known grave.

Pte Harold Pearcey   6th Battalion Somerset Light Infantry

Service No.:	28861	Age:	19
Place of birth:	Salisbury, Wiltshire	Home country:	England
Date of death:	23/10/17	Cause of death:	Killed in action
Memorial:	Salisbury, Wiltshire		
War cemetery:	Hooge Crater Cemetery, Belgium		
Theatre of war:	Belgium		
Next of kin:	Emma Philpott (grandmother)		
Address:	3 Curtiss Court, Endess Street, Salisbury, Wiltshire		

Nineteen-year-old Harold Pearcey was killed in action on Tuesday 23 October 1917, probably by German shelling, during actions that took place to the south-east of Ypres.

Cpl William Charles Beaven   Central Ontario Regiment 4th Canadian Mounted Rifles

Service No.:	172007	Age:	24
Place of birth:	Salisbury, Wiltshire	Home country:	England
Date of death:	26/10/17	Cause of death:	Killed in action
Memorials:	Salisbury, Wiltshire		
	St Martin's Church Memorial		

War cemetery: Tyne Cot Cemetery
Theatre of war: Belgium
Next of kin: Michael & Alice Beaven (parents)
Address: The Close, Salisbury, Wiltshire

William Beaven was killed on Friday 26 October in the area of Passchendale, north of Ypres. He is remembered on the Tyne Cot Memorial and has no known grave.

Pte Harold Stanley Gale   *2nd Battalion Royal West Surrey Regiment*

Service No.:	G/5397	Age:	28
Place of birth:	Salisbury, Wiltshire	Home country:	England
Date of death:	26/10/17	Cause of death:	Killed in action
Memorials:	Salisbury, Wiltshire		
	St Thomas Church Memorial		
War cemetery:	Tyne Cot Cemetery, Belgium		
Theatre of war:	Belgium		
Next of kin:	Leonora Gale (wife); James & Matilda Gale (parents)		
Address:	5 The Drove, West Harnham, Salisbury, Wiltshire		
	10 Nelson Road, Salisbury, Wiltshire		

Harold Gale had originally joined the 13th Hussars but was transferred to the 2nd Battalion Royal West Surrey Regiment. He was the third son of James and Matilda and had married Leonora Earney early in 1908. He was killed in action on Friday 26 October 1917, probably in the unsuccessful attack south of the Menin Road, near Polygon Wood, east of Ypres.

Pte Reginald Godfrey Harris   *9th Battalion Devonshire Regiment*

Service No.:	204924	Age:	21
Place of birth:	Fordingbridge, Hampshire	Home country:	England
Date of death:	26/10/17	Cause of death:	Killed in action
Memorials:	Salisbury, Wiltshire		
	St Martin's Church Memorial		
War cemetery:	Hooge Crater Cemetery, Belgium		
Theatre of war:	Belgium		
Next of kin:	William & Kate Harris (parents)		
Address:	125 Gigant Street, Salisbury, Wiltshire		

Reginald Harris was killed in action on Friday 26 October 1917 on the first day of the Battle of Passchendale, during the attack south of the Menin Road, south of Polygon Wood, during the unsuccessful attack made by the 7th Division.

Sgt William Charles Coombes   *14th Royal Defence Corps*

Service No.:	48955	Age:	57
Place of birth:	Fisherton, Wiltshire	Home country:	England
Date of death:	28/10/17		
Memorial:	Salisbury, Wiltshire		
War cemetery:	Salisbury (Devizes Road) Cemetery, England		
Theatre of war:	Home		
Next of kin:	Fanny Coombes (wife); John & Emily Coombes (parents)		
Addresses:	25 High Street, Salisbury, Wiltshire		
	Fisherton, Salisbury, Wiltshire		

William Coombes.

William Coombes had been a soldier in the Wiltshire Regiment and was too old to go to war. He did, however, join the Royal Defence Corps, which was a form of home guard. He died on Sunday 28 October 1917, either of illness or from natural causes.

Pte Victor James		*2nd Battalion Wiltshire Regiment*	
Service No.:	24529	Age:	20
Place of birth:	Newton Abbot, Devon	Home country:	England
Date of death:	29/10/17	Cause of death:	Died of wounds
War cemetery:	Trois Arbres Cemetery, Steenwerck, France		
Theatre of war:	France		
Next of kin:	Henry David & Flora Almeda Asenath James (parents)		
Address:	40 Abbotsbury Road, Newton Abbot, Devon		

L/Cpl Victor James, whilst serving with the Wilts Regiment, died from wounds received in action. L/Cpl James was, until joining the Army in May 1916, on the staff of the London City & Midland Bank Ltd, Salisbury, where he was much esteemed. He was brought into a clearing-station hospital on Monday 29 October 1917, suffering from internal injuries received in action and, although everything possible was done for him, there was no hope for him from the first, and he passed away the same day. He was buried at Trois Arbres Cemetery and a cross was erected over the grave. The official intimation has been accompanied by a message of sympathy from the King and Queen. He had been in France since December 1916, and had experienced some of the hottest fighting.

31 OCTOBER 1917 – BRITISH OCCUPY BEERSHEBA

Able Seaman Cecil Victor Simmonds		*Drake Battalion Royal Navel Division Royal Naval Voluteer Reserve*	
Service No.:	R/990	Age:	20
Place of birth:	Salisbury, Wiltshire	Home country:	England
Date of death:	01/11/17	Cause of death:	Died of wounds
Memorials:	Salisbury, Wiltshire		
	Baptist Church Memorial & St Martin's Church Memorial		

War cemetery: Mendingham Military Cemetery, Belgium
Theatre of war: Belgium
Next of kin: William Carey & Louisa Jane Simmonds (parents)
Address: 93 Rampart Road, Salisbury, Wiltshire

Cecil Simmonds died of wounds on Thursday 1 November 1917 at 46th Casualty-Clearing Station, who were based at Mendinghem, north-west of Ypres.

Pte William Thomas Larkam   *2/4th Battalion Dorsetshire Regiment*
Service No.:   202303   Age: 32
Place of birth: Salisbury, Wiltshire Home country: England
Date of death: 03/11/17   Cause of death: Killed in action
Memorials: Salisbury, Wiltshire
                  St Martin's Church Memorial & St Paul's Church Memorial
War cemetery: Gaza War Cemetery, Israel
Theatre of war: Palestine
Next of kin: Annie Edith Larkham (wife); Eli & Harriet Larkham (parents)
Addresses: 48 Sydney Street, Salisbury, Wiltshire
                  St Martin, Salisbury, Wiltshire

Pte Larkham, known as Thomas, had originally joined the Wiltshire Regiment but was transferred to the 2/4th Battalion Dorsetshire Regiment. He had married his wife, Edith Annie Blake, at the start of 1909 in Salisbury and in November 1917 he found himself in Palestine, preparing for the attacks on Gaza. He was killed in action on Saturday 3 November 1917 and was subsequently buried in Gaza War Cemetery.

Cpl Sidney Ernest Matthews   *121st Battery 27th Brigade Royal Field Artillery*
Service No.:   19980   Age: 40
Place of birth: Salisbury, Wiltshire Home country: England
Date of death: 04/11/17   Cause of death: Killed in action
Memorials: Salisbury, Wiltshire
                  St Paul's Church Memorial
War cemetery: La Clytte Military Cemetery, Belgium
Theatre of war: Belgium
Next of kin: The late Frank William & Sarah Matthews (parents)
Address: Britford, Wiltshire

Sidney Matthews was killed in action on Sunday 4 November 1917, during the Second Battle of Passchendale. He is buried in La Clytte Military Cemetery, west of Ypres. During the Third Battle of Ypres the Salient was packed with British Forces, which made an easy target for German artillery gunners or bombing from German aircraft. It is likely that one of these methods caused Matthew's death.

Pte Tom Zebedee   *2nd Royal Marine Battalion Royal Marine Light Infantry*
Service No.:   CH/2006(S)   Age: 37
Place of birth: Salisbury, Wiltshire Home country: England
Date of death: 06/11/17   Cause of death: Killed in action
Memorial: Salisbury, Wiltshire
War cemetery: Tyne Cot Memorial, Belgium

Theatre of war: Belgium
Next of kin: Sophie Zebedee (wife); late William & Mary Kate Zebedee
                  (parents)
Address: 22 Harnham Road, Salisbury, Wiltshire
                  St Edmunds, Salisbury, Wiltshire

Pte Zebedee was the only son of the late William and Mary Zebedee and the husband of Sophie Zebedee. He was killed in action on Tuesday 6 November 1917 during the Second Battle of Passchendale.

> 6 NOVEMBER 1917 – PASSCHENDALE WAS CAPTURED, BRINGING TO AN END THE THIRD BATTLE OF YPRES, BELGIUM – 7 NOVEMBER 1917 – BRITISH CAPTURE GAZA

Pte Bert Edward Cornish   *1/4th Battalion Wiltshire Regiment*
Service No.:   201848   Age: 20
Place of birth: Salisbury, Wiltshire. Home: Country: England
Date of death: 07/11/17   Cause of death: Killed in action
Memorials: Salisbury, Wiltshire
                  St Paul's Church Memorial & St Martin's Church Memorial
War cemetery: Gaza War Cemetery, England
Theatre of war: Palestine
Next of kin: Sarah Hayter (mother)
Address: 8 Meron Row, Gas Lane, Salisbury, Wiltshire

The 1/4th Battalion Wiltshire Regiment had spent most of the First World War in India, but in September 1917 the Wiltshires arrived in Egypt where they would remain for the remainder of the conflict. On 7 November the Wiltshires were advancing against Turkish forces and had been continuously shelled. Pte Cornish was a casualty of the Turkish shelling: he was killed in action on Wednesday 7 November 1917, on the last day of the Third Battle of Gaza, when the British captured Gaza from the Turkish. Seven other members of the 1/4th Battalion Wiltshire Regiment were also killed during this action.

Cpl Wilfred Fry   *1/4th Battalion Wiltshire Regiment*
Service No.:   200672   Age: 27
Place of birth: Salisbury, Wiltshire   Home country: England
Date of death: 07/11/17   Cause of death: Killed in action
Memorial: Salisbury, Wiltshire
War cemetery: Gaza War Cemetery, Israel
Theatre of war: Palestine
Next of kin: Stephen W. & Elizabeth Fry (parents)
Address: St Edmund, Salisbury, Wiltshire

Wilfred Fry was killed in the same action as Bertie Cornish, and was killed in action due to Turkish shell fire on Wednesday 7 November 1917. Both are buried in Gaza War Cemetery, Israel.

Sgt Arthur George Howes   *1/4th Battalion Wiltshire Regiment*
Service No.:   200121   Age: 26
Place of birth: Laverstock, Wiltshire   Home country: England

Above: *Paschendaele Memorial.*

Right: *Sgt Arthur George Howes in a trench in Gaza. (Photograph courtesy Wiltshire Military Museum, Wardrobe)*

Date of death: 08/11/17   Cause of death: Died of wounds
Memorials: Salisbury, Wiltshire
                          St Mark's Church Memorial
War cemetery: Deir El Belah War Cemetery, Israel
Theatre of war: Palestine
Next of kin: Edith Howes (wife); William & Clara Howes (parents)
Addresses: 58 Park Street, Salisbury, Wiltshire
                          58 Park Street, Salisbury, Wiltshire

In mid-November 1917 official news was received of the death from wounds in Palestine of Sgt Howes, who was a member of the local company of the Territorial Army when war broke out, and proceeded to India with the Wiltshire Regiment.

At Christmas 1917, Edith Howes received the following letter from the officer under whom her husband served:

Dear Mrs Howes,
I am writing to express my deepest sympathy with you in the loss of your husband on the evening of November 6th–7th. He was my platoon sergeant, and a better one no-one could wish for. Always extremely cheery, always willing to help others, and his numerous other qualities combined, caused everyone to admire him, and owing to his kindly disposition and many other sterling qualities he became a great favourite in the sergeants' mess. I have never heard him spoken of except in the highest terms by anyone, and not only the platoon have lost a thoroughly competent sergeant and friend, but also the battalion. Owing to my absence in the recent attack, he was in command of the platoon, and led them to within an ace of the objective when he was struck down by a bursting shell, after having shown great courage and leadership. Please accept my sincere sympathy in your great loss.

Cpl Ewart Frederick Parfitt   *1/4th Battalion Dorsetshire Regiment*
Service No.:   202958   Age: 19
Place of birth: Salisbury, Wiltshire   Home country: England

Date of death: 13/11/17   Cause of death: Died of illness
Memorials: Salisbury, Wiltshire
                 St Mark's Church Memorial
War cemetery: Baghdad North Gate War Cemetery, Iraq
Theatre of war: Mesopotamia
Next of kin: Frank H. & Eveline A. Parfitt (parents)
Address: 12 Albany Road, Salisbury, Wiltshire

Ewart Parfitt died, probably from disease, on Tuesday 13 November 1917 in Baghdad.

Pte Bertram Frank Shergold   *A Company 1/4th Battalion Wiltshire Regiment*
Service No.:   20081   Age: 36
Place of birth: Manton, Wiltshire   Home country: England
Date of death: 13/11/17   Cause of death: Died of wounds
Memorials: Salisbury, Wiltshire
                 St Martin's Church Memorial
War cemetery: Jeruslam Memorial, Israel
Theatre of war: Egypt
Next of kin: Annie Louise Shergold (wife); William & Emma Shergold (parents)
Address: 27 Rampart Road, Salisbury, Wiltshire

Pte Shergold died of his wounds received the wounds during the action to capture the villages of El Rustinineh and El Mesmiyeh, in what was then Palestine, on Tuesday 13 November 1917. The casualty total for that day was ninety wounded and ten killed. Bertram Shergold is remembered on the Jerusalem Memorial, Israel, and has no known grave.

17 NOVEMBER 1917 – BRITISH CAPTURE JAFFA

A British tank captured by the Germans.

10

CAMBRAI

On 20 November 1918 the British mounted a surprise tank attack between the River Scarpe and St Quentin, France. This was the first time a massed tank attack had taken place and 378 machines went into action at what was to be known as the Battle of Cambrai.

2nd-Lt Harold Stokes		*E Battalion Tank Corps*		
Place of birth:	Salisbury, Wiltshire	Home country:	Dorset	Age: 25
Date of death:	20/11/17	Cause of death:	Killed in action	
War cemetery:	Cambrai Memorial, Louverval, France			
Theatre of war:	Cambrai, France			
Next of kin:	Robert & Fanny Stokes (parents)			
Address:	Laverstock, Boscombe, Bournemouth, Dorset			

2nd-Lt Harold Stokes, youngest son of Mr and Mrs Robert Stokes, of Laverstoke, Boscombe, Bournemouth, and formerly of Salisbury, was killed in action in France on Tuesday 20 November 1917. This was the first day of the Battle of Cambrai. Stokes had enlisted in 1914 and had served with the Natal Carbineers in German South West Africa. As a second lieutenant, Stokes would have commanded a tank and it is likely he was killed in action near Flequieres Ridge, south-west of Cambrai, where twenty-seven tanks were knocked out by German guns. Stokes is remembered on the Cambrai Memorial and has no known grave.

L/Cpl William Charles Hawkins		*1/4th Battalion Wiltshire Regiment*	
Service No.:	200870	Age:	25
Place of birth:	Salisbury, Wiltshire	Home country:	England
Date of death:	22/11/17	Cause of death:	Died of wounds
Memorials:	Salisbury, Wiltshire		
	St Martin's Church Memorial		
War cemetery:	Ramleh War Cemetery, Israel		
Theatre of war:	Palestine		
Next of kin:	George & Caroline Hawkins (parents)		
Address:	Salisbury, Wiltshire		

William Hawkins died of his wounds on Thursday 22 November 1917, received in action as the British Army fought their way through Palestine. He probably died in the field hospital that was based at Ramleh and was buried in the cemetery of the same name.

Pte William Henry Thring		*7th Battalion East Surrey Regiment*	
Service No.:	G/14963	Age:	28
Place of birth:	Salisbury, Wiltshire	Home country:	England
Date of death:	22/11/17	Cause of death:	Died of wounds
Memorial:	St Mark's Memorial		
War cemetery:	Tin Court New British Cemetery, France		
Theatre of war:	France		

Next of kin: Frederick William & Mary Ann Thring (parents)
Address: 2 Campbell Road, Salisbury, Wiltshire

On 20 November 1917 the 7th Battalion East Surrey Regiment were in action during the Battle of Cambrai, advancing and capturing the area east of Perrone. William Thring died of his wounds on Thursday 22 November 1917, probably suffered during fighting on the first day of the action.

Cpl John William Leahy   *14th Battalion Durham Light Infantry*
Service No.:   11246   Age: 19
Date of death: 25/11/17   Cause of death: Killed in action
Place of birth: Newcastle-upon-Tyne, Northumberland
Home country: England
Memorials: Salisbury, Wiltshire
                  St Paul's Church Memorial
War cemetery: Marcoing British Cemetery, France
Theatre of war: France
Next of kin: Regimental Quartermaster, Sgt Patrick & Mrs Florence Leahy (parents)
Address: 78 Meadow Road, Salisbury, Wiltshire

On Sunday 25 November 1917, the 14th Battalion Durham Light Infantry was in the British line between Cantaing, Noyelles and Marcoing, which lie south-west of Cambrai. Nineteen-year-old John Leahy was killed in action soon after the Germans counter-attacked. Marcoing was evacuated by the British in December 1917 and was held by the Germans until 28 September 1918.

Pte Francis Charles Badder   *1/4th Battalion Wiltshire Regiment*
Service No.:   200946   Age: 20
Place of birth: Salisbury, Wiltshire   Home country: England
Date of death: 28/11/17   Cause of death: Died of wounds
Memorials: Salisbury, Wiltshire
                  Bishop Wordsworth's School Memorial
War cemetery: Gaza War Cemetery, Israel
Theatre of war: Palestine
Next of kin: Samuel & Ellen Badder (parents)
Address: St Edmund, Salisbury, Wiltshire

When the war broke out, Pte Badder was employed in the office of Messrs Hodding & Jackson. He joined the local company of the Territorial Army, and proceeded to India. He was wounded in action during the fighting that took place at Gaza, in November 1917. He died at one of the casualty-clearing stations based in the area and was buried in the Gaza War Cemetery.

Rifleman Reginald James Clark   *12th Battalion Rifle Brigade*
Service No.:   S/33649   Age: 32
Place of birth: Salisbury, Wiltshire   Home country: Egypt
Date of death: 30/11/17   Cause of death: Killed in action
Memorials: Salisbury, Wiltshire
                  St Martin's Church Memorial
War cemetery: Cambrai Memorial, Louverval, France
Theatre of war: France
Next of kin: Millicent Clark (wife); Harry & Elizabeth Clark (parents)
Address: Rosebank, Easton, Winchester, Hampshire

On Friday 30 November 1917, the 12th Battalion Rifle Brigade were near La Vacquerie south-west of Cambrai. Reginald Clark was killed in action during this day as the Germans counterattacked in force, sweeping through the British lines and almost routing the defenders. He is remembered with over 7,000 men who died during the Battle of Cambrai on the Cambrai Memorial and has no known grave.

Pte William Reuben Morris   *2nd Battalion Wiltshire Regiment*

Service No.:	22922
Place of birth:	Idmiston, Wiltshire
Date of death:	03/12/17
Memorials:	Salisbury, Wiltshire
	St Paul's Church Memorial
War cemetery:	Hooge Crater Cemetery, Belgium
Theatre of war:	Belgium
Next of kin:	James & Fanny Morris (parents)
Address:	Idmiston, Wiltshire

Age:	25
Home country:	England
Cause of death:	Killed in action

On Monday 3 December 1917 the 2nd Battalion Wiltshire Regiment were in trenches east of Ypres. At noon the 2nd New Zealand Infantry Brigade attacked Polderhoek Chateau and the Germans retaliated by shelling the Wiltshires' support lines and causing seven casualties. One of the casualties was William Morris who was killed outright during the shelling.

Pte George Henry Saunders   *2nd Battalion Wiltshire Regiment*

Service No.:	33220
Place of birth:	Bemerton, Wiltshire
Date of death:	04/12/17
Memorials:	Salisbury, Wiltshire
	St Mark's Church Memorial
War cemetery:	Tyne Cot Cemetery, Belgium
Theatre of war:	Belgium
Next of kin:	George W. & Alice M. Saunders (parents)
Address:	Fisherton, Salisbury, Wiltshire

Age:	28
Home country:	England
Cause of death:	Killed in action

George Saunders was killed in action on Tuesday 4 December 1917, in the trenches south-east of Ypres, near Hollebeke. He fell during the afternoon under a bombardment of German trench mortars. George Saunders is remembered on the Tyne Cot Memorial and has no known grave.

L/Cpl Sydney Rowthorn   *15th Battalion London Regiment (Civil Service Rifles)*

Service No.:	532134
Place of birth:	Salisbury, Wiltshire
Date of death:	06/12/17
Memorials:	Salisbury, Wiltshire
	St Martin's Church Memorial
War cemetery:	Cambrai Memorial, Louverval, France
Theatre of war:	France
Next of kin:	Harry & Kate Rowthorn (parents)
Address:	4 Kelsey Road, Salisbury, Wiltshire

Age:	29
Home country:	England
Cause of death:	Killed in action

Sydney Rowthorn was listed as missing on 6 December 1917, during the German counterattack at the Battle of Cambrai, his unit was operating south-east of Cambrai, near

Anneux. He was the third son of Harry and Kate Rowthorn, and in late October 1918, their hopes were dashed when they received an official report. Rowthorn was presumed killed in action on or about 6 December 1917. He is remembered on the Cambrai Memorial and has no known grave.

Pte Richard Salisbury   *Royal Army Service Corps 884th Coy Mechanical*
                                                 Transport

Service No.:	M2/226823	Age:	23
Place of birth:	Sedgehill, Wiltshire	Home country:	England
Date of death:	07/12/17	Cause of death:	Died of wounds
Memorials:	Salisbury, Wiltshire		
	St Martin's Church Memorial		
War cemetery:	Dozinghem Military Cemetery, Belgium		
Theatre of war:	Belgium		
Next of kin:	Lily Salisbury (wife); Henry & Lizzie Salisbury (parents)		
Address:	52 St Ann Street, Salisbury, Wiltshire		

Pte Salisbury died of his wounds on Friday 7 December 1917 at a casualty-clearing station based at Dozinghem, Belgium. He had been attached to the XIX Corps Heavy Artillery and it is likely his wounds were received during a German bombardment on the Ypres Salient.

Pte Ernest Victor Targett   *5th Battalion Wiltshire Regiment*

Service No.:	03/9982	Age:	20
Date of death:	07/12/17	Cause of death:	Died of wounds.
Place of birth:	Morgans Vale, Wiltshire	Home country:	England
Memorials:	Salisbury, Wiltshire		
	St Martin's Church Memorial		
War cemetery:	Baghdad North Gate, Iraq		
Theatre of war:	Mesopotamia		
Next of kin:	Henry G. & Kate Targett (parents)		
Address:	Salisbury, Wiltshire		

At 6.45 a.m. on Wednesday 5 December 1917 the 5th Battalion Wiltshire Regiment crossed the River Nahrin with orders to attack the Turkish position at Kara Tepe. The War Diary states: 'The attack was carried out in splendid style, the men going forward with great dash over most difficult country and driving the enemy from successive ridges in irresistible fashion.' Twenty-year-old Ernest Targett died of his wounds on Friday 7 December 1917, received during the action at Kara Tepe. He was probably wounded by shrapnel during the advance.

9 DECEMBER 1917 – JERUSALEM SURRENDERS TO BRITISH FORCES

Guardsman Thomas Francis Witt   *1st Battalion Grenadier Guards*

Service No.:	29253	Age:	19
Place of birth:	Fyfield, Hampshire	Home country:	England
Date of death:	13/12/17	Cause of death:	Died of wounds
Memorials:	Salisbury, Wiltshire		
	St Mark's Memorial		
War cemetery:	St Sever Cemetery Extension, Rouen, France		

Theatre of war: France
Next of kin: Thomas & Fanny Witt (parents)
Address: 21 Park Street, Salisbury, Wiltshire

Nineteen-year-old Tom Witt was the eldest son of Thomas and Fanny Witt. He died on Thursday 13 December 1917, at the hospital centre of Rouen, most likely from wounds received at the Battle of Cambrai. His parents' thoughts can be felt in these words: 'We do not know what pain he bore; we never saw him die; we only know he passed away; and never said goodbye.'

Capt. Christopher Ken Merewether   *1/4th Battalion Wiltshire Regiment*
Place of birth: North Bradley, Wiltshire   Home country: England   Age: 27
Date of death: 19/12/17   Cause of death: Died of wounds
Memorials: Salisbury, Wiltshire
                  St Thomas Church Memorial
War cemetery: Port Said War Memorial Cemetery, Egypt
Theatre of war: Palestine
Next of kin: Canon Wyndham Arthur Seinde Merewether & Harriot Edith Merewether
                  (parents)
Address: Langton House, Salisbury, Wiltshire

News reached Salisbury at the end of November 1917 that Capt. C.K. Merewether of the Wiltshire Regiment had been dangerously wounded in Palestine. Capt. Merewether, who was in command of the Bradford-on-Avon company of the Wiltshire Territorials before the war, was employed in connection with the White Star Line, Liverpool, when war broke out and he joined his regiment and proceeded to India, where he commanded two companies that included many men from the neighbourhood of Salisbury and Wilton. He was wounded in the fighting about Katrah and Mughar on 13 November and was subsequently admitted to Kantara Hospital, from where he was transferred to the 31st General Hospital at Port Said. He was reported dangerously wounded in the right shoulder and spine and on Monday 26 November 1917, news was received stated that his condition was still grave, but that he was cheerful and had practically no pain.

Capt. Christopher Ken Merewether, of the Wiltshire Regiment, died on Wednesday 19 December 1917 of wounds received in action, was born at North Bradley Vicarage on 26 May 1890, the only son of Revd W.E.S. Merewether, vicar of St Thomas's, Salisbury and grandson of the late Henry Alworth Merewether, Q.C., of Bowden Hill, Chippenham – formerly chairman of the Wiltshire Quarter Sessions and Recorder of Devizes. Merewether was educated at St Aubyn's, Rottingdean, and Winchester College, where he was in the Senior Division Sixth Book, and head of his house (Revd J.T. Branston's). Matriculating at Oriel College, Oxford, he took Honours in Modern History and upon leaving the university, was selected by the directors of the White Star Line of Liverpool for training as an assistant manager. Having passed through the Officer Training Corps at Winchester, he was appointed to the command of the Bradford-on-Avon half company of the Wiltshire Territorials. On the outbreak of war he left his appointment with the White Star Company and joined the Wiltshire Regiment, with which he served continuously from August 1914 until his death. He took a prominent place in all school games, played for his college XI, was a member of the Vincent's and the Authentic's Cricket Club, and at hockey represented Oxford University against Cambridge. He was an original member of the Cavendish Club, London.

Pte Ernest William Best   *6th Battalion Wiltshire Regiment*
Service No.:   204053   Age: 23
Place of birth: Salisbury, Wiltshire   Home country: England
Date of death: 23/12/17

Left: *The cross that marked the grave of Capt. Christopher Ken Merewether now hangs in the cloisters at Salisbury Cathedral.*

Above: *Capt. Merewether sitting 8th from left. (Photograph courtesy Wiltshire Military Museum, Wardrobe)*

Far left: *Portrait of Capt. Merewether. (Photograph courtesy Wiltshire Military Museum, Wardrobe)*

Left: *Capt. Christopher Ken Merewether was seriously wounded during the 1st/4th Battalion Wiltshire Regiment's attack at El Mesmiyeh on 13 November 1917. Evacuated to Port Said, Merewether died of his wounds a week later. He was described by his men as 'Our gallant Captain'. (Photograph courtesy Wiltshire Military Museum, Wardrobe)*

Memorial: Salisbury, Wiltshire
War cemetery: Ribecourt Road Cemetery, Trescault, France
Theatre of war: France

Ernest Best died, most likely of illness or disease, the day before Christmas Eve, Sunday 23 December 1917, in the area of Trescault village, south-west of Cambrai.

Pte Harry George Hart   *5th Battalion Wiltshire Regiment*
Service No.:   25812   Age: 32
Place of birth: Longham, Dorset   Home country: England
Date of death: 25/12/17   Cause of death: Died of illness
Memorials: Salisbury, Wiltshire
                 St Mark's Church Memorial
War cemetery: Kirkee 1914–18 Memorial, India
Theatre of war: Mesopotamia
Next of kin: Bessie Hart (wife)
Address: 69 Park Street, Salisbury, Wiltshire
Next of kin: John & Mary S. Hart (parents)

Harry Hart had married Bessie Smith in the summer of 1915 in Salisbury. Two years later was he evacuated from Mesopotamia due to illness and died in India on Christmas Day, Tuesday 25 December 1917. He is remembered on the Kirkee 1914–18 Memorial, India.

L/Cpl Francis Henry Smith   *Royal Military Police Military Foot Police*
Service No.:   P/3075   Age: 40
Place of birth: Upavon, Wiltshire   Home country: England
Date of death: 27/12/17   Cause of death: Died of illness
Memorials: Salisbury, Wiltshire
                   St Paul's Church Memorial
War cemetery: Cairo War Memorial Cemetery, Egypt
Theatre of war: Egypt
Next of kin: Henry Oram & Jane Smith (parents)
Address: Netheravon, Wiltshire

Francis Smith, the second son of Henry Oram and Jane Smith, died of pneumonia at the military hospital in Cairo on Thursday 27 December 1917.

Pte Bertram Arthur Heath   *15th Battalion London Regiment (Civil Service Rifles)*
Service No.:   532878   Age: 23
Place of birth: Guildford, Surrey   Home country: England
Date of death: 27/12/17   Cause of death: Killed in action
Memorials: Salisbury, Wiltshire
                   St Thomas Church Memorial & St Mark's Church Memorial
War cemetery: Jerusalem War Cemetery, Israel
Theatre of war: Palestine
Next of kin: Quarter Master Sgt Alfred & Annie Maria Heath (parents)
Address: 2 Queens Road, Salisbury, Wiltshire

In mid-January 1915 news was received in Salisbury that Pte Bertram Arthur Heath, London Regiment (Civil Service Rifles), youngest son of Mrs Heath, 2 Queen's Road, Salisbury, was killed in action on Thursday 27 December 1917. Deep sympathy was felt for Mrs Heath and the members of the family in this, the second bereavement sustained by them during the war. Ernest Heath, one of two sons, who had belonged to the 'old army' and fought at Mons, had been killed in September 1914. Pte Bertram Heath had fought in France and was then transferred to the Salonika front, where he took part in engagements around Monastir. Heath then proceeded to Palestine, where he was killed. He was a Lewis machine-gunner. Three brothers were serving in France at this time.

Capt. William Walter Morrice   *3rd Battalion Wiltshire Regiment*
Place of birth: Longbridge Deverill, Wiltshire   Home country: England   Age: 37
Date of death: 30/12/17   Cause of death: Killed in action
Memorial: Salisbury, Wiltshire
War cemetery: Rocquigny Equancourt Road British Cemetery, Mananco, France
Theatre of war: France
Next of kin: Cannon John David & Jessie Fenton Morrice
Address: St Edmunds Rectory, Salisbury, Wiltshire

In January 1918, news reached Salisbury that Capt. William Walter Morrice, Wiltshire Regiment, attached to the Labour Corps, was killed in action on Saturday 30 December 1917. Capt. Morrice, thirty-seven, was educated at Connaught House, Weymouth and at Rossall, subsequently was a scholar at Clare College, Cambridge. He was articled to the late Mr R.A. Malden of Salisbury. He obtained a commission in the Wilts Regiment in 1915, and was in command of a Labour Company in France. Canon and Mrs Morrice had another son, a captain in the ASC, MT, serving in Palestine.

11
1918

Gunner Charles William Horton   *B Battery 285th Brigade Royal Field Artillery*

Service No.:	65233	Age:	29
Place of birth:	West Harnham, Wiltshire	Home country:	England
Date of death:	12/01/18	Cause of death:	Killed in action
Memorial:	Salisbury, Wiltshire		
War cemetery:	Anzac Cemetery, Sailly Sur La Lys, France		
Theatre of war:	France.		
Next of kin:	William & Emily Horton (parents)		
Address:	West Harnham, Salisbury, Wiltshire		

Charles was killed in action on Saturday 12 January 1918 probably due to German shell fire in the area around Bethune, France. He is buried in the Anzac Cemetery, Sailly Sur La Lys, France, named after the Australian units which began to use the area to bury fallen soldiers in July 1916.

Pte Ernest James Evemy   *24th Battalion Manchester Regiment*

Service No.:	55356	Age:	29
Place of birth:	Leamington Spa, Warwickshire	Home country:	England
Date of death:	14/01/18	Cause of death:	Died of illness
Memorials:	Salisbury, Wiltshire		
	St Mark's Church Memorial		
War cemetery:	Altivole Communal Cemetery, Italy		
Theatre of war:	Italy		
Next of kin:	Annie Evemy (wife); William J. & Emma Evemy (parents)		
Addresses:	79 Park Street Salisbury, Wiltshire		
	Milford Hill, Salisbury, Wiltshire		

Commonwealth forces were sent to Italy in November 1917 to aid the Italian forces fighting the Austrians in the north of the country. Ernest Evemy had originally joined the Devonshire Regiment, but was transferred to the 24th Battalion Manchester Regiment. He died after a few hours of illness on Monday 14 January 1918 at a field hospital near Altivole, north-west of Treviso, Italy.

Pte Alfred George Foreman   *6th Battalion Wiltshire Regiment*

Service No.:	204162	Age:	21
Place of birth:	Salisbury, Wiltshire	Home country:	England
Date of death:	14/01/18	Cause of death:	Died of illness
Memorials:	Salisbury, Wiltshire		
	St Paul's Church Memorial & St Martin's Church Memorial		
War cemetery:	Rocquigny Equancourt Road British Cemetery, Mananco, France		
Theatre of war:	France		
Next of kin:	Samuel & Emma Foreman (parents)		
Address:	Salisbury, Wiltshire		

Twenty-one-year-old Alfred Foreman died, most likely of illness, on Monday 14 January 1918 at a casualty-clearing station between the villages of Rocquigny and Equancourt, north of Peronne, France.

Pte William Goodfellow		*2nd Battalion Coldstream Guards*	
Service No.:	212120	Age:	33
Place of birth:	Harnham, Wiltshire	Home country:	England
Date of death:	16/01/18	Cause of death:	Killed in action
Memorials:	Salisbury, Wiltshire		
	St Martin's Church Memorial		
War cemetery:	Fampoux British Cemetery, France		
Theatre of war:	France		
Next of kin:	Mrs A. Goodfellow (wife); William & Mary Goodfellow (parents)		
Address:	38 Milford Street, Salisbury, Wiltshire		
	East Harnham, Salisbury, Wiltshire		

In late January 1918 William Goodfellow's wife received the news that he had been killed in action on Wednesday 16 January 1916. He was serving with the 2nd Battalion Coldstream Guards, which he had joined in January 1917 and had been on active service for about three months. He was well known in football circles, having played for Salisbury and also for Croydon Common in the Southern League. He fell in the area around Arras. He left a widow and child in Salisbury.

> The call was short the shock severe
> To part with one we loved so dear
> Our hopes in Heaven that we may meet
> And then our joy will be complete

Pte Arthur Edward Butt		*6th Battalion Wiltshire Regiment.*	
Service No.:	204055	Age:	20
Place of birth:	Salisbury, Wiltshire	Home country:	England
Date of death:	22/01/18	Cause of death:	Killed in action
Memorial:	Salisbury, Wiltshire		
War cemetery:	Thiepval Memorial, France		
Theatre of war:	France		
Next of kin:	Albert Thomas & Eva Beatta Butt (parents)		
Address:	8 Bridge Street, Salisbury, Wiltshire		

In the first week of February 1918, Mr and Mrs Thomas Butt, of 8 Bridge Street, were officially informed that their eldest son, Pte Arthur Butt, had been killed on post duty on Tuesday 22 January 1918, within a week of his return from home leave. Pte Butt joined the Yeomanry early in the war and after training at home was drafted to an infantry battalion in France. His parents learnt of his death through a letter from a comrade received on 29 January, the twenty-first anniversary of their son's birth. He was killed during German shelling near the Hindenburg Line, France, and he is remembered on the Thiepval Memorial and has no known grave.

Pte Robert J. Warren		*24th Battalion London Regiment*			
Service No.:	721573	Home country:	England	Age:	22
Date of death:	22/01/18	Cause of death:	Died of wounds		
War cemetery:	Salisbury (Devizes Road) Cemetery, England				
Theatre of war:	Home				

Above: *British troops in Italy.*

Right: *Robert Warren, who died of his wounds.*

Pte R.J. Warren, London Regiment, died in the Salisbury Infirmary on Tuesday 22 January 1918. Warren was twenty-two years of age and was wounded in France and came to Salisbury by convoy. The funeral took place at the Devizes Road Cemetery on the afternoon of Friday 25 January 1918, Revd D. Macperson, rector of Nunton and Odstock, officiating. The coffin, covered with a Union Jack, was borne on a gun carriage drawn by six horses of a Reserve Brigade, R.H.A., Bulford, and the firing party was provided by the Hampshire Regiment. After the committal, three volleys were fired and the bugler sounded the *Last Post*.

Pte John Edward Peters		*1st Battalion Australian Infantry Australian Imperial Force*	
Service No.:	7550	Age:	31
Date of death:	27/01/18	Cause of death:	Died of illness
Home country:	Australia		
War cemetery:	Salisbury (London Road) Cemetery, England		
Theatre of war:	Home		
Next of kin:	Henrietta Peters (wife)		
Address:	1 Thynnes Court, St John Street, Salisbury, Wiltshire		

On Tuesday 29 January 1918 the funeral took place of John Peters, who died the previous Sunday at the Isolation Hospital in Salisbury of Cerebro Spinal Meningitis. He had enlisted at Orange, New South Wales, on 29 April 1917 and was the husband of Hettie Peters. The coffin was borne on a gun carriage and was accompanied by the band of the 1st Training Battalion, Australian Imperial Force.

The internment took place at the London Road Cemetery, Salisbury, in the Roman Catholic section. The ceremony was conducted by Chaplain O'Hare, and three volleys were fired at the grave side and the *Last Post* was sounded. Pte Peters was a most popular presence amongst his comrades.

After John's death, his wife Hettie asked for his personal effects and medals to be sent to her, but she moved to different towns in Australia and, in 1920, left for a new life with her child in England. In 1935 she wrote the following letter:

11 Waters Road
Salisbury
Wilts
Dear Sirs

Far left: *The original private memorial to John Peters.*

Middle: *The Commonwealth War Graves headstone for John Peters.*

Left: *William Leaver died at the Royal Naval Hospital, Haslar.*

When leaving Sydney in 1920 I was told that the badge would be sent in England, but it has not arrived yet. It is the only medal I got of my late husband, John Edward Peters 7550, 1st Battalion AIF. I would like it for my child's sake. I though it would have been here by now.

Thanking you

Yours Truly
Hettie Peters.

Chief Stoker William Charles Leaver   *Royal Navy HMS* Vernon
Service No.:   141283   Age: 54
Place of birth: Salisbury, Wiltshire   Home country: England
Date of death: 28/01/18
                  Bishop Wordsworth's School Memorial
War cemetery: Salisbury (Devizes Road) Cemetery, England
Theatre of war: Home
Next of kin: The late William & Elizabeth Leaver (parents)
Address: Fisherton, Salisbury, Wiltshire

Leaver died at the Royal Naval Hospital, Haslar, Gosport, on Monday 28 January 1918. He was the only son of the late William Leaver of Wilton Road and Bemerton, Salisbury. He was interred at the Salisbury (Devizes Road) Cemetery on 1 February 1918. He had a long career in the Navy and had been awarded the Long Service and Good Conduct Medal.

Lt Harold Sidney Rogers   *Royal Naval Volunteer Reserve HM Trawler*
                                                     Remindo
Home country: England   Age: 36
Date of death: 02/02/18   Cause of death: Killed in action
Memorial: St Mark's Church Memorial
War cemetery: Chatham Naval Memorial, England
Theatre of war: At sea
Next of kin: Helena May Rogers (wife); Herbert & Grace Mary Rogers (parents)
Addresses: 5 Harvey Road Boscombe, Bournemouth, Dorset
                  Westgate-on-Sea

Far left: Tom Speechly, victim of an air accident.

Left: American Luke Brennan, who was killed in a flying accident near Stalbrigde, Dorset.

During the First World War, trawlers were used to sweep for sea mines. Lt Rogers was killed in action on Saturday 2 February 1918 when HM Trawler *Remindo* sank after an explosion, which was likely to have been a mine.

2nd-Lt Tom Martindale Speechly   *Royal Flying Corps*
Place of birth: Uttoxeter, Staffordshire   Age: 20
Home country: England   Date of death: 08/02/18
War cemetery: Salisbury (London Road) Cemetery, England
Theatre of war: Home
Next of kin: Tom Burge & Jessie Speechly (parents)
Address: Uttoxeter, Staffordshire

On Friday 8 February 1918 four aircraft took off from Old Sarum Airfield, on a planned flight to Warminster-Trowbridge-Chippenham-Swindon and then return to Old Sarum. The flyers were with an instructor who was teaching the young pilots to fly in formation. Tom Speechly's plane was on the left and he had been flying well until they reached Chippenham, where he had too much speed on and, instead of throttling back, he zig-zagged the machine to lessen the speed. The planes had been ordered to fly 100ft apart, but it seemed Tom Speechly lost control and flew in front of one of the other aircraft and his machine was struck by its propeller, just behind the observer's seat. The aircraft had been flying at about 6,000ft and after the collision, Tom Speechly's plane went into a spin, disappearing through the clouds. Speechly had been flying with a passenger, Air Mechanic Greenlay, and the machine crashed 3 miles from Chippenham at Sutton Lane. The pilot was killed in the impact and his air mechanic was found two fields away. Both men received what was described as frightful injuries, and death was instantaneous.

Speechly had originally joined the Canadian Mounted Rifles on 8 December 1914 at the age of sixteen and lied about his age. He had alredy served at Ypres in Belgium when he transferred to the Royal Flying Corps.

Leading Seaman Albert Stephen F. Gay   *Royal Navy HMS* Cullist
Service No.:   235675   Age: 28
Place of birth: Winchester, Hampshire   Home country: England
Date of death: 11/02/18
Decorations: Distinguished Service Medal
Memorial: Salisbury, Wiltshire

War cemetery: Portsmouth Naval Memorial, England
Theatre of war: At sea
Next of kin: Lucy Emily Gay; Robert & Minnie Gay (parents)
Address: Buckland, Faringdon, Berkshire
                Winchester, Hampshire

Albert Gay was drowned on Monday 11 February 1917 when HMS *Cullist*, an armed admiralty store carrier, was sunk of the coast of Ireland by a German U–boat. Albert Gay was mentioned in dispatches and was awarded the Distinguished Service Medal. He is remembered on the Portsmouth Naval Memorial.

2nd-Lt Lester Luke Brennan   *99th Squadron Royal Flying Corps*
Place of birth: Minneapolis, United States   Age: 25
Date of death: 25/02/18   Cause of death: Accidental
Home country: United States of America
War cemetery: Salisbury (London Road) Cemetery, England
Next of kin: Mr & Mrs L.T. Brennan (parents)
Address: 1406 Fremont Avenue North, Minneapolis, Minnesota

Lester was a part of the American draft to raise men to fight in Europe. He had been a business manager with the Walker Stephone Opera Company. He arrived in England and transferred to the Royal Flying Corps. He was killed in a flying accident in the Stockbridge area on Monday 25 February 1918.

Ordinary Telegraphist George James Thomas Sanger   *Royal Navy HM Submarine D3*
Service No.:   J/42592   Age: 18
Place of birth: Salisbury, Wiltshire   Home country: England
Date of death: 15/03/18   Cause of death: At sea
Memorial: Salisbury, Wiltshire
War cemetery: Chatham Naval Memorial, England
Theatre of war: At sea
Next of kin: Thomas Sanger (father)
Address: Wishford, Salisbury, Wiltshire

ROYAL FLYING CORPS.

RECRUITS, SKILLED or UNSKILLED (the latter must be Clerks, Storemen, &c.). Men of almost any occupation are wanted at once for the various Branches of the Royal Flying Corps.

Men of military age and up to fifty years of age accepted.

Corps rates of pay.

Apply personally, or in writing, to the nearest Recruiting Officer who will put applicants into touch with the Special Recruiting Officer of the Royal Flying Corps in this District.

GOD SAVE THE KING.   [2296]

Advert for the Royal Flying Corps, accepting recruits up to the age of fifty. On 1 April 1918 the Royal Air Force was formed.

Above: *Advert for the Army Service Corps.*

Right: *Walter Bennett, a member of the Royal Defence Corps.*

Eighteen-year-old George Sanger was a member of the crew of the British Submarine D3, which set off from Gosport on 7 March 1918 to patrol the English Channel. A French airship AT-o was on patrol and spotted a submarine. The French commander stated that the submarine fired rockets at the airship. In reply the French dropped four bombs, the submarine disappeared and after a short time men were seen in the water. By the time a rescue vessel arrived all the men had drowned. It was found that the men came from HM Submarine D3, the identification rockets set off by the British had been mistaken for gun fire by the French.

George Sanger is remembered on the Chatham Naval Memorial; he died at sea.

2nd-Lt William Everett Sinclair		*Royal Air Force*		
Place of birth:	Derby, Canada	Home country:	Canada	Age: 21
Date of death:	15/03/18	Cause of death:	Accidental	
War cemetery:	Salisbury (London Road) Cemetery, England			
Next of kin:	Donald Alexander & Laura Belle Sinclair (parents)			
Address:	84 Furby Street, Winnipeg			

Twenty-one-year-old William Sinclair was killed in a flying accident in the Salisbury area on Friday 15 March 1918. Official records state he was a member of the Royal Air Force; if this is the case, he must be regarded as one of their first casualties as the RAF was formed on 1 April 1918.

Pte Walter W. Bennett		*157th Protection Company Royal Defence Corps*	
Service No.:	62187	Age:	51
Place of birth:	Glastonbury, Somerset	Home country:	England
Date of death:	20/03/18	Cause of death:	Died of illness
Memorials:	Salisbury, Wiltshire		
	St Paul's Church Memorial		
War cemetery:	Salisbury (Devizes Road) Cemetery, England		
Theatre of war:	Home		
Next of kin:	Edith Bennett (wife)		
Address:	8 Brandon Cottages, Highfield, Devizes Road, Salisbury, Wiltshire		

Walter Bennett was a member of the Royal Defence Force Corps, formed in August 1917. It came into being to replace garrison battalions and was composed of older soldiers or those who were medically unfit. Bennett had formerly been a member of the Gloucester Regiment and he died, most likely of Illness, in Salisbury, on Wednesday 20 March 1918.

12

KAISERSCHLACT

Pte Charles Munday   *10th Battalion Royal Fusiliers*

Service No.:	53217	Age:	35
Place of birth:	Salisbury, Wiltshire	Home country:	England
Date of death:	21/03/18	Cause of death:	Killed in action
Memorial:	Salisbury, Wiltshire		
War cemetery:	The Huts Cemetery, Belgium		
Theatre of war:	Belgium		
Next of kin:	Alice Maria Munday (wife); Robert & Sarah Munday (parents)		
Addresses:	38 Rampart Road, Salisbury, Wiltshire		
	Shrewton, Wiltshire		

Charles Munday had originally joined the Royal Army Service Corps but was transferred to the 10th Battalion Royal Fusiliers, probably due to a lack of replacements for the infantry units. On Thursday 21 March 1918 the Germans launched their Spring Offensive with a bombardment followed by Storm troops who had been trained to penetrate the frontline and advance quickly through the British and French rear and communication trenches. Munday was killed in action along with nearly one hundred other members of the 10th Battalion Royal Fusiliers. He is buried at the Huts Cemetery, Dikkebus, Belgium.

Pte Sidney Harry Scammell   *1st Battalion Wiltshire Regiment*

Service No.:	26160	Age:	41
Place of birth:	Salisbury, Wiltshire	Home country:	England
Date of death:	21/03/18	Cause of death:	Killed in action
Memorial:	Salisbury, Wiltshire		
War cemetery:	Arras Memorial, France		
Theatre of war:	France		
Next of kin:	Ibena Martha Scammell (wife); Edwin & Maria Scammell (parents)		
Addresses:	83 Montagu Street, Swindon, Wiltshire		
	135 Castle Street, Salisbury, Wiltshire		

The Germans had commenced their Spring Offensive at 4.40 a.m. on Thursday 21 March 1918, and bombarded the British frontline and rear areas. The 1st Battalion Wiltshire Regiment were at camp at Achiet le Grand, north-east of the town of Bapaume. At 5 a.m. the Germans started to bombard the railway station at Achiet le Grand, with large-calibre, high-velocity shells. One of the shells fell within the Wiltshires' camp, causing fifty-seven casualties. One of the casualties was Sidney Scammell; he is remembered on the Arras Memorial and has no known grave.

British Artillery in action at Pozieres, France.

Sgt Herbert Job Weeks   *2nd Battalion Wiltshire Regiment*

Service No.:	27035	Age:	36
Place of birth:	Salisbury, Wiltshire	Home country:	England
Date of death:	21/03/18	Cause of death:	Killed in action
Memorial:	Salisbury, Wiltshire		
War cemetery:	Pozieres Memorial, France		
Theatre of war:	France		
Next of kin:	Job & Emily H. Weeks (parents)		
Address:	St Edmund, Salisbury, Wiltshire		

On Thursday 21 March 1918 the 2nd Battalion Wiltshire Regiment were in trenches east of Ham, south-east of Peronne. At 4.30 a.m. the German offensive began with a bombardment consisting of high-explosive and gas shells. At 10 a.m., with the aid of a dense mist, the Germans broke through the British line and the 2nd Battalion Wiltshire Regiment found themselves surrounded. At 1.30 p.m. news was received via a carrier pigeon from Lt Col. Martin to the effect that he was still holding out in a redoubt with about fifty men. Herbert Weeks was killed in action during the German advance, he is remembered on the Pozieres Memorial and has no known grave. Weeks's brother, Arthur Reginald Weeks, was killed in action at the Somme in September 1916.

Pte James Blake   *Royal Army Medical Corps 8th Field Ambulance*

Service No.:	3263	Age:	30
Place of birth:	Bishop's Down, Wiltshire	Home country:	Wales
Date of death:	21/03/18	Cause of death:	Killed in action
Memorial:	St Martin's Church Memorial		
War cemetery:	Arras Memorial, France		
Theatre of war:	France		
Next of kin:	Jenny Blake (wife)		
Address:	Cardiff, Glamorganshire		

James Blake had lived in Salisbury prior to the First World War and he was killed in action on the first day of the German Spring Offensive. He is remembered on the Arras Memorial and has no known grave.

Lt Arthur Frowde Dickinson

		14th Battalion Northumberland Fusiliers		
Place of birth:	Brockley, London	Home country: England	Age:	22
Date of death:	22/03/18	Cause of death: Killed in action		
Memorials:	Salisbury, Wiltshire			
	St Thomas Church Memorial			
War cemetery:	Pozieres Memorial, France			
Theatre of war:	France			
Next of kin:	Arthur H. & Blanche E. Dickinson (parents)			
Address:	Fisherton Street, Salisbury, Wiltshire			

Lt Arthur Frowd Dickinson, son of Mr and Mrs A.H. Dickinson of 52 Fisherton Street, was killed in action on Friday 22 March 1918 on the Western Front. He was educated at Bishop's Wordsworth's School, and spent some years in the London City and Midland Bank. He joined the Wiltshire Yeomanry in August 1914 and after training, served with a dismounted unit in France. Dickinson was given a commission in the Northumberland Fusiliers. He was mentioned in despatches.

Lt Dickinson's commanding officer wrote to Mrs Dickinson, stating:

It is with the deepest regret that I write to tell you of your son's death. I know full well that no words of mine can ameliorate your loss, but I can tell you that he died , as he had lived, with the utmost gallantry. His death was instantaneous and in the thick of one of the strongest attacks the German's have yet launched, an attack which he and his company met in the most splendid way. Your son was beloved by all, and his unfailing cheerfulness and ready wit, as well as his soldierly qualities, were a great asset to his battalion. I shall personally miss him very much as I have seen a great deal of him both on parade and off. He was a son to be proud of, and I wish it had pleased providence to spare him.

Much sympathy was given to Mr and Mrs Dickinson, who had another son serving in the East.

Pte Frederick James Bennett

		6th Battalion Wiltshire Regiment	
Service No.:	203229	Age:	23
Place of birth:	Downton, Wiltshire	Home country: England	
Date of death:	22/03/18	Cause of death: Died of wounds	
Memorial:	Salisbury, Wiltshire		
War cemetery:	Queant Road Cemetery, Buissy, France		
Theatre of war:	France		

On the second day of the German Spring Offensive, the 6th Battalion Wiltshire Regiment were at the sugar beet factory on the Bapaume to Cambrai road, south of the village of Morchies. It is likely Frederick Bennett died of his wounds and was buried in this area, and his remains were moved to the cemetery of Buissy at the end of the conflict.

Pte Alfred Edward Curtis

		59th Battalion Yorkshire Light Infantry	
Service No.:	44012	Age:	42
Place of birth:	Portsmouth, Hampshire	Home country: England	
Date of death:	22/03/18	Cause of death: Killed in action	
Memorials:	Salisbury, Wiltshire	Theatre of war: France	
	St Martin's Church Memorial		
War cemetery:	Pozieres Memorial, France		
Next of kin:	William Lucius & Harriet Elizabeth Curtis (parents)		
Address:	101 St Andrews Road, Southsea, Hampshire		

Left: *British soldiers in the trenches.*

Above: *The site of some First World War trenches today.*

Alfred Curtis was killed on the second day of the German Spring Offensive, south of Marcoing. He is remembered on the Poziers Memorial and has no known grave.

L/Cpl Herbert Harrison	*6th Battalion Wiltshire Regiment*
Service No.: 203204	Age: 23
Place of birth: Salisbury, Wiltshire	Home country: England
Date of death: 23/03/18	Cause of death: Killed in action

Memorials: Salisbury, Wiltshire.
                 Bishop Wordsworth's School Memorial & St Mark's Church Memorial.
War cemetery: Arras Memorial, France
Theatre of war: France
Next of kin: Percy & Alice Harrison (parents)
Address: 99 Park Street, Salisbury, Wiltshire

On the third day of the German offensive, the 6th Battalion Wiltshire Regiment were surrounded at the sugar beet factory on the Bapaume to Cambrai road, south of the village of Morchies. It is likely Herbert Harrison died at this place. He is remembered on the Arras Memorial and has no known grave.

Pte Archibald Frank Burt	*1st Battalion Wiltshire Regiment*
Service No.: 33305	Age: 20
Place of birth: Salisbury, Wiltshire	Home country: England
Date of death: 24/03/18	Cause of death: Killed in action

Memorial: Salisbury, Wiltshire
War cemetery: Arras Memorial, France
Theatre of war: France
Next of kin: Henry Frank & Emma Jane Burt (parents)
Address: 18 Ashfield Road, Salisbury, Wiltshire

On the morning of Sunday 24 March 1918 the 1st battalion Wiltshire Regiment were in the trenches east of Achiet le Grand. Subjected to German shelling throughout the day, the British guns retaliated but a considerable amount of friendly shells fell short, causing several casualties. During the afternoon there was an intensive bombardment by the Germans who attacked at around 4 p.m. but it was repulsed on the Wiltshires' front. Shortly after this the Wiltshires were ordered to retire, however, the supporting battalions on the right flank broke and retired leaving the Wiltshires' forward companies in an exposed position. The War Diary describes the consequences: 'They attempted to come back as ordered but were practically exterminated by machine-gun fire.' When the 1st Battalion Wiltshire regiment returned to Achiet le Petit they numbered fifty-seven, the casualties suffered during the fighting since 21 March 1918 were 413. One of these casualties was Archibald Burt, who killed in action on 24 March 1918. He is remembered on the Arras Memorial and has no known grave.

Archibald Burt was the second son of Henry and Emma Burt; all they knew at the time was that their son had fallen somewhere in France.

> Safely safely gathered in
> No more sorrow, No more Sin
> Him God called from weary strife
> In his dawn this young bright life

L/Cpl Charles Hall

Service No.:	22236	

Place of birth: Harnham, Wiltshire
Date of death: 24/03/18
Decorations: Military Medal
Memorial: Salisbury, Wiltshire
War cemetery: Arras Memorial, France
Theatre of war: France
Next of kin: Harry & Mary Hall (parents)
Address: Salisbury, Wiltshire

1st Battalion Wiltshire Regiment
Age: 20
Home country: England
Cause of death: Killed in action

L/Cpl Hall was killed in action on Sunday 24 March 1918 (see Archibald Burt). He is remembered on the Arras Memorial and has no known grave.

Sgt Harry Musselwhite

Service No.: 14262
Place of birth: Homington, Wiltshire
Date of death: 24/03/18
Memorial: Salisbury, Wiltshire
War cemetery: Pozieres Memorial, France
Theatre of war: France
Next of kin: Henry & Mary A. Musselwhite (parents)
Address: 25 Milford Street, Salisbury, Wiltshire

3rd Dragoon Guards
Age: 38
Home country: England
Cause of death: Killed in action

Harry Musselwhite had a long career in the Army and from 1901 he was a member of the 6th Dragoon Guards. He was killed in action on the third day of the German Spring Offensive. He is remembered on the Pozieres Memorial and has no known grave.

Pte Walter Usher

Service No.: 33132
Place of birth: Salisbury, Wiltshire
Date of death: 24/03/18
Memorial: Salisbury, Wiltshire

2/4th Battalion Oxfordshire and Buckinghamshire Light Infantry
Age: 28
Home country: England
Cause of death: Died of wounds

War cemetery: St Souplet British Cemetery, France
Theatre of war: France
Next of kin: William & Elizabeth Usher (parents)
Address: 79 Castle Street, Salisbury, Wiltshire

In May 1918 William and Elizabeth Usher received official intimation that their son Walter Usher was posted as missing on 21 March 1918. It was not until some time later that they found their son had died of head wounds at a field hospital at St Quentin on 24 March 1918.

Pte William Charles Veck   *3rd Battalion Worcestershire Regiment*
Service No.:   23683   Age: 20
Place of birth: Salisbury, Wiltshire   Home country: England
Date of death: 24/03/18   Cause of death: Killed in action
Memorials: Salisbury, Wiltshire
                  St Martin's Church Memorial
War cemetery: Ontario Cemetery, Sains Les Marquion, France
Theatre of war: France
Next of kin: Mary Veck (mother)
Address: St Edmund, Salisbury, Wiltshire

William Veck was killed in action on Sunday 24 March 1918, during the German Spring Offensive. His battalion were being used to reinforce the lines at the Bapaume to Cambrai road. He is buried at Sains Les Marquion, which, on the date of his death, was in German hands. It is likely his remains were moved into the cemetery after the end of the war.

Pte Theodore Frank Tudgay   *7th Battalion Somerset Light Infantry*
Service No.:   28994   Age: 19
Place of birth: Salisbury, Wiltshire   Home country: England

Above: *Henry Lund Eaton.*

Left: *British prisoners of war captured during a German offensive.*

Date of death: 26/03/18   Cause of death: Killed in action
Memorial: Salisbury, Wiltshire
War cemetery: Foreste Communal Cemetery, France
Theatre of war: France
Next of kin: William & Eliza Tudgay (parents)
Address: 7 Husseys Almshouses, Castle Street, Salisbury, Wiltshire

Theodore Tudgay was killed in action during the first few days of the German offensive west of St Quetin, most likely in the action at Rosieres en Stanterre, along with three other members of the 7th Battalion Somerset Light Infantry.

Mr Henry Lund Eaton   *Australian Munitions Worker*
Home country: Australia   Age: 42
Date of death: 26/03/18
War cemetery: Salisbury (Devizes Road) Cemetery, England

Henry Lund was an Australian munitions worker who had come to Salisbury because of the war. He died on 26 March 1918 in Salisbury.

L/Cpl Frederick Witt   *6th Battalion Wiltshire Regiment*
Service No.:   21269   Age: 31
Place of birth: Bickton, Hampshire   Home country: England
Date of death: 27/03/18   Cause of death: Killed in action
Memorials: Salisbury, Wiltshire
                   St Martin's Church Memorial
War cemetery: Arras Memorial, France
Theatre of war: France
Next of kin: Harry Witt (father)
Address: Fryern Court, Fordingbridge, Hampshire

Frederick Witt was killed in action on Wednesday 27 March 1918 in the area around the villages of Hebuterne, Fonqvillers and Bayencourt, west of Bapaume. During the previous days the 6th Battalion Wiltshire Regiment had withdrawn from the east of Bapaume, the Germans in pursuit.
    Frederick Witt is remembered on the Arras Memorial and has no known grave.

Flight Sub Lt Edward Cuthbert Stocker   *5 (Naval) Squadron Royal Naval Air Service*
Place of birth: Clevedon, Somerset   Home country: England   Age: 18
Date of death: 27/03/18   Cause of death: Killed in action
War cemetery: Arras Flying Services Memorial, France
Theatre of war: France
Next of kin: Maj. Edward G. & Ethel Stocker (parents)
Address: 50 Albany Road, Salisbury, Wiltshire

The German Spring Offensive was the first time large-scale air power had a direct influence on a battle. On 23 March, seventy machines were involved in a single air engagement. Royal Naval Air Squadrons were used to carry out low-level attacks against German ground targets.
    Eighteen-year-old Edward was the younger and only surviving child of Maj. Edward and Ethel Stocker. He was reported missing on 27 March 1917 while flying near Dompierre-Bequincourt, south-east of Albert, France. In April 1919 news reached Edward's parents that he was presumed killed on 27 March 1918.

2nd-Lt John Ferdinando Collins   *56th Company Machine Gun Corps*

Place of birth:	Reading, Berkshire	Home country:	England	Age: 19
Date of death:	28/03/18	Cause of death:	Killed in action	
Memorials:	Salisbury, Wiltshire			
	St Martin's Church Memorial			
War cemetery:	Roclincourt Military Cemetery, France			
Theatre of war:	France			
Next of kin:	The late Henry John & Jane F.L. Collins (parents)			
Address:	24 St Mark's Road, Salisbury, Wiltshire			

Nineteen-year-old John Collins, an only son, was killed in action north-east of Arras on Thursday 28 March 1918.

Capt. Charles Basil Mortimer Hodgson   *3rd Battalion Royal West Surrey Regiment*

Place of birth:	Kingston, Middlesex	Home country: England Age: 37	
Date of death:	01/04/18	Cause of death: Died of wounds	
War cemetery:	Cairo War Memorial Cemetery, Egypt		
Theatre of war:	Egypt		
Next of kin:	Charles Durant & Emily Hodgson (parents)		
Address:	Hallams Shamley Green, Guildford, Surrey		

Capt. Charles Basil Mortimer Hodgson, the Queen's Royal West Surrey Regiment, was reported dangerously ill from wounds on 9 March 1918 and died in hospital at Cairo, on Monday 1 April 1918. It was a mere ten days after the death of his brother, Capt. Cyril Hodgson.

Capt. C.B.M. Hodgson was married on 3 August 1911 to Mary Alice (Molly), eldest daughter of the Archdeacon of Sarum and Mrs Carpenter and was born in September 1881. Educated at Eton (Mr Willaims' House) and Magdalen College, Oxford, he was called to the Bar and practised at the Inner Temple, and in July 1907 was gazetted to the Special Reserve Battalion of The Queen's, obtaining his company in 1913. Soon after the outbreak of war he joined his regiment at the front and took part in the Battle of the Aisne and the First Battle of Ypres. He was invalided home after being injured at Langemarck, and during his convalescence he spoke in various parts of the country for the Parliamentary Recruiting Committee. In February 1915 he was appointed to the staff in Mesopotamia, but was invalided to Egypt with typhoid. Later he became GSO3 and served through the campaign against the Senussi. He was mentioned twice in despatches and was awarded the *Croix de Guerre*. He served on the staff of the Western Frontier Force in Cairo until he went to Palestine, where he was attached to the London Regiment.

Rifleman Horace Percy Williams   *18th Battalion Kings Royal Rifle Corps*

Service No.:	R/39084	Age: 19	
Place of birth:	Dover, Kent	Home country: England	
Date of death:	01/04/18	Cause of death: Died of wounds	
Memorials:	Salisbury, Wiltshire		
	St Paul's Church Memorial		
War cemetery:	Cabaret Rouge British Cemetery, Souchez, France		
Theatre of war:	France		
Next of kin:	George & Annie Williams		
Address:	52 George Street, Salisbury, Wiltshire		

Nineteen-year-old Horace Williams had originally joined the Royal Army Service Corps but was transferred to the 18th Battalion Kings Royal Rifle Corps. He was killed in action on Monday 1 April 1918, during the German Spring Offensive north of Arras.

Pte Charles Goodridge		*85th Battalion Nova Scotia Regiment*	
Service No.:	150418	Age:	43
Place of birth:	Dowton, Wiltshire	Home country:	Canada
Date of death:	03/04/18	Cause of death:	Killed in action
Memorials:	Salisbury, Wiltshire		
	St Mark's Memorial		
War cemetery:	Orchard Dump Cemetery, Arleux en Gohelle, France		
Theatre of war:	France		
Next of kin:	William & Elizabeth Goodridge (parents)		
Address:	71 Park Street, London Road, Salisbury, Wiltshire		

Charles Goodridge joined the Canadian Army on 25 September 1915 at the age of forty years and eleven months. Prior to the war he had been a labourer. He was killed on Wednesday 3 April 1915, north-east of Arras.

Pte William Hayter		*5th Battalion Oxfordshire and Buckinghamshire Light Infantry*	
Service No.:	33106	Age:	28
Place of birth:	Salisbury, Wiltshire	Home country:	England
Date of death:	04/04/18	Cause of death:	Killed in action
Memorials:	Salisbury, Wiltshire		
	St Paul's Church Memorial		
War cemetery:	Pozieres Memorial, France		
Theatre of war:	France		
Next of kin:	Frederick & Ellen Hayter (parents)		
Address:	St Edmund, Salisbury, Wiltshire		

Above: *British casualties during a German offensive.*

Left: *The original cross that marked the grave of Capt. Charles Basil Mortimer Hodgson.*

William Hayter had originally joined the Gloucester Regiment but was transferred to the 5th Battalion Oxfordshire and Buckinghamshire Light Infantry. He was killed in action on Thursday 4 April 1918 at the Battle of Avre, east of Amiens, he was one of nineteen other members of his battalion to die on that day – the 14th Light Division of which Hayter's battalion were part, had suffered almost 6,000 casualties in the period fron 21 March 1918 to 4 April 1918.

2nd-Lt Henry Edwardes Palmer   *5th Battalion Royal Berkshire Regiment*
Place of birth: Alton, Hampshire   Home country: England   Age: 34
Date of death: 05/04/18   Cause of death: Died of wounds
War cemetery: Bouzincourt Ridge Cemetery, Albert, France
Theatre of war: France
Next of kin: Elizabeth Palmer (wife); William H. & Diana Palmer (parents)
Addresses: Uplands Ovingdean, Brighton, Sussex
                  11 Milford Street, Salisbury, Wiltshire

In late April 1918 the news reached Salisbury that 2nd-Lt H.E. Palmer, Berkshire Regiment, the only son of Mr W H Palmer, of 11 Milford Street, Salisbury, was reported missing in action since 5 April, near Warloy, south-east of Amiens.

No further news was heard until the end of January 1919 when his parents were informed that Henry Palmer was reported to have died of his wounds on the day he was reported missing: Friday 5 April 1918.

9 APRIL 1918 – 'GEORGETTE' THE SECOND GERMAN SPRING OFFENSIVE IS LAUNCHED

Cpl Alexander George Baugh   *6th Battalion Wiltshire Regiment*
Service No.:   9272   Age: 30
Place of birth: Gosport, Hampshire   Home country: England
Date of death: 10/04/18   Cause of death: Killed in action
Memorial: Salisbury, Wiltshire
War cemetery: Tyne Cot Memorial, Belgium
Theatre of war: Belgium
Next of kin: Alexander & Sarah A. Baugh (parents)
Address: 413 North Tidworth, Tidworth, Hampshire

On the night of 9/10 April 1918 the 6th Battalion Wiltshire Regiment were east of the Messines, Wytschatete Ridge, holding the trenches. At 3.30 a.m. the Germans started shelling the British lines with high-explosive and gas shells, with the high-explosive shells falling throughout the day. At 6 a.m., the Germans attacked, under the cover of a mist, to the right of the Wiltshires and forced their way through the British lines. At 4.30 p.m. orders were given to the British front to retire, but the orders were not received by the forward companies of the Wiltshires. They held out for a number of German attacks but were surrounded. Later some survivors managed to work their way through the lines.

Cpl Baugh was one of forty-two men killed on Wednesday 10 April 1918; he is remembered on the Tyne Cot Memorial and has no known grave.

L/Cpl Frederick Stewart Hunphries   *6th Battalion Wiltshire Regiment*
Service No.:   204136   Age: 21

Place of birth:	New Sarum, Wiltshire	Home country:	England
Date of death:	10/04/18	Cause of death:	Killed in action
Memorials:	Salisbury, Wiltshire		
	St Paul's Church Memorial		
War cemetery:	Tyne Cot Cemetery, Belgium		
Theatre of war:	Belgium		
Next of kin:	Henry & Henrietta Humphries (parents)		
Address:	10 Hartington Road, Salisbury, Wiltshire		

Frederick Humpries was killed in action during the fighting on Wednesday 10 April 1918 (see Alexander Baugh). He is remembered on the Tyne Cot Memorial and has no known grave.

Pte Desmond Light   *6th Battalion Wiltshire Regiment*

Service No.:	203309	Home country:	England	Age:	21
Date of death:	10/04/18	Cause of death:	Killed in action		
Memorials:	Salisbury, Wiltshire				
	St Mark's Church Memorial				
War cemetery:	Tyne Cot Memorial, Belgium				
Theatre of war:	Belgium				
Next of kin:	Charles & Jessie Light (parents)				
Address:	62 College Street, Salisbury, Wiltshire				

Desmond Light was formerly a member of the Wiltshire Yeomanry, which was merged with the 6th Battalion Wiltshire Regiment in September 1917. He was killed in action on Wednesday 10 April 1918 (see Alexander Baugh). He is remembered on the Tyne Cot Memorial and has no known grave.

L/Cpl Frederick Alfred Humby   *1/4th Battalion Wiltshire Regiment*

Service No.:	200914	Age:	25
Place of birth:	Salisbury, Wiltshire	Home country:	England
Date of death:	10/04/18	Cause of death:	Killed in action
Memorial:	Salisbury, Wiltshire		
War cemetery:	Jerusalem Memorial, Israel		
Theatre of war:	Palestine		
Next of kin:	William Frank & Eliza Humby (parents)		
Address:	29 Bedwin Street, Salisbury, Wiltshire		

On 10 April 1918 the 1/4th Battalion Wiltshire Regiment were attacking Turkish positions at Sheikh Subih Ridge. As soon as the action began the Wiltshires found themselves under fire from Turkish artillery and machine-gun fire which halted the attack. The Wiltshires fell back to positions at the head of the Wadi Arak.

During the night, parties went out to bring in the wounded but were shelled by the Turks and, later on, Turkish bombers crept up to the Wiltshires' forward observation post; one of the Wiltshires was killed and around him were lying the bodies of three Turkish Soldiers.

Frederick Humby was the second son of William and Eliza Humby, and was reported wounded and missing on Wednesday 10 April 1918 in Palestine. In January 1919 official news was received informing his parents he had been killed in action on that day. He is remembered on the Jerusalem Memorial and has no known grave.

Pte Harold William Pistell   *1/4th Battalion Wiltshire Regiment*

Service No.:	200456	Age:	25
Place of birth:	Salisbury, Wiltshire	Home country:	England
Date of death:	10/04/18	Cause of death:	Killed in action
Memorials:	Salisbury, Wiltshire		
	St Paul's Church Memorial and Dews Road Primitive Methodist Memorial		
War cemetery:	Jerusalem Memorial, Israel		
Theatre of war:	Palestine		
Next of kin:	Albert William & Phoebe Emily Pistell (parents)		
Address:	15 South Street, Salisbury, Wiltshire		

Harold Pistell was killed in action on Wednesday 10 April 1918 (see Frederick Humby). He is remembered on the Jerusalem Memorial and has no known grave.

L/Cpl Gilbert Robins   *1/4th Battalion Wiltshire Regiment*

Service No.:	200474	Age:	28
Place of birth:	Salisbury, Wiltshire	Home country:	England
Date of death:	10/04/18	Cause of death:	Died of wounds
Memorial:	Salisbury, Wiltshire		
War cemetery:	Jerusalem Memorial, Israel		
Theatre of war:	Palestine		
Next of kin:	George H. & Annie Robins (parents)		
Address:	Bentley Downton Road, Salisbury, Wiltshire		

Gilbert Robins died of his wounds on Wednesday 10 April, from wounds received on the same day (see Frederick Humby). He is remembered on the Jerusalem Memorial and has no known grave.

Cpl John Thomas Harry Staples   *A Company 1/4th Wiltshire Regiment*

Service No.:	200099	Age:	31
Place of birth:	Bulford, Wiltshire	Home country:	England
Date of death:	10/04/18	Cause of death:	Killed in action
Memorial:	Salisbury, Wiltshire		
War cemetery:	Ramleh War Cemetery, Israel		
Theatre of war:	Palestine.		
Next of kin:	Mary Emma Staples (wife); Harry & Sarah Staples (parents)		
Addresses:	The Terraces, Cadnam, Hampshire.		
	Salisbury		

John Staples was killed in action on Wednesday 10 April, (see Frederick Humby). He was one of twenty-four members of the 1/4th Wiltshire Regiment to be killed on this day. He is buried in Ramleh War Cemetery.

Pte William Charles Knight   *11th Battalion Lancashire Fusiliers*

Service No.:	33489	Age:	20
Place of birth:	Shaftsbury, Dorset	Home country:	England
Date of death:	10/04/18	Cause of death:	Killed in action
Memorials:	Salisbury, Wiltshire		
	St Paul's Church Memorial		
War cemetery:	Ploegsteert Memorial, Belgium		

Theatre of war: France
Next of kin: Charles & Elizabeth Ann Knight (parents)
Address: 42 Meadow Road, Salisbury, Wiltshire

William Knight had originally joined the Royal Field Artillery, but was transferred to the
11th Battalion Lancashire Fusiliers. On 9 April the Germans commenced the second Spring
Offensive against positions in northern France and Belgium. William Knight was killed
in action on Wednesday 10 April 1918, during the Battle on Lys, at Estaires, south-east of
Aementieres, France. He is remembered on the Ploegsteert Memorial, Belgium, and he has
no known grave.

Pte Walter Ernest Bond		*2nd Battalion Hampshire Regiment*	
Service No.:	381303	Age:	19
Place of birth:	Salisbury, Wiltshire	Home country:	England
Date of death:	11/04/18	Cause of death:	Killed in action
Memorial:	Salisbury, Wiltshire		
War cemetery:	Haverskerque British Cemetery, France		
Theatre of war:	France		
Next of kin:	William & Elizabeth Harriet Bond (parents)		
Address:	17 Farthing Street, Salisbury, Wiltshire		

Nineteen-year-old Walter Bond was killed in action on Thursday 11 April 1918, on the third
day of the second German Spring Offensive, in the area of the town of Estaries, northern
France. He was of twenty-eight men of the 2nd Battalion Hampshire Regiment killed on
this day.

L/Cpl Sidney Edward Moorhouse		*2nd Battalion Hampshire Regiment*	
Service No.:	355222	Age:	28
Place of birth:	Salisbury, Wiltshire	Home country:	England
Date of death:	11/04/18	Cause of death:	Killed in action
Memorials:	Salisbury, Wiltshire		
	St Martin's Church Memorial		
War cemetery:	Ploegsteert Memorial, Belgium		
Theatre of war:	France		
Next of kin:	Jessie Mabel Pernell Moorhouse (wife); Edward & Elizabeth Moorhouse (parents)		
Addresses:	Invergelder Walford, Wimborne, Dorset		
	Eversley, Elm Grove, Salisbury, Wiltshire		

Lance-Cpl Sydney Moorhouse (Hants Regiment), a native of Salisbury, was officially reported
to have been killed in action on the Western Front on Thursday 11 April . He was a clerk in
Lloyds Bank at Southampton (to which he had been transferred from Wimborne) prior to
joining up. He was only twenty-seven years of age, and had been married a year and a half.
His wife has been living with her father, Mr Henry King, at Walford.

Sidney Moorhouse is remembered on the Ploegsteert Memorial in Belgium; he has no
known grave.

Pte Arthur Ernest Davis		*6th Battalion Wiltshire Regiment*	
Service No.:	36095	Age:	18
Place of birth:	Trowbridge, Wiltshire	Home country:	England

Date of death:	11/04/18	Cause of death:	Killed in action
Memorials:	Salisbury, Wiltshire		
	St Paul's Church Memorial and Dews Road Primitive Methodist Memorial		
War cemetery:	Tyne Cot Cemetery, Belgium		
Theatre of war:	Belgium		
Next of kin:	Hedley Herbert & Lucy Miles Davis (parents)		
Address:	53 St Paul's Road, Salisbury, Wiltshire		

Eighteen-year-old Arthur Davis was killed in action on Thursday 11 April 1918, probably due to shell fire, in trenches around Wijtschate, south of the town of Ypres Belgium.

He is remembered on the Tyne Cot memorial, and has no known grave.

L/Cpl Percy William Simmons   *57th Field Company Royal Engineers*

Service No.:	28631	Age:	25
Date of death:	11/04/18	Cause of death:	Killed in action
Place of birth:	Weymouth, Dorset	Home country:	England
Memorial:	Salisbury, Wiltshire		
War cemetery:	Croix Du Bac British Cemetery, Steenwerck, France		
Theatre of war:	France		
Next of kin:	John & Ellen Simmons (parents)		
Address:	St Edmund, Salisbury, Wiltshire		

Percy Simmons was killed in action on 11 April 1918 in the area of Estaires. He is buried at Steenwerck, which was in German hands on the 10 April 1918.

Pte Frederick Douglas Percy   *2/4th Battalion Oxfordshire and Buckinghamshire Light Infantry*

Service No.:	34440	Age:	18
Place of birth:	Streatham, Middlesex	Home country:	England
Date of death:	13/04/18	Cause of death:	Died of wounds
Memorial:	Salisbury, Wiltshire		
War cemetery:	Lapugnoy Military Cemetery, France		
Theatre of war:	France		
Next of kin:	Ernest Walter & Sarah Ann Percy (parents)		
Address:	158 Devizes Road, Salisbury, Wiltshire		

In early May 1918 news was received from the War Office, that Frederick Douglas Percy, son of Mr and Mrs E.W. Percy, Fisherton Farm, and grandson of Mr H.G. Percy, who was only eighteen years and eight months, and was serving in the Oxfordshire and Buckinghamshire Light Infantry, had died from wounds received in action in France. The young man joined the Army in August 1917 and had only been in France eleven days when he was wounded. Much sympathy was felt for the bereaved parents.

Lt Col. George Koberwein Fulton   *9th Battalion Cheshire Regiment*

Place of birth:	Downton, Wiltshire	Home country:	England	Age: 33
Date of death:	14/04/18	Cause of death:	Killed in action	
Decorations:	Distinguished Service Order			
Memorial:	Salisbury, Wiltshire			
War cemetery:	Tyne Cot Memorial, Belgium			

Theatre of war: Belgium
Next of kin: Eleanore Fulton (wife); Hamilton & Rosa Fulton (parents)
Addresses: The Manor House, Wilton, Wiltshire
The Close, Salisbury

Lt-Col. George Koberwein Fulton, Cheshire Regiment, was killed in action on Sunday 14 April 1918, was thirty-three years of age and the younger son of Mr Hamilton Fulton, of the Close, Salisbury. He was educated at Connaught House (Morgan's), Weymouth, Marlborough, and Brasenose College, Oxford. He was in the OTC, at Marlborough, and was coxswain of the Brasenose boat. On leaving Oxford he was, for some time, engaged in forestry in the Caucasus, but on the bombardment of Batoum in 1904 he escaped in an oil ship. Soon after reaching England he joined his father, and was in partnership with him at his death. Lt-Col. Fulton received a commission in 1914, and was gazetted captain in the Wiltshire Regiment a few weeks later. He went on service with that regiment in August 1916, and was, with the exception of a few weeks, almost continuously fighting at the front until his death. In 1917 he was sent on a senior officers' course at Aldershot, and was recommended for a command. On his return to the front he was gazetted a major in the Wiltshire Regiment, and soon afterwards was transferred to the Cheshire Regiment, a battalion of which he commanded at his death. He had some marvellous escapes, and was 'a cool and fearless officer, beloved by his brother officers and men'. His battalion was fighting from 21–28 of March 1918 without cessation, and the fighting in which his regiment was engaged on 12, 13 and 14 April was described by the special correspondent of the *Times* as follows:

> The fighting about Neuve Eglise seems to have been of the most heroic character against great odds, the troops engaged being those which had already had many continuous days of hard fighting. Yesterday, especially, there was a time when some Cheshires and Wiltshires fought in a hollow square including part of the village. The fighting was of the most ruthless character, and our men not only held their formation till other troops coming up drove the enemy forward and relieved the flanks, but when that was done they broke into a counterattack and killed great numbers of the enemy, who were driven back in confusion. From officers' accounts, it seems to have been an extraordinary exhibition of gallantry and unquenchable determination. Some King's Royal Rifles behaved no less finely, holding part of this line against overwhelming numbers of the enemy, who at one time threatened completely to encircle them by a temporary penetration of the line.
>
> Tales are told of a colonel with machine guns, who fought most gallantly, even after he was wounded, continuing to hold the Germans back at a critical point and killing great numbers of the enemy.

In August 1912 Lt-Col. Fulton married Eleanore, younger daughter of the late Dr Mackay of Elgin, NB, and left one daughter.

In September 1918 Lt-Col. G.K. Fulton, Cheshire Regiment (formerly Wiltshire Regiment), was awarded a DSO:

> For conspicuous gallantry and devotion to duty in handling his battalion in a most skilful manner. He set a splendid example of courage and disregard of danger, and was indefatigable in arranging the battalion dispositions, and personally supervising its movements. At all times when the situation was critical he was up in the frontline encouraging the men and taking part in the fighting.

Lt-Col. Fulton was killed on 14 April 1918, while personally making a reconnaissance of the area in front of his battalion. He is remembered on the Tyne Cot Memorial and has no known grave.

Pte Henry George White   *D Company 7th Battalion Kings Shropshire*
                                            Light Infantry
Service No.:   27655   Age: 19
Place of birth: Salisbury, Wiltshire   Home country: England
Date of death: 14/04/18   Cause of death: Killed in action
Memorials: Salisbury, Wiltshire
                   St Mark's Church Memorial
War cemetery: Ploegsteert Memorial, Belgium
Theatre of war: Belgium
Next of kin: Harry Ernest & Ellen Marrion White (parents)
Address: 90 Wyndham Road, Salisbury, Wiltshire

Nineteen-year-old Henry White was killed in action on Sunday 14 April 1918, during the Battle of Hazebrouck, northern France, which lies south-west of Ypres. He is remembered on the Plogsteert Memorial and has no known grave.

Pte William James Stout   *1st Battalion Wiltshire Regiment*
Service No.:   22092   Age: 20
Place of birth: Argentina   Home country: England
Date of death: 15/04/18   Cause of death: Died of illness
Memorials: Salisbury, Wiltshire
                   St Mark's Memorial
War cemetery: Cologne Southern Cemetery, Germany
Theatre of war: Germany, as a prisoner of war
Next of kin: Mr J. & Mrs M. Stout (parents)
Address: 2 Helena Terrace, College Street, Salisbury, Wiltshire

In late May 1918 news reached Salisbury of William Stout, Wiltshire Regiment, eldest son of Mr J. Stout, 2 Helen Terrace, Salisbury, who had been reported missing on 24 March – he was a prisoner of war. Previous to joining the Army he had been employed by the London & South West Railway. After the war his parents found out the truth: Stout was captured by the Germans on 24 March in fighting east of Fremicourt, France. However, he died of illness in a German prisoner of war camp on Monday 15 April 1918.

2nd-Lt Harold Cox   *12th Battalion London Regiment (The Rangers)*
Place of birth: Salisbury, Wiltshire   Home country: England   Age: 27
Date of death: 16/04/18   Cause of death: Died of wounds
Memorial: Salisbury, Wiltshire
War cemetery: Messines Ridge British Cemetery, Belgium
Theatre of war: Belgium
Next of kin: Frank William & Sarah Jane Cox (parents)
Address: Avon House, Castle Street, Salisbury, Wiltshire

Harold Cox was reported missing on 16 April 1918. He was the eldest son of Frank and Sarah Cox. He had joined the 12th Battalion London Regiment but was on attachment to the Machine Gun Corps. In May 1919 his parents received the official report that Cox had died of wounds received in action on Tuesday 16 April 1918 at Wychaete Ridge, south of Ypres.

L/Cpl Sidney George Orchard   *7th Battalion Royal West Surrey Regiment*
Service No.:   G/7626   Age: 27

British prisoners of war captured during a German offensive.

Place of birth:	Salisbury, Wiltshire	Home country:	England
Date of death:	26/04/18	Cause of death:	Killed in action
Decorations:	Military Medal	Theatre of war:	France
Memorials:	Salisbury, Wiltshire		
	St Mark's Church Memorial		
War cemetery:	Pozieres Memorial, France		
Next of kin:	William J. & Rosa Orchard (parents)		
Address:	100 Radnor Park Road, Folkestone, Kent		

In June 1916 news was received concerning Sidney Orchard, MM, Royal West Surrey Regiment. He was the son of Mr and Mrs Orchard, of Folkestone, formerly of Salisbury, and was killed in action on 26 April 1918. His father was, for many years, Band Sergeant in the 4th Wiltshre Regiment, and was then with the Canadian Forces.

Sidney Orchard enlisted in February 1916 and had been twice wounded and gained the Military Medal in April 1917 for gallantry in the field. Much sympathy was expressed with his parents, who had lost three sons in a ten-month period; the eldest, William Orchard, being killed while doing volunteer work in Belgium in June 1917 and the youngest, Alfred Orchard,, drowned at sea in September 1917.

2nd-Lt Percy Stuart Gaster   *Royal Air Force No.18 Training Squadron*

Place of birth:	Camberwell, London	Home country:	England	Age:	18
Date of death:	21/04/18	Cause of death:	Accidental		
Memorial:	Choir School Memorial				
War cemetery:	Camberwell Old Cemetery, England				
Theatre of war:	Home				
Next of kin:	Percy & Mabel Sherwood Gaster (parents)				
Address:	20 Strafford Road, Twickenham, Middlesex				

Eighteen-year-old Percy Glaster was killed on Sunday 21 April 1918, in an aircraft accident.

Pte Arthur James Smith   *2/4th Battalion Royal Fusiliers*

Service No.:	90061	Age:	18
Place of birth:	Salisbury, Wiltshire	Home country:	England
Date of death:	25/04/18	Cause of death:	Killed in action
Memorial:	Salisbury, Wiltshire		
War cemetery:	Pozieres Memorial, France		

Theatre of war: France
Next of kin: George & Edith Smith (parents)
Address: 32 St Edmunds, Church Street, Salisbury, Wiltshire

Arthur Smith had originally joined the Somerset Light Infantry, but was transferred to the 2/4th Battalion Royal Fusiliers. He was killed in action on 25 April 1918, when he was one of eight members of his battalion who died on that day. Arthur Smith is remembered on the Pozieres Memorial, and has no known grave.

Maj. Richard Fielding Morrison   *51st Brigade Royal Field Artillery*
Place of birth: Mhow, India   Age: 27
Date of death: 25/04/18   Cause of death: Died of wounds
Decorations: Military Cross
War cemetery: Haringhe (Bandaghem) Military Cemetery: Belgium
Theatre of war: Belgium
Next of kin: E.J. Morrison (wife); Lt-Col. Richard Hobart Morrison & Louise C.C. Morrison (parents)
Addresses: 53, Eglinton Road, Donnybrook, Dublin
Johnstown House, Cabinteely, Co. Dublin

Maj. Richard Fielding Morrison, MC, Royal Field Artillery, whose death from wounds received in action on the same day is reported to have taken place on Thursday 25 April 1918, he was the eldest son of Lt-Col. Hobart Morrison, late of the 18th (QMO) Hussars, and Mrs Morrison of Johnstown House, Cabinteely, Ireland and Clayton Croft, Salisbury. Richard Morrison was born at Mhow, India, in 1890, and was within five days of completing his twenty-eighth year. He was educated at Wellington College, where he was captain of the 'shooting eight', and afterwards at the Royal Military Academy, Woolwich, he obtained his commission in the Royal Field Artillery in July 1910, passing out at the head of the Gunners, and obtaining the 'Tombs Memorial Prize.' He joined the 129th Howitzer Battery at Dundalk, and went with it subsequently to Bulford, proceeding with it to France at the outbreak of the war, and receiving his 'baptism of fire' in the retreat from Mons. He was present in all the subsequent fighting in which his division, the 3rd, took part.

In 1915, he was posted to the Royal Horse Artillery, and served for some time as Adjutant of his Brigade. On appointment as acting captain he was re-posted to the Field Artillery, and on promotion to captain in July 1916, he was given the command of a howitzer battery, with the acting rank of Major, and commanded it throughout the British offensive on the Somme in that year, and in the battles of 1917, being wounded in October by a shell. From the outbreak of the war until his death he served continuously at the front, and was in, practically, all the most severe fighting that took place. He was mentioned in despatches in 1915 and received the Military Cross in January 1917. He also had the 1914 Star to his credit. He was married in 1916, to Effie, elder daughter of Mr A.F. Ferrier, Ash Hurst, Killiney, Co. Dublin. Maj. Morrison was universally popular: he was a keen soldier and a good sportsman, and had one of the most efficient batteries, both as regards gunnery and horsemanship, believing as he did that the day would come (as it has) when the wagon line would again become an essential in the fighting of the guns themselves. He was a good man to hounds and loved his horses.

In Maj. Morrison the 'Royal Regiment' lost a smart and promising officer, and all who knew him a cheery, genial and unselfish friend, whose loss was much felt.

Pte Frederick Charles Edward Gamblin   *12th Battalion Gloucestershire Regiment*

Service No.:	44372	Age:	18

Service No.:   44372   Age: 18
Place of birth: Salisbury, Wiltshire   Home country: England
Date of death: 26/04/18   Cause of death: Died of wounds
Memorials: Salisbury, Wiltshire
                    St Paul's Church Memorial
War cemetery: Aire Communal Cemetery, France
Theatre of war: France
Next of kin: William & Sarah Gamblin (parents)
Address: 36 Meadow Road, Salisbury, Wiltshire

During the German offensive of 1918, the age for serving on the continent was lowered from nineteen to eighteen and a half and this released replacement troops who had been in training in England. Frederick Gamblin had originally joined the Devonshire Regiment but was transferred to the 12th Battalion Gloucestershire Regiment. He died of his wounds on Friday 26 April 1918 at one of the medical units based in the town of Aire. His wounds were probably received in fighting around Hazebrouck, northern France, in mid-April.

Sapper David Baird   *107th Field Company Royal Engineers*

Service No.:   56830   Age: 40
Place of birth: Monkwearmouth, Durham   Home country: England
Date of death: 27/04/18   Cause of death: Died of illness
War cemetery: Salisbury (Devizes Road) Cemetery, England
Theatre of war: Home
Next of kin: Mary Jane Baird (mother)
Address: Monkwearmouth, Durham

David Baird died most likely from illness at one of the military hospitals in the Salisbury area on Saturday 27 April 1918.

Pte Robert I. Wade   *1/5th Battalion York & Lancaster Regiment*

Service No.:   33068   Age: 33
Place of birth: Southgate, Middlesex   Home country: England

David Baird, who died in the Salisbury area.

Date of death: 29/04/18   Cause of death: Killed in action
Memorials: Salisbury, Wiltshire
                   St Thomas Church Memorial & St Mark's Church Memorial
War cemetery: Tyne Cot Cemetery, Belgium
Theatre of war: Belgium
Next of kin: Winifred C. Wade (wife)
Address: Kirkley, 11 Victoria Road, Salisbury, Wiltshire

Robert had originally joined the Royal Army Service Corps, but he was transferred
to the 1/5th Battalion York & Lancaster Regiment. He was killed in action on Monday
29 April 1918 and is remembered on the Tyne Cot Memorial; Robert has no known grave.

Pte Percy Francis Gale   *6th Battalion Dorsetshire Regiment*
Service No.:   20719   Age: 19
Place of birth: Salisbury, Wiltshire   Home country: England
Date of death: 30/04/18   Cause of death: Died of wounds
Memorials: Salisbury, Wiltshire
                   St Martin's Church Memorial
War cemetery: Doullens Communal Cemetery, Extension No.2, France
Theatre of war: France
Next of kin: Francis & Henrietta Gale (parents)
Address: 104 Milford Hill, Salisbury, Wiltshire

Nineteen-year-old Percy Gale died of wounds on Tuesday 30 April 1918 from wounds
received during the second German Spring Offensive.

RSM Frank William Leach   *1/4th Battalion Hampshire Regiment*
Service No.:   200025   Age: 30
Place of birth: Salisbury, Wiltshire   Home country: England
Date of death: 02/05/18   Cause of death: Died of illness
Memorial: Bishop Wordsworth's School Memorial
War cemetery: Baghdad North Gate War Cemetery, Iraq
Theatre of war: Mesopotamia; Prisoner of War
Next of kin: William & Alice Mary Leach (parents)
Address: 1 Montgomery Terrace, Bemerton, Wiltshire

Frank Leach died, most likely of illness, on Thursday 2 May 1918 as a prisoner of war at
Nasebin, Turkey. He was the only son William and Alice Leach and grandson of the late Mr
W. Leach of the Old Rectory, Caste Street, Salisbury.

Pte Frederick James Foyle   *2nd Battalion Lancashire Fusiliers*
Service No.:   53024   Age: 33
Place of birth: Broadchalke, Wiltshire   Home country: England
Date of death: 03/05/18   Cause of death: Killed in action
Memorials: Salisbury, Wiltshire
                   St Thomas Church Memorial
War cemetery: Loos Memorial, France
Theatre of war: France
Next of kin: Isaac & Harriet Foyle (parents)
Address: Broadchalke, Wiltshire

Frederick Foyle had originally joined the Dorset Regiment but was transferred to the 2nd Battalion Lancashire Fusiliers. He was killed in action on 3 May 1918, south of Bethune, France. Foyle is remembered on the Loos Memorial and has no known grave.

Pte John William Lyons   *53rd Battalion Australian Infantry Australian Imperial Force*

Service No.:   3344   Age: 26
Place of birth: Sydney, Australia   Home country: Australia
Date of death: 03/05/18   Cause of death: Died of wounds
War cemetery: Salisbury (London Road) Cemetery, England
Next of kin: William & Mary Lyons (uncle & aunt)
Address: Sydney, Australia

John Lyons had joined the Australian Army on 4 August 1915 along with his brother Reginald. They had consecutive service numbers – John's was 3344 and Reginald's 3345. The brothers had been orphaned and were raised by their uncle.

John Lyons arrived in France during July 1916; he was gassed on 14 April 1918 and evacuated to the 9th General Hospital at Rouen. He was then transferred to the military hospital at Fovant, where he died of bronchial pneumonia caused by gas poisoning.

John Lyons's brother was stationed at the Codford camp attached to 14th Australian Training Battalion and was consulted concerning the funeral arrangements.

On 14 August 1918 John Lyons's uncle received the following letter:

Dear Sir

With reference to the report of the regrettable loss of your nephew, the late 3344 Pte J.W. Lyons, 53rd Battalion. I am now in in receipt of advice which shows that he died at the Military Hospital, Fovant, Salisbury, on 03/05/18, of Brocho-pneumonia, and was buried at London Road Cemetery, Salisbury, consecrated ground, section – Roman Catholic. Grave No.17, on 07/05/1918.

The deceased soldier was buried with full Military Honours, the coffin being of good polished elm with brass mounts. The band of the Training Brigade preceded the funeral which was attended by a firing party, Pall bearers and two officers also a platoon of men from the Australian Training Battalion. A wreath from the deceased's comrades and a cross of flowers from his late ward mates were placed on the grave.

The grave was blessed by the chaplain, the Rev. John Lee, according to the Roman Catholic Church.

The deceased was very popular with both officers and men and his loss as a soldier and comrade is very keenly felt.

The utmost care and attention is being devoted where possible to the graves of our soldiers. It is understood photographs of graves are being taken as soon as possible and these will be transmitted to the next of kin when available.

These additional details are furnished by direction, it being the policy of the department to forward all information received in connection with deaths of members of the Australian Imperial Force.

Yours faithfully
Base Records.

Reginald Lyons, John's brother, was to go on to win the Military Medal and survived the war.

Far left: *John Lyons, who died after gas poisoning.*

Left: *American Harry Preston.*

2nd-Lt Harry Dennis Preston		Royal Air Force	
Place of birth:	Manitoba, Canada	Age:	22
Date of death:	14/05/18	Cause of death:	Accidental
Home country:	United States of America		
War cemetery:	Salisbury (London Road) Cemetery, England		
Next of kin:	Robert K. & Ada Preston (parents)		
Address:	804 Monadnock Building, Chicago, Illinois		

Harry Preston was drafted to the American forces on 5 June 1917. On reaching England he transferred to the Royal Air Force. He died on Tuesday 14 May 1918, most likely as a result of a accident while flying in the Salisbury area.

27 MAY 1918 – 'BLUCHER' THIRD GERMAN SPRING OFFENSIVE

Pte Herbert Walter Fay		1st Battalion Wiltshire Regiment	
Service No.:	21869	Age:	26
Place of birth:	Montisfont, Hampshire	Home country:	England
Date of death:	27/05/18	Cause of death:	Killed in action
Memorials:	Salisbury, Wiltshire		
	St Paul's Church Memorial		
War cemetery:	Soissons Memorial, France		
Theatre of war:	France		
Next of kin:	Walter & Emma Fay (parents)		
Address:	78 St Paul's Road, Salisbury, Wiltshire		

On Monday 27 May 1918 the Third German Spring Offensive was launched along the Chemin des Dames on the Aisne. The 1st Batalion Wiltshire Rgiment were at Guyencourt, north-west of Reims. At 1 a.m. the Germans started a heavy gas bombardment which lasted until 5 a.m. At 10.30 a.m. the Wiltshires moved forward and held a line in front of the village of Bouffignereux.. The Germans attacked at 5.30 a.m. in great force and the Wiltshires were compelled to retire, splitting into small groups.

Herbert Fay was killed in action on 27 May 1918 in the action near Bouffignereux. He is remembered on the Soissons Memorial and has no known grave.

Gunner Fred Hutchins   *74th Company Royal Garrison Artillery*
Service No.:   357003   Age: 31
Place of birth: Salisbury, Wiltshire   Home country: England
Date of death: 31/05/18   Cause of death: Died of wounds
Memorials: Salisbury, Wiltshire
                    Salisbury United Methodists Memorial
War cemetery: Baghdad North Gate War Cemetery, Iraq
Theatre of war: Mesopotamia
Next of kin: Thomas & Elizabeth Hutchins (parents)
Address: Milford, Salisbury, Wiltshire

Fred Hutchins had been a member Hampshire Territorial Royal Garrison Artillery. He died of his wounds on Friday 31 May 1918 at one of the medical units based in Baghdad.

Pte Percy Pike   *2nd Battalion Wiltshire Regiment*
Service No.:   203341   Age: 28
Place of birth: Woodborough, Wiltshire   Home country: England
Date of death: 31/05/18   Cause of death: Killed in action
Memorial: Salisbury, Wiltshire
War cemetery: Chambrecy Britsh Cemetery, France
Theatre of war: France
Next of kin: Ellen E.J. Pike (wife); Thomas & Annie Pike (parents)
Address: Hill View, Shrewton Road Chitterne, Codford, Wiltshire
                    Woodborough, Wiltshire

Percy Pike was killed in action during heavy fighting on Friday 31 May between Sarcy, Bligny and Chambercy West of Reims, France. The Germans attacked under the cover of a smoke screen forcing the British to withdraw, a retreat during which they were shelled and machine gunned by the Germans. During the evening a counter-attack took place in conjunction with French forces and recovered some of the ground lost to the Germans.

Pte Albert Edward Young   *10th Battalion Royal Warwickshire Regiment*
Service No.:   50762   Age: 18
Place of birth: Salisbury, Wiltshire   Home country: England
Date of death: 31/05/18   Cause of death: Killed in action
Memorials: Salisbury, Wiltshire
                    St Paul's Church Memorial
War cemetery: Marfaux British Cemetery, France
Theatre of war: France
Next of kin: George Henry & Edith Emma Young (parents)
Address: 55 Windsor Street, Salisbury, Wiltshire

Albert Young was killed in action on Friday 31 May 1915, during the heavy fighting west of Reims (see Percy Pike). He was one of ten members of his battalion to die on that day.

A British machine-gun crew under instruction.

Pte George Henry Gelliffe   *6th Battalion Wiltshire Regiment*
Service No.:   22751   Age: 23
Place of birth: Lockerley, Hampshire   Home country: England
Date of death: 03/06/18   Cause of death: Died of illness
Memorial: Salisbury, Wiltshire
War cemetery: Cologne Southern Cemetery, Germany
Theatre of war: Germany, as a prisoner of war
Next of kin: Alice Gelliffe (mother)
Address: St Edmunds, Salisbury, Wiltshire

George Gelliffe died on Monday 3 June 1918, most likely of illness, to which malnutrition contributed, while a prisoner of war. The British blockade of German ports was causing serious food shortages. He is buried in Cologne Southern Cemetery, Germany.

Lt Mervyn Sydney Wilkins   *6th Battalion Gloucestershire Regiment*
Place of birth: Bath, Somerset   Home country: Wales   Age: 25
Date of death: 16/06/18   Cause of death: Killed in action
                    Choir School Memorial Salisbury
War cemetery: Magnaboschi British Cemetery, Italy
Theatre of war: Italy
Next of kin: Gladys M.G. Wilkins (wife); Walter Sydney & Helen Wilkins (parents)
Address: Ffynone Pencaerau, Neath, Wales.
                    Bristol

Mervyn Wilkins was killed in action on Sunday 16 June 1918; on the previous day the Austrian army had launched a massive attack during the Second Battle of Pave River, Italy. The Austrians penetrated the Allied lines and it is likely Mervyn Wilkins was killed during this action.

Pte William Charles Edwards   *2nd Battalion Wiltshire Regiment*
Service No.:   29821   Age: 27
Place of birth: Fordingbridge, Hampshire   Home country: England

Date of death: 21/06/18   Cause of death: Killed in action
Memorial: Salisbury, Wiltshire
War cemetery: Soissons Memorial, France
Theatre of war: France

William Edwards was killed in action on Friday 21 June 1918, south of Reims. He is remembered on Soissons Memorial and has no known grave.

Gunner Ernest George Steer   *D Battery 18th Brigade Royal Field Artillery*
Service No.:   831310   Age: 29
Place of birth: Salisbury, Wiltshire   Home country: England
Date of death: 03/07/18   Cause of death: Accidental
Memorial: Salisbury, Wiltshire
War cemetery: Aubigny Communal Cemetery Extension, France
Theatre of war: France
Next of kin: Walter & Alice Steer (parents)
Address: 43 Bedwin Street, Salisbury, Wiltshire

Ernest Steer was the second son of Walter and Alice Steer. Prior to joining the artillery he had been a constable with Worcester City Police. He died on Wednesday 3 July 1918 in an accident.

   'Till the day break
   And the Shadows flee away'

2nd-Lt John Stewart Macdonald   *15th Battalion London Regiment (Civil Service Rifles)*
Place of birth: Darlington, Durham   Home country: England   Age: 33
Date of death: 05/07/18   Cause of death: Accidental
Memorial: Salisbury, Wiltshire
War cemetery: Houchin British Cemetery, France
Theatre of war: France
Next of kin: Constance Macdonald (wife); Stewart Muir & Lillian A. Macdonald
                    (parents)
Addresses: 10 St Andrews Mansions, Dorset Street, London
                    Salisbury, Wiltshire

John was the elder son of Stewart and Lillian Macdonald and the husband of Constance Macdonald. He had served as a private in the London Scottish from 1914 to 1917 and was wounded at the Battle of the Somme of July 1916. He died as the result of an accident on Friday 5 July 1918, south of the town of Bethune, France.

Pte Victor Henry Cowmeadow   *1/1st Battalion Derbyshire Yeomanry*
Service No.:   76067   Age: 21
Place of birth: Salisbury, Wiltshire   Home country: England
Date of death: 08/07/18   Cause of death: Died of illness
Memorials: Salisbury, Wiltshire
                    Bishop Wordsworth's School Memorial & St Martin's Church Memorial
War cemetery: Mikra British Cemetery, Greece
Theatre of war: Salonika
Next of kin: Frederick James & Catherine Eliza Cowmeadow (parents)
Address: 70 St Anne Street, Salisbury, Wiltshire

Victor Cowmeadow was the third son of Frederick and Catherine Cowmeadow. He died of disease on Monday 8 July 1918, at Salonika, Greece.

Pte George Sylvester Ward McCudden	*33rd Battalion Australian Infantry Australian Imperial Force*	
Service No.:	2919	Age:	21
Place of birth:	Johns River, Australia	Home country:	Australia
Date of death:	14/07/18	Cause of death:	Died of illness
War cemetery:	Salisbury (London Road) Cemetery, England		
Next of kin:	Randolph & Mary McCudden (parents)		
Address:	Beechwood, New South Wales, Australia		

George McCudden enlisted in the Australian Imperial Force on 5 October 1915 at the age of nineteen; he had previously been employed as postal assistant. He arrived in England in January 1918 and went to France in November 1917. In mid-April 1918 he was gassed and evacuated to England. He spent the next two months in Norfolk War Hospital, Thorpe, Norwich, and was returned to the Australian Depot in the UK on 13 June 1918. On the 28 June 1918, McCudden was admitted to the military hospital, Fovant, where he died of influenza on Sunday 14 July 1918, at the age of twenty-one. It is likely that the influenza was an effect of George being gassed earlier that year.

2nd-Lt Henry Leopold Breakey	*Royal Air Force*		
Place of birth:	Monoghan, Ireland	Home country:	Ireland	Age:	25
Date of death:	15/07/18	Cause of death:	Died of wounds		
War cemetery:	Salisbury London Road Cemetery, England				
Next of kin:	H. J. & Alice M Breakey (parents)				
Address:	Hillside, Monoghan, Ireland				

Henry Breakey joined the Canadian Army on 29 August 1918 in British Columbia. Prior to the war his profession was a bank accountant. While in England he transferred to the Royal Air Force where he died of wounds at Amesbury on Monday 15 July 1918.

18 JULY 1918 – ALLIES MOUNT A MASSIVE COUNTERATTACK

Gunner Albert Edward Bowey	*RA Command Depot Royal Garrison Artillery*	
Service No.:	116903	Age:	39
Place of birth:	Salisbury, Wiltshire	Home country:	England
Date of death:	29/07/18		
Memorial:	Salisbury, Wiltshire		
War cemetery:	East Harnham All Saints Churchyard, England		
Theatre of war:	Home		
Next of kin:	Rose Emily Bowey (wife); William J. & Mary Bowey (parents)		
Addresses:	12 Old Street Harnham, Salisbury, Wiltshire		
	St Thomas, Salisbury, Wiltshire		

Albert Edward Bowey, of Harnham, who died while on service, was apprenticed in the composing department of the *Salisbury and Winchester Journal*, and had worked for the firm ever since he left school, until he joined the RGA in 1916. He underwent his military

Far left: *George McCudden, after he was gassed he died of influenza.*

Middle: *Henry Breakey from Ireland, who died of his wounds.*

Left: *Albert Bowey, who died while on service and is remembered on the Salisbury Memorial.*

training at Plymouth, in Ireland and at Lydd, and proceeded to France with his battery in due course.

He was invalided home after about twelve months' service, and was in various military hospitals until – his health having apparently improved – he was on the point of rejoining his battery overseas. Unfortunately he had a relapse, and died suddenly on Monday 29 July 1918. at the Command Depot, Rippon, Yorkshire. He was thirty-nine years of age, and left a widow and five children. The funeral took place at East Harnham churchyard on the afternoon of 2 August 1918.

Pte George Brown		*2nd Battalion Wiltshire Regiment*	
Service No.:	33035	Age:	26
Place of birth:	Salisbury, Wiltshire	Home country:	England
Date of death:	07/08/18	Cause of death:	Killed in action
Memorials:	Salisbury, Wiltshire		
	St Mark's Church Memorial		
War cemetery:	Le Vertannoy British Cemetery, Hinges		
Theatre of war:	France		

On Wednesday 7 August 1918 the 2nd Battalion Wiltshire Regiment were near the village of Hinges, north-west of Bethune. At 6 a.m. the Germans began to retire and the Wiltshires sent out patrols to establish the enemy's position.

George Brown was killed in action on 7 August 1918 and is buried in Le Vertannoy British Cemetery, Hinges, along with two other members of the 2nd Battalion who fell on that day. It is interesting to note that the online Commonwealth War Graves Register states he died on 7 August 1915.

13

A BLACK DAY FOR THE GERMAN ARMY

Pte Sidney Richard Perry Grant — *B Company 16th Battalion Lancashire Fusiliers*

Service No.:	62608	Age:	18
Place of birth:	East Stoke, Dorset	Home country:	England
Date of death:	10/08/18	Cause of death:	Killed in action
Memorials:	Salisbury, Wiltshire		
	St Thomas Church Memorial		
War cemetery:	Vis En Artois Memorial, France		
Theatre of war:	France		
Next of kin:	Thomas M. & Hannah Letitia Grant (parents)		
Address:	11 New Street, Salisbury, Wiltshire		

On 8 August 1918 the 16th Battalion Lancashire Fusiliers were part of the allied advance at the Somme. On the first day the Germans were pushed back 8 miles and sustained 27,000 casualties. The General Ludendorff, described it as the 'Black Day' of the German army.

Sidney Grant was killed in action on Saturday 10 August 1918 in the Bapaume area, as the British continued the advance. He is remembered on the Vis En Artois Memorial, with almost 10,000 other men who were to fall between 8 August 1918 and the Armistice Day and have no known grave.

Pte Ernest John Sheppard — *A Company 5th Battalion Saskatchewan Regiment*

Service No.:	466631	Age:	24
Place of birth:	Salisbury, Wiltshire	Home country:	Canada
Date of death:	10/08/18	Cause of death:	Killed in action
Memorial:	Salisbury, Wiltshire		
War cemetery:	Rosieres Communal Cemetery Extension, France		
Theatre of war:	France		
Next of kin:	Thomas & Martha Sheppard (parents)		
Address:	10 College Street, Salisbury, Wiltshire		

Ernest Sheppard left his job as a hotel porter to enlist in the Canadian army during July 1915. On 9 August 1918 the 2nd Canadian Division, with the aid of tanks, captured the village of Rosieres, east of Amiens. Sheppard was killed in action on Saturday 10 August 1918 and is buried at Rosieres.

Pte William Ewart G. Rake — *2nd Battalion Wiltshire Regiment*

Service No.:	36229	Age:	18
Place of birth:	Salisbury, Wiltshire	Home country:	England

Date of death: 17/08/18   Cause of death: Killed in action
Memorial: Salisbury, Wiltshire
War cemetery: Le Vertannoy British Cemetery, Hinges, France
Theatre of war: France
Next of kin: Edward John & Lizie Emma Rake (parents)
Address: 61 Trevor Street Nechells, Birmingham, Worcester

On Saturday 17 August 1918 the 2nd Battalion Wiltshire Regiment were in the trenches at Hinges, a village north-west of Bethune. Eighteen-year-old William Rake was killed in action on this day and was buried locally.

Able Seaman Albert Victor Weeks   *Royal Navy HMS Apollo*
Service No.:   J/24452   Age: 21
Place of birth: Newton, Wiltshire   Home country: England
Date of death: 17/08/18
War cemetery: Netherhampton St Katherine Churchyard, England
Theatre of war: Home
Next of kin: James & Maria Weeks (parents)
Address: Hurdcott South Lodge, Barford St Martin, Wiltshire

Albert Weeks died on Saturday 17 August 1918 at Weymouth; he is buried in Netherhampton St Katherine Churchyard.

21 AUGUST 1918 – SECOND BATTLE OF ALBERT

2nd-Lt Cecil Keith Foyle Wright   *10th Battalion Royal Fusiliers*
Place of birth: Salisbury, Wiltshire   Home country: England   Age: 28
Date of death: 21/08/18   Cause of death: Killed in action
Memorials: Salisbury, Wiltshire
                    St Thomas Church Memorial and Dews Road Primitive Methodist
                    Memorial
War cemetery: Douchy Les Ayette British Cemetery, France
Theatre of war: France
Next of kin: Thomas & Alice Georgiana Wright (parents)
Address: The Poplars Crane Bridge Road, Salisbury, Wiltshire

News was received that 2nd-Lt Cecil K.F. Wright, ARCM, FRCO, Royal Fusiliers, son of Thomas and Alice Wright, the Corn & Forage Merchants of Byfield, Mill Road, Salisbury, had been killed in action on Wednesday 21 August 1918 during the first day of the Battle of Albert on the Somme.

Rifleman Benjamin J. Bucknall   *C Company 16th London Regiment (Queens*
                                                     Westminster Rifles)
Service No.:   554035   Age: 20
Place of birth: Yeovil, Somerset   Home country: England
Date of death: 28/08/18   Cause of death: Killed in action
Memorial: Salisbury, Wiltshire
War cemetery: Queant Road Cemetery, Buissy, France
Theatre of war: France

Next of kin: John & Alice Bucknall (parents)
Address: 3 Montgomery Terrace Bermerton, Salisbury, Wiltshire

In mid-September 1918 John and Alice Bucknall received the news that their son, Benjamin, was killed in action somewhere in France, while serving with the Queens Westminster Rifles. He fell near the village of Buissy, on the Arras-Cambrai Road on Wednesday 28 August 1918.

Pte Victor Frederick Saunders   *1st/5th London Field Ambulance Royal Army Medical Corps*
Service No.:   536412   Age: 28
Home country: England   Place of birth: Barnet, Hertfordshire
Date of death: 28/08/18   Cause of death: Died of illness
Memorials: Salisbury, Wiltshire
                          St Paul's Church Memorial
War cemetery: Salisbury (Devizes Road) Cemetery, England
Theatre of war: Home
Next of kin: Frederick & Mary Saunders (parents)
Address: 41 Hartington Road, Salisbury, Wiltshire

Victor Saunders died on Wednesday 28 August 1918 in Manchester, most likely of disease.

Pte William George Vater   *3rd Water Tank Company Royal Army Service Corps*
Service No.:   M/338314   Age: 30
Place of birth: Hilton, Dorset   Home country: England
Date of death: 30/08/18   Cause of death: Killed in action
Memorial: Salisbury, Wiltshire
War cemetery: Albert Communal Cemetery Extension, France
Theatre of war: France
Next of kin: Matilda C.E. Vater (wife); William & Ellen Vater (parents)
Addresses: 13 St Mark's Road, Salisbury, Wiltshire
                          Whitechurch, Dorset

Victor Saunders, who died in Manchester.

William Vater was killed in action on Friday 30 August 1918 near the town of Albert north-east of Amiens, France, most likely by German shelling.

Pte Reginald Arthur Randall		1st Battalion Wiltshire Regiment	
Service No.:	207726	Age:	22
Place of birth:	Poole, Dorset	Home country:	England
Date of death:	31/08/18	Cause of death:	Killed in action
Memorials:	Salisbury, Wiltshire		
	St Mark's Church Memorial		
War cemetery:	Warlencourt British Cemetery, France		
Theatre of war:	France		
Next of kin:	Walton & Eliza Randall (parents)		
Address:	8 Wyndham Terrace, Salisbury, Wiltshire		

Reginald Randell was killed in action on Saturday 31 August 1918. The 1st Battalion Wiltshire Regiment were west of the village of Beaulencourt, south of Bapaume, moving into position for an attack. Reginald Rendell was one of three members of the Wiltshires killed on that day.

2nd-Lt John Leopold Look		1st Battalion Gloucestershire Regiment	
Place of birth:	Sutton Dicheat, Somerset	Age:	31
Date of death:	01/09/18	Cause of death:	Died of wounds
Home country:	England	Memorial:	Salisbury, Wiltshire
War cemetery:	Bagneux British Cemetery, Gezaincout, France		
Theatre of war:	France		
Next of kin:	George & Anna Couzens Look (parents)		
Address:	Alhampton Court, Dicheat, Somerset		

John Look was attached to the 1/5th Battalion Devonshire Regiment when he was wounded during the Second Battle of Bapaume on Saturday 31 August 1918. He died of his wounds at one of the casualty-clearing stations near Gezaincourt, France.

Pte Reginald Penny		1st Battalion Wiltshire Regiment	
Service No.:	32660	Age:	20
Place of birth:	Bishopstone, Wiltshire	Home country:	England
Date of death:	01/09/18	Cause of death:	Killed in action
Memorial:	Salisbury, Wiltshire		
War cemetery:	Beaulencourt British Cemetery, Ligny Thilloy, France		
Theatre of war:	France		
Next of kin:	Harry & Alice Penny (parents)		
Address:	Salisbury, Wiltshire		

At 2 a.m. on 1 September 1918, the 1st Battalion Wiltshire Regiment were preparing to attack the village of Beaulencourt, south of Bapaume. The action started with a British creeping barrage and heavy British artillery concentrating on Beaulencourt. The Wiltshires then advanced under cover of the creeping barrage and attacked the village.

The village had been fortified with many enemy machine guns but German resistance was overcome and by 5.30 a.m. the village was in the Wiltshires' hands.

At 6.30 a.m. the Germans attempted a counter-attack to retake the village but it was easily repulsed by the Wiltshires.

An extract from the War Diary informs us of the items captured in the attack:

The following war material was captured in the village:
Two Field Guns (Damaged) Twenty-one Light Machine Guns
Two Light Field Pieces
Five Anti-Tank Rifles
Two Heavy Machine Guns
Approx 100 Prisoners were captured including four officers

Reginald Penny was one of nineteen members of the Wiltshires killed during this action.

The British advance also captured Perrone, south of Bapaume on Sunday 1 September. Overall, during August over 57,000 German prisoners of war were captured.

2nd-Lt Victor Charles Prince		*2/4th Battalion London Regiment*	
Place of birth:	Salisbury, Wiltshire	Home country:	England
Date of death:	01/09/18	Cause of death:	Killed in action
Age:	20	Decorations:	Military Cross
Memorials:	Salisbury, Wiltshire		
	St Martin's Church Memorial & the Choir School Memorial		
War cemetery:	Vis En Artois Memorial, France		
Theatre of war:	France		
Next of kin:	William John & Agnes Jane Prince (parents)		
Address:	66 St Ann Street, Salisbury, Wiltshire		

Mr W.J. Prince of St Ann Street received news in mid-September 1918, that his second son, 2nd-Lt V.C. Prince, London Regiment, was killed in action. 2nd-Lt Prince was educated at the Cathedral Chorister's School and Shaftesbury Grammar School. He joined the London Rifle Brigade in August 1916, obtained his commission the following year, proceeding to France in December 1917. Mr Prince has received the following letter from his commanding officer:

> It is with the greatest sorrow that I have to write and tell you the sad news that your son was killed in action whilst gallantly leading his company to the attack on 1 September. He had only recently taken over command of the company and had already proved himself to be both a gallant and able leader. I really cannot tell you in words what a splendid lad he was, and how much he will be missed by myself and his brother officers. He was always so cheery, and never happy unless seeing to the comfort and welfare of his men, with whom he was a great favourite. I am sure it will be a solace to you in your deep grief to know that your son died at the head of his company, in an attack which was a great success, gallantly doing his duty.

In January 1919 Victor Prince was posthumously awarded the Military Cross. The decoration was awarded:

> For conspicuous gallantry and able leadership, on 1 September 1918. His company was held up in heavy machine-gun fire 400 yards from it's objective; he went forward to the frontline and personally led a platoon with great dash, causing heavy casualties to the enemy. His example at a critical moment was worthy of high praise.

Victor Prince was killed in action on Sunday 1 September 1918, south-east of Arras; he is remembered on the Vis En Artois Memorial and has no known grave.

Pte Frank Rose · *16th Battalion Royal Warwickshire Regiment*

Service No.: 28051
Place of birth: Bemerton, Wiltshire
Date of death: 02/09/18
Memorials: Salisbury, Wiltshire
St Martin's Church Memorial & St Mark's Church Memorial
War cemetery: Bailleul Road East Cemetery, St Laurent Blangy, France
Theatre of war: France
Next of kin: William & Elizabeth Rose (parents)
Address: Fisherton Anger, Salisbury, Wiltshire

Age: 25
Home country: England
Cause of death: Killed in action

Frank Rose was killed in action on Monday 5 September 1918 near Arras, during what came to be known as the Second Battle of Bapaume. He was one of fourteen members of his battalion killed in action on that day.

Pte Bertram James Smith · *2nd Battalion Royal Fusiliers*

Service No.: 83164
Place of birth: Salisbury, Wiltshire
Date of death: 02/09/18
Memorial: Salisbury, Wiltshire
War cemetery: St Sever Cemetery Extension, Rouen, France
Theatre of war: France
Next of kin: Robert & Alice Smith (parents)
Address: 72 St Edmunds, Church Street, Salisbury, Wiltshire

Age: 19
Home country: England
Cause of death: Died of wounds

Bertram had originally joined the Devonshire Regiment but was posted to the 2nd Battalion Royal Fusiliers. He died of wounds on Monday 2 September 1918 at one of the casualty-clearing stations based in the Rouen area. The wounds he died of were most likely received during the British advance during August 1918.

Cpl Stephen Collinson · *18th Hussars*

Service No.: 20364
Home country: England
Date of death: 02/09/18

Age: 38

Stephen Collinson, who died in Salisbury.

War cemetery: Salisbury (London Road) Cemetery, England
Theatre of war: Home
Next of kin: Nellie Collinson (wife)
Address: Salisbury, Wiltshire

Cpl Collinson married Nellie Smith in Salisbury in spring 1915, not knowing that in just over three years he would be dead. He died at one of the hospitals in the Salisbury area on Monday 2 September 1918.

Pte Henry Stagg   *2/7th Battalion Hampshire Regiment*
Service No.:   307159   Age: 30
Place of birth: Winchester, Hampshire   Home country: England
Date of death: 03/09/18   Cause of death: Died of illness
Memorial: Salisbury, Wiltshire
War cemetery: Amara War Cemetery, Iraq
Theatre of war: Mesopotamia
Next of kin: Henry & Flora Stagg (parents)
Address: Winchester, Hampshire

Henry Stagg died, most likely of illness or disease, on Tuesday 3 September 1918 at one of the medical units based at Amara, Mesopotamia, in modern-day Iraq.

Gunner Leopold George Weston   *5th Brigade Canadian Field Artillery*
Service No.:   1263308
Place of birth: Salisbury, Wiltshire   Home country: England
Date of death: 03/09/18   Cause of death: Died of wounds
Memorial: Salisbury, Wiltshire
War cemetery: Ligny St Flochel British Cemetery, Averdoingt, France
Theatre of war: France
Next of kin: Arthur Henry & Elizabeth Anne Weston (parents)
Address: Dunreven House, Salisbury, Wiltshire

In 1900 Leopold Weston had joined the 8th Hussars in which he served for seven years prior to the outbreak of the war. He had been a clerk. Leopold's brother, Norman, had been living in Canada and in December 1914 joined the 1st Canadian Mounted Rifles, and most likely persuaded his brother to enlist in the Canadian Cavalry. On 23 June 1915, Leopold joined Lord Strathcona's Horse, the Royal Canadians. Norman Weston was killed in action during June 1916 and Leopold himself was probably wounded; he was transferred to the 2nd Reserve Cavalry being unfit for frontline service. He attained the rank of second lieutenant.

   On 7 November 1917 Leopold effectively rejoined the Canadian Artillery as a gunner, a rank equivalent to a private soldier, and was declared fit for service. Leopold died of his wounds on Tuesday 3 September 1918 at one of the casualty-clearing stations at Ligny St Flochel, near St Pol, east of Arras.

Pte Frederick George Chatfield   *7th Battalion Royal Sussex Regiment*
Service No.:   266523   Age: 33
Place of birth: Wimbledon, Surrey   Home country: England
Date of death: 05/09/18   Cause of death: Killed in action
Memorials: Salisbury, Wiltshire
                   St Paul's Church Memorial

War cemetery: Peronne Communal Cemetery Extension, France
Theatre of war: France
Next of kin: William H. and Louisa Chatfield (parents)
Address: 39 George Street, Salisbury, Wiltshire

On 4 September 1918 the 7th Battalion Royal Sussex Regiment, were in the area east of the Canal du Nord and south of Manancourt. They were preparing for an attack on Nurlu, which lies north-east of Peronne. Frederick Chatfield was killed in action on Thursday 5 September during the action at the German fortified village of Nurlu. He was one of seven members of the battalion to die on that day.

Pte Joseph John Skinner   *8th Battalion Gloucestershire Regiment*

Service No.:	44566		
Place of birth:	Eastbourne, Sussex	Home country:	England
Date of death:	09/09/18	Cause of death:	Killed in action
Memorials:	Salisbury, Wiltshire		
	St Thomas Church Memorial		
War cemetery:	Loos Memorial, France		
Theatre of war:	France		

Joseph Skinner had formerly been a member of the Hampshire Carabineers prior to joining the 8th Battalion Gloucestershire Regiment. He was killed in action on Monday 9 September 1918 during the British advance. He was one of six members of the battalion who were killed in action on that day. All six are remembered on the Loos Memorial and have no known grave.

Pte William Powrie   *1st Battalion Wiltshire Regiment*

Service No.:	204644	Age:	28
Home country:	England.	Cause of death:	Killed in action
Date of death:	10/09/18		
Memorials:	Salisbury, Wiltshire		
	St Paul's Church Memorial		
War cemetery:	Grand Seraucourt British Cemetery, France		
Theatre of war:	France		
Next of kin:	Mildred Powrie (wife)		
Address:	Brookside, Nether Wallop, Stockbridge, Hampshire		

William Powrie was killed in action on Tuesday 10 September near Sorel Le Grand while taking up position on the frontline.

Pte Montague Jesse Welch   *2/4th Battalion Hampshire Regiment*

Service No.:	44766	Age:	19
Place of birth:	Crowds Hill, Hampshire	Home country:	England
Date of death:	12/09/18	Cause of death:	Killed in action
Memorials:	Salisbury, Wiltshire		
	St Paul's Church Memorial		
War cemetery:	Lowrie Cemetery, Havrincourt, France		
Theatre of war:	France		
Next of kin:	Charles Henry & Rosa Emily Welch (parents)		
Address:	Twyford, Hampshire		

Montague Welch was killed in action on 12 September during the capture of Havrincourt by the British. It lies south-west of Cambrai and just north of Havrincourt Wood.

L/Cpl Charles William Johnston   *41st Battalion Australian Infantry Australian Imperial Force*

Service No.:	1851	Age:	23
Place of birth:	Rock Hampton, Australia	Home country:	Australia
Date of death:	12/09/18	Cause of death:	Died of illness
War cemetery:	Salisbury (London Road) Cemetery, England		
Next of kin:	John & Margaret Johnston (parents)		
Address:	Rock Hampton, Queensland, Australia		

Charles Johnston joined the Australian Imperial Force on 10 January 1916. Prior to the war he had been a fitter and was engaged to be married to Miss E. Carson. He arrived in England in October 1916 and proceeded to France during February 1917.

On 16 October 1917 he was wounded in action with a gun shot to the thigh and evacuated to hospital in England. On 7 September 1918 he was admitted to hospital at Fovant, where he died of appendicitis on Thursday 12 September 1918. He was buried at London Road Cemetery on 16 September 1918 with full military honours.

Driver John Biles Kingsbury   *14th Brigade Australian Artillery Australian Imperial Force.*

Service No.:	5405	Home country:	Australia	Age:	23
Date of death:	17/09/18	Cause of death:	Died of illness		
War cemetery:	Salisbury (London Road) Cemetery, England				
Next of kin:	John Biles Kingsbury & Sarah Kingsbury (parents)				
Address:	Douglas Street, Clermont, Queensland, Australia				

John Kingsbury enlisted in the Australian Imperial Force on 5 January 1916 and arrived in France the following June. In August 1917 he was wounded in action with a shell wound to the right arm. On 29 October 1917 he was wounded again with a bullet to the chest, but he had recovered enough by 8 November to be put on a charge for drunkenness. On 28 November he was on charge again, for being AWOL for an hour and lost two days pay. He died on Tuesday 17 September 1918 of endocarditis, an inflammation of the inside lining of the heart chambers, at the military hospital, Sutton Veny. Kingsbury was buried at London Road Cemetery with full military honours on 21 September 1918.

In January 1919 Kingsbury's father wrote the following letter to the Austalian Records Office:

To Maj. J.M. Dean
Officer in Charge Base Records
Melbourne

Dear Sir
Please accept my sincerest thanks for your report of the death of my son No.5405 Driver John Biles Kingsbury. It is a great comfort to his mother and myself to know where he is buried, especially myself as I lived in the place named for many years before coming to Queensland and have still a few friends there. Yet, again thanking you Sir.

Yours Obediently
J.B. Kingsbury

Far left: *Charles Johnston, who died of appendicitis.*

Left: *John Kingsbury, who died of heart disease.*

2nd-Lt John Folliott

Place of birth:	Salisbury, Wiltshire		
Date of death:	19/09/18		
Memorials:	Salisbury, Wiltshire		
	Wilsford Wiltshire & St Martin's Church Memorial		
War cemetery:	Trefcon British Cemetery, Caulaincourt, France		
Theatre of war:	France		
Next of kin:	John Alfred & Amy Folliott (parents)		
Address:	Tamerton, Salisbury, Wiltshire		

2nd Battalion Durham Light Infantry

Home country:	England	Age:	20
Cause of death:	Killed in action		

Mr and Mrs J.A. Folliott, of Tamerton, London Road, Salisbury, had by October 1918, received many messages of sympathy on the death of their only son, 2nd-Lt John Folliott of the Durham Light Infantry, who was killed in action in France on Thursday 19 September. With the expressions of sympathy was associated the name of Miss Folliott by whom the loss of an only brother is keenly felt. 2nd-Lt Folliott was educated at the Modern School, Salisbury and Sherborne, and after a school career of high promise, entered Sandhurst. He passed out of Sandhurst in December 1917 and was commissioned to the Durham Light Infantry. Up to April 1918 he was training with a reserve battalion at South Shields. He was detailed for the Western Front in the middle of April 1918, and within a month was commended for gallantry in action, a rare distinction for so young an officer. Upon the parchment, which is an official record of conspicuous bravery, his brigadier-general notified that 2nd-Lt John Folliott's endeavours: 'on 21 May, 1918, near ----- whilst in charge of a raiding party and in the previous preliminary recognisances has been reported to me, and I have much pleasure in reading the record of your gallantry.'

Letters from officers of the regiment and others are testimony of the high regard 2nd-Lt Folliott had won during his period of service. His colonel had written to his father:

You will already have heard of the death of your son John in action on the morning of the 19 September. Will you allow me to express my sympathy at your great loss of such a splendid boy. He died leading two platoons into action, being killed almost instantaneously by a machine-gun bullet. He is a very great loss to us all, both as a very capable officer and a very charming friend. His loss has been felt very deeply by his men, who were devoted to him. He was buried by our chaplain last night, who has, I understand, written to you. A cross will also be erected tomorrow on his grave. I shall personally miss very deeply your son, who has repeatedly displayed great gallantry, and who has died, as he lived, a very fine example to all.

Lt Folliott's company commander wrote to his mother:

You son was killed at five minutes to seven on the morning of the 19th. He died without pain, and I am very glad to say that I was able to get his body back. He is buried near ---------- I can only repeat that we have lost one of the most popular officers of the battalion and one who was beloved by his men. Please accept my deepest sympathy in your very great sorrow.

The chaplain of the battalion has also written a deeply sympathetic letter, in which he speaks of Lt Folliott's high character, his splendid example to the regiment and the devotion of his men. Typical of the letters from personal friends is one written from one friend on active service to another and since forwarded to the bereaved mother, in which the writer says: 'I was never so miserable in all my life. He was a multitude of friends all rolled in one.'

In October 1918, John Folliott's father received the following message of condolence upon the death in action of his only son: 'The King and Queen deeply regret the loss you and the army have sustained by the death of you son in the service of his country. Their Majesties truly sympathise with you in your sorrow.'

John Folliott was killed in action on Thursday 19 September 1918 and is buried in Trefcon British Cemetery, Caulaincourt, France.

Capt. Robert Halley Knight		*4th Battalion Wiltshire Regiment*			
Place of birth:	Keswick, Cumberland	Home country:	England	Age:	25
Date of death:	19/09/18	Cause of death:	Killed in action		
Memorial:	Salisbury, Wiltshire				
War cemetery:	Ramleh War Cemetery, Israel				
Theatre of war:	Palestine				
Next of kin:	Dr Alexander & Elizabeth Anne Knight (parents)				
Address:	Bolton-le-Sands, Carnforth, Lancashire				

Capt. R.H. Knight, Wiltshire Regiment, was well known in Salisbury, where he had lived for about four years prior to the outbreak of war; he was killed in action in Palestine on 19 September 1918. He was the son of Dr and Mrs Knight, of Keswick, Cumberland, and was educated at Fettes. He became an articled pupil of Messrs Fletcher & Fletcher, chartered accountants, of Salisbury, in 1911 and passed the intermediate examination of the Institute of Chartered Accountants in 1913. He was a private in the Wiltshire Territorials on the outbreak of war, and before his regiment proceeded to India he received a commission. While in India he was promoted to lieutenant, and was made a captain earlier in 1914. In 1917 he went to Palestine and was slightly wounded. The news of the death of Capt. Knight was received with much regret by his many friends in Salisbury. He was held in the highest respect, and enjoyed great popularity in sporting circles. He was a keen member of the South Wiltshire Golf Club.

Robert Knight was killed in action on Thursday 19 September 1918 while attacking Turkish trenches at Et Tireh, north-east of Jaffa, in modern-day Israel.

L/Cpl Sidney George Lear		*1/4th Battalion Wiltshire Regiment*	
Service No.:	201412	Age:	21
Place of birth:	Salisbury, Wiltshire	Home country:	England

Date of death:	19/09/18	Cause of death:	Killed in action
Memorials:	Bishop Wordsworth's School Memorial & St Mark's Church Memorial		
War cemetery:	Ramleh War Cemetery, Israel		
Theatre of war:	Palestine		
Next of kin:	Edward & Agnes Lear (parents)		
Address:	41 St Mark's Road, Salisbury, Wiltshire		

On Thursday 19 December 1918 the 1/4th Battalion Wiltshire regiment were in action against entrenched Turkish forces 1½ miles south-west of Et Tireh (north-east of Jaffa). The Turks were forced out of the trenches, but at a cost to the Wiltshires of seventy-seven casualties. Sixteen members of the battalion were killed in action including Sidney Lear and Col. Armstrong, the commanding officer of the 1/4th Battalion.

Sgt James Richard Garland   *10th Battalion East Kent Regiment (The Buffs)*

Service No.:	T/270604	Age:	28
Place of birth:	Tadnole, Dorset	Home country:	England
Date of death:	21/09/18	Cause of death:	Killed in action
Memorial:	Salisbury, Wiltshire		
War cemetery:	Vis En Artois Memorial, France		
Theatre of war:	France		
Next of kin:	Thomas Richard Garland (father)		
Address:	Fisherton Brewery Stores, Salisbury, Wiltshire		

James Garland was a member of the West Kent Yeomanry which, along with the Royal East Kent Yeomanry, became the 10th Battalion East Kent Regiment. He was killed in action on Saturday 21 September 1918, during the fighting that took place around Epehy, north-east of the town of St Quentin. Garland was one of twenty-two members of the Buffs to be killed on that day and he is remembered on the Vis En Artois Memorial. John Garland, the only son of Thomas and the late Alice Garland, has no known grave.

Pte Alan Brooks   *14th Battalion London Regiment (London Scottish)*

Service No.:	514800	Age:	19
Place of birth:	Salisbury, Wiltshire	Home country:	England
Date of death:	27/09/18	Cause of death:	Killed in action
Memorials:	Salisbury, Wiltshire		
	St Thomas Church Memorial		
War cemetery:	Vis En Artois British Cemetery, Haucourt, France		
Theatre of war:	France		
Next of kin:	Harry & Frances E. Brooks (parents)		
Address:	45 High Street St Thomas, Salisbury, Wiltshire		

Nineteen-year-old Alan Brooks was killed in action on Friday 27 September 1918 in the action that took place to the west of Cambrai at the Battle of Canal Du Nord. He is buried in the Vis En Artois British Cemetery, Haucourt, which is situated on the Arras to Cambrai Road.

Company Quartermaster Sgt George Ralph Singleton   *5th Battalion Saskatchewan Regiment*
Canadian Infantry

Service No.:	81804	Age:	29
Place of birth:	Salisbury, Wiltshire	Home country:	Canada

Date of death: 28/09/18   Cause of death: killed in action
Memorials: Salisbury, Wiltshire
                    Bishop Wordsworth's School Memorial
War cemetery: Haynecourt British Cemetery, France
Theatre of war: France
Next of kin: Edith A. Singleton (wife); Harry Sidney & Amelia Singleton (parents)
Address: 31 Endless Street, Salisbury, Wiltshire
                    79 College Street, Salisbury, Wiltshire

George Singleton joined the Canadian Infantry on 12 December 1914 at Winnipeg, Canada. He had formerly been a member of the 3rd Battalion Wiltshire Regiment. Prior to the war he had been a farmer. On 27 September 1918 the 1st Canadian and 11th Divisions attacked and captured Haynecourt, north-west of Cambrai. The following day, Saturday 28 September, George Singleton was killed in action during the action at Sailly, which was successfully captured by the Canadians.

Pte Lionel Cecil Trubridge   *1st Battalion Lancashire Fusiliers*
Service No.:   28542   Age: 21
Place of birth: Fisherton, Wiltshire   Home country: England
Date of death: 28/09/18   Cause of death: Killed in action
Memorials: Salisbury, Wiltshire
                   St Paul's Church Memorial
War cemetery: Hooge Crater Cemetery, Belgium
Theatre of war: Belgium
Next of kin: William & Jane Trubridge (parents)
Address: Fisherton Anger, Salisbury, Wiltshire

On Saturday 28 September 1918 King Albert of Belgium led an Anglo-Belgian attack along a 23-mile front from Dixmunde to Ploegsteert, Belgium, Pte Trubridge was killed in action along with ten other members of the 1st Battalion Lancashire Fusiliers. His brother Thomas Trubridge was killed in France in October 1914.

Pte Albert Henry Sheppard   *7th Battalion Shropshire Light Infantry*
Service No.:   27604   Age: 21
Place of birth: Tidworth, Wiltshire   Home country: England
Date of death: 01/10/18   Cause of death: Killed in action
Memorial: Salisbury, Wiltshire
War cemetery: Flesquieres Hill British Cemetery, France
Theatre of war: France
Next of kin: William & Mary J. Sheppard (parents)
Address: New Court Down Buildings, Downton, Wiltshire

Albert Sheppard had originally joined the Wiltshire Regiment and was transferred to the 7th Battalion Shropshire Light Infantry. He was killed in action on Tuesday 1 October 1918 during the action to the east of Cambrai, along with seven other members of the 7th Battalion.

Pte Thomas Butler   *32nd Battalion Australian Infantry Australian Imperial Force 32nd*
Service No.:   3521   Age: 32
Place of birth: Wallaroo, Australia   Home country: Australia

Australian Thomas Butler died in Salisbury.

Date of death:	04/10/18	Cause of death:	Died of illness
War cemetery:	Salisbury London Road Cemetery, England.		
Next of kin:	John & Kate Butler (parents)		
Address:	Cannon Street, Wallaroo, South Australia		

Thomas Butler enlisted in the Australian Imperial Force on 10 April 1916 and arrived in England at the end of September 1916, embarking for France on 5 December 1916. He returned to England sick with varicose veins before rejoining the front in France during May 1917.

He was wounded by accident in May 1918 with a bullet to the foot and evacuated to England. In September 1918 he was admitted to the Military Hospital at Fovant with perforated stomach ulcers, where he died on Friday 4 October 1918.

He was buried with full military honours, at London Road Cemetery on 8 October 1918.

Guardsman Charles Douglas Turner		*2nd Battalion Grenadier Guards*		
Service No.:	30409	Age:		29
Place of birth:	Pimlico, London	Home country:		England
Date of death:	05/10/18	Cause of death:		Died of wounds
Memorials:	Salisbury, Wiltshire			
	Bishop Wordsworth's School Memorial & St Thomas Church Memorial			
War cemetery:	St Sever Cemetery Extension, Rouen, France			
Theatre of war:	France			
Next of kin:	Charles & Martha Turner (parents)			
Address:	15 Church Street, Fisherton Anger, Salisbury, Wiltshire			

News was received that Pte Douglas Turner (Grenadier Guards), only son of Mr and Mrs Charles Turner, of Church Street, Fisherton, died of his wounds during fighting in October 1918. He was an Bishop's School old boy, who after leaving school, held an appointment in the Goods Traffic Department in the South Western Railway, which brought him into contact with a wide district around the city. Before the war he was in the Wiltshire Yeomanry, and soon after the outbreak of hostilities endeavoured to rejoin a mounted unit, but his services were retained on the railway. He enlisted under the Derby scheme in 1916 and joined a Household Brigade Regiment, subsequently transferring to the Grenadier Guards. He went through much fighting with the Guards Division and earlier in 1918 was in hospital suffering from shell shock. In the fighting during the previous week his left leg was shattered, and he died in hospital at Rouen on Saturday 5 October 1918.

2nd-Lt Bertrand John Young   *B Company 6th Battalion Royal Warwickshire*
                                                Regiment

Place of birth: Alvediston, Wiltshire   Home country: England   Age: 36
Date of death: 05/10/18   Cause of death: Killed in action
Memorials: Salisbury, Wiltshire
                    St Martin's Church Memorial
War cemetery: Bellicourt British Cemetery, France
Theatre of war: France
Next of kin: John & Louisa Young (parents)
Address: Pound Street, Ebbesbourne Wake, Salisbury, Wiltshire

2nd-Lt Young was killed in action on Saturday 5 October 1918, north of the town of St Quentin, France. This day marked the end of the Battles of Cambrai and St Quentin and the German forces retreated to positions along the River Suippe.

2nd-Lt Charles Hedley Edgecombe   *11th Squadron Royal Air Force*
Home country: Canada   Age: 30
Date of death: 06/10/18   Cause of death: Died of shock
War cemetery: Salisbury (London Road) Cemetery, England
Next of kin: Frederick & Helen Edgecombe (parents)
Address: Fredericton, New Brunswick, Canada

An inquiry was held on the afternoon of Monday 7 October 1918 into the death of Lt Edgecombe by the deputy coroner, Mr H.C. Wyld. Capt. Collett, RAF, of Old Sarum, stated the airmen left the aerodrome on Saturday at 10.35 a.m. The aeroplane was then in good order. Cpl Charles Hesketh, RAF, stated that he was sent with a party to attend to the machine on Sunday. There was nothing seriously wrong, and it was put in order ready to start. At 3.30 p.m. on Sunday, Lt Edgecombe ascended to 300 or 400ft, and when a half mile from where they started the machine made a steep bank, the wind seemed to get under it, turned it over , and it came nose down in a spin. Mr Tom Ridout, farmer, and PC Fudge also gave evidence. The coroner recorded as the verdict that the deceased died from shock caused by a violent fall to the ground in an aeroplane.

Pte William Moncrieffe Macey   *7th Battalion Wiltshire Regiment*
Service No.:   32048   Age: 22
Place of birth: Salisbury, Wiltshire   Home country: England
Date of death: 07/10/18   Cause of death: Killed in action
Memorials: Salisbury, Wiltshire
                    St Paul's Church Memorial & St Martin's Church Memorial
War cemetery: Templux Le Guerard British Cemetery, France
Theatre of war: France
Next of kin: Sidney & Ada Blanche Macey (parents)
Address: 70 York Road, Salisbury, Wiltshire

William Macey was killed in action on Monday 7 October 1918 near the village of Bony, north of St Quentin, which was part of the German defence systen known as the Hindenburg Line. He was one of forty-two members of the 7th Battalion to be killed on that day. Macey's brother Alwyn Sidney Macey was killed near Arras in May 1917.

Cpl Frank Noke   *2nd Battalion Royal Dublin Fusiliers*
Service No.:   14938   Age: 25

Charles Edgecombe, who died in a tragic air crash.

Place of birth:	Salisbury, Wiltshire	Home country:	England
Date of death:	07/10/18	Cause of death:	Killed in action
Memorial:	Salisbury, Wiltshire		
War cemetery:	Vis En Artois Memorial, France		
Theatre of war:	France		
Next of kin:	Frank & the late Mary Noke (parents)		
Address:	21 Guilder Lane, Salisbury, Wiltshire		

Cpl Noke had originally joined the Wiltshire Regiment but was transferred to the 2nd Battalion Royal Dublin Fusiliers. He was the second son of Frank Noke and the late Mary Noke. He was killed on Monday 7 October 1918 during the action to retake Cambrai. He was one of twenty-three members of the 2nd Battalion to be killed on that day. Noke is remembered on the Vis En Artois Memorial and has no known grave.

2nd-Lt Douglas Gilbert Hayward Aldworth   *3rd Battalion Royal Berkshire Regiment*

Home country:	England	Age:	19
Date of death:	10/10/18	Cause of death:	Died at sea
Memorials:	Salisbury, Wiltshire		
	St Martin's Church Memorial		
War cemetery:	Grange Gorman Military Cemetery, Ireland		
Theatre of war:	Ireland		
Next of kin:	Arthur E. & E.R. Aldworth (parents)		
Address:	Laverstock Vicarage, Laverstock, Wiltshire		

Nineteen-year-old Douglas Hayward was drowned on Thursday 10 October 1918 when the SS *Leinster*, a troop ship on its way to France, was sunk by a German U-boat.

Pte Edward Waters   *2nd Battalion Coldstream Guards*

Service No.:	18199	Age:	23
Place of birth:	Highfield, Wiltshire	Home country:	England
Date of death:	11/10/18	Cause of death:	Died of wounds
Memorials:	Salisbury, Wiltshire		
	St Paul's Church Memorial		

War cemetery: Grevillers British Cemetery, France
Theatre of war: France
Next of kin: Beat Waters (wife); Edward & Agnes Waters (parents)
Addresses: 23 Beaumont Street, London
                  30 George Street, Salisbury, Wiltshire

Edward Waters, known as Teddy, died of his wounds on Friday 11 October 1918, at one of the casualty-clearing stations based at Grevillers, east of Bapaume. His wounds were most likely received during the actions against the Hindenburg Line. His wife wrote the following:

> It's only a wife that knows the sorrow
> It's only a widow that knows the pain
> of losing a husband she loved so dearly
> And knows she can never see him again
> With heart so loving and actions so kind
> It would be hard in this world his equal to find
> A loving husband one of the best
> From his sorrowing wife Beat

Pte Frederick Allan Vincent   *2nd Battalion Australian Reinforcement Australian Imperial Force*

Service No.:	56619	Age:	21
Place of birth:	Burnie, Tasmania	Home country:	Australia
Date of death:	11/10/18	Cause of death:	Died of illness
War cemetery:	Salisbury London Road Cemetery, England		
Next of kin:	Henry & Alice Vincent (parents)		
Address:	Burnie, Tasmania		

Frederick Vincent had joined the Australian Imperial Force on 28 May 1915 and arrived in England on 27 September 1917 He was admitted to the military hospital at Sutton Veny on 10 October 1918, seriously ill. He died the follwing day of pneumonia. He was buried with full military honours on 17 October 1918 at London Road Cemetery.

In August 1919 Alice Vincent, his mother, received a parcel of Frederick Vincent's personal possessions consisting of: one disc, three postage stamps, two keys and two letters.

Pte Douglas Wornell Harding   *53rd Battalion Royal Warwickshire Regiment*

Service No.:	TR/28234	Age:	18
Place of birth:	Salisbury, Wiltshire	Home country:	England
Date of death:	13/10/18	Cause of death:	Died of illness
Memorial:	Salisbury, Wiltshire		
War cemetery:	Salisbury (London Road) Cemetery, England		
Theatre of war:	Home		
Next of kin:	Edwin W. & Alice M. Harding (parents)		
Address:	33 Wyndham Road, Salisbury, Wiltshire		

Eighteen-year-old Douglas Harding was the eldest son of Edwin and Alice Harding. He died, most likely of disease, at Amesbury, on Sunday 13 October 1918.

Pte Lewis Charles Jackson   *1/4th Battalion Hampshire Regiment*

Service No.:	201986	Age:	21

Place of birth:	Salisbury, Wiltshire	Home country:	England
Date of death:	15/10/18	Cause of death:	Died of illness
Memorials:	Salisbury, Wiltshire		
	St Mark's Church Memorial		
War cemetery:	Kirkee 1914–18 Memorial, India		
Theatre of war:	India		
Next of kin:	Edwin Robert & Amelia Bessie Jackson (parents)		
Address:	81 London Road, Salisbury, Wiltshire		

Lewis Jackson had originally joined the Wiltshire Regiment but was transferred to the 1/4th Battalion Hampshire Regiment. He was the second son of Pte and Mrs Jackson – Edwin, his father was serving in the British Army.

Lewis Jackson died of pneumonia following influenza, at Deccan War Hospital, Poona, India, on Tuesday 15 October 1918. He is remembered on the Kirkee 1914–18 Memorial. It commemorates over 1,800 servicemen who died in India during the First World War, and are buried in cemeteries in India and Pakistan where their graves can no longer be properly maintained.

Gunner Anthony Austin Street		*Australian Field Artillery Australian Imperial Force*	
Service No.:	63787	Age:	20
Place of birth:	Sydney, Australia	Home country:	Australia
Date of death:	16/10/18	Cause of death:	Died of illness
War cemetery:	Salisbury (London Road) Cemetery, England		
Next of kin:	John William & Mary Veronica Street (parents)		
Address:	Sydney		

Anthony Street, a clerk, joined the Australian Imperial Force on 11 February 1918. His brother was a major in the Army and already in Europe. He left Sydney on 5 June 1918 and arrived in England on 12 August 1918. He reported sick, with influenza, to Sutton Veny Military Hospital on 9 October 1918 and was admitted to the military hospital, and was described as seriously ill, on 12 October 1918. He died on Wednesday 16 October 1918 of pneumonia caused by influenza. He was buried at 3 p.m. on 19 October 1918, at London Road Cemetery.

One of the Wreaths on the grave had a simple note: 'From Father & Mother, Jack, Maude and Margery.'

Far left: *Frederick Vincent, who died of pneumonia – itself a terrible killer in the First World War.*

Left: *Anthony Street, who died of pneumonia caused by influenza.*

L/Cpl Walter Reginald Hazel　　　　　　　*1/1st Battalion Nottinghamshire Yeomanry*

Service No.:	320356	Age:	21
Place of birth:	Bournemouth, Dorset	Home country:	England
Date of death:	18/10/18	Cause of death:	Died of illness
Memorials:	Salisbury, Wiltshire		
	St Thomas Church Memorial		
War cemetery:	Damascus Commonwealth War Cemetery, Syria		
Theatre of war:	Palestine		
Next of kin:	Walter & Isabell Hazel (parents)		
Address:	118 Old Christchurch Road, Bournemouth, Dorset		

L/Cpl Walter Reginald Hazel, of the Royal Wiltshire Imperial Yeomanry, was the only son of Mr and Mrs W. Hazel, of Bournemouth, and brother of Mrs M.J. Keevil, of High Street, Salisbury. He joined the OTC at the Bournemouth School in 1911. Two years later he came to Salisbury in his father's business and joined the Wiltshire Yeomanry. He was mobilised with his unit in August 1914. After training in Sussex, he went to France with the British Expeditionary Force and he experienced two years fighting that finished at the Battle of the Somme. In this action he was severely wounded, and it took him three months at Netley Hospital to recuperate. He then joined the Cavalry unit at Aldershot, where he won his cross swords and guns. After completing his five years' service he was drafted into the Sherwood Rangers Yeomanry and sent to Egypt with the Egyptian Expeditionary Force. He was there only a few weeks before he succumbed to an attack of malaria.

Walter Hazel died in a military hospital in Damascus on 10 October 1918.

L/Cpl Frederick James Moore　　　　　　　*Royal Army Service Corps Mechanical Transport*

Service No.:	M2/153799	Age:	24
Place of birth:	Exeter, Devon	Home country:	England
Date of death:	18/10/18	Cause of death:	Killed in action
Memorials:	Salisbury, Wiltshire		
	St Paul's Church Memorial		
War cemetery:	Carnieres Communal Cemetery Extension, France		
Theatre of war:	France		
Next of kin:	William & Mary Jane Moore (parents)		
Address:	7 Ashfield Road, Salisbury, Wiltshire		

Frederick Moore was attached to 'R' Siege Park, XVII Corps, Heavy Artillery. He was killed in action on 18 October 1918, east of Cambrai.

2nd-Lt Dudley Victor Druery　　　　　　　*13th Battalion London Regiment*

Place of birth:	Putney, London	Home country:	England	Age: 21
Date of death:	18/10/18	Cause of death:	Died of wounds	
Memorial:	Choir School Memorial			
War cemetery:	St Sever Cemetery Extension, Rouen, France			
Theatre of war:	France			
Next of kin:	Henry & Cecile C.L. Druery			
Address:	Putney, London			

Dudley Druery died of his wounds on Friday 18 October at one of the medical units based in the Rouen area.

Pte Ethelbert Edward Henry Gale

Service No.:   M2/035166
Place of birth: Cowley, Oxfordshire
Date of death: 19/10/18
Memorials: Salisbury, Wiltshire
                  St Thomas Memorial
War cemetery: Mikra British Cemetery, Greece
Theatre of war: The Balkans
Next of kin: Beatrice Gale (wife); James & Matilda Gale (parents)
Addresses: 7 Wood Street, Kettering, Surrey.
                  Cowley, Oxfordshire

Royal Army Service Corps 1083rd Mechanical Transport Coy

Age: 38
Home country: England
Cause of death: Died of illness

Ethelbert Gale died of illness on 19 October 1918 at Mikra, Greece, at one of the hospitals based in the town.

Pte Frank Seviour

Service No.:   37041
Place of birth: Salisbury, Wiltshire
Date of death: 20/10/18
Memorials: Salisbury, Wiltshire
                  St Martin's Church Memorial & Salisbury United Methodists Memorial
War cemetery: St Aubert British Cemetery, France
Theatre of war: France
Next of kin: Frank George Seviour (father)
Address: 1 Meadow Cottage, Friary, Salisbury, Wiltshire

2nd Battalion Wiltshire Regiment

Age: 18
Home country: England
Cause of death: Killed in action

Just before 3 a.m. on Sunday 20 October 1918, 2nd Battalion Wiltshire Regiment were advancing under a British artillery barrage towards the railway embankment at St Aubert east of Cambrai. Unfortunately, the barrage did not lift adequately causing some shells to fall short. Sixteen members of the battalion were killed in the 'friendly fire' incident. Eighteen-year-old Frank Seviour was killed in action on that day and is buried in St Aubert British Cemetery. His brother William Serviour would be killed in action in Russia, during June 1919.

Pte Edward Percy Robinson

Service No.:   43537
Place of birth: Salisbury, Wiltshire
Date of death: 23/10/18
Memorial: Salisbury, Wiltshire
War cemetery: Croix Churchyard, France
Theatre of war: France
Next of kin: Albert & Mary A. Robinson (parents)
Address: 6 George Street, Salisbury, Wiltshire

1st Battalion Middlesex Regiment

Age: 19
Home country: England
Cause of death: Killed in action

Nineteen-year-old Edward Robinson had originally joined the Wiltshire Regiment but was transferred to the 1st Battalion Middlesex Regiment. He was killed in action on 23 October 1918 during the advance between Le Cateau and Valenciennes, east of Cambrai, in the process pushing the German forces back 3 miles. He was one of thirty-two members of the 1st Battalion to be killed on that day and is buried in the churchyard at Croix, a village north-east of Cateau.

Pte Harry Sturgess   *4th Reserve Battalion Wiltshire Regiment*

Service No.:   09   Age: 18
Place of birth: Kensington, London   Home country: England
Date of death: 24/10/18   Cause of death: Died of illness
Memorials: Salisbury, Wiltshire
                   St Martin's Church Memorial
War cemetery: Grange Gorman Military Cemetery, Ireland
Theatre of war: Ireland
Next of kin: Adopted son of John & Elizabeth Bell
Address: Salisbury, Wiltshire

In May 1918 the 4th Reserve Battalion Wiltshire Regiment moved to Ireland. Eighteen-year-old Harry Sturgess died of illness on Thursday 24 October 1918 and is buried in Grange Gorman Military Cemetery,

Pte Frederick Bailey   *60th Mobile Workshop Royal Army Ordinance Corps*

Service No.:   025261   Age: 26
Place of birth: Salisbury, Wiltshire   Home country: England
Date of death: 25/10/18   Cause of death: Died of illness
Memorial: Salisbury, Wiltshire
War cemetery: Montecchio Precalcino Communal Cemetery Extension, Italy
Theatre of war: Italy
Next of kin: Fredrick & Mary Ann Bailey (parents)
Address: Castle Street, Salisbury, Wiltshire

Frederick Bailey died of illness on Friday 25 October 1918, at one of the casualty-clearing stations based at the town of Montecchio Precalcino, Italy. The inscription of the original wooden cross erected by his comrades read: 'from Comrades of Nos.62 and II Ordnance Workshops.'

Pte Albert Fullford   *1st Battalion Wiltshire Regiment*

Service No.:   4752   Age: 40
Place of birth: Salisbury, Wiltshire   Home country: England
Date of death: 27/10/18   Cause of death: Died of illness
Memorials: Salisbury, Wiltshire
                   St Martin's Church Memorial
War cemetery: Cologne Southern Cemetery, Germany
Theatre of war: Germany
Next of kin: William P. & Elizabeth J. Fullford (parents)
Address: Salisbury, Wiltshire

Albert Fullford died on Sunday 27 October 1918, most likely due to illness as a prisoner of war in Germany. At this stage of the war, food shortages were rife in Germany and this had great effect on the health of British prisoners of war.

Pte Gilbert Charlie Hibberd   *9th Company (Colchester) Royal Army Medical Corps*

Service No.:   132934   Age: 25
Place of birth: Salisbury, Wiltshire   Home country: England
Date of death: 27/10/18   Cause of death: Died of illness
Memorial: Salisbury, Wiltshire
War cemetery: St Albans Cemetery, England

British artillery in Italy.

Theatre of war: Home
Next of kin: George & Anna Hibberd (parents)
Address: St Edmund, Salisbury, Wiltshire

Gilbert Hibberd died of illness on Sunday 27 October 1918 at St Albans. His brother, Frank Albert Hibberd, was killed in action at Arras in April 1917.

L/Cpl Joseph Arthur Hearn		*1st Battalion Royal Munster Fusiliers*	
Service No.:	G/921	Age:	20
Place of birth:	Salisbury, Wiltshire	Home country:	England
Date of death:	28/10/18	Cause of death:	Died of illness
Memorial:	Salisbury, Wiltshire		
War cemetery:	Arquata Scrivia Communal Cemetery Extension, Italy		
Theatre of war:	Italy		
Next of kin:	William & Ada Hearn (parents)		
Address:	8 Richmond Terrace, Gramshaw Road, Bemerton, Wiltshire		

Joseph had originally joined the Wiltshire Regiment but was transferred to the 1st Battalion Royal Munster Fusiliers. He died of illness at one of the military hospital bases in Arquata Scrivia, Italy, on Monday 28 October 1918.

Pte William George Bell		*2nd Battalion Wiltshire Regiment*	
Service No.:	7536	Age:	28
Place of birth:	Salisbury, Wiltshire	Home country:	England
Date of death:	29/10/18	Cause of death:	Died of illness
Memorials:	Salisbury, Wiltshire		
	St Paul's Church Memorial		
War cemetery:	Niederzwehren Cemetery, Germany		
Theatre of war:	Germany		
Next of kin:	John & Elizabeth Bell (parents)		
Address:	St Martin, Salisbury, Wiltshire		

Pte Bell, known as George, died as a prisoner of war in Germany, on Tuesday 10 October 1918. He is most likely to have died of disease.

Maj. Henry Wyndam Francis Blackburn Farrer   *39th Brigade Royal Field Artillery*

Place of birth:	Ireland	Home country:	England	Age: 24
Date of death:	30/10/18	Cause of death:	Killed in action	

Decorations: Military Cross, *Croix de Guerre* (Belgium)
Memorial: Salisbury, Wiltshire
War cemetery: La Vallee Mulatre Communal Cemetery Extension, France
Theatre of war: France
Next of kin: Canon Henry R.W. & Georgina B. Farrer (parents)
Address: South Canonry, Salisbury, Wiltshire

Maj. Henry Wyndham F.B. Farrer, MC. A brilliant officer, who had been three times mentioned in despatches and had been awarded the Military Cross and two bars – immediate rewards for gallantry in field – and also the Belgian *Croix de Guerre*, was killed in action on Wednesday 30 October 1918. He was second son of Canon and Mrs Farrer, of South Canonry, the Close, Salisbury, to whom the deepest sympathy was extended in their sad bereavement.

Henry Farrer, who was killed instantaneously by a shell, had been wounded on six occasions, four times seriously. He was only twenty-four years of age. He was educated at Sandroyd and Bedford Grammar School, where he was a mathematical scholar. At both schools he obtained first colours for cricket and football and, developing into a fine athlete, he got his cap for Dorset cricket, playing the last three seasons before the war. While he was still at school, Farrer was asked to play in the Midland Counties Rugby XV against the New Zealand All Blacks.

He passed twenty-eighth into Woolwich in December 1912, and immediately got his rugby XV colours. Owing to the war, he was given his commission in August 1914 and went to France in the following October, serving there continuously until he was killed.

Rifleman John James Adlam   *B Company 22nd Battalion Rifle Brigade*

Service No.:	204508	Age:	34
Place of birth:	Salisbury, Wiltshire	Home country:	England
Date of death:	31/10/18	Cause of death:	Died of illness

Memorial: Salisbury, Wiltshire
War cemetery: Dorian Memorial, Greece
Theatre of war: Balkans
Next of kin: John & Mary Anne Adlam (parents)
Address: 117 Gigant Street, Salisbury, Wiltshire

John Adlam originally joined the Wiltshire Regiment but was transferred to the 22nd (Wessex Welsh) Battalion, the Rifle Brigade. He died of pneumonia at a hospital in Salonika on Thursday 31 October 1918.

Pte Harry Waters   *22nd Battalion Tank Corps*

Service No.:	311461	Age:	29
Place of birth:	Salisbury, Wiltshire	Home country:	England
Date of death:	31/10/18	Cause of death:	Died of illness

Memorials: Salisbury, Wiltshire
                 St Paul's Church Memorial
War cemetery: Salisbury (Devizes Road) Cemetery, Wiltshire
Theatre of war: Home
Next of kin: Rosa Ellen Waters (wife); George & Jane Waters (parents)
Addresses: 23 George Street, Salisbury, Wiltshire
                 30 George Street, Salisbury, Wiltshire

Harry Waters died of illness at Wareham, Dorset, on Thursday 31 October 1918.

Capt. Tom Geoffrey Milsome Parker		*Royal Army Medical Corps*		
Place of birth:	Salisbury, Wiltshire	Home country:	England	Age: 28
Date of death:	03/11/18	Cause of death:	Died of illness	
Memorials:	Salisbury, Wiltshire			
	Choir School Memorial			
War cemetery:	Christchurch Cemetery, England			
Theatre of war:	Home			
Next of kin:	Lewis Jacques Parker & Emily Parker (parents)			
Address:	26 Castle Street, Salisbury, Wiltshire			

Just before the Armistice was announced news was received by Mr and Mrs Lewis J. Parker, of 26 Castle Street, Salisbury, of the sad death of their eldest son, Capt. Tom G.M. Parker, LDS, RCS, Royal Army Medical Corps, which occurred at the military hospital, Christchurch, from pneumonia following influenza.

Capt. Parker was educated at the Choristers School, Salisbury, and Dean Close School, Cheltenham, and subsequently proceeded to the Royal Dental and Middlesex Hospitals to qualify as a surgeon-dentist. Afterwards he assisted his father in his practice. He joined the Canadian Army Dental Corps in 1915 and was subsequently transferred to the RAMC, and was stationed at Christchurch, where he was held in the highest respect. Two years previously, Mr and Mrs Parker received news that their other son, George Alec Parker, who had won the DSO and the MC, had gone down in German lines and was missing, and no further news had been heard of him.

The funeral of Capt. Parker took place at Christchurch Cemetery and was attended with full military honours. The cortege left the Royal Military Hospital, the coffin being placed on a gun carriage, covered with the Union Jack.

At the conclusion of the service, Mr Pennington, in addressing the large gathering around the grave, said the circumstances under which they were present that day were truly tragic. They were laying to rest with full military honours one of the multitude of patriotic sons who had stood by their country in her hour of need. He was certain, however, that all those noble young men who had sacrificed their earthy life in this way would live forever in the Paradise of God, kin fulfilment of the Master's words: 'He that saveth his life shall lose it, but he that loseth his life for my sake and the Gospel's shall find it.' The firing party was furnished by fifty men of the Royal Engineers, under Lt R.U. Thorn, Headquarters, and the *Last Post* was sounded by a detachment of buglers of the Royal Engineers.

Air Mechanic First Class Edwin Hopkins		*Royal Air Force Artillery Co-operation*	
		Squadron	
Service No.:	44440	Age:	26
Home country:	England		
Date of death:	04/11/18	Cause of death:	Died of illness
War cemetery:	Salisbury (Devizes Road) Cemetery, England		
Theatre of war:	Home		
Next of kin:	Cecilia Mary Hopkins (wife); Edwin & V. Hopkins		
Address:	22 Tamar Street, Charlton, London		

Edwin Hopkins died of illness on Monday 4 November 1918 in one of the hospitals in the Salisbury area.

Far left: *The grave of Air Mechanic Edwin Hopkins.*

Left: *Reginald Monk, who died from sleeping sickness.*

Shipwright 1st Class Bertram Henry Symes   *Royal Navy HMS* Nimrod

Service No.:	342477
Place of birth:	St Mawes, Cornwall
Date of death:	07/11/18
War cemetery:	Edinburgh Seafield Cememtery, Scotland
Theatre of war:	Home
Next of kin:	The late Revd Charles & Susan G. Symes (parents)

Age:	42
Home country:	England
Cause of death:	Died of illness

Bertram Symes was the third surviving son of the late Revd Charles Symes, who had formerly been a Wesleyan Minster at Salisbury. He died of illness, on Thursday 7 November 1918, at the American Naval Base Hospital, Leith.

He had been chief petty officer of HMS *Woowich*, and of his twenty years in the Royal Navy he spent the last four on active service in the North Sea: 'Having fought a good fight he has finished his course.'

Sapper Reginald Monk   *Signal Service Training Centre Royal Engineers*

Service No.:	548902
Place of birth:	Salisbury, Wiltshire
Date of death:	08/11/18
Memorials:	Salisbury, Wiltshire
	Bishop Wordsworth's School Memorial
War cemetery:	East Harnham All Saints Churchyard, England
Theatre of war:	Home
Next of kin:	William & Sarah Jane Monk (parents)
Address:	18 Bouverie Avenue, Salisbury, Wiltshire

Age:	20
Home country:	England
Cause of death:	Died of illness

Reginald Monk originally joined the London Scottish Regiment but was transferred to the Royal Engineers. He was the younger son of William and Sarah Monk. He died at Royal Albert Dock Hospital, London, from sleeping sickness contracted in German East Africa on Friday 8 November 1918.

Walter Jacob, who died of illness in the Salisbury area.

Driver Walter Jacob   *11th Field Company Royal Engineers*

Service No.:	141462	Age:	26
Place of birth:	Bishopstone, Wiltshire	Home country:	England
Date of death:	09/11/18	Cause of death:	Died of illness
Memorial:	Salisbury, Wiltshire		
War cemetery:	Salisbury London Road Cemetery, England		
Theatre of war:	Home		
Next of kin:	Maud Jacob (wife); Samuel & Sarah Jacob (parents)		
Addresses:	17 Green Croft Street, Salisbury, Wiltshire		
	23, Milford Hill, Salisbury		

Walter Jacob died of illness on Saturday 9 November at one of the hospitals in the Salisbury area.

14

ARMISTICE DAY –
MONDAY 11 NOVEMBER 1918

The War is Over but the Deaths Continue:

Pte Clarence William Yacamini

Service No.:	66045
Place of birth:	Watford, Herefordshire
Date of death:	13/11/18
Memorials:	Salisbury, Wiltshire
	St Thomas Memorial
War cemetery:	Archangel Memorial, Russia
Theatre of war:	Russia
Next of kin:	Francis Dudley & Stella Yacamini (parents)
Address:	2 Water Lane, Salisbury, Wiltshire

2/10th Battalion Royal Scots

Age:	19
Home country:	England
Cause of death:	Killed in action

Clarence Yacamini originally joined the Norfolk Regiment but was transferred to the 2/10th Battalion Royal Scots. In August 1918 his battalion left England for northern Russia, as part of the Archangel Force. He was killed in action on Wednesday 13 November 1918 fighting the 'Bolos' (Bolsheviks).

While others celebrated the end of the war, his parents – Francis and Stella Yacamini – were grief stricken.

Capt. Guy Dodgson

Place of birth:	Hampstead, London
Date of death:	14/11/18
Memorial:	Salisbury, Wiltshire
War cemetery:	Caudry British Cemetery, France
Theatre of war:	France
Next of kin:	The late Henley F. Dodgson & Helen Fulton (parents)
Address:	The Close, Salisbury, Wiltshire

1st Battalion Hertfordshire Regiment

Home country:	England	Age:	23
Cause of death:	Died of wounds		

Capt. Guy Dodgson, Hertfordshire Regiment, who died at a casualty-clearing station at Candry, France, on Thursday 14 November 1918, from pneumonia after being wounded whilst leading his company in action on 4 November 1918. He was the youngest son of the late Mr Henley F. Dodgson, of Bovingdon, Hertfordshire, and Mrs Hamilton-Fulton, of the Close, Salisbury. He was educated at St Christopher's, Eastbourne, and Winchester College, where he was in the Officer Training Corps. On leaving Winchester in 1913 he went to Stuttgart to study music at the *Conservatoire*. Whilst at home for his first vacation in 1914, war broke out, and he received a commission in the Hertfordshire Regiment. He was gazetted as captain in 1916, and went to France in June 1917. He was with his brigade headquarters as an intelligence officer from October 1917 until May 1918, when he rejoined his battalion, and was gassed soon afterwards and invalided home. He rejoined his regiment in France again in September. His

Right: *This photograph shows the battlefield graves of soldiers who fell fighting for their country.*

Right: *A war cemetery in Belgium.*

Above: *Zillebeke, Belgium.*

Right: *Zonnebeke, Belgium.*

colonel wrote: 'He was hit in the last battle the battalion took part in, and he did magnificently. His loss to the unit is tremendous. He was so keen and a splendid boy. He was a great favourite of mine, and, in fact, of everybody's in the battalion.'

Above: *The original cross that marked the grave of Guy Hodgson can be seen in the cloisters at Salisbury Cathedral.*

Left: *A ruined church on the Somme.*

His brigade major had also written: 'On his return from leave this year, he insisted on returning to his battalion, which was typical of his very fine spirit. I was very sorry he decided to do so, as he was always keen and ready for work.'

A brother officer wrote: 'We shall all miss him more than I can say, especially his company, who thought the world of him.'

His eldest brother, Capt. Francis Dodgson, was killed in action in France on 15 July 1916.

Capt. Claude Elwin Abell	No. 11 Training Depot Squadron Royal Air Force		
Place of birth: Brighton, Sussex	Home country: England	Age: 19	
Date of death: 14/11/18	Cause of death: Accidental		
War cemetery: Salisbury (London Road) Cemetery, England			
Theatre of war: Home			
Next of kin: Percival James & Mary D. Abell (parents)			
Address: 87 Buckingham Road, Brighton, Sussex			

A very distressing aviation accident occurred at an aerodrome near Salisbury on Thursday 14 November 1918. A collision between two aeroplanes caused the deaths of Capt. Claude Elwin Abell, RAF, aged nineteen, of Brighton; Lt Ian Redulf Mees, RAF, aged twenty, of London; and Sgt John Rufus Williams, attached to a USA Aero Squadron, also aged twenty, who was from Alabama, USA. A fourth airmen had a narrow escape from a similar fate.

Lt Ian Rudolph Mees	48th Squadron, Royal Air Force		
Place of birth: Glasgow, Scotland	Home country: England	Age: 20	
Date of death: 14/11/18	Cause of death: Accidental		
War cemetery: Salisbury (Devizes Road) Cemetery, England			
Theatre of war: Home			
Next of kin: A.R. & Florence M. Mees (parents)			
Address: Pembridge Gardens Hotel, Notting Hill Gate, London			

Twenty-year-old Ian Mees died as the result of an accident on Thursday 14 November 1918, in the same incident as Claude Abell.

Sgt William McCubbin   *10th Battalion Labour Corps*

Service No.:	295196	Age:	51
Place of birth:	Stranraer, Scotland	Home country:	England
Date of death:	17/11/18	Cause of death:	Died of illness

Memorials: Salisbury, Wiltshire
                   Baptist Church Memorial
War cemetery: Sutton In Ashfield Cemetery, England
Theatre of war: Home
Next of kin: Emily Ann Spencer (formerly McCubbin) (wife); William & Mary
                   McCubbin (parents)
Addresses: 59 Brookdale Road, Sutton in Ashfield, Nottinghamshire.
                   Stranraer, Scotland

William McCubbin died in Mansfield, most likely of illness, on Sunday 17 November 1918. He had originally joined the Royal Engineers but transferred to the Labour Corps working at the Southern Command. On the memorials in Salisbury he is listed as R. McCubbin.

Cpl Sydney Denzil Oliver   *34th Div. Signal Company Royal Engineers*

Service No.:	32046	Age:	29
Place of birth:	Wandsworth, London	Home country:	England
Date of death:	18/11/18	Cause of death:	Died of illness

Memorial: Salisbury, Wiltshire
                   St Thomas Church Memorial
War cemetery: Terlincthun British Cemetery, Wimille, France
Theatre of war: France
Next of kin: Olive Mary Oliver (wife); Arthur & Annie Oliver (parents)
Addresses: Topps Cottage, Breamore, Salisbury, Wiltshire
                   Salisbury, Wiltshire

Sydney Oliver married Olive Mary Glass early in 1915, and he survived the end of the war in which he served for four years, in the Royal Engineers as a despatch rider. He died on Monday 18 November of pneumonia, after contracting influenza at a hospital in Boulogne.

Far left and left: Claude Abell and Ian Mees died in the same air accident.

Pte Alfred Walter Noble   *30th Company Royal Army Ordinance Corps*

Service No.:   07549   Age: 34
Place of birth: Salisbury, Wiltshire   Home country: England
Date of death: 24/11/18   Cause of death: Died of illness
Memorial: Salisbury, Wiltshire
War cemetery: Baghdad North Gate War Cemetery, Iraq
Theatre of war: Mesopotamia
Next of kin: Alfred John & Emma Noble (parents)
Address: 84 York Road, Fisherton, Salisbury, Wiltshire

Alfred Noble died, likely of disease, at a Baghdad military hospital on Sunday 24 November 1918.

2nd-Lt Seward Biggs   *332nd Company Royal Army Service Corps*

Place of birth: Farmborough, Somerset   Home country: England   Age: 36
Date of death: 26/11/18   Cause of death: Died of illness
Memorials: Salisbury, Wiltshire
                  St Mark's Church Memorial
War cemetery: Caudry British Cemetery, France
Theatre of war: France
Next of kin: Lilian Adelize Gilson Biggs (wife)
Address: 55 Castle Road, Salisbury, Wiltshire

Seward Biggs, known as Jim, died of bronchial pneumonia at 21st Casualty-Clearing Station, Caudry, on Tuesday 26 November 1918.

Pte Walter Frederick Hardy   *Wiltshire Regiment Depot*

Service No.:   202786   Age: 34
Place of birth: Dorchester, Dorset   Home country: England
Date of death: 27/11/18   Cause of death: Died of illness
Memorial: Salisbury, Wiltshire
War cemetery: Salisbury (London Road) Cemetery, England
Theatre of war: Home
Next of kin: Elizabeth Hardy (wife); Arthur Cornelius Hardy (father)
Addresses: 5 St Huberts Cottages, Gerrards Cross, Buckinghamshire
                  Salisbury, Wiltshire

Walter died of illness on Wednesday 27 November 1918 at a hospital in the Salisbury area.

Pte Bertie Ryall Dart   *8th Battalion Oxfordshire and Buckinghamshire Light Infantry*

Service No.:   28134   Age: 36
Place of birth: Fulham, London.   Home country: England
Date of death: 01/12/18   Cause of death: Died of illness
Memorials: Salisbury, Wiltshire
                  St Martin's Church Memorial
War cemetery: Sofia War Cemetery, Bulgaria
Theatre of war: Balkans
Next of kin: Ellen Blake (formerly Dart) (wife); John & Elsie Jane Dart (parents)
Addresses: 112 Castle Street, Salisbury, Wiltshire
                  St Martin, Salisbury, Wiltshire

Bertie Dart had been captured during fighting against Bulgarian forces and was a prisoner of war. He died, most likely from illness, on Sunday 1 December 1918 and he was buried in Sofia War Cemetery, Bulgaria.

Capt. Cuthbert Francis Hodding   *4th Battalion Wiltshire Regiment*

Place of birth:	Salisbury, Wiltshire	Home country:	England
Date of death:	08/12/18	Cause of death:	Died of illness
Memorial:	Salisbury, Wiltshire		
War cemetery:	Salisbury (London Road) Cemetery, England		
Theatre of war:	Home		
Next of kin:	Beryl Anstruther Dean (formerly Hodding) (mother)		
Address:	Rose Cottage, Aldbourne, Wiltshire		

Capt. Cuthbert Francis Hodding was the only child of Mr F. Hodding, the town clerk of Salisbury, and of Mrs Hodding of the Retreat, Castle Road, Salisbury. His death occurred at his parents residence, from pneumonia following influenza, on the morning of 8 December 1918. The deepest sympathy of a large number of friends and acquaintances was extended to Capt. Hodding's widow, to whom he was married in September 1917, and to his father and mother in their sad bereavement. Capt. Hodding was of an amiable disposition and was very popular, and his death is deeply regretted. Educated at Marlborough College, Capt. Hodding was subsequently articled to Messrs Hodding & Jackson, solicitors, of Salisbury. After serving his articles with the firm, he acted as managing clerk to solicitor's at Reading and Oxford. On the outbreak of war he accompanied the 4th Wiltshire Territorials, with which he had been connected for some time and held a commission in the battalion, to India, and shortly afterwards received his captaincy.

Later he was attached to a Gurkha Battalion on the North West Frontier, where he suffered from a severe attack of dysentery, which incapacitated him from duty, and he was invalided home. He had some exciting experiences on the journey home, the boat in which he was a hospital patient being torpedoed off Crete. Capt. Hodding remained in hospital in Malta for some time, and his health slowly, but gradually improved, and he was at length able to resume duty with a Reserve Battalion of the Wiltshire Regiment in Dublin.

A few months ago, however, he was discharged to the Territorial Reserve of Officers, and resumed his legal work in Messrs Hodding & Jackson's offices. He was, however, very far from well, and when attacked with influenza about a fortnight ago and pneumonia supervened, his condition became critical, and despite every attention he succumbed on Sunday morning. Before the war Capt. Hodding was an enthusiastic hockey player, and gained more than a local reputation, playing as center-half back for the West of England. He also took a keen interest in boxing.

The funeral took place on Wednesday afternoon, the first part of the service being conducted at St Edmund's Church, where a representation of the congregation attended to pay tribute to the memory of the deceased officer.

The internment took place in the London Road Cemetery, Canon Morris officiating at the graveside. Owing to illness neither Capt. Hodding's wife or mother was able to be present at the church or the graveside. The coffin was inscribed: 'Cuthbert Francis Hodding, Died December 8th, 1918, Aged 35 years.'

Salisbury Journal 1918

Pte Stephen Walter Dyer   *2/4th Battalion Wiltshire Regiment*

Service No.:	202075	Age:	21
Place of birth:	Salisbury, Wiltshire	Home country:	England
Date of death:	09/12/18	Cause of death:	Died of illness

Memorials: Salisbury, Wiltshire
                    St Paul's Church Memorial
War cemetery: Madras 1914–18 War Memorial, Chennai, India
Theatre of war: India
Next of kin: James & Emily Dyer (parents)
Address: Salisbury, Wiltshire

Stephen died of illness on Monday 9 December 1918 and he is remembered in Madras 1914–18 War Memorial, Chennai, India.

Lt George Thornhill Ritchie   *Royal Air Force*
Place of birth: Kilmarnock, Ayrshire   Home country: South Africa   Age: 23
Date of death: 13/12/18
War cemetery: Salisbury (London Road) Cemetery, England
Theatre of war: Home
Next of kin: Andrew & Isabella Ritchie (parents)
Address: 5 Johannes Street, Troyeville, Johannesburg

Lt Ritchie had served in East Africa with the 7th Battalion South African Infantry and transferred to the RAF. He died in one of the hospitals in the Salisbury area on Friday 13 December 1918.

Capt. Clerke Colqhoun Burton   *Headquarters Transport Sect Australian Infantry*
                                                                 Australian Imperial Force
Place of birth: Australia   Home country: Australia   Age: 35
Date of death: 14/12/18   Cause of death: Died of illness
War cemetery: Salisbury (London Road) Cemetery, England
Next of kin: Francis Charles & Mary M. Burton (parents)
Address: Tynowg Bay Road, Sandingham, Victoria, Australia

Much regret was caused by the news of the death at Hendon on Saturday 14 December of Capt. Clerke C. Burton, Austrailian Imperial Force, who, during his residence in Salisbury, which extended for a period of over two years, had made many friends by his genial personality and manner, and was everywhere held in respect and esteem. Capt. Burton, who was thirty-

South African George Ritchie.

five years of age, died from pneumonia, following influenza. Prior to the war he resided at Melbourne, Australia, where he was engaged as an insurance broker and adjuster, and for some years lived at Camberwell, and later at Sandingham, Victoria. He joined the Australian Imperial Forces as a private in February 1915, and served in the Gallipolli Campaign with the 5th Infantry Battalion. He was invalided to Egypt and was subsequently transferred to ths staff of the AIF Canteens, on the arrival of the Australians in England in June 1916.

Capt. Burton took up the duties of officer in charge AIF Canteens, Salisbury area, having his offices at 108 Fisherton Street, Salisbury. He held this position until August, when he was detailed for special duty in France. Whilst in Salisbury, where he was very popular, Capt. Burton became a member of the Elias De Derham (Salisbury) Lodge of Freemasons. He took a keen interest in bowling, and often took part in local games.

The funeral took place in Salisbury on the afternoon of Wednesday 18 December 1918, with full military honours. The coffin, covered with the Australian flag and several wreaths, was borne on a gun carriage, drawn by four horses. A firing party of 100 Australians and 100 Australian soldiers as mourners, accompanied by two Australian bands, marched in procession with the coffin from the railway stations to the London Road Cemetery, where the interment took place in the presence of a large gathering of sympathisers.

Salisbury Journal 1918

1919

Pte Arthur Henry Elkins   *5th Battalion Wiltshire Regiment*

Service No.:	202850	Age:	39
Place of birth:	Bishopstone, Wiltshire	Home country:	England
Date of death:	04/01/19	Cause of death:	Died of illness
Memorials:	Salisbury, Wiltshire		
	St Paul's Church Memorial		
War cemetery:	Mikra British Cemetery, Greece		
Theatre of war:	Salonika		
Next of kin:	Florence E. Elkins (wife); Thomas & Anna Elkins (parents)		
Addresses:	2 Middleton Road, Fisherton, Salisbury, Wiltshire		
	Bishopstone, Wiltshire		

Arthur Elkins died from illness on Saturday 4 January 1919 at a hospital in the Mikra area, Greece.

Pte Edward James Harwood   *1/4th Battalion Somerset Light Infantry*

Service No.:	201138	Age:	25
Place of birth:	Salisbury, Wiltshire	Home country:	England
Date of death:	06/01/19	Cause of death:	Died of illness
Memorial:	Salisbury, Wiltshire		
War cemetery:	Mikra British Cemetery, Greece		
Theatre of war:	Salonika		
Next of kin:	William & Sarah Harwood (parents)		
Address:	Willow Grove, 28 Wilton Road, Salisbury, Wiltshire		

Edward Harwood, who known as James, died of illness at one of the hospitals based in the Mikra area, Greece, on Monday 6 January 1919.

Pte Albert Edward Patience · *2nd Battalion Wiltshire Regiment*

Service No.:	203077	Age:	28
Place of birth:	East Harnham, Wiltshire	Home country:	England
Date of death:	08/01/19	Cause of death:	Died of illness
Memorial:	Salisbury, Wiltshire		
War cemetery:	Copenhagen Western Cemetery, Denmark		
Theatre of war:	Germany		
Next of kin:	Albert E. & Bessie Patience (parents)		
Address:	East Harnham, Salisbury, Wiltshire		

Albert Patience had originally joined the Somerset Light Infantry but was transferred to the 2nd Battalion Wiltshire Regiment. He was captured by the Germans and had been a prisoner of war. After his release he died of illness at Copenhagen, Denmark, on Wednesday 8 January 1919.

2nd-Lt Frank Percy Goodyear · *Royal Army Service Corps*

Home country:	England	Age:	39
Date of death:	08/02/19	Cause of death:	Died of illness
War cemetery:	Salisbury (Devizes Road) Cemetery, England		
Theatre of war:	Home		
Next of kin:	Mabel Goodyear (wife)		
Address:	2 Brights Villas, Bemerton, Wiltshire		

Frank Goodyear died of illness in one of the hospitals in the Salisbury area on Saturday 8 February 1919.

Pte Ernest Meaby Horder · *Royal Army Service Corps Mechanical Transport*

Service No.:	M/298124	Age:	35
Place of birth:	Wimborne, Dorset	Home country:	England
Date of death:	16 /02/19	Cause of death:	Died of illness
Memorials:	Salisbury, Wiltshire		
	St Mark's Church Memorial		
War cemetery:	Les Baraques Military Cemetery, Sangatte, France		
Theatre of war:	France		
Next of kin:	Winifred Fanny Horder (wife); Mr & Mrs G. Horder (parents)		
Addresses:	58 Hamilton Road, Salisbury, Wiltshire		
	Bere Regis, Dorset		

The death of driver Ernest Mabey Horder, of the Mechanical Transport of the RASC, occurred in hospital at Calais, from bronchio-pneumonia, following influenza. Horder was the second son of Mr and Mrs G. Horder of Bere Regis, and formerly of the Manor Farm, Kingston Lacy. The deceased was in his thirty-sixth year and was about to be demobilised, his papers having actually been received. He had been serving for nearly two years. Prior to enlisting he was with Messrs Wilkes, Son & Casey, ironmongers, of Salisbury. He served an apprenticeship with Mrs F.W. Barratt at his ironmongery shop in Wimborne. He married Winifred, third daughter of Mr and Mrs H Mead, of AImborne, eight years ago next Easter, and sincere sympathy was felt for the widow and members of the family. The deceased, who passed peacefully away on Sunday 16 February 1919, was buried at Calais. The service at St Mark's' Church, Salisbury, of which Mr Horder had been a sidesman, was of a memorial character on Sunday evening, and as a tribute to the deceased, who was held in high esteem. Mr and Mrs Horder lost their fourth son (Frank) whilst he was serving at Blandford Camp last year.

Staff Sgt Lionel John Lancaster

Attached 4th Cyclist Brigade Royal Army Service Corps

Service No.:	S4/247344	Age:	34
Place of birth:	Battersea, London	Home country:	England
Date of death:	20/02/19	Cause of death:	Died of illness
Memorials:	Salisbury, Wiltshire		
	St Mark's Church Memorial		
War cemetery:	Salisbury (London Road) Cemetery, England		
Theatre of war:	Ireland		
Next of kin:	E.M. Lancaster (wife); Henry T. & Eliza A. Lancaster (parents)		
Addresses:	58 Belle Vue Road, Salisbury, Wiltshire		
	Marlborough Road, Salisbury, Wiltshire		

Lionel Lancaster was the eldest son of Henry and Eliza Lancaster. Prior to the war he had been a printworker. He died of illness, at King George V Hospital, Dublin, on Thursday 22 February 1919.

Pte William Albert Victor Quant

3rd Division Motor Transport Company Royal Army Service Corps

Service No.:	M2/050300	Age:	27
Place of birth:	Exeter, Devon	Home country:	England
Date of death:	23/02/19		
Memorials:	Salisbury, Wiltshire		
	St Martin's Church Memorial		
War cemetery:	Huy La Sarte Communal Cemetery, Belgium		
Theatre of war:	Belgium		
Next of kin:	Sarah E. Quant (wife); Mr W. Quant (father)		
Addresses:	91 Milford Hill, Salisbury, Wiltshire		
	28 Poltimore Square, Exeter, Devon		

William Quant was known as Victor and he married Sarah E. Searle in the spring of 1915 at Hungerford. He died on Sunday 23 February 1919 at the 50th (Northumbrian) Casualty-Clearing Station, based at Huy, Belgium.

Lionel Lancaster, who died in Dublin.

Officers Steward 1st Class Joseph Henry Doel   *Royal Navy HMS* Victory

Service No.:	364987	Age:	31
Place of birth:	Wilton, Wiltshire	Home country:	England
Date of death:	15/03/19	Cause of death:	Died
Memorials:	Salisbury, Wiltshire		
	St Paul's Church Memorial		
War cemetery:	Portsmouth Kingston Cemetery, England		
Theatre of war:	Home		
Next of kin:	Joseph H. & Jane Doel (parents)		
Address:	Fisherton, Salisbury, Wiltshire		

Joseph Doel died on Saturday 15 March 1919 at Portsmouth.

Pte Louis William Ernest Stokes   *Royal Army Service Corps 116th Aux Petrol Coy MT*

Service No.:	M/339912	Place of birth:	Wilton, Wiltshire	Age: 20
Date of death:	02/04/19	Cause of death: Died of illness		
Home country:	England			
Memorial:	Salisbury, Wiltshire			
War cemetery:	Arquata Scivia Communal Cemetery Extension, Italy			
Theatre of war:	Italy			
Next of kin:	William F. & Annie Stokes (parents)			
Address:	2 College Street, Salisbury, Wiltshire			

Louis Stokes, known as Ning, was the eldest son of William and Annie Stokes. He died of pneumonia at 38th Stationary Hospital, Arquata, Italy.

Pte Francis James Fletcher   *7th Battalion Wiltshire Regiment*

Service No.:	20902	Age:	35
Place of birth:	Deane, Wiltshire	Home country:	England
Date of death:	14/04/19		
War cemetery:	Salisbury (Devizes Road) Cemetery, England		
Theatre of war:	Home		
Next of kin:	James & Anna Fletcher (parents)		
Address:	1 Sunny Cottage, Ashley Road, Salisbury, Wiltshire		

Francis Fletcher died on Monday 14 April 1919 at Devizes Wiltshire.

Pte William John Amor   *Hampshire Regiment Depot*

Service No.:	26936	Age:	26
Place of birth:	Salisbury, Wiltshire	Home country:	England
Date of death:	16/05/19		
Memorials:	Salisbury, Wiltshire		
	St Martin's Church Memorial		
War cemetery:	Alton Cemetery, England		
Theatre of war:	Home		
Next of kin:	Henry & Julia Amor (parents)		
Address:	18 Milford Hill, Salisbury, Wiltshire		

Francis Fletcher, who died in Devizes, Wiltshire.

William Amor died on Friday 16 May 1919 in the Alton area. He was the brother of Henry Giles Amor, who died in Singapore during July 1917.

Pte Reginald John Witt   *3rd Battalion Wiltshire Regiment*

Service No.:   32325   Age: 26
Place of birth: Salisbury, Wiltshire   Home country: England
Date of death: 14/06/19
Memorial: Devizes, Wiltshire
War cemetery: Grange Gorman Military Cemetery, Ireland
Theatre of war: Ireland
Next of kin: Rose A. Witt (mother)
Address: 69 Milford Hill, Salisbury, Wiltshire

Reginald Witt died on Saturday 14 June 1919, at King George V Hospital, Dublin. Prior to the First World War he had lived at Milford Hill, Salisbury.

Pte William Seviour   *2nd Works Company Wiltshire Regiment*

Service No.:   9170   Age: 21
Place of birth: Harnham, Wiltshire   Home country: England
Date of death: 20/06/19   Cause of death: Killed in action
Memorials: Salisbury, Wiltshire
                  Salisbury United Methodists Memorial
War cemetery: Archangel Memorial, Russia
Theatre of war: Russia
Next of kin: Frank George Seviour (father)
Address: 1 Meadow Cottage, Friary, Salisbury, Wiltshire

William Seviour was part of the Russian Relief Force which consisted of a detachment of 200 regular soldiers from the Wiltshire Regiment, sent to Archangel in 1919 to protect British interests during the Russian Revolution. Serviour was killed in action during fighting against the 'Bolos' on Friday 20 June 1919. He is remembered on the Archangel Memorial, Russia, with 219 British soldiers who died during the northern Russian campaign, He has no known grave. His brother, Frank Seviour, as recorded above, was killed in action in France during October 1918.

Sgt Ernest Fryer   *B Company 1st Garrison Battalion Somerset Light Infantry*

Service No.:	34811	Age: 40
Place of birth:	Salisbury, Wiltshire	Home country: England
Date of death:	21/06/19	Cause of death: Died of illness
Memorial:	Salisbury, Wiltshire	
War cemetery:	Karachi 1914–18 War Memorial, Pakistan	
Theatre of war:	India	
Next of kin:	Alice Fanny Fryer (wife); Sophia Fryer (mother)	
Addresses:	Bicton, Fordingbridge, Hampshire	
	Salisbury, Wiltshire	

In July 1919 news reached Salisbury of the death of Ernest Fryer, who had died of illness at the Station Hospital, Lahore, in what was then India.

Ernest Fryer was buried in one of the cemeteries in Lahore, which is modern-day Pakistan.

Pte Arthur Scott   *Royal Army Ordinance Corps Depot*

Service No.:	O/233	Age: 47
Home country:	England	
Date of death:	14/09/19	
Memorials:	Salisbury, Wiltshire	
	St Paul's Church Memorial	
War cemetery:	Salisbury (London Road) Cemetery, England	
Theatre of war:	Home	
Next of kin:	Rose Maria Scott (wife)	
Address:	22 Coldharbour Lane, Salisbury, Wiltshire	

Arthur had married Rose Maria Hughes in Salisbury at the start of the year during 1901. He died in Salisbury on Sunday 14 September 1919.

Pte William George Andrews   *1/4th Battalion Wiltshire Regiment*

Service No.:	202032	Place of birth: East Harnham, Wiltshire
Home country:	England	Age: 32
Date of death:	25/10/19	
Memorial:	Salisbury, Wiltshire.	
War cemetery:	Cheltenham Cemetery, England	
Theatre of war:	Home	
Next of kin:	George & Mary J. Andrews (parents)	
Address:	East Harnham, Salisbury, Wiltshire.	

William George Andrews died in Gloucester on Saturday 25 October 1919; he was buried at Cheltenham Cemetery.

Cpl George C. Rance   *Royal Army Pay Corps*

Service No.:	10890	Age: 31
Home country:	England	
Date of death:	16/12/19	
War cemetery:	Salisbury (Devizes Road) Cemetery, England	
Theatre of war:	Home	

Next of kin: Maj. George & Ada Rance (parents)
Address: Stamford, Lincolnshire

George Rance died at one of the hospitals in the Salisbury area on Tuesday 16 December 1919.

Pte William George Flowers   *South Staffordshire Regiment*
Service No.:   204658   Age: 23
Place of birth: Bath, Somerset   Home country: England
Date of death: 24/01/1920
Memorial: Salisbury, Wiltshire.
War cemetery: Salisbury (London Road) Cemetery, England
Theatre of war: Home
Next of kin: Ethel Emily Flowers (wife); Frederick & Georgina Flowers (parents)
Address: 15 The Close, St Anne Gate, Salisbury, Wiltshire.

William Flowers died at one of the hospitals in the Salisbury area on Saturday 24 January 1920.

Right: *Arthur Scott's original grave marker.*

Far right: *The headstone of Arthur Scott, who died in Salisbury.*

George Rance, who worked at Southern Command Headquarters.

Harry Liversridge, who died in Salisbury.

Sgt William Henry Weeks   *13th Battalion Royal Berkshire Regiment*
Service No.:   30935   Age: 37
Place of birth: Salisbury, Wiltshire   Home country: England
Date of death: 15/02/20
Memorials: Salisbury, Wiltshire
                    St Paul's Church Memorial
War cemetery: Salisbury (Devizes Road) Cemetery, England
Theatre of war: Home
Next of kin: Alice Weeks (wife); Alfred & Harriett Weeks (parents)
Addresses: 18 Gas Lane, Salisbury, Wiltshire
                    28 Ashfield Road, Salisbury, Wiltshire

Sgt Weeks died on Sunday 15 February 1920 at one of the hospitals in the Salisbury area.

Leading Telegraphist Harry Thomas Liversridge   *Royal Navy HMS Victory*
Service No.:   J/30404   Age: 23
Place of birth: Salisbury, Wiltshire   Home country: England
Date of death: 25/04/1920
War cemetery: Salisbury (London Road) Cemetery, England
Theatre of war: Home
Next of kin: George & Ellen Liversidge (parents)
Address: 55 Culver Street, Salisbury, Wiltshire

Harry Liversridge died at one of the hospitals in the Salisbury area on Sunday 25 April 1918.
His brother Reginald Liversidge was killed in action during October 1914.

Pte George Compton   *1st Battalion Wiltshire Regiment*
Service No.:   7931   Age: 34
Place of birth: Bower Chalke, Wiltshire   Home country: England
Date of death: 22/05/1920
War cemetery: Salisbury London Road Cemetery, England
Theatre of war: Home

Next of kin: Edgar & Sarah A. Compton (parents)
Address: Broadchalke, Wiltshire

George Compton died at one of the hospitals in the Salisbury area on Saturday 22 May 1920.

Pte William Henry Holloway   *4th Hussars*
Service No.:   532307   Age: 28
Home country: England
Date of death: 18/09/1920
War cemetery: Salisbury (London Road) Cemetery, England
Theatre of war: Home
Next of kin: Caroline Holloway (mother)
Address: 74 Park Street, Salisbury, Wiltshire

William Holloway died while serving with the 4th Hussars on Saturday 18 September 1918.

Col. Arthur F. Hamilton-Cox   *Royal Army Pay Corps Southern Command*
                                            (Salisbury)
Date of death: 05/03/1921   Age: 59
War cemetery: Salisbury (London Road) Cemetery, England
Theatre of war: Home

Arthur Hamilton-Cox died while serving at the Southern Command Headquarters in Salisbury on Saturday 5 March 1921.

Flying Officer Bernard Frederic Deane   *Royal Air Force School of Artillery Co-operation*
Place of birth: Chungkingsickwan, China Home country: England   Age: 24
Date of death: 15/04/1921   Cause of death: Accidental
War cemetery: Salisbury (London Road) Cemetery, England
Theatre of war: Home
Next of kin: Violet E. Deane (wife); Frederick Salter & Alice Mary Deane (parents)
Addresses: Hartfield Square, Eastbourne, Sussex
                Whaddon, Gloucestershire

Right: *The grave of George Compton.*

Far right: *The grave of William Holloway.*

Far left and left: *Flying Officer B.F. Deane and Air-Mechanic P.F. Elliott died in the same aircraft accident.*

Flying Officer B.F. Deane and Air-Mechanic P.F. Elliott, both belonging to Old Sarum Aerodrome, were killed in an air disaster near Andover, on the afternoon of Friday 4 April 1921. They were carrying out a routine flight in a Bristol fighter to Andover. At 1.15 p.m. they left for the return journey in a high wind. All went well until they were a little more than a mile away. They were flying at a low altitude, about 600ft, and were over Mr Hartigan's gallops, near Weyhill, when the machine got out of control. Mr Deane tried to glide the plane to ground, but he was unsuccessful, and the machine crashed to earth in a nose dive, killing the occupants instantaneously and damaging the craft. John Cook, a labourer, of Kimpton, saw the accident and hastened to the spot, only to find that his help was to no avail.

Capt. Clarke, the deputy coroner for North West Hampshire, held an inquest, without a jury, at Andover Aerodrome, on Saturday afternoon, when he returned a verdict of 'accidental death' and expressed his sympathy with the relatives.

The funeral of both the deceased airmen took place at the London Road Cemetery, Salisbury, on 19 April 1921. Both coffins were brought from the aircraft centre at Old Sarum by an RAF tender.

Flying Officer Deane had not long been married. Mrs Deane's parents lived at Eastbourne, and Mr and Mrs Elliott at Northwood, Middlesex.

Aircraftsman 2nd Class Philip Frederick Elliott		*RAF*	
Service No.:	326121	Age:	20
Place of birth:	Hendon, Middlesex	Home country:	England
Date of death:	15/04/1921	Cause of death:	Accidental
War cemetery:	Salisbury (London Road) Cemetery, England		
Theatre of war:	Home		
Next of kin:	Frederick & Clara H. Elliott (parents)		
Address:	60 Reginald Road, Northwood, Middlesex		

Philip Elliott died as the result of an aircraft accident on Friday 15 April 1921 (see Bernard Frederic Deane for details of the accident).

Driver Francis Henry Paice		*Royal Army Service Corps*	
Service No.:	T4/211123	Age:	35

Place of birth: Guildford, Surrey   Home country: England
Date of death: 11/05/21
War cemetery: Salisbury (London Road) Cemetery, England
Theatre of war: Home
Next of kin: Nellie Maud Paice (wife); Thomas Edward Paice (father)
Address: 5 The Friary, Salisbury, Wiltshire

Francis Paice married Nellie M. Sanger at Salisbury in the summer of 1910. He survived the war and died on Wednesday 11 May 1921 at Bath, Somerset, while serving with the Royal Army Service Corps.

Company Quarter Sgt Alfred William Meech   *4th Battalion Dorsetshire Regiment*
Service No.:   201012   Age: 49
Place of birth: Dorchester, Dorset   Home country: England
Date of death: 14/06/21
War cemetery: Salisbury (Devizes Road) Cemetery
Theatre of war: Home
Next of kin: Ellen Meech (wife)
Address: 31 Highfield Road, Salisbury, Wiltshire

Company Quarter Sgt Alfred Meech died at one of the hospitals in the Salisbury area on Tuesday 14 June 1921.

The original grave marker for Francis Paice.

Far left: *The grave of F.H. Paice.*

Left: *Alwyne Topham, who died locally.*

Sgt Alwyne Topham   *1/5th Loyal North Lancashire Regiment*

Service No.:	38972	Age:	22
Place of birth:	Hales Worth, Suffolk	Home country:	England
Date of death:	22/07/21		
Memorials:	Salisbury, Wiltshire		
	St Mark's Church Memorial		
War cemetery:	Salisbury (London Road) Cemetery, England		
Theatre of war:	Home		
Next of kin:	John Henry & Gertrude Rosa Topham (parents)		
Address:	51 Albany Road, Salisbury, Wiltshire		

Alwyne Topham died at one of the hospitals in the Salisbury area on 22 July 1921.

Pte Ernest Burrington   *1st Labour Company Hampshire Regiment*

Service No.:	35045	Age:	45
Place of birth:	Exeter, Devon	Home country:	England
Date of death:	19 August 1921		
War cemetery:	Salisbury London Road Cemetery, England		
Theatre of war:	Home		
Next of kin:	Elizabeth Lilian Burrington (wife)		
Address:	25 Bedwin Street, Salisbury, Wiltshire		

Ernest Burrington married Elizabeth Roberts in 1902. He originally joined the Hampshire Regiment but transferred to the 178th Labour Coy Labour Corps. Ernest Burrington died on 19 August 1921 at Salisbury.

15
REMEMBRANCE

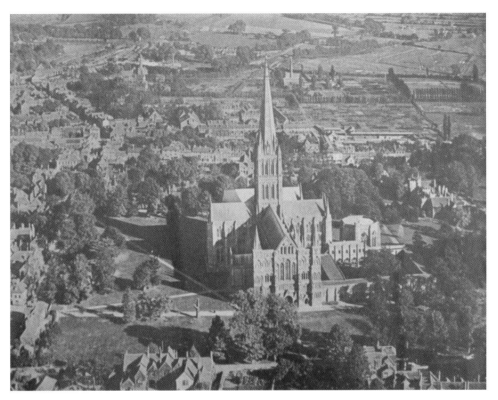

Salisbury Cathedral planned to call its North Aisle, Warriors' Aisle, with a stained-glass window and book of Remembrance.

Salisbury's proposed memorial.

The Salisbury 1914–19 War Memorial unveiled in February 1922 by Lt Tom Edwin Adlam, VC.

Lt Tom Edwin Adlam was the first Salisbury soldier to receive the VC in the First World War. He led an attack in October 1916 near Thiepval during the Battle of the Somme, on a German position which had to be captured for a major attack to begin. He was wounded in the leg but carried on leading his men, capturing the position and killing all the occupants. The son of John and Eva Adlam of Farley Road, Waterloo Gardens, Salisbury, he was an assistant master at Basingstoke School prior to the war and a corporal at Winchester Training College Corps at its outbreak, attached to the Hampshire Regiment. When the regiment mobilised he was promoted to sergeant and posted to India. He was granted a commission in 1915 and was top of the class on his officer's course. He married Ivy Mace on 21 June 1916 and proceeded to France in early July 1916. His mother died shortly afterwards and he returned home for the funeral.

Above: *St Paul's Church Memorial.*

Right: *St Mark's Church Memorial.*

Right: *London Road Cemetery's Cross of Sacrifice.*

Below left: *East Harnham Church Memorial.*

Below right: *Dedication on London Road Cemetery's Cross of Sacrifice.*

IN REMEMBRANCE OF
DR. CHARLES BEAVEN.   R.Engineers
SERGT. WILLIAM EDWARD W. BLENCOWE.   2nd Wilts.
PTE. JOSEPH BOLWELL.   2nd Wilts.
GNR. ALBERT EDWARD BOWEY.   R.M.L.I.
LCE.CPL. CHARLES WILLIAM BROOKSON.   R.G.A.
LCE.CPL. AUGUST FRANK BUTLER.   A.P.C.
SERGT. ALBERT EDWARD CARD.   5th Wilts.
PTE. FRANK NEWTON COOKE.   4th Wilts.
GNR. HARRY CRUMPLIN.   A.I.F.
GNR. ERNEST ELLERY.   R.F.A.
PTE. JOHN FRANCIS FREESTONE.   R.F.A.
PTE. HAROLD STANLEY GALE.   1st Wilts.
PTE. WILLIAM GOODFELLOW.   R.W.Surrey.
PTE. GILBERT CHARLES GREEN.   Coldstream Guards.
MAJOR PHILIP GEOFFY POWYS HILL.   A.I.F.
SPR. REGINALD MONK.   R.Engineers.
PTE. ALBERT EDWARD PATIENCE.   2nd Wilts.
PTE. ERNEST GEORGE READ.   R.Wilts Yeo.
PTE. ERNEST EDWIN ROWE.   10th Middlesex.
PTE. FRANK SEVIOUR.   2nd Wilts.
PTE. WILLIAM SEVIOUR.   2nd Wilts.
DR. DAVID HERBERT SQUIRES.   R.F.A.
CPL. FREDERICK W. STOKES.   2nd Wilts.
2ND LIEUT. HAROLD PERCY TOZER D.L.I. and R.F.C.
PTE. HARRY WHITE.   1st Wilts.
LCE.CPL. BRIAN MORAW WILLIAMS.   13th R.Fus.

Who gave their lives for their Country in the
GREAT WAR. 1914-1919.

TO THE HONOURED
MEMORY OF EIGHTY
SAILORS AND SOLDIERS
WHO GAVE THEIR
LIVES FOR THEIR
COUNTRY DURING THE
GREAT WAR 1914-1918
FIFTY-TWO OF WHOM
LIE IN THIS CEMETERY
AND TWENTY-EIGHT
IN DEVIZES ROAD
CEMETERY ADJOINING
THE CITY OF
SALISBURY

Above: *A dugout at Sanctuary Wood.*

Left: *Delville Wood Memorial, Somme, France.*

Below: *Ypres Menin Gate Memorial, Ieper, Belgium.*

Above left: *The 'Iron Harvest' unearthed by farmers today at Ypres, Belgium.*

Above right: *Some of the shells that did not explode, Ypres, Belgium.*

Below: *This book is dedicated to all those men who gave their lives.*

MAPS

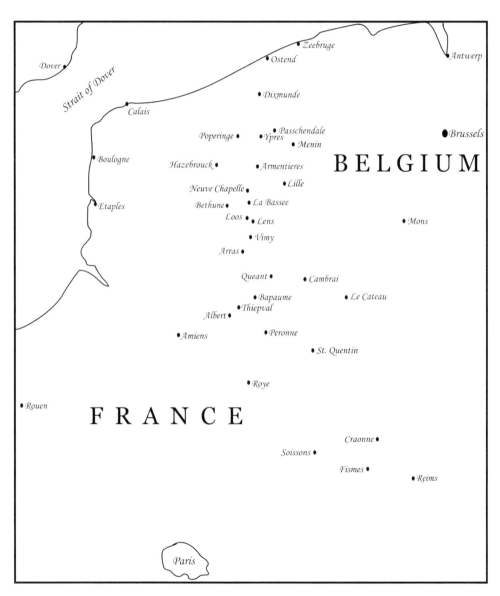

The Western Front.

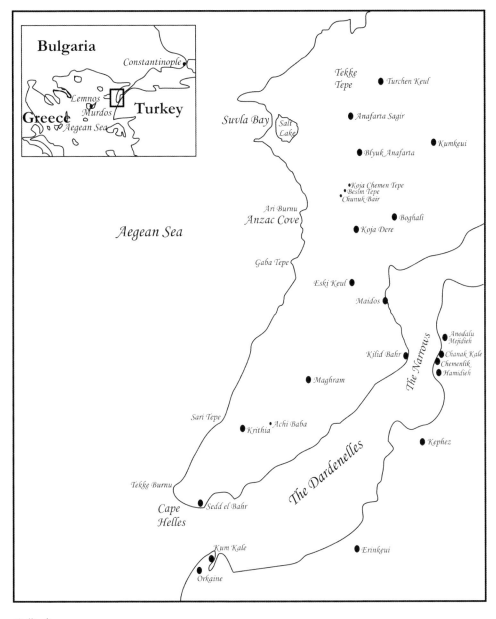

Gallipoli.

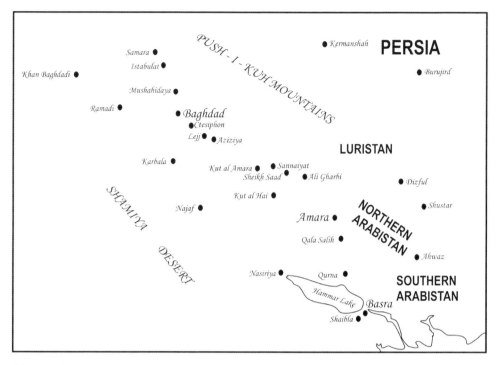

Mesopotamia.

Salonika.

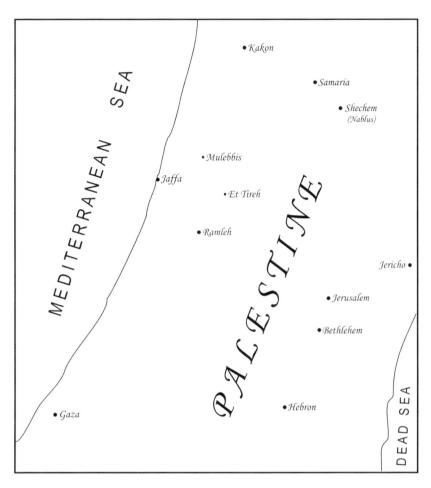

Palestine.

A–Z of Memorials

AIF Burial Ground, Flers
Leonard Justly Rawlings
Walter John Sanger
Frederick Stevens

Abbeville Communal Cemetery Extension
Albert James Baugh
Robert William Webb

Aire Communal Cemetery
Frederick Charles Edwards Gamblin
Aix Noulette Communal Cemetery Extension
Henry J. Batt

Albert Communal Cemetery Extension
William George Vater

Alexandria Chatby Military and War Memorial
Henry Bowey

Altivole Communal Cemetery
Ernest James Evemy

Alton Cemetery
William Jon Amor

Amara War Cemetery
Frank Augustus Butler
Arthur Reginald Cannings
Alfred Steven Drake
James Kiddle
William Lowne Smith
Henry Stagg
Francis Newton Talbot
Maurice George Edward Watts

Ancre British Cemetery, Beamont Hamel
Alfred Blake

Anzac Cemetery, Sailly Sur La Lys
Charles William Horton

Archangel Memorial
William Seviour
Clarence William Yacamini

Arquata Scivia Communal Cemetery Extension
Louis William Ernest Stokes

Arras Flying Services Memorial
George Alec Parker
Edward Cuthbert Stocker

Arras Memorial
Harry Bell
James Blake
Archibald Frank Burt
Ernest Samuel Butcher
Charles Hall
Herbert Harrison
Frank Albert Hibberd
Sidney Charles Laurence
Alwyn Sidney Macey
Thomas George Marchant
Ernest Edward Rowe
George Robert Rowe
Sidney Harry Scammell
Raymond Walter Welch
Harry Victor White
Frederick Witt
Osmund Bartle Wordsworth

Artillery Wood Cemetery
Gilbert Charles Green
Ernest Sidney Phillips

Aubigny Communal Cemetery Extension
Edward John Besent
Ernest George Steer

Baghdad North Gate War Cemetery
Fred Hutchins
Frank William Leach
James Musselwhite
Alfred Walter Noble
Ewart Frederick Parfitt
Henry Charles Scutt
Ernest Victor Targett
Henry Richard T. Woolford

Bagneux British Cemetery, Gezaincourt
John Leopold Look

Bailleul Communal Cemetery Extension Nord
Bertrum Frederick Ernest Jerrard
Harry Shergold

Bailleul Road East Cemetery, St Laurent Blangy
Frank Rose

Bard Cottage Cemetery
Herbert Arthur Rendell

Basra Memorial
Gilbert Aplin
Alfred Edward V. Beck
George Sidney B. Burbage
Albert Edward Card
Sidney Caleb Cox
John Davis
John Hopgood
Edmund James Leaver
Philip Owen
Reginald Stone
Henry Tucker
Walter John Tucker
Joseph Tyler
Alfred Arthur Vicary
Leslie James Maskett Webb
Henry James Witt

Basra War Cemetery
Henry Morris Facey
Harry Jenkins
Albert Bert Sherlock

Bavay Communal Cemetery
Edward John Ezard

Beaulencourt British Cemetery, Ligny Thilloy
Reginald Penny

Becourt Militry Cemetery, Becordel Becourt
Eric Noel Player

Belford House Cemetery
Edward Maj.

Bellicourt British Cemetery
Bertrand John Young

Berks Cemetery Extension
Sidney Martin

Berlin South Western Cemetery
Arthur Frederick Randell

Bethune Town Cemetery
William Benjamin Powney

Blighty Valley Cemetery, Authuile Wood
Frederick Short

Boulogne Eastern Cemetery
Frederick Charles Nash
Henry Palmer
Charles Lloyd Sanctuary

Bournemouth East Cemetery
Percy Edwin Victor Briant

Bouzincourt Ridge Cemetery, Albert
Henry Edwardes Palmer

Braine Communal Cemetery
William Stevens

Bulls Road Cemetery, Flers
John Philip Morton Carpenter
Harry Taylor

Bully Grenay Communal Cemetery, British Extension
Henry Sidney Williams

Cabaret Rouge British Cemetery, Souchez
Hedley Charles Sainsbury
Horace Percy Williams

Cairo War Memorial Cemetery
Charles Basil Mortimer Hodgson
Francis Henry Smith

Camberwell Old Cemetery
Percy Stuart Gaster

Cambrai War Memorial, Louverval
Reginald James Clark
Sydney Rowthorn
Harold Stokes

Canada Farm Cemetery
Henry Joseph Harfitt

Carnieres Communal Cemetery Extension
Frederick James Moore

Carnoy Military Cemetery
Alfred Ernest Hart

Caterpillar Valley Cemetery, Longueval
Eric Walace Ware

Caudry Britsih Cemetery
Guy Dodgson
Seward Biggs

Cement House Cemetery
Thomas Edward Dunning

Cerisy Gailly Military Cemetery
Alfred Wells

Chambrecy British Cemetery
Percy Pike

Chatham Naval Memorial
Edward Tyrrell Inman
Alfred Harold Orchard
Harold Sidney Rogers
George James Thomas Sanger

Cheltenham Cemetery
William George Andrews

Chilli Trench Cemetery, Gavrelle
Joseph Plumbtre Gilbert

Chocques Military Cemetery
Frederick Cutcher
William Finlay Partridge
William Neville Pitt
Ernest Robins

Christchurch Cemetery
Tom Geoffrey Milsome Parker

City of Paris Cemetery
Ernest Alfred Heath

Cologne Southern Cemetery
Albert Fullford
George Henry Gelliffe
William James Stout

Contalmaison Chateau Cemetery
Frederick William Burges

Copenhagen Western Cemetery
Albert Edward Patience

Corbie Communal Cemetery
Charles Frederick Bunsell
Frank Gatford

Croix Churchyard
Edward Percy Robinson

Croix Du Bac British Cemetery, Steenwerck
Percy William Simmons

Damascas Commonwealth War Cemetery
Walter Reginald Hazel

Dantzig Alley British Cemetery, Mametz
William Bramwell Pepper

Deir El Belah War Cemetery
Arthur George Howes

Delville Wood Cemetery, Longueval
William James Clare

Dive Copse British Cemetery, Sailly Le Sec
Stanley Edward Penny

Divisional Collecting Post Cemetery and Extension
Arthur Douglas Pile

Dorian Memorial
John James Adlam
Rupert Eustace Akers
Ernest Higgs
Thomas Penruddocke
Ernest George Read
George Edward Sennett
Harry Alfred Stone

Dorian Military Cemetery
William Arthur Grace

Douchy Les Ayette British Cemetery
Cecil Keith Foyle Wright

Doullens Communal Cemetery Extension No.2
Percy Francis Gale

Dozinghem Military Cemetery
Edward Frank Eyres
Harold Percival Morris
Richard Salisbury

Dranoutre Military Cemetery
Reginald Frank Gordon Bush

Dulhallow ADS Cemetery
Reginald Witt

Duisans British Cemetery, Etrun
Elliot Walter Grace
Claude Romako a'Beckett Terrell

*East Harnham All Saints
   Churchyard*
Albert Edward Bowey
Charles William Brookson
Ernest Walter Ellery
Reginald Monk
Harold Percy Tozer

Eastry Churchyard
William Warner Lassetter

Edinburgh Seafield Cemetery
Bertram Henry Symes

Etaples Military Cemetery
Claude Herbert Cox
John Lawrence Morey

*Euston Road Cemetery,
   Colincamps*
Alfred Leopold Burrough

Fampoux British Cemetery
William Goodfellow

*Feuchy Chapel British
   Cemetery, Wancourt*
Edward Percy Lott Horne

*Fins New British Cemetery,
   Sorel Le Grand*
Andrew John Clyde
Arthur Brindley Johnson

*Flesquieres Hill British
   Cemetery*
Albert Henry Sheppard

Foreste Communal Cemetery
Theordore Frank Tudgay

Gaza War Cemetery
Francis Charles Badder
Bert Edward Cornish
Wilfred Fry
William Thomas Larkam
Kenneth Felix Wilson

*Godewaersvelde British
   Cemetery*
Donald Horder

*Gordon Dump Cemetery,
   Ovillers La Boisselle*
Edward James Goff

*Gorre British and Indian
   Cemetery*
Harry Sheldrake

*Grand Seraucourt British
   Cemetery*
William Powrie

*Grange Gorman Military
   Cemetery*
Douglas Gilbert Hayward
   Aldworth
Harry Sturgess
Reginald John Witt

Grevillers British Cemetery
Edward Waters

Guards Cemetery Lesboeufs
Hercules Hopkins

*Guillemont Road Cemetery,
   Guillemont*
Edward Wyndham Tennant

Hamburg Cemetery
Robert John Huggins

*Harringhe (Bandaghem)
   Military Cemetery*
Richard Fielding Morrison

Haverskerque British Cemetery
Walter Ernest Bond

Haynecourt British Cemetery
George Ralph Singleton

Helles Memorial
Sidney Andrews
Frederick Hamilton Bates
Albert Edward Brown
Charles Cobb
William Henry John Fry
Alfred James Hinxman
Frederick Arthur Horton
Albert Edward Humphries
Albert William James
William Yonge Radcliffe
Charles James Sewell
William Wells

Hooge Crater Cemetery
Francis George Harper
Reginald Godfrey Harris
William Rueben Morris
Harold Pearcey
Lionel Cecil Trubridge

Houchin British Cemetery
John Stewart MacDonald

*Huy La Sarte Communal
   Cemetery*
Willaim Albert Victor Quant

Jerusalem War Cemetery
Bertram Arthur Heath
Hugh Gordon Sutton

Jerusalem Memorial
Frederick Alfred Humby

Harold William Pistell
Gilbert Robins
Bertram Frank Shergold

Karachi 1914–18 Memorial
Ernest Fryer

Kirkee 1914–18 Memorial
William James Crotty
Harry George Hart
Lewis Charles Jackson
Stanley John Swayne

Kranji War Cemetery
Henry Giles Amor

La Clytte Military Cemetery
Sidney Ernest Matthews

*La Ferte Sous Jouarre
   Memorial*
Alfred George Stickland

*La Vallee Mulatre Communal
   Cemetery Extension*
Henry Wyndham Francis
   Blackburn

Lapugnoy Military Cemetery
Frederick Douglas Percy

*Laventie Military Cemetery La
   Gorgue*
Ernest Edward Whitlock

Le Touret Memorial
William Oliver Chapman
Sgt Wilfred Ralph Crockett
Albert George Victor Crook
Lewis Joseph Daniels
George Hawkins
William King
Reginal William Liverridge
Ishmael Newbury
James Newman
James Albert Penny
Sidney William Jack Pitman
Thomas J. Truebridge
Thomas Williams
Frank Vincent

*Le Touret Military Cemetery,
   Richelbourg L Avoue*
Malcolm A.R. Bell

*Le Vertannoy British Cemetery,
   Hinges*
George Brown
William Ewart G. Rake

*Les Baraques Military
   Cemetery, Sangatte*
Ernest Maby Horder

*Ligny St Flochel British
    Cemetery, Averdoingt*
Leopold George Weston

Lijssenthoek Military Cemetery
Ronald Henry Spinney

Lilliers Communal Cemetery
Walter Taylor Habgood

*London Rifle Brigade
Cemetery*
Charles Harry Robinson

Lone Pine Memorial
Frank Newton Cooke

*Longuenesse St Omer Souvenir
    Cemetery*
Brian Moray Williams

Lonsdale Cemetery, Authuile
William Frank Welsh

Loos British Cemetery
Frederick William Stokes

Loos Memorial
Frank Thomas Anscombe
Albert Edward Burbage
John Harold Clark
William Fletcher
Frederick James Foyle
Joseph John Skinner

Lowrie Cemetery, Havrincourt
Montague Jesse Welch

*Madras 1914–18 War Memorial,
    Chennai*
Steven Walter Dyer

Magnaboschi British Cemetery
Mervyn Sydney Wilkins

Marcoing British Cemetery
John William Leahy

Marfaus British Cemetery
Albert Edward Young

*Mendingham Military
    Cemetery*
Cecil Victor Simmonds

*Menin Road South Military
    Cemetery*
Walter Charles Shergold

*Messines Ridge British
    Cemetery*
Harold Cox

Mikra British Cemetery
Bertie Francis Andrews
Victor Henry Cowmeadow
Arthur Henry Elkins

Ethelbert Edward Henry
    Gale
Edward James Harwood

*Mount Huon Military
    Cemetery, Le Treport*
Reginald Claude Hawkins

*Montecchio Precalcino
    Communal Cemetery
    Extension*
Frederick Bailey

*Montreuil Aux Lions British
    Cemetery*
Sidney Charles Allen

*Netherhampton St Katherine
    Churchyard*
Albert Victor Weeks

Netley Military Cemetery
Willis Manks

*Neuville En Ferrain
    Communal Cemetery*
James Cromwell Bush

New Irish Farm Cemetery
Harry Brown
Felix George Buckley

Niederzwehren Cemetery
William George Bell
William Augustus Portman
    Foster

*Noeux Les Mines Communal
    Cemetery*
Henry Robert Miles

Nouvelles Communal Cemetery
Walter Richard Aston Dawes

*Ontario Cemetery, Sains Les
    Marquion*
William Charles Veck

Oosttaverne Wood Cemetery
Charles William Andrews

*Orchard Dump Cemetery,
    Arleux en Gohelle*
Charles Goodridge

*Outterstreene Communal
    Cemetery, Extension Bailleul*
Sidney New Massey
Harry Osmund

Ovillers Military Cemetery
Siegfried Thomas Hinkley

*Peronne Communal Cemetery
    Extension*
Frederick George Chatfield
Robert Buchanan Wilkes Gosse

*Perrone Road Cemetery,
    Maricourt*
Robert Bright

Pieta Military Cemetery
George Leslie Ferrey
George Benjamin Hodson

Ploegsteert Memorial
William Charles Knight
Sidney Edward Moorhouse
Henry George White

Plymouth Naval Memorial
Kenneth Alder

Poelcapelle British Cemetery
Roger Alvin Poore

*Pont D Achelles Military
    Cemetery, Nieppe*
Richard Philip Hodgson

*Pont D Hem Military
    Cemetery, La Gorgue*
Horace Frank Brown Dredge

*Port Said War Memorial
    Cemetery*
Christopher Ken Merewether

Portsmouth Kingston Cemetery
Joseph Henry Doel

Portsmouth Naval Memorial
Percy Beck
Henry Gordon Blackburn
Joseph Bolwell
Leslie Arthur Claridge
Henry George Elliott
Albert Steven F. Gay
John Reginald George
Walter Edmund George
Sydney Hazel
Henry George Head
Fred Hibberd
Ewart William Hill
Harry Daniel West

Pozieres Memorial
Alfred Edward Curtis
Arthur Frowde Dickinson
William Hayter
Harry Musselwhite
Sidney George Orchard
Arthur James Smith
Herbert Jobs Weeks

Queant Road Cemetery, Buissy
Frederick James Bennett
Benjamin J. Bucknall

Ramleh War Cemetery
William Charles Hawkins

Robert Halley Knight
Sidney George Lear
John Thomas Harry Staples

*Regina Trench Cemetery,
   Grandcourt*
William Richard Whitehead

*Ribecourt Road Cemetery,
   Trescault*
Ernest William Best

Roclincourt Military Cemetery
John Ferdinando Collins

*Rocquigny Equancourt Road
   British Cemetery, Mananco*
Alfred George Foreman
William Walter Morrice

*Rosieres Communal Cemetery
   Extension*
Ernest John Sheppard

*Rosskeen Parish Churchyard
   Extension or Burial Ground*
Sidney Emm

*Rue David Military Cemetery,
   Fleuxbaix*
Edward Hamilton Westrow
   Hulse
Albert Edward Mortimer

*Sally Sur La Lys Canadian
   Cemetery*
Arthur James Irish
Edwin James Witt

*Salisbury (Devizes Road)
   Cemetery,*
David Baird
Walter W. Bennett
Thomas Brady
Arthur Bloy Buckle
William Charles Cain
William Charles Coombes
Edward Daniel Curtlin
Athur Cudmore
Henry Lund Eaton
Francis James Fletcher
Herbert Thomas Geater
Frank Percy Goodyear
Edwin Hopkins
William Charles Leaver
John A. Mates
Alfred W. Meech
Ian Rudolph Mees
Herbert John Meigh
George C. Rance
Victor Frederick Saunders

Philip Sellers
David Reat Smith
Herbert Frederick Taylor
Joseph Tiffin
John Thresher
Robert J. Warren
Harry Waters
William Henry Weeks
William White
William Frank Wise

*Salisbury London Road
   Cemetery*
Claude Elwin Abell
Hnery Leopold Breakey
Lester Luke Brennan
Thomas Butler
Ernest Burrington
Clerke Colqhourn Burton
William Constantine Campbell
Arthur Edward Chambers
Stephen Collinson
George Compton
James Cull
Bernard Frederick Deane
Charles Hedley Edgecombe
Philip Frederick Elliott
George Duncan Findlay
William George Flowers
George Gray
Arthur F. Hamilton-Cox
Douglas Wornell Harding
Walter Frederick Hardy
Cuthbert Francis Hodding
William Henry Holloway
James Francis Hope
Harry Edgar Randolph Jackson
Walter Jacob
Charles William Johnston
Albert George William Jones
Joseph Francis Mary Kelly
John Biles Kingsbury
Lionel John Lancaster
Harry Thomas Liversidge
John William Lyons
Frederick William Mayor
James Hannay Stewart McClure
George Sylvester Ward
   McCudden
Arthur William Mitchell
George Mullins
Francis Henry Paice
John Edward Peters
Harry Dennis Preston
Thomas Read

George Thornhill Ritchie
Arthur Scott
William Everett Sinclair
Robert John Smith
Tom Martindale Speechly
Anthony Austin Street
Alfred Thomas Sturgess
Alwyne Topham
Frederick Allan Vincent

*Salonika Lembet Road Military
   Cemetery*
Charles Hazel Beaven

Sanctuary Wood Cemetery
Cecil George Sandbrook
   Rawlings

*Sarigol Military Cemetery,
   Kriston*
Leonard Wheeler

Serre Road Cemetery No.2
Francis Dodgson
Alfred Henry Wisdom

Shotley St Mary Churchyard
Francis Henry Jolliffe

Sofia War Cemetery
Bertie R. Dart

Soissons Memorial
William Charles Edwards
Herbert Walter Fay

Southampton Old Cemetery
Arthur Lionel Chappell

St Albans Cemetery
Edward Graham
Gilbert Charlie Hibberd

St Aubert British Cemetery
Frank Seviour

*St Nazaire Toutes Aides
   Cemetery*
Thomas James Gascoigne

St Nicholas British Cemetery
Frank Albert Symons

*St Sever Cemetery Extension,
   Rouen*
Dudley Victor Druery
William Ralph Mould
Leslie Eneas Phillimore
Bertram James Smith
Charles Douglas Turner
Thomas Francis Witt

St Souplet British Cemetery
Walter Usher

St Symphorien Military Cemetery
George Green

Ste Marie Cemetery, Le Havre
Herman Theodore Wells

Struma Military Cemetery
Edgar Robert Foakes

Sutton in Ashfiled Cemetery
William McCubbin

Templux Le Guerard British Cemetery
William Moncrieffe Macey
Charles Penruddocke

Tenby St Mary Church Cemetery
Henry Simeon Burton

Terlincthun British Cemetery Wimille
Sydney Denzil Oliver

The Huts Cemetery
Leslie Vivian Hurle Bath
Charles Munday

Thiepval Memorial
Albert John Andrews
Victor George Besant
William John Blake
William John Brock
William Harry Bush
Lionel William Bushrod
Arthur Edward Butt
Frank William Dredge
William M. Farr
William Gaisford
John Gatford
Frederick Charles Giddings
Stanley Glover
Basil Austin Gummer
Ernest Leonard Holcombe
Ernest Frank House
Albert Charels Massey
Edgar Percy Rousell
Frederick Murray Sainsbury
Frederick Clarence Scott
Ernest Frank Viney
Arthur Reginald Weeks
Cecil Jack Wort

Tin Court New British Cemetery
William Henry Thring

Tourcoing Pont Neuville Communal Cemetery
Sidney Hubert Uphill

Trefcon British Cemetery, Caulaincourt
John Folliott

Trois Arbres Cemetery Steenwerck
Bertram T. Collier
Victor James

Tyne Cot Cemetery
Wilfred Gordon Anson
Alexander George Baugh
William Charles Beaven
William James Burton
Robert Henry Curtis
Arthur Ernest Davis
George Koberwein Fulton
Harold Stanley Gale
Bertram John Gardner
Frederick Stewart Hunphries
William Richard John James
Desmond Light
Percival Edward Rattue
George Henry Saunders
Wilfred Henry Scott
Harry William Stagg
Charles Alfred Tilley
Robert I. Wade
Tom Zebedee

Vailly British Cemetery
John Francis Freeston

Vimy Memorial
Alfred Frimston Williams

Vis En Artois British Cemetery, Haucourt
Alan Brooks

Vis En Artois Memorial
James Richard Garland
Sidney Richard Perry Grant
Frank Noake
Vivtor Charles Prince

Vlamertinghe Military Cemetery
Cyrill Henry Cooper

Voomezeele Enclosure No.3
Frederick Massey

Wancourt British Cemetery
William Charles Burrough

Warlencourt British Cemetery
Reginald Arthur Randall

Warlincourt Halte British Cemetery, Saulty
Wilfred Louis Bradshaw
Bertie James Fiander

West Harnham St George Churchayrd
David Herbert Squires

Wimereux Communal Cemetery
Ernest Cassey

Wulverghem Lindenhoek Road Military Cemetery
Alfred Conduit

Ypres Menin Gate
Frederick James Allen
Harry Victor Beaven
William Edward Walley Blencowe
John Thomas Cook
Charles Cropp
Fred Crouch
Albert John Gray
Leonard Walter Oram Head
Albert George Kimber
Hugh Arthur Grenville Malet
James Herrick Mcgregor
Alfred Morris
Frederick Arthur Newton
William Samuel Orchard
Charles Palmer
Albert Robinson
Frank Reginald Safe
Reginald Sheppard
James Smith
William Henry Smith
William Sutton
Norman Froud Weston
Frederick William Young

Ypres Reservois Cemetery
Walter Musselwhite

Zandvoorde British Cemetery
Harry Batt

BIBLIOGRAPHY

Books read as general interest and research material during the writing of this book:

Battleground Europe series by Pen and Sword Books Ltd:
  The Battle of Neuve Chapelle, French Flanders, Geoff Bridger, 2000
  Sanctuary Wood & Hooge, Ypres, Nigel Cave, 1993
  Hill 60, Ypres, Nigel Cave, 1998
  Walking the Salient, Paul Reed, 1999
The Wiltshire Regiment, 1914-1959, Martin McIntyre, 2006, Tempus Publishing
A Serious Disappointment, The Battle of Aubers Ridge 1915 and the Munitions Scandal, Adrian Bristow, 1995, Pen and Sword Books
Outrage at Sea, Naval Atrocities in the First World War, Tony Bridgland, 2002, Pen and Sword Books
The Ironclads of Cambrai, The First Great Tank Battle, Bryan Cooper, 1967, Cassell Military Paperbacks
The War the Infantry Knew, Captain J.C. Dunn, 1987, Jane's Publishing Company Ltd
Christmas Truce, The Western Front, December 1914, Malcolm Brown and Sherley Seaton, 2001, Pan Books
Jutland, The German Perspective, V.E. Tarrant, 1995, Cassell Military Paperbacks
Kitchener's Army, Ray Westlake, 1989, Spellmount Ltd

In addition original newspapers papers of the *Wiltshire Times* and *Salisbury Journal* from between 1914 and 1919 have been extensively researched to ascertain much additional personal information relating to the soldiers listed herein.